THE
RELATIONSHIP
TOOLBOX

ROBERT ABEL

VALENTINE PUBLISHING HOUSE
DENVER COLORADO

The Scripture quotations contained herein are from the New Revised Standard Version Bible, Copyright © 1989 by the Division of Christian Education of the National Council of the Churches of Christ in the USA, and are used by permission. All rights reserved.

Grammatical Note: To address the problematic use of the generic pronoun "he", the author has chosen to use the plural pronoun "they" when referring to a singular noun of common gender (usually "partner"). The generic alternative "he or she" was too distracting and the choice of "they" fits with the conversational style of the book. It also acknowledges the perspective of readers who do not find that the generic pronoun "he" applies equally to females and males.

Editing: Richard Haugh
Graphic Design: Mary Sue Alexander
Page Design: Deborah Gotto
Cover Illustrations: Hugh B. Alexander
Interior Illustrations: Casey Keeler
Photography: Larry Sampson
Proof Reading: Phyllis Hunt
Technical Support: Brenda Mumma, Jeanne Wills

Publisher's Cataloging-in-Publication Data

Abel, Robert A.

The relationship toolbox : 72 tools to keep your relationship running and tune-up your love life / Robert Abel ; [edited by Richard Haugh]. — 1st ed.

p. cm.
Preassigned LCCN: 97-71726
ISBN: 0-9657666-2-4

1. Interpersonal relations. 2. Psychology, Applied.
3. Spiritual healing.   I. Title

BF636.A34 1998   158.2
                                  QB197-40862

02 01 00 99 98 * 10 9 8 7 6 5 4 3 2 1

Printed in the United States of America.

In dedication and honor to all who walk the road of love, healing, growth and personal empowerment. By doing so, you create a better world for all of us.

Happy are those who find wisdom, and those who get understanding, for her income is better than silver, and her revenue better than gold. She is more precious than jewels, and nothing you desire can compare with her. Long life is in her right hand; in her left hand are riches and honor. Her ways are ways of pleasantness, and all her paths are peace. She is a tree of life to those who lay hold of her; those who hold her fast are called happy.

Proverbs 3: 13-18

TABLE OF CONTENTS

FOREWORD

When you bought this book, you probably thought you were getting a great deal on a lot of powerful information that would help improve your everyday interactions and relationships. But actually you are getting two books for the price of one. Yes, it's true the first book was written on "How to have a failed marriage and broken relationship." But after the editors finished cleaning up the language, it only turned out to be four sentences long. So here it goes:

THE RELATIONSHIP BREAKUP BOX

Chapter One: If you want your business to fail and end up in bankruptcy, don't bother going into work.

Chapter Two: If you want your children to grow up doing drugs, going to jail or ending up in the hospital, or worse, don't do any parenting work.

Chapter Three: If you want to go from one unsuccessful personal relationship to the next, until you finally end up old, bitter, isolated and lonely, don't do any personal or mutual relationship work.

Chapter Four: If you want your marriage to end up in divorce, don't do any relationship, healing, forgiveness or maintenance work.

THE END

Wow, that was easy! You just completed the first book on how not to have a successful or fulfilling relationship. So, let's start out the second book by looking at a few sentences that will help in its introduction.

Success in your relationships, just like anything else in life, will require hard work and personal growth. There is no such thing as a fairy tale relationship. It is not possible to magically find that perfect person who will instantly make all your problems and worries in life disappear. No person on the face of this planet can bring you internal happiness, peace, joy and contentment unless you are able to find it inside of yourself first. Finding the perfect mate will not guarantee anyone a lifetime of paradise, in the garden of Eden. In fact, we all got kicked out of the garden a long time ago, when God personally gave us the boot.

If you want to live happily ever after in paradise, it will be necessary to create your own garden through hard work. Once you accept that life is difficult, and relationships require some effort on your part, you have already completed half the journey down the road of successful relationships.

After beginning the process of working on your life and relationships, you may realize it's a lot like working on a car. If your car is broken, you could read a million self-help books and repair manuals and your car would still be in the same condition it was when you started. You could also pay a thousand experts for their advice, but your car's condition will not change. You could try a quick-fix solution using duct tape and chicken wire, but how long do you think that would last?

Usually when our cars experience mechanical problems, we can have them fixed at any shop in town. But that is not true when it comes to relationships, because you are your own relationship mechanic. You are the only person in this world who can make changes and adjustments inside yourself. Once you assume the role of the master mechanic, you may find yourself looking for a collection of powerful tools to assist in the process.

That is where this book comes into play. Every chapter presents a powerful tool that can be used in your everyday interactions and repair procedures. Every chapter was prepared in an easy-to-understand, condensed, inspirational and empowering format. All the fillers and unimportant stories were left out in an effort to save time and provide you with only the necessary information. The tools that these chapters contain are designed to flow together and, at the same time, stand on their own. So feel free to jump into your reading anywhere you like. You can begin in the front, or combine chapters to fit your specific relationship needs. It's even possible to substitute healing procedures to create your own personalized methods.

A car theme has been used throughout the book as an easier method of relating to the subjects. Enjoy its content while traveling down the road of life. Welcome!

ADDICTIONS

TOOL 1

*I*magine for a minute that your car developed a problem in the carburetor or fuel injection system. Let's say it leaked gasoline every time it was running. As you continued to drive the vehicle, the leak would grow bigger and bigger. You know something is seriously wrong with the car because it's not running very well and is getting terrible gas mileage.

If this situation happened in your life, what would you do? Would you ignore the problem and continue to fill up the gas tank twice a day? Or would you fix the spot where the fuel is leaking and resolve the problem? Do you think the problem is going to fix itself? Do you think a stronger type of gas will solve your problem and make the car run better? Do you realize the longer you drive the car, the worse the problem is going to get? What would happen if the leaking gasoline ignited? Do you realize you are risking a possible engine fire that could destroy the entire vehicle?

Well, the same situation applies to addictions because the car's problem (the leaking fuel system) is similar to our own personal problems. The car's ability to run well depends on a lack of mechanical problems just as our ability to feel good depends on a lack of personal problems. We're designed to feel good when our lives are devoid of problems. God engineered our bodies to experience negative emotions so we would quickly recognize our problems and deal with them in a healthy manner. The addictions we use to make ourselves feel better work just like adding more gasoline to the car in an attempt to make it run better. Everyone wants to feel good, but what are you going to do the next time you experience negative emotions or a leaking carburetor? Are you going to deal with the problems directly, or turn to something that temporarily makes you feel better?

All addictions are mood altering. In other words, they temporarily make us feel good. Once the high wears off, we usually don't feel any better, because the original problem is still there and now we have added pain and guilt from the hangover. After using an addiction to deal with negative emotions or problems in life, we usually feel twice as bad. No one likes feeling bad or dealing with problems, so once again we turn back to the addiction in an attempt to make ourselves feel better. After the high wears off again, we now feel three times as bad. So once again we run to the addiction in a compulsive manner to make ourselves feel better. This process keeps getting worse and worse, and eventually the addiction cycle is born.

Turning to your addiction instead of dealing with whatever is causing your pain is just like putting gas in your car twice a day to avoid fixing the carburetor. Eventually you will need more and more gas to run your car just as you will need more and more compulsive fixes to make yourself feel better. Eventually your car will catch fire and burn up. In the same way, an addict crashes and hits bottom. Your car will end up in the junkyard. An addict will end up in the hospital, if they're lucky.

There's only one way to fix your car, and that's to stop putting gas in it and repair the underlying problems. Depending on the severity of the leak it might be necessary to have it towed to a mechanic. There's only one way to break your addiction cycle, and that's to stop participating in obsessive or compulsive behavior and deal with whatever is causing you to experience negative emotions, pain or problems in life. Depending on the severity of your addiction it may be necessary to reach out for medical or psychological assistance, or to a support group tow truck.

It's possible to become addicted to almost anything. You can become addicted to anything you obsessively think about or compulsively do to distract yourself from your negative feelings. Some addictions are extremely hard to recognize. Usually when we think of addictions, we picture drug and alcohol abusers. But we can become addicted to something as healthy as exercise. That's because when we overextend ourselves in physical exercise, our brains release an opiate-like chemical to which obsessive fitness enthusiasts can become addicted.

Some typical addictions are alcohol, illegal drugs, doctor-prescribed medications, food, compulsive overeating, caffeine, nicotine, work, success, money, our spouses, codependent relationships, perfectionism, materialism, gambling, consumerism, religion, power, sex, thrill seeking, risk taking, lust, control, exercise, dieting, cleanliness, obsession with physical beauty, academic pursuits, preoccupation with entertainment, television, and even sports.

What do you use to make yourself feel better? Do you try to hide your addiction from others? Does the drive to make yourself feel better come before your own well-being, children, partner, others or God? Are you experiencing intimacy problems in your relationship because your addiction is preventing you from truly connecting with your Inner Self? Can you recognize any obsessive or compulsive behaviors in your partner as they attempt to make themselves feel better? If so, the following steps are designed to help you and your partner overcome an addiction.

Steps to Overcoming an Addiction

Step 1: Recognize and Admit Your Addiction

The first step is recognizing your addiction and admitting you have a problem. When we deny our addictions, they become impossible to deal with. When we bring them out into the open and tell other people about our problems, we empower ourselves to overcome and deal with these obsessive and compulsive tendencies. Take a close look at your life for anything that keeps you from dealing with your problems and shameful, worthless, fearful or uncomfortable feelings.

Has your life become unmanageable? Are you comfortable with yourself? Are you connected to your Inner Self and spiritual source? Can you be by yourself without any distractions, feeling comfortable and peaceful for extended periods of time? If not, what do you use to make yourself feel better? What do your close friends and family say regarding any of your obsessive or compulsive behaviors? What would they say if you asked them?

Step 2: Recognize the Damage

The next step is looking at the amount of damage your addictions are causing to your life. Many times we become so consumed by our addictions that we fail to recognize the damage they cause. Take a close look at every aspect of your life: physical, mental, emotional and spiritual. How does this addiction affect your physical health, your social life, your ability to think and work, your emotional abilities to connect with others and your ability to love? How is the addiction affecting your relationship with God and what He's trying to communicate to you through your Inner Self?

It might be helpful to make a list of all the negative aspects and disadvantages that you experience as a result of your addiction. After you've evaluated your own life, try asking the people you are closest to for their opinion. Ask your friends, family members, relatives and coworkers how your obsessive or compulsive behaviors affect their lives. How many times have they been isolated, abandoned, inconvenienced, worried, scared, neglected, abused or threatened because of this problem? If you are a drug- or alcohol-abusing parent trying to raise a child, you are probably causing serious emotional damage which your children may spend the rest of their life trying to overcome. If your children are too young to share with you how much damage your addiction is causing, contact a local Al-Anon group and ask any one of its members.

Step 3: Take Action

Next you need to free yourself from the compulsive behavior or addictive substances. Begin by making a commitment to yourself and anyone else you feel would be a good support system. It might be helpful to write down on paper your commitment to overcome the addiction and display it in a prominent area where everyone can see it.

Next, start eliminating the compulsive behavior or addictive substances from your life. Every situation needs to be treated differently in this process. Try starting small, since every step in the right direction will eventually get you where you want to go. For example, if you are a shopaholic, try leaving your credit card home all week. If that step is too large to take on all at once, try reducing it to just the weekend. Look for any other ways you can cut back or slowly reduce the amount of your addiction. Setting up a gradual reduction schedule or similar plan might be helpful.

Other times it might be necessary to go through a detoxification program especially for substance abuse. Hospitalization, medical treatment and prevention are very helpful and many times necessary to treat withdrawal symptoms. In detox you will be medically treated with other nonaddictive drugs to safely reduce your body's chemical dependency.

Keeping track of your obsessive or compulsive behaviors by using a log is also helpful in eliminating an addiction. Many times we have a way of exaggerating the truth or minimizing our problems. A written log will help you keep track of what you actually do and record your progress. Make the necessary plans (almost like setting a goal) to reduce and eventually eliminate the addiction from your life.

Step 4: Monitor and Correct Your Thinking Patterns

Next it's necessary to identify and change your thinking patterns that contribute to the obsessive or compulsive behavior. By writing down your thoughts before, during, and after your participation in the addictive behavior you will have an easier time eliminating it from your life. A written log will help identify destructive self-talk that calls or encourages you to participate in the unhealthy behavior. It will also be helpful to identify your true needs as well as any distorted thought patterns that might be contributing to the compulsive behaviors.

Begin by carrying around a small log everywhere you go. Whenever you start thinking about the opportunity of your addiction, simply write down your thoughts, feelings and true needs. Identify the reasons why you are feeling down, depressed, upset, uncomfortable or frustrated. How would you like to be feeling? What else could you do to help yourself feel better without turning to the addiction?

Try to recognize the self-talk voice calling you to the destructive behavior. What is it saying to you? Become familiar with this voice so you can recognize it whenever it presents itself. If the voice appears loud and powerful, go into your imagination and picture the voice coming from a scared and frightened child hiding inside a big monster costume. The big monster only has one purpose, and that's self-destruction. All it knows is drink, drug, destroy and die. The scared child will only come out of the monster costume when they feel loved. Try creating and recording in your log some loving statements, words and feelings which help bring the child out from inside of the monster disguise.

Another way to use the log is by looking at any distorted perceptions that you may be using. For example: Suppose you are driving home from work and something happens to upset you, like a traffic jam. Some distorted thoughts that can lead to your addiction might be: "Traffic is always terrible. No one knows how to drive in this city." (All or none thinking.) "This really sucks." (Failure to recognize the positive.) "I will never get home." (Predicting the future.) "I should never have gotten on the highway. It's all my fault." (Martyrdom.) "My life sucks. I'm a loser." (Name calling.) "I must get out of here before I lose my mind." (Authoritative.) "I need another fix to relax or else I'll go crazy."

As you can see, this type of distorted thinking would drive anyone to drink. The log will help you identify these kinds of distorted thinking patterns, and the information in the Perceptions chapter will help you convert them into the truth. Identify your distorted thinking patterns in the log, and counteract them with positive self-talk that helps you overcome your obsessive and compulsive behaviors.

If you give in to your addiction, write down in the log how terrible it makes you feel afterward. When you successfully avoid a calling for the addiction by embracing that hurt part from inside yourself, write down in your log all of your positive feelings of accomplishment, self-worth, happiness and personal success.

Step 5: Do Inner-Self Work

Many times addictions start out because we don't like the way we are feeling or the problems we are experiencing. Then in an attempt to relieve the pain and problems, we turn to our mood-altering addictions to make ourselves feel better. Unfortunately, the problems and negative emotions we are trying to avoid only grow worse. Eventually they consume us almost like the addiction itself. It's necessary to confront these negative feelings and problems head-on. You need to embrace and accept whatever it is you have been running from.

This can be easily accomplished by getting in touch with your Inner Self. We are all spiritual beings, existing in this physical world. Your Inner Self is the spiritual part of your being that is connected to God. When there is a problem in our lives, God speaks to us through our Inner Self — through our conscience, intuition and self-awareness. So instead of running from your problems, negative feelings and God's will, get in touch with this part of your being. Find out what the real issues are and deal with them directly so you won't need to cover them up with your addiction any longer.

Spend some time every day in meditation and prayer. Ask God to give you the courage necessary to uncover and identify your issues. Look deep inside yourself and discover the underlying reasons that had previously been avoided. Make a fearless and intensive search of your past and write down in a log the real issues, problems and past traumatic experiences that are in need of resolution. (See Inner Self, Prayer and Meditation chapters for more information.)

Step 6: Resolve the Issues

Next it's necessary to resolve any underlying issues that have been uncovered in your life. If the carburetor in your car leaks fuel, it's necessary to rebuild or replace it with a new one. If any negative childhood memories arise from your Inner Self work, make a list of them and heal them by using the techniques in the Healing chapter. If you remember any unforgiving people from your past, forgive them using the procedure in the Forgiveness chapter. If there are any past mistakes that cause you to experience negative feelings, it's necessary to forgive yourself. Making amends to other people whom you have hurt in the past is also a very powerful method of healing yourself, not to mention others. Direct amends can be made, but only when doing so won't cause additional harm to others.

If you are using your addiction to avoid problems in your current relationships, you may need to do some work to strengthen your bonds, grow closer and reconcile the differences with your partner. If you are participating in an unhealthy or destructive relationship, it may be necessary to remove yourself and set up some protective boundaries. Do whatever it takes to get your life back together, without turning to the addiction.

Step 7: Fill the Void

Once you start eliminating the addiction from your life, it becomes necessary to fill the void it leaves by replacing it with something positive, loving and healthy. For example, if you are eating to make yourself feel better, loved, and nurtured, replace the false comfort that food offers with some self-concept work or some loving affirmations. If you use alcohol as a crutch for dealing with people at social events, replace the alcohol with new social skills. Give yourself the love, comfort and support you need in healthy methods instead of turning to the addiction. Remember that people can become addicted to almost anything. Be careful not to replace one addiction with another.

Step 8: Seek Support Systems

Seeking out support systems is essential in your healing and recovery process. Many times addictions cannot be treated in isolation. Talking about and sharing our situation with others, especially those who have overcome similar experiences, is very empowering. Reach out to friends, family, counselors, therapists, churches, help hot lines, medical facilities, or alcoholics and narcotics anonymous programs. This step will help ensure and guide your well-being.

Step 9: Make Daily Efforts

Overcoming addictions will require daily efforts. It's important to reward yourself for progress made along the road to recovery. Be forgiving and patient with yourself in case you experience any temporary regressions or setbacks. Many times they occur, and when they do, it won't help anything if you are hard, critical and nonloving with yourself.

Avoid any unnecessary temptations. Start socializing with nonabusers. Remove any paraphernalia like ashtrays, matches, bottles and reminders from your environment. Change your old habits or environment to make access to the addiction more difficult. Prepare your mental, emotional and physical defenses and responses when unexpected temptations occur in the future. If you feel the anxiety or temptation arising, stop yourself and take a break. Remove yourself from the situation immediately. Call a friend, mentor or someone who will hold you accountable. Go for a walk. Get in touch with your feelings by using the self-awareness exercise. Practice positive self-talk or affirmations. Focus on relaxation exercises and your deep-breathing techniques wherever a temptation occurs.

Ask God for His daily assistance in overcoming your addiction. Pray through the entire process for strength, courage, insight, healing and willpower. God is our greatest strength, hope and empowerment in dealing with addictions.

Visions of Inspiration

Who has woe? Who has sorrow? Who has strife? Who has complaining? Who has wounds without cause? Who has redness of eyes? Those who linger late over wine, those who keep trying mixed wines. At the last it bites like a serpent, and stings like an adder. Your eyes will see strange things, and your mind utter perverse things. "They struck me," you will say, "but I was not hurt; they beat me, but I did not feel it. When shall I awake? I will seek another drink."

Proverbs 23: 29,30,32,33,& 35

Blessed is anyone who endures temptation. Such a one has stood the test and will receive the crown of life that the Lord has promised to those who love him. No one, when tempted, should say, "I am being tempted by God": for God cannot be tempted by evil and he himself tempts no one. But one is tempted by one's own desire, being lured and enticed by it; then, when that desire has conceived, it gives birth to sin, and that sin, when it is fully grown, gives birth to death. Do not be deceived, my beloved.

James 1: 12-16

When you stop drinking, you have to deal with this marvelous personality that started you drinking in the first place.

Jimmy Breslin

AFFIRMATIONS

TOOL 2

*H*ave you ever listened to a car salesman talk about his products? It does-n't matter if the car he's trying to sell is a junker from the 1970s, or a lemon with transmission problems. He can still talk for hours about its posi-tive qualities. He will tell you all of the features or advantages the car has to offer, like rack-and-pinion steering, anti-lock brakes — even the vanity mirror. A good salesman will relate how the car meets your personal situation and needs. He may even take time to learn about any problems you might have experienced with your last car in an effort to overcome objections you might have concerning the new purchase.

The salesman's most powerful tool is his ability to motivate you to view the product in a positive manner. If he criticized the car, called it names and pointed out all its negative points, you probably wouldn't be the least bit interested, would you? Who would want to be associated with such a negative piece of scrap metal if that's how the salesman described it to you? Who would want to drive a car like that around town — or even worse, buy it?

The same situation applies to our own lives and relationships because we all have a little car salesman inside our heads. This little salesman is known as our inner dialogue or inner voice, and it can sell us on either the positive or the negative. Picture for a minute a tiny car salesman inside your head who looks exactly like you, except this little person has a switch on his back with two settings: one for positive sales pitches and one for negative sales pitches. The negative setting promotes negative self-talk and self-defeating criticism about you and your life. The positive setting promotes positive self-talk, encouragement and enthusiasm about you and your life.

Practicing positive mental affirmations every day is just like offering that little internal salesman a big incentive package to sell yourself to the world. If you don't offer your salesman an incentive, they will become angry and flip that switch over to the negative sales pitch setting. A positive internal dialogue based on optimism and truth will produce a more positive life. A negative internal dialogue based on fear and false assumptions will produce emotional misery. It's that simple. The choice is yours, and you are in charge of placing the switch on — positive sales pitches, or the negative sales pitches. Are you going to empower yourself or defeat yourself? If a car salesman can talk eight hours a day about how great their products are, don't you think everyone should be able to talk eight hours a day about how great they are themselves? Besides, who's more valuable — you or a car?

Imagine for a minute that you're about to start an important project and the little voice inside your head (the salesman) starts speaking negatively: "You're a loser. You're not good enough. You're overweight and stupid. No one likes you, and you're going to fail." You're going to feel worthless and self-defeated, and the important project you're about to start may already be pre-destined to fail, all because you neglected your responsibility to maintain a positive internal dialogue.

On the other hand, we can empower ourselves and increase our chances for success if we give ourselves some positive mental affirmations, like: "You are a very talented, smart, beautiful person. Everyone likes you, supports you and is counting on you to succeed with this important project." The positive switch setting will empower your life and relationships and the negative switch setting will destroy your life and relationships. By repeating positive messages over and over to yourself, your life will eventually begin to reflect that reality.

If you find yourself having a hard time practicing or believing in your positive affirmations, first convert your negative self-talk into its positive intentions. (See the Criticism chapter for more information.) For example, you might actually be overweight, and your internal voice has a loving intention or a good reason behind why it's saying this to you. Maybe the little salesman inside you believes you would be healthier and happier by taking better care of your body. Now, if you are overweight and your internal dialogue is letting you know for a good reason, you probably won't be able to change your emotional outlook by repeating skinny affirmations over and over again. If a car has a bad transmission, a good salesman will confront the truth and still sell the car with a warranty program or by working the future repairs into the price somehow. The same is true by finding the positive intentions behind our internal voice when it's speaking negatively.

God put you in charge of your own life and your own internal car dealership. God created you with unlimited power and potential. You can run a successful dealership with positive self-talk or a bankrupt dealership with negative self-talk. If you find yourself sitting on a lot full of junkers, that's okay. Simply motivate your sales force by flipping the switch over to the positive by practicing positive affirmations every day. One by one those junkers will disappear, allowing room for better and better opportunities to arrive on the lot. God wants you to view yourself and your lot in the same loving manner that He does. All you have to do is accept responsibility for your own internal dialogue. The following items will help you practice positive self-talk and affirmations on a regular basis.

Practicing Affirmations

Creating Affirmations

There are an unlimited number of ways affirmations can be created. They can be short and simple like, "I love myself," or more complex and intentionally designed for a specific purpose.

It's helpful to keep in mind the seven basic ingredients that make up a motivating affirmation. They are personal, emotional, visual, motivating, positive, present tense, frequently practiced and purposeful. They *personally* apply to your life and are usually spoken from the first person or your name. They *emotionally* touch a part of your being or describe an emotional response which you enjoy experiencing. They can be *visualized* to increase their effectiveness. They are *motivating,* using powerful meanings and statements spoken with great emphasis. They promote the *positive* and are based on loving intentions. They are spoken from the *present tense* describing your actions or intentions as you would like them to accrue in the present. They are *frequently* repeated throughout the day or used when specific negative situations occur in your life.

Standard Affirmations

Standard affirmations can be used to promote your self-concept, improve your abilities to perform successfully, create a personal sense of peace and confidence in your life, and increase your internal happiness.

It's helpful to practice standard affirmations every day. Say at least ten in the morning, ten around noon, and ten in the evening. If there are certain times of day you regularly find yourself getting upset or unhappy, focus more affirmation efforts toward those specific times. For example, a good time for morning affirmations might be during rush hour traffic if it is stressful for you. Try to cover all areas of your life with the standard affirmations, including your personal appearance, work and social concerns, home and environment issues, God, your talents and abilities, and the roles you fulfill in life (like father, mother, teacher, student, giver, receiver). Any aspect concerning your physical, mental, social, emotional or spiritual self can be converted into a standard affirmation.

Some physical affirmations might be: "I am beautiful. I love my eyes, hair, smile, wardrobe, looks, and best features." Think about all the ways you look good and let yourself know. "I am grateful for the body God has given me. I look great. I have outstanding (fill in a characteristic). I deeply value my life, efforts, and abilities. I am a great father, mother, firefighter, scientist, cook, or assistant."

Some mental affirmations might be: "I'm very intelligent, creative, smart and hardworking." Think of your best mental advantages and let yourself know. "I deserve financial success, to succeed in all my efforts."

Some social affirmations might be: "I'm friendly and outgoing. I'm well accepted and many people like me. I'm connected to everyone else in life. We are all brothers and sisters, and children of God. I'm a good boyfriend/girlfriend and my partner loves me."

Some emotional affirmations might be: "I love myself. I deserve to be happy and healthy. I am a lovable, useful and valuable person." Look for the tiniest of efforts to reward yourself with another encouraging affirmation. "I feel good about myself for these actions. I am a very loving and lovable person. I am important and my feelings matter. God loves me unconditionally. Life is great; everything is as it should be. God is my divine protector and I am safe. God forgives me and I accept that forgiveness. God gives me the strength to overcome all the problems that I may encounter."

Affirm something nice to yourself for any reason, regardless of how insignificant it may seem at the time. State your standard affirmations with force and enthusiasm. Try to create a mental image in your mind that represents what you are saying. Allow yourself to feel the emotional response stemming from your mental image. Remember, it only takes 28 days to form new habits.

Special Affirmations

It's helpful to practice special affirmations any time you want to correct, improve or modify a specific negative thought, problem or behavior in your life.

For example, let's say you want to modify your impatience and irritable behavior whenever your children start misbehaving. A good affirmation that uses the seven basic ingredients might be: "I will personally feel better about myself when I respond in a loving and wise manner whenever my children are misbehaving." Repeat your affirmation frequently throughout the day and visualize yourself interacting with your children in that manner. Experience the feelings related to that mental and verbal image, and before long you'll notice a considerable difference in your behavior.

If you want assistance in modifying unhealthy thoughts and behaviors that are leading to an addiction, a good affirmation might be: "Because I love and respect myself, I will take great personal satisfaction in overcoming any form of temptation in my life. With God's help I will prevail. I will walk in faith and maintain my internal strength, courage and persistence." Try creating your own personalized special affirmations to counteract anything you want to change in your life or relationships.

Parental Affirmations

It's helpful to practice parental affirmations in connection with your past healing work. Parental affirmations are spoken directly to the inner childlike part of yourself that suffered a harmful experience in your past. You can speak directly to that little boy or girl, or you can imagine your parents, guardians or role models speaking these affirmations to your child self.

For example, if you were abandoned a lot as a child, it's possible you have present-day abandonment issues. You might find yourself experiencing sick feelings any time your partner is late. Usually, 10 percent of the hurt feelings come from the actual inconvenience and 90 percent of the hurt feelings come from the unhealed past experiences. Your inner child may feel that if he or she was loved and wanted, they would never have been abandoned. Once you are aware of these issues, you can start practicing parental affirmations by giving that hurt child part of yourself some positive words of reassurance. Imagine your parents speaking directly to your inner child using reassuring words like, "We love you and would never abandon you," "We will always be with you in our hearts and thoughts," or "You're very special and precious to us." Allow your inner child to vividly imagine the conversation and to feel the words.

Once you determine your negative past experiences, you can heal them using the information listed in the Healing chapter and create parental affirmations to help reinforce the healing process. Allow your adult self, parents, or role models to give your child self all the love and support he or she never received but always deserved.

Visions of Inspiration

Speak the affirmative; emphasize your choice by utter ignoring of all that you reject.

Emerson

He said to them, "Then do you also fail to understand? Do you not see that whatever goes into a person from outside cannot defile, since it enters, not the heart but the stomach, and goes out into the sewer?" And he said, "It is what comes out of a person that defiles. For it is from within, from the human heart, that evil intentions come: fornication, theft, murder, adultery, avarice, wickedness, deceit, licentiousness, envy, slander, pride, folly. All these evil things come from within, and they defile a person."

Mark 7: 18-23

Affirmation of life is the spiritual act by which man ceases to live unreflectively and begins to devote himself to his life with reverence in order to raise it to its true value. To affirm life is to deepen, to make more inward and to exalt the will to live.

Albert Schweitzer

ANGER

TOOL 3

*I*magine driving down a highway, when suddenly another motorist's reckless driving puts your life in danger. Your car swerves out of control and winds up in a ditch. Luckily for you there wasn't any physical damage, but there probably was a lot of emotional damage in the form of hurt and threatened feelings. What would you do if this situation happened to you? How would you deal with your anger?

Unfortunately, there are many unhealthy responses to anger, both aggressive and passive, that many people choose every day. For example, if someone cut you off on the road, an unhealthy aggressive response would be to recklessly speed through traffic, endangering other motorists in the same manner you were hurt. An unhealthy passive response would be to drive unreasonably slowly, inconveniencing other drivers traveling behind your vehicle.

The only healthy way to deal with your anger is mentally and verbally. But before you can do that, it's necessary to discover the source of your anger. That isn't difficult, as there are only two things in life that have the potential to make us angry: being hurt and being threatened. When you see a person become angry or you yourself become angry, there are only two possible issues that need to be dealt with: Why do you feel hurt? Why do you feel threatened? It's that simple. If another motorist caused your anger, he either endangered your life (threatened you) or disrespected your rights (hurt you). If you want to convert your anger into personal growth, you need to discover what caused you to feel hurt and threatened, then verbally express yourself in an attempt to resolve the situation.

Anger is probably one of the most misunderstood tools in your relationship tool box. It's like a hammer: It can be used to carefully build and repair your relationships, or it can be used in a reckless manner, causing a lot of damage and destruction. God gave us the powerful tool of anger to be used as an opportunity for change. Anger acts almost like an internal warning sign that helps us protect our rights. It helps us define what is and what isn't acceptable and tolerable in our relationships. When things are unacceptable or intolerable, they are quickly brought to our attention through anger. Anger helps us establish who we are in relation to what other people are trying to make us be. If your relationship partner is trying to force you to do or be something you don't want to do or be, it quickly comes to your attention through your angry emotions.

Anger helps us determine our limits regarding how much we are able to do and give. When we overextend ourselves, anger lets us know through our hurt feelings of being used. Anger helps protect our individual identities. It helps us protect who we are and what we stand for. It will help promote intimacy, growth and boundaries whenever problems arise if it is used by the master mechanic. Anger helps protect us from danger because it serves as an early warning sign that identifies anything that has the potential to hurt or threaten our well-being.

God gave us the beautiful gift of anger and designed it with a lot of horsepower for a reason: It takes a lot of power to look inside yourself and find the cause of your hurt and threatened feelings so the other party can be respectfully confronted. This is not always easy and requires a strong person who knows how to focus and direct this abundance of power in a healthy manner. The best part of verbally expressing your anger is finding out (most of the time) that the other party had no idea their actions were harmful or threatening. The driver who cut you off probably just spilled his soda and had no idea his action almost caused an accident. After using your horsepower in a healthy manner to verbally express your concerns, you will quickly realize that it was just a simple, forgivable mistake.

Take a look at your hammering experiences, as well as those of your relationship partner. How was your anger used in the past? How did your parents use their hammers? What skills are necessary to use your hammer like a master mechanic? If you or your relationship partner have been using anger like a 20-pound sledge hammer, the following steps will help convert it into personal and mutual growth, problem-solving abilities, and productive changes.

Steps in Transforming Anger

Step 1: Recognize Your Unhealthy Anger Styles

How do you now respond to your anger? There are many unhealthy responses and behaviors you can choose. Some styles are passive and others are more aggressive. It helps to identify your past responses, make a list of your behaviors, and let others around you know that you are working on changing them. Look through the following list of unhealthy uses of anger to see if you can identify with any of these behaviors:

❖ **Unhealthy Passive Responses:** Attempting to hide your anger. Being afraid of your anger or that of other angry people. Repressing your anger because of the potential to lose control and harm others. Being fearful that others won't like you if you show your anger. Believing that anger is bad, sinful, ugly or destructive. Showing your anger in an indirect manner by intentionally forgetting to do something you promised to do. Trying to make the other person lose their temper first. Intentionally stalling, playing helpless or inconveniencing another with your anger. Ignoring others who hurt you. Rebelling, isolating yourself, pouting, acting rejected or getting even by hurting another behind their back.

❖ **Unhealthy Aggressive Responses:** Shouting, yelling, swearing, making threats, throwing and breaking objects. Physically fighting with another. Door slamming. Getting even. Destroying the property of others. Losing control, acting on the spur of the moment and later regretting your actions. Getting impatient with people when you don't get your way. Using anger to intimidate others to get what you want. Pretending you're angry, and acting tough in order to display an image of strength and power. Using anger to keep others from getting too close, or to establish emotional distance. Feeling justified in your anger and destructive actions because of superior beliefs, moral righteousness, arrogance or a "They started it first" attitude.

Step 2: Identify Your Anger at the First Possible Sign

It's very important to identify your angry feelings as soon as they arise. Many times we are well into a fight before we realize, "Hey, I'm really angry and upset here." The faster you can identify your angry feelings, the sooner you can analyze and resolve the situation. It's helpful to remember the principle of stimulus and response: Something happens to hurt or threaten you, and you respond in anger. Something outside of you cannot force you to be angry. It's generated within you, and is a gift that is controllable.

Identifying your angry feelings quickly will make it easier to detect and confront the outside stimulus of hurt and threat before it turns into anger. Don't let any emotions take control of your actions, because anger usually begets more anger.

Step 3: Express Your Hurt or Threatened Feelings

Once you have identified your anger at the first possible sign, next verbally express why you felt hurt or threatened. This is the ultimate key in transforming your anger. Once you verbally express your feelings and thoughts concerning how, where, when and why you were hurt and threatened, your anger will disappear.

Unfortunately, this is harder than it sounds. You might need to take a few minutes alone to get in touch with your true feelings. Try to discover the underlying intentions that brought about the hurt or threatened feelings. Are these true or just speculation?

Once you have determined and pinpointed the actual hurt or threat, express yourself, using "I" statements whenever possible. (See the Communication chapter for more information.) It's helpful to have the other party listen and respond to you, but it's not necessary. For example, if you're driving on the highway and someone cuts you off, causing angry emotions, instead of acting passively or aggressively (getting even or taking it out on other people later), simply identify your feelings and verbally express them: "I feel hurt because I perceived the other motorist's actions as very disrespectful," or "I feel threatened because the other motorist's actions might have caused an accident or damaged my vehicle." Once you verbally express yourself, your anger will automatically dissipate.

Step 4: Promote the Positive and Minimize the Negative

After you have worked through the hurt and threatened feelings, it's helpful to promote the positive and avoid the negative. Every situation you encounter will need to be treated differently. For example, if you're driving and another motorist cuts you off, try to find a loving way to view their actions. Maybe something is wrong with their alignment and they could not control the vehicle. Maybe they accidentally overdosed on drugs, or someone in their family just died. Maybe they didn't see you or even realize what happened.

In the same way, try to find a loving approach to viewing your partner's actions. Try taking turns empathetically listening to one another. When two people try to work through their anger, both want to be heard and understood. Try to find and acknowledge some form of truth in whatever your partner is saying. It might be helpful to work through the conflict resolution exercise located in the Problems/Conflict chapter whenever a domestic dispute arises. Working through the steps in the Compromise chapter will also be helpful in resolving any underling issues that keep surfacing in your relationship.

It's also important to avoid negative forms of dealing with the situation. Raising your voice only causes more tension and anxiety. Acting out your anger physically only causes your body to produce more energy, power and potential for violence. The endorphins your mind produces can't tell the difference between fighting off a mountain lion when you're angry and throwing a pillow across the room when you're angry at the children. When you physically act on your anger, your body responds by producing more power and energy. It's like throwing gas on a fire. So instead of getting physical with your anger, try to quiet your body through some breathing exercises.

Don't violate your partner when you are angry. Name calling, mocking, talking down, ridiculing, being critical or sarcastic, exaggerating the circumstances, blaming, preaching or lecturing only extend the problem. Try not to leave your partner hanging. Abandoning and walking out on your partner without letting them know when you will be back only causes more hurt. Don't force anyone to stay in a conflict with you. Usually nothing can be resolved when tensions are running high. Try not to make any major decisions or participate in any dangerous activities when you're consumed by anger; it's not worth the risk.

If you are trying to help an angry person, try explaining that you are willing to hear and accept what they have to say. Use statements like, "What happened to make you this angry?" or "What upset you the most?" or "Who else are you angry at?" Help them locate the source of who, what, where, when and why they feel hurt and threatened so it can be expressed in a healthy manner.

Visions of Inspiration

I was angry with my friend; I told my wrath, my wrath did end. I was angry with my foe; I told it not, my wrath did grow.

William Blake

A soft answer turns away wrath, but a harsh word stirs up anger.

Proverbs 15: 1

Be angry but do not sin; do not let the sun go down on your anger.

Ephesians 4: 26

Anger is what arouses you to challenge a situation. Aim to use it to improve things. Often, with it, you can change things.

Walter McQuade and Anna Aikman

ANXIETY

TOOL 4

*A*nxiety is like the electrical operating system in your car. Once the key is inserted in the ignition switch and turned on, electricity from the battery flows to all the operating systems throughout the vehicle. When we turn the switch off, most of the electrical applications like the radio and power windows stop operating. The electrical current in your car can be used for healthy purposes like making music with the radio or moving the windows up and down, or for unhealthy purposes like short-circuiting your car's electrical parts and shocking the driver.

We don't worry about getting shocked in our car, because its electrical system was designed by the factory to be used in a safe, specific and limited manner. But many times our lives and relationships aren't so simple.

Any time you experience anxiety in life, it's a form of electrical energy being generated inside your body that's not being used. This unused energy — anxiety — can be identified by those short-circuited, over-energized shocking feelings. Your body works the same way as a car, except there are no switches to turn on and off. The electrical energy your body generates is controlled by the thoughts produced by your conscience and subconscious mind.

God perfectly designed your internal operating system to run automatically. We only need to think certain thoughts and our brain automatically produces an appropriate amount of electricity to handle the upcoming situation. If your mind produces a thought regarding an upcoming dangerous situation, like a mountain lion is going to eat you for lunch, your body will instantly produce the appropriate amount of energy for you to respond accordingly. This is known as the "fight or flight" response. By the thoughts we think, our body creates the energy necessary for us to either defend ourselves from the mountain lion (fight) or run from him (flight).

Generally when we experience anxiety, it is considered unhealthy, because it is energy that has been created in our bodies but is not being used. Unused energy can be recognized in those uncomfortable feelings and moods like uneasiness, dread, concern, tension, apprehension, restlessness and worry. This unused energy or anxiety can short-circuit your internal electrical system, causing insomnia, lack of concentration, impatience, headaches, relationship problems, impaired judgment, increased blood pressure, shortness of breath, muscle tightness, sweating, butterflies in the stomach, lack of appetite, irritability, over-dependence, poor memory, unhappiness, dizziness or fainting. The next time you experience anxiety in your life and relationships, remember that it's a form of energy that's being generated by your body but not being used. There are two possible reasons why this is happening.

First, the heightened sense of electricity you are experiencing can be a form of personal power allowing you to do the right things at the right time. For example, let's say you notice something in your control that's not morally or ethically proper, like child abuse. Your brain would automatically think thoughts producing the proper amount of electrical power. This energy will be created because consciously or subconsciously you feel obligated to take some form of action. Maybe you realize that the child is helpless, and by turning your back on this situation, you are just as responsible as if you were participating in the behavior yourself. The heightened sense of electricity (anxiety) your body produces is actually calling you to do the right things at the right times, like contacting the proper authorities or personally confronting the abuser. Once you do what you know to be the right thing, regardless of how hard or uncomfortable it might be, the energy will be consumed, producing the appropriate actions, and your anxiety will disappear.

God asks that we all live with integrity — that is, doing the right things at the right times. He knows this isn't always easy and it takes great courage to confront difficult situations in life. That is why He designed your electrical system to run automatically. Many times when we experience that heightened sense of electrical energy, it's God's calling to do the right thing at the right time. If you fail to use that energy when it's available, it will sit inside your body in the form of anxiety, which when prolonged can begin to short-circuit your electrical system.

The second reason anxiety may be produced is thinking distorted or false thoughts about stressful or dangerous situations. For example, if in your mind you thought a mountain lion was about to eat you and your children for lunch, the ignition switch inside of your brain, not knowing if this situation is real or not, would automatically produce the necessary energy for you to either fight or flee. If your thoughts and perceptions are distorted (based on fear and not facts), your brain — not knowing the difference — will automatically produce the electrical energy it thinks is necessary. Usually when this happens, we are safe and sound and are just imagining upcoming dangerous situations beyond our control. Our brains don't know if there is a mountain lion loose in the office, or just paperwork to do and deadlines to meet. If there's nothing to fight off or run from, the unused energy (anxiety) will sit inside your body, and over time may cause severe damage.

If you are experiencing anxiety in your life or relationships, it is a calling for action. You can take action by doing the right things at the right times. Or you can take action by monitoring your thoughts and perceptions to make sure they accurately represent the true situation. God designed your electrical system to run in a healthy manner. He wants you to use your energy along with the radio to make music, not to shock yourself and other drivers on the road of life.

If you are experiencing anxiety and can't resolve it by doing what you know to be the right thing, try writing an anxiety letter at least once a day. It will help you get in touch with any possible distorted or irrational forms of thinking.

Steps to Writing an Anxiety Letter

Step 1: Make a Commitment

Most of us experience some type of anxiety or tension on a daily basis. At first it might be difficult to recognize the low levels of tension that build into unhealthy situations of anxiety. That's why it's helpful to write at least one anxiety letter per day. Try to record your information immediately after you realize your anxious feelings so the thoughts and behaviors that created this internal energy can be identified.

Step 2: Rate the Subject

Begin your letter by writing down a brief description of the events that created the unused personal power and energy you are experiencing. Then rate the intensity of these anxious feelings on a scale of one to ten. For example, a traffic jam might be rated four and being late to an appointment might be rated an eight for intensity.

Step 3: Recognizing Your Irrational Thoughts

Many times we automatically think distorted and irrational thoughts when we experience feelings of anxiety. It's helpful to identify any forms of distorted perceptions and write down a brief description of what you were thinking whenever anxious feelings arise.

There are ten common forms of distorted thinking patterns, all of which will cause your brain to produce an overabundance of unusable energy. A good example of this can be taken from the thoughts of a person late to an appointment due to a traffic jam:

* All or none thinking — "Because I'm late, my whole day is ruined."
* Perfectionism — "I'll look like a failure if I don't get to my appointment on time."
* Predicting the future — "This delay will take hours."
* Blaming — "It's my fault because I chose this route."
* Failure to recognize the positive — "I can't do anything right."
* Justification through our feelings — "I feel like a loser, so it must be true."
* Mind reading — "I know people at the meeting hate me already."
* Martyrdom — "I know God is trying to make me lose out on this deal."
* Name calling — "I wish these stupid reject construction workers would get out of my way."
* Authoritative — "I will *never* again do that. I *must* get out of here. This *always* happens to me."

Thinking in this manner will only make the situation worse. These thoughts are harmful because they do not accurately represent the truth. If you find yourself thinking like this, try to identify the distorted thinking patterns and record your thoughts in the anxiety letter. For more information on distorted thinking patterns, please see the Perceptions chapter.

Step 4: Study Your Behavior

Next write a brief description of how you were acting. How did you react to the situation that caused those anxious feelings? It might be helpful to imagine how someone else would describe your behavior; for example, I was constantly changing the radio station and dangerously cutting other drivers off to get to my appointment on time.

Step 5: Decide on Future Thoughts

It's helpful to write down some rational thoughts that would be more appropriate for this situation in the future. Rational thoughts during anxiety experiences will help reduce and manage that overabundance of unused electrical current your body is generating. Some useful and calming mental perception might be, "It's okay, I can handle this. It's not my fault. I'll find a different way. I'll make a call and let the other people know I will be arriving 20 minutes late."

Since many forms of distorted perceptions are based on fears and not facts, it's helpful to find the truth about a situation — for example, "I may or may not be late. If I had known about the traffic delay, I would have chosen a different route. I don't know what effects, if any, this inconvenience will have on my future deals. It's even possible that the people I am meeting are caught up in the same traffic jam."

Step 6: Decide on Future Behavior

Now write down some ways you might handle this situation in the future. What would be the ideal reaction to this type of situation? What behavior would be the most appropriate? For example, "Next time I will focus my attention on the tenseness in my body and stay in one lane in traffic. Then I will practice breathing techniques, do affirmations and monitor my perceptions to make sure they represent the truth."

Step 7: Make Daily Efforts

Changing behavior is not always easy. Many times we behave the only way we know how. By writing daily anxiety letters, we can begin to see patterns, solutions and changes we can make that will minimize the amount of anxiety in our lives and relationships. Many times our anxiety is closely related to and caused by some form of fear. It might be necessary to transform and heal any underlying fears responsible for your recurring anxiety attacks. If your anxiety letters help you recognize a pattern of fearful events or thoughts, please see the Fear chapter for ideas on how to get rid of them.

It's important to turn to God for wisdom, knowledge and understanding on a daily basis. Ask for assistance in determining the proper course of action to take if your anxiety is a calling to do the right things at the right times. If your anxiety is being caused by distorted thinking patterns, ask God for assistance in recognizing unhealthy thought patterns and changing your behavior. God will be there for you in either situation, helping eliminate anxiety from your life and relationships.

Visions of Inspiration

Therefore I tell you, do not worry about your life, what you will eat or what you will drink, or about your body, what you will wear. Is not life more than food, and the body more than clothing? Look at the birds of the air; they neither sow nor reap nor gather into barns, and yet your heavenly Father feeds them. Are you not of more value than they?

Matthew 6: 25-26

Worry a little bit every day and in a lifetime you will lose a couple of years. If something is wrong, fix it if you can. But train yourself not to worry. Worry never fixes anything.

Mary Hemingway

Rule Number 1 is, don't sweat the small stuff. Rule Number 2 is, it's all small stuff. And if you can't fight and you can't flee, flow.

Dr. Robert S Eliot

Humble yourselves therefore under the mighty hand of God, so that he may exalt you in due time. Cast all your anxiety on him, because he cares for you.

1 Peter 5: 6-7

BEHAVIOR

TOOL 5

A great way to study behavior is to look at people when they are behind the wheel of a car. If we placed today's drivers into three different categories, we would probably end up with passive, aggressive and assertive.

Usually the aggressive driver recklessly violates other people on the road by traveling at a high rate of speed, cutting off others, failing to signal and tailgating. Aggressive behavior is dangerous, violating and unhealthy because the driver might not be able to stop or control the car in time to prevent a crash.

The same is true of passive drivers. They violate other people on the road by traveling too slow. They inconvenience the people behind them as everyone is forced to maneuver around a slower obstacle. It's necessary to plan ahead for them, wait, and in many cases stop for them, because a crash may also occur. Passive behavior is dangerous, unhealthy, violating to self and violating to others.

The third driving style is assertive. This is where a driver keeps up with traffic and remains in control of the vehicle. Assertive drivers don't drive too fast, endangering others, and they don't drive too slow, inconveniencing others. They realize some situations require aggressiveness, like making way for a fire truck at a blocked intersection, while other situations require passiveness, like letting another car merge in front of them.

Assertive behavior is healthy; passive and aggressive behaviors are both equally destructive, dangerous, violating and unhealthy. Passive people violate themselves first and then indirectly violate others later. Aggressive people violate others first and then indirectly violate themselves later.

Every motorist on the road today at one time learned how to drive a car. No one was born with that ability. In the same way, most of our human behavior is learned. Usually we all had to study a motor vehicle instruction manual and pass written and road side tests before we could get our licenses.

If we all learned how to drive in an assertive manner, why do people cause accidents and violate others every day with their aggressive and passive behaviors? What makes one driver aggressive and another passive, when our driving behavior is a learned response? There are only two possible reasons: The lack of a spiritual connection or negative subconscious programming. Let's look at how these conditions affect our unhealthy and violating behaviors.

People who lack a spiritual connection might not believe in God or have a very close relationship with God. If they don't, why would they care if their actions violated another person? If these people avoided a connection with their Inner Self, their conscience might have a hard time communicating feelings of guilt to them. They might even be able to cause an accident and not even care, if they got away with it. God teaches us right from wrong, using our conscience through our Inner Self. People devoid of their spirituality might violate others with their passive or aggressive behaviors without any consideration for anything besides their own interests.

Negative subconscious programming from our past is the second possible reason behind our unhealthy or violating behaviors. Usually we all start out driving assertively, just as we learned in the driving manual. Then maybe an aggressive driver cut us off and forced us off the road and into a ditch. If we did not do the necessary healing and forgiveness work, this experience could affect our behavior in either a passive or aggressive manner. We might become aggressive drivers ourselves, making sure "nothing like that ever happens to us again." In an attempt to protect ourselves, we might drive around violating others in the same way we ourselves were violated. Or if another motorist sent our car into a ditch, we might fear the situation and drive extra carefully, making sure the same thing never happens again. In an attempt to protect ourselves, we might drive very slowly, inconveniencing others in the same way we ourselves were inconvenienced and hurt. Usually when our behavior turns passive or aggressive, it stems from some form of subconscious hurt that remains unhealed.

Many times passive and aggressive people are attracted to each other in their relationships for the sole purpose of helping each other grow in their abilities to be assertive. For instance, a passive driver who completely stops his vehicle at the bottom of a freeway on-ramp might be attracted to an aggressive driver who quickly accelerates while looking back to search for an opening in the oncoming traffic. When they meet, the passive driver might learn the importance of merging assertively and the aggressive driver might learn the importance of yielding to others assertively.

In the same way, passive and aggressive behaviors can be just as destructive to your life and relationships. Aggressive people make choices for others by infringing on their rights. They usually get their way by demanding, criticizing, blaming, accusing, hurting and verbally abusing others. Aggressive people achieve their goals and needs at the expense of others.

When we are too passive, we can violate ourselves. Passive people allow others to make decisions for them without considering their own needs. This self-sacrificing and self-denying behavior is unhealthy because it allows other people to take advantage of us and violate our rights. Passive behavior usually results in frustration, anger and resentment.

Because passive and aggressive behaviors can cause a lot of problems in relationships, the following steps have been designed to help you be more assertive in your own interactions.

Steps to Creating Assertive Behavior

Step 1: Identify Unhealthy Behaviors

If you want to act more assertively, it's necessary to first identify any unhealthy behaviors in your life and relationships. Most of us know which side of the line our tendencies seem to reside. If we behave in a passive manner, we usually realize it through the disrespect and pain that accompanies our actions. People who are aggressive might not be aware that their actions are violating others unless they have been confronted in the past. Aggressive people who always seem to get their way have little incentive to change their behavior unless they're told and shown the damage that it causes. If you are unsure whether your behavior is excessively passive or aggressive, ask a trusted friend, coworker or your relationship partner.

Step 2: List Unhealthy Behaviors

Create a list of unhealthy passive or aggressive behaviors you would like to change. Begin by writing down any recurring behaviors or conflicts from your past where you were overly passive or aggressive. What happened in your past when you failed to act assertively? What similar actions or situations would you like to change in the future? Look at your interactions with other people such as salespeople, coworkers, restaurant servers, family, relatives, friends and strangers. If you are working with a partner, try to help them identify any areas in their own life where more assertiveness could be beneficial.

Step 3: Consider Advantages and Disadvantages

Now consider the advantages and disadvantages of your unhealthy behaviors. By taking the time and effort to study the consequences of your unhealthy behavior, you may be more motivated to change it in the future. Start by making a list that describes all the harm your nonassertive behavior causes to yourself and others. What effect does your aggressive behavior have on your marriage or relationship partner when you violate their rights through aggression? How does the other person's anger come back to affect your relationship? If you act in a passive manner, list all the disadvantages you personally experience. How does the loss of your self-respect, self-worth and unfulfilled needs affect other people around you?

Next, address all the positive advantages you can gain by acting more assertively. What benefits will you experience in your life and relationships by changing your behavior? Make sure you address both the positive and negative aspects of each item listed in Step 2.

Step 4: Heal the Past

Look at your past conditioning to determine where your unhealthy behaviors were learned. Many times our passive and aggressive tendencies stem from our childhood. As children, we naturally presented our needs to our care-givers in a direct and assertive manner. We cried when we were hungry and asked to have ice cream whenever we wanted it. If our requests and needs were unfulfilled, we probably learned other indirect methods to get what we wanted. Maybe we learned to act aggressively by being very demanding in order to receive the attention we needed. Or maybe we learned to act passively by playing the helpless victim in order to receive what we wanted.

Many times those learned behaviors from our childhood accompany us into our adult lives. If you have been acting in a nonassertive manner for a long time, it's helpful to go back and heal your past where these unhealthy behaviors were learned. For more information on how to do this, see the Power chapter, which deals with the victim or helpless role (passive behavior), the demanding persecutor role (aggressive behavior) and the enabler or rescuer role (which can be either passive or aggressive). If necessary, follow the instructions and healing procedures before continuing to Step 5.

Step 5: Learn New Behaviors

Once you have healed and reprogrammed any subconscious tendencies to act in a nonassertive manner, your next step is to learn new assertive behaviors. There are several ways you can learn to behave assertively:

❖ **Select a good role model** — Learning to act assertively becomes easier when we have a good role model to follow. Most of our behaviors are simply a learned or conditioned response. By following the example of assertive role models, we can change our behaviors. Try to pick someone you feel is very assertive. Whom do you know who handles situations, conflicts or confrontations efficiently? Study your role model's behavior and ask yourself: How do they express themselves, listen to others and make decisions? How do they act compassionately toward others and at the same time stand up for what is right? How would your role model handle the situations described in the list in Step 2? Once you have identified assertive qualities in your role model, look within yourself to discover and develop those identical attributes.

❖ **Use imagination techniques** — A very powerful way to change your behavior is through imagination techniques. Begin with a relaxed, meditative state of mind. Take one of the items from the list in Step 2 that you wish to improve on. In your imagination re-create the situation so it produces the results you desire. For example, let's say you would like to be more assertive in meeting people at parties. In your imagination visualize a party scene with someone you would like to meet. At first it might be helpful to study your role model's behavior. Vividly imagine your role model as they confidently and assertively interact with other people at the party. Next, envision someone who looks like you interacting in the same scene. Finally, envision yourself acting assertively and accomplishing the desired results. Allow your subconscious to experience how good it feels to act assertively and meet new people at the party. The more often you create positive, healthy and assertive behavior in your imagination, the more your external reality will begin to reflect those same results.

❖ **Try role-playing** — Role-playing is another powerful way to change your behavior. Many times opposites in relationships are drawn to each other because they are attracted to those qualities in their partner that they themselves lack. If your partner's tendencies are at the opposite extremes of your own, they could be an excellent teacher. By working together, you can create more assertiveness in both of your lives. Other methods of role-playing could include the slave/master game. Try playing it for an hour at a time before reversing roles with your partner. One person agrees to be the slave and the other person the master. The master gives orders and the slave performs the specified duties. The passive partner hopefully learns more about being aggressive, and the aggressive person can experience how it feels to be ordered around. Other forms of role-playing that may be helpful in changing your behavior might include gradual exposure. If you are intimidated and passive around auto mechanics, make it a personal assignment to stop by a local garage every night after work for a week and get an estimate or ask questions. By gradually exposing yourself to situations where you lack assertiveness, you will become more assertive in dealing with those situations. Look at the items listed in Step 2 and create some different methods of behavior modification through role playing.

❖ **Check body language** — It's important to check and monitor your body language to be sure you're presenting an assertive image to others. For example, if you are really angry and upset but portray humorous and silly body language, other people will probably have a hard time taking you seriously. Many times we don't know how we look or appear to others unless we get direct feedback. It might be helpful to have a friend record, tape or critique your behavior to see how you are interacting and presenting yourself to others. Direct eye contact portrays the seriousness of your message. Intention of your message can be adjusted by hand gestures for added emphasis. Try to use your entire body to establish the amount of distance between you and other people. Depending on your situation, leaning in closer or pulling yourself away can generate an assertive expression to your message. Tone and volume of your voice, along with the content and timing of your messages, are also important factors to consider when portraying an assertive image.

❖ **Make daily efforts** — Changing our passive or aggressive behaviors requires daily efforts. Many times we will experience temporary setbacks as we revert to our conditioned tendencies. When this happens, it's important to forgive ourselves and others. If you have allowed yourself to be violated, make amends to yourself. If you have violated another through aggression, make the necessary retributions. In either event it's important to learn from those mistakes to prevent their recurrence in the future. God will help you throughout life, especially when you call on Him through your daily actions, words and thoughts.

Visions of Inspiration

Keep your heart with all vigilance, for from it flow the springs of life. Put away from you crooked speech, and put devious talk far from you. Let your eyes look directly forward, and your gaze be straight before you. Keep straight the path of your feet, and all your ways will be sure.

Proverbs 4: 23-26

We should behave to our friends as we would wish our friends to behave to us.

Aristotle

BLAME

TOOL 6

*I*magine driving around town when suddenly your car crashes into another motorist. Whose fault would it be? Surely someone is to blame — is it your fault or theirs? Usually our first response is to blame the other party. But before that can happen, you will need some facts and rules to prove your point. If both parties agree to a specific set of rules, like traffic laws, and someone violates a specific rule, clearly everyone knows whose insurance company will pay the bill. But what happens when there aren't any clearly defined rules?

Let's say that your car crashes into another person's car while driving across private property. If the traffic laws did not apply in this situation, who would you blame? Should the bigger car have the right-of-way? Or should the faster car? Can you imagine how childish the conversation would sound if both drivers blamed one another? "It's your fault!" "No, it's your fault!" "I was here first!" "No, you weren't. I was here first!" "My car is bigger!" "So, who cares? My car is faster!" "My dad is going to beat up your dad!" "No, my lawyer is going to beat up you and your dad!" Even if one party got tired of blaming the other and accepted responsibility for their actions, wouldn't both cars still be damaged? Even if you blamed the other party for the accident, wouldn't both cars still need to be fixed?

How does blame and the lack of personal responsibility help repair the emotional and physical damage incurred in an automobile accident? The answer is, it doesn't. The only way you are going to fix your emotional damage is through some healing and forgiveness work. The only way you are going to fix your physically damaged car is by being responsible enough to get it into an auto body shop. Blame, therefore, is a calling for forgiveness work and responsibility, all of which happens inside yourself. It's not necessary to make someone say, "I'm sorry, it's my fault," before you can forgive them. It's not necessary to make someone acknowledge their mistakes before you assume responsibility for your own circumstances.

Whenever you blame another person or situation for problems affecting your life, you surrender to them your own personal power of responsibility. Blame is a waste of valuable time and energy that could be used in the forgiveness process and in following through with responsible behaviors. Any time you hear your relationship partner blaming anyone or anything, you know they really need to take some form of responsibility and perform some type of forgiveness work. And of course, the same is true for every motorist on the road of life, including yourself. The following steps are designed to help you transform blame into forgiveness and responsibility.

Steps to Transforming Blame

Step 1: Make an Identification List

First, make a written list describing all the situations where blame is present in your life. Try to include all the people, places, things, events or circumstances you blame yourself or others for. List anyone or anything in your life that you are dissatisfied with or unhappy about. Think of as many circumstances as possible and write them down in one large list.

Step 2: Assign Reasons

Next, explain the reasons behind your blame. Describe why these other people, places, things, events or circumstances are at fault. Why do you blame them? Why are they responsible? What did they do to cause you to feel this way? Write down a reason for every item on your identification list.

Step 3: Heal Experiences

Now you're ready to heal any unjust or unfair experiences, events or circumstances that you have suffered. Begin by writing a healing letter for every item on your identification list. (Instructions for the healing letter can be found in the Healing chapter.) This letter can be addressed and written to anyone or anything you blame. For example, if you blame government or society, address your letter to a political leader or to the people in your community. Address your letters to whomever you feel is at fault: God, yourself, parents, family, old friends, ex-relationship partners, television, media or the human race. Take the time necessary to complete this forgiveness process to the best of your abilities.

Step 4: Determine Responsibility

To determine which aspects of responsibility lie within your direct control, break the blamed situation into smaller parts. There are three possible actions to choose from: *internal actions,* which involve our behaviors, such as what we can do about the situation and the ways we think, act and perceive things; *external actions,* which involve the ways we act and interact with other people and the ways we can influence, motivate and direct their behaviors; and *acceptance,* where we learn to accept situations that lie beyond our direct control.

For example, let's say you blame a flat tire on roofers who left nails in your driveway. You can take some *internal* actions like changing the tire yourself and forgiving the roofers; you can take some *external* actions like having a tow truck driver to help with the flat; or you can influence the roofers to pay compensation for the damages. If you have exhausted all your internal and external actions, you can always *accept* the situation and entrust it to God.

It's helpful to study the blamed situations on your identification list from Step 1 to determine which internal, external or acceptance actions lie within your direct control. Once you have a list of these available options, all you need do is follow through with responsible actions.

Visions of Inspiration

Each man is questioned by life; and he can only answer to life by answering for his own life; to life he can only respond by being responsible.

Dr. Viktor Frankl

I will sing of loyalty and of justice; to you, O Lord, I will sing. I will study the way that is blameless. When shall I attain it? I will walk with integrity of heart within my house; I will not set before my eyes anything that is base.

Psalm 101: 1-3

People are always blaming their circumstances for what they are. I don't believe in circumstances. The people who get on in this world are the people who get up and look for the circumstances they want, and , if they can' find them, make them.

George Shaw

BOUNDARIES

TOOL 7

*I*magine you parked your car in a high crime area. Now picture a person about to break into your vehicle and steal the stereo. At first you watch this person case out the situation, then they walk up to the driver side window to get a closer look. At this point do you think the burglar has done anything wrong? Next, they check the door to see if it's locked. Now have they done something wrong? What would you say to a person who has checked the door handle on your car? Would you view them as a threat or a friend? Are they trying to steal your radio, or were they attempting to turn off your head lights in hopes of preventing a dead battery? If someone opened your car's door, are they doing something wrong? Do they need to remove your stereo and run away down the street before you consider it a personal violation?

Where would you draw your boundary line in this situation? At what point would you take action to protect yourself and your car? The choice will be different for everyone. If you have had a stereo stolen in the past, your boundary line might be drawn once the person looked through the glass window. If you never had anyone break into your car, your boundary line might be once someone climbed into the front seat.

Boundaries are mental lines we draw to protect ourselves from being hurt, used, abused, threatened or encroached upon. Your car has specific safety devices like the air bag to protect you from danger. In the same way, you will need to set up your own specific safety devices and boundaries to help protect yourself from danger. Boundaries are like personal laws that help us determine who we are, where we stand, how we will react, how much we can give and what we will and will not tolerate. When these personal lines are crossed, we know it's time to take action to protect ourselves. When these lines are not crossed, we can allow ourselves to be free, open and loving in our relationships.

Cars are easier to protect than people because your vehicle only exists in a physical realm. If your car is violated in any way, there's always some kind of physical evidence of the crime. People, on the other hand, can be hurt mentally, emotionally, spiritually and physically. Therefore, our boundaries or protective devices will need to be much more elaborate and maintained on a regular basis to provide adequate protection. If someone opens your car door, the alarm will go off. When someone violates you emotionally, like with negative criticism, your internal alarm will warn you through your negative feelings. If you are not well connected to your emotions and Inner Self, you might have a hard time responding to the early warning signs. People who suffered a traumatic childhood might have grown up accustomed to having their alarm go off all the time. Unfortunately, these people usually travel from one abusive relationship to the next and might not be able to set healthy boundaries for themselves without first doing some healing work.

God loves each and every one of us deeply. He is always there to help maintain and enforce our personal safety equipment. All you need to do is listen to your Inner Self and express your rights in an assertive manner. If your alarm system has been deactivated, the following steps will help evaluate your current boundaries.

Steps to Evaluating the Lack of Boundaries

Step 1: List Harmful Aspects

First, make a list of all the people, places, events or things that take advantage of you. Write down situations where you experience mental, physical, spiritual or emotional abuse in your life. What makes you feel empty inside? What makes you sick? What makes you angry? What hurts you? Take a look at anything that you despise, dislike, hate, cannot stand or are offended by. Identify any situations that cause anxiety, fear or panic or scare you somehow.

Step 2: Recognize the Damage

Next, describe why the items in the harmful aspect list are damaging to you. Write down an explanation for every item, and describe how and why you suffer or feel hurt, used or abused.

Step 3: Evaluate the Situation

Now evaluate the items in your harmful aspect list. By self-examination you can determine if there is a rational need for additional boundaries in your life. Ask yourself the five questions listed below regarding every item on your list. If you answer "yes" to any of these questions, adding additional boundaries might help you protect yourself. If so, move on to Step 4 for assistance in developing additional protective boundaries. If you have answered "no" to any of these questions, you might want to review information in the Blame chapter.

* ❖ Is there something you can do to protect yourself from being taken advantage of in this situation?
* ❖ Do other people make personal decisions for you?
* ❖ Does it seem like you are the only one giving and not receiving in return?
* ❖ Do you feel consumed and overwhelmed by other people's wishes and demands?
* ❖ Do you feel as though God doesn't want you to protect yourself, only to self-sacrifice?

Step 4: Develop Protective Boundaries

After you have evaluated the need for additional protective boundaries, it's necessary to create some personal laws that are designed out of love and protection for everyone involved. Begin creating your personal laws by writing down a list of rules that will protect you from the violations you are experiencing. Make sure these rules are designed out of love and protection for everyone involved.

It's important to share these laws with anyone who has the potential to violate them in the future. If you suffer from emotional, physical or mental abuse, it's important to take action immediately. Refer to the Abuse chapter for more information and steps. Learning to act assertively will help maintain your protective boundaries in the future. See the Behavior chapter for more information.

Visions of Inspiration

Do not stand in a place of danger trusting in miracles.

Arab proverb

Do you not fear me? says the Lord; Do you not tremble before me? I placed the sand as a boundary for the sea, a perpetual barrier that cannot pass; though the waves toss, they cannot prevail, though they roar, they cannot pass over it.

Jeremiah 5: 22

Only those means of security are good, are certain, are lasting, that depend on yourself and your own vigor.

Machiavelli

CHANGE

TOOL 8

*H*ave you ever turned on to a one-way street going the wrong direction? Almost instantly we know something is wrong, as cars head straight at us. Apparently we were mentally, emotionally and physically prepared to go one direction, but through some unforeseen circumstances we are now being forced to make some changes. If you have ever made this wrong turn mistake, you have only two options from which to choose.

Your first choice is to refuse to make changes. All you need to do is think the same mental thoughts, deny and repress any emotions that arise as warning signs, and drive your car head-on into the oncoming traffic. Your second choice will produce less damage to your car, life and relationships, but will require a little more work. Here it will be necessary to change your mental thoughts, vent any negative emotions that may arise and turn your car around to avoid a crash. If this situation happened to you tomorrow, would you try to fight the changes or would you do the necessary work and flow with them?

Life is a constant process of change. Every day, everything is constantly changing around us. If we fail to adjust ourselves mentally, physically and emotionally, we will end up looking like a car that has been driven the wrong way down a one-way street. Usually the more time and energy we invest in creating a pre-determined reality, the harder it is for us to change. For example, a motorist who drives the wrong way down a one-way street apparently has not invested much time or mental energy into the decision. Because the investment is small, it will be relatively easy making the adjustments required to change the course of the vehicle. All that driver needs to do is acknowledge a mistake and make a U-turn.

But changes can be extremely difficult to deal with when they occur after we have invested years of our time and energy in a marriage, career or relationship. If you have put years of your life into the community where you live, what are you going to do when your partner gets a job transfer? The changes of buying a new house and calling a moving van can happen very quickly compared with the emotional and mental adjustments that will be necessary to change your life. Unfortunately, it's not so easy to let go of the friends, family and community you will be leaving behind.

It's important to remember that change brings with it the opportunity for new growth. Whenever a part of your life is left behind, an equal amount of space is opened up for something new. We can't experience the brightness of a new day without passing through the night. Life is a constant process of growth, which can only take place through changing events and circumstances. If you find your life changing in new directions, it will be necessary to grow and change if you want to avoid a head-on collision. The following steps have been designed to help you in that process.

Steps to Benefiting From Change

Step 1: Express Your Feelings

Confronting and expressing all your feelings is the first step in dealing with changes. Begin by writing down all your feelings and thoughts regarding the events in your life when you are facing changes. Describe what's happening, how it's affecting your life and who is at fault. Explain any feelings of anger, frustration and resentment that you may be experiencing. Next, write down all your concerns, fears or regrets. What are you concerned about, and what don't you want to happen? Make a list that describes ten of the worst possible outcomes. What would happen if all ten of these outcomes became reality? Write down how you could survive even the worst-case scenario.

Step 2: Be Patient With Yourself

We are all capable of adapting to changes; all we need is time. By accepting the uncomfortable feelings that surround new situations, we begin the process of acceptance. Allow yourself time for that readjustment process. Because the physical changes happen quickly doesn't mean the emotional and mental adjustments will automatically keep pace. If you are having a hard time with the readjustment process, try cultivating some interests, activities or friendships you haven't had time for in the past.

Step 3: Leave the Negative Behind

Now make a list of items about yourself, life and relationships that you want to leave behind. Many times with changes come the opportunities to free yourself from old expectations, ways of thinking and patterns of behavior. Write down any aspects about yourself or life you would be better off without. What responsibilities, commitments or bad habits are you willing to let go? Simplifying your life can be very fulfilling, peaceful and satisfying. Remember — change opens up the chance to start over.

Step 4: Create New Opportunities

Whenever changes present themselves in life, new growth and opportunities are right there as well. Make a list of items about your life and relationships that you want to improve, advance or re-create. Take a look at every aspect of your life for anything that you have always wanted to do or develop. Through these current changes, you may now have the opportunity and freedom to accomplish the things you have always wanted. Write down all your proposed changes, advantages, freedoms, gifts and positive aspects that are possible now that your situation is open to change.

Step 5: Make Daily Efforts

Benefiting from change requires daily effort. Concentrating and thinking positive thoughts about the future and yourself is very important. By looking ahead, thinking successful thoughts and practicing daily affirmations, you can empower yourself to do anything. Try to establish a clear perspective between cherishing your past and clinging to things that keep you from moving forward in life. It's all right to treasure, value and cherish your old job, the house you left behind, your old city and town, distant friends, family and past memories, but it's unhealthy to cling to them. Try to focus your attention on your new plans and future. Set goals and share your plans, hopes and dreams with other people. By expressing your new plans to others, you publicly commit yourself to their accomplishment and at the same time include those other people into your life.

Turning to God in prayer is essential during times of change. Ask for strength, courage and detaching love in dealing with the past, and guidance, understanding and direction for dealing with the future.

Visions of Inspiration

God is our refuge and strength, a very present help in trouble. Therefore we will not fear, though the earth should change, though the mountains shake in the heart of the sea.

Psalm 46: 1-2

Do not remember the former things, or consider the things of old. I am about to do a new thing; now it springs forth, do you not perceive it? I will make a way in the wilderness and rivers in the desert.

Isaiah 43: 18-19

God please grant me the serenity to accept the things I cannot change. The courage to change the things I can, and the wisdom to know the difference.

The Serenity Prayer

Keep constantly in mind in how many things you yourself have witnessed changes already. The universe is change, life is understanding.

Marcus Aurelius

CLOSURE

TOOL 9

*I*magine for a minute that God owned a giant car lot, and one day He loaned you one of the vehicles. At first this new car was great — it was exciting, clean and valuable. But like everything else in the world, this car would need maintenance. Now let's pretend that you neglected to maintain God's car. You knew the oil needed to be changed regularly but hoped the car would change its own oil or hoped that God would secretly do the maintenance work for you somehow. After all, He was nice enough to let you borrow the car in the first place. Wouldn't He be nice enough to maintain it for you as well?

Then after neglecting God's car over a period of time, it started developing transmission and clutch problems. The gears constantly made a loud, grinding noise whenever you tried to shift. Sometimes when you carefully used the proper combination of gas pedal and clutch pedal, the car shifted smoothly. Other times when you failed to use the clutch, the car made the loud, unpleasant grinding noise. "Something must be wrong with this car," you thought. Sometimes you felt it was easier to leave the car in first gear than to go through the hassle of shifting. The only problem with leaving the car in first gear was the engine made a really loud noise whenever you started going very fast.

After a while in this vehicle any motorist would be frustrated, right? The question is, would you ask God for a faster car that didn't make those funny engine and transmission noises? Or would you be mad at God for letting you borrow it in the first place? Would you dump the car in a ditch somewhere and grab another vehicle off God's lot without bothering to ask His permission? And why did God give you a standard transmission instead of an automatic transmission in the first place? If you keep blaming the car, will you ever learn how to properly maintain, drive and take care of any vehicle? If you get another new car, will the same thing happen to it if it isn't maintained and driven properly?

If you're wondering what this situation has to do with relationships, it's simple. The car borrowed from God in this analogy represents our personal relationships. The inability to properly drive the vehicle represents our personal shortcomings. Usually God handpicks cars with standard transmissions because He wants you to learn how to drive a five-speed. Sure, an automatic transmission might seem easier, but God would rather have His children learn, grow and develop their abilities than take the easy way out. God is loving and He wants us, as His children, to be just as loving.

There is no better way to learn how to be more loving than to be in a committed relationship or marriage. This is because relationships and marriages require only two things to be successful: self-love and love of others. If you are experiencing relationship problems, one or both of you are lacking in your abilities to be loving. If you and your partner love each other and maintain enough self-love, the relationship will flourish and function beautifully. If you are involved in a loving relationship, you will be enjoying its tremendous value, and both parties will not want it to end in closure. If you are involved in a relationship that lacks love, it is a calling for more personal growth and a deeper ability to practice self-love and love of others.

The only reason to intentionally end a relationship is that something is preventing your efforts to grow spiritually in a loving manner. Usually we can be loving toward our partner regardless of any circumstances. If your partner is emotionally, physically or mentally abusive, your self-love will demand that you remove yourself from the situation until your partner can get help to be more loving in return. If you are involved in a physically abusive or emotionally or spiritually destructive relationship, it will be necessary to remove yourself from the relationship immediately.

If your partner wants to end your relationship and you don't, unfortunately there isn't a lot you can do. Almost all states allow for no-fault divorce, where either party can divorce the other without their consent. If your partner wants to see other people, it's not possible to stop them. If you find yourself in a forced breakup, you are probably experiencing a lot of pain. You can do some healing work, forgive your partner, rebuild your self-concept, learn from your mistakes, grow spiritually and ask God for another car. Or you can live life being hurt, wounded, resentful, angry and afraid to get another vehicle because of the pain and damage the last one has caused.

Relationships are made for growth, and breakups are also made for growth. When a relationship comes to an end, you might find yourself compulsively consumed with the other person. Many times you can't stop thinking about the good times you shared, wondering why the breakup happened, feeling sorry for yourself, replaying old memories and feeling rejected and abandoned. The situation will inevitably feel worse if you loved your partner more than they loved you. If that's the case, it's helpful to work your way through the following process so that you can properly grieve your loss and restore your peace of mind.

Steps to Getting Over a Relationship

Step 1: Grieve Your Loss

It's helpful to work your way through the grieving process after experiencing the loss of your partner. The greater our efforts and abilities to love, the greater our abilities to experience the pain of the loss. The more time, energy and love you invested in the relationship, the more it hurts when you break up. By working through the grieving process, you will be converting the negative pain into positive experiences and growth. The grieving process has four parts or stages:

- **Confrontation** — Acknowledging, recognizing, defining and admitting your loss.
- **Confusion** — Working through the emotional turmoil that arises.
- **Change** — Reinvesting your love, time and energy into another partner or situation.
- **Contentment** — Finding a positive way to view the situation and grow from the experience.

The amount of time you will need to work through these stages will depend on your loss. The harder you work, the faster you can recover. The information listed in the Grieving/Loss chapter will help you through this process.

Step 2: Monitor and Change Your Thoughts

Next it will be helpful to control any compulsive thoughts and change your perceptions. Many times we increase our pain and suffering by dwelling on unnecessary thoughts regarding our ex-partner. Not only are these thoughts unpleasant, but by allowing their existence, we surrender our present and future over to that person as well. It's necessary to start monitoring and changing your thinking patterns. When you find yourself thinking about your ex-partner, try to figure out why. If you are fantasizing and dreaming about the good times you shared, change your thoughts to ones that will create and promote good times for yourself or someone else in your life. If you find yourself thinking loving thoughts about your ex-partner, convert them to loving thoughts about yourself. If you find yourself thinking angry thoughts about your ex-partner, then some forgiveness work will be necessary (see Step 4).

Other times we may overvalue our ex-partner in our minds, thinking of them almost in terms of gods. No one is perfect and it's very destructive to honor another person in place of God. If you find yourself worshipping your ex-partner, convert your worship to your Heavenly Father. It's important to realize that it was your own ability to love your ex-partner that created such a high perception in your mind. By changing your perceptions of the person, you can change the amount of value they represent. The less value your ex-partner represents, the easier you will get over them.

Other ways of changing your perceptions can include imagination techniques. If you were attracted to the seriousness of your ex-partner, try imagining them acting silly. If your ex-partner was very athletic, try imaging what they would look like as a couch-potato.

Step 3: Perform Self Work

Next it will be helpful to perform some self work. You can begin by changing your thoughts and perceptions from how much you love this person to how much you need this person. Usually our hurt stems from how much the person was needed and how much it hurts now that they're gone. You can still continue your love for them in your heart, but it's unlikely that will help you with your pain. Once you get in touch with how much the former partner was needed, you can identify those needs and fulfill them for yourself. See the Primary Human Needs chapter for a list of those needs. It will also be beneficial to work on your self-concept and self-acceptance at this time.

Step 4: Forgive

The next step in getting over a relationship is working through the forgiveness process. Many times we blame ourselves or our partners for events that happened in the past. Any time blame is present in our lives, it's a calling for forgiveness and responsibility. You might have made some serious mistakes in the past that contributed to the breakup. If so, it will be empowering to work through the healing steps listed in the Forgiveness or Guilt chapters. If you find yourself consumed with anger and resentment toward your ex-partner, some healing work will help restore your own personal peace and well-being. Refer to the healing steps listed in the Resentment/Revenge, Healing or Forgiveness chapters for more information. Begin by writing a list of all the mistakes you made and all the damage you suffered from your ex-partner's actions. Then write some forgiveness and healing letters to help free yourself from this emotional turmoil.

Step 5: Make Daily Efforts

Getting over the pain involved in breakups requires daily effort. Make a commitment to focus some of your time and energy on the future. Those who live in the past can't experience the present. Breakup times are an excellent opportunity to set new goals and reestablish direction, potential and purpose for your life. Turning to old friends and creating new friends is essential. When you're in need, nothing is as comforting as empathetic friends, family and support systems. Loneliness and isolation are very common feelings, after breakups and divorces. The Loneliness/Isolation chapter will help you meet and make new friendships.

Don't forget to turn to God in your times of need. Ask Him for strength, courage, guidance, peace of mind, understanding and the opportunity to grow from your recent breakup and all the lessons that it provides.

Visions of Inspiration

After the relationship has ended: Feel what you are feeling. Mourn. Take time to think about yourself. Denying what you feel doesn't work. Figure out what you have learned by being in this relationship. Only then will you be free to move on.

Dr. Elaine Hatfield

Do not think that I have come to bring peace to the earth; I have not come to bring peace, but a sword. For I have come to set a man against his father, and a daughter against her mother, and a daughter-in-law against her mother-in-law; and one's foes will be members of one's own household. Whoever loves father or mother more than me is not worthy of me; and whoever loves son or daughter more than me is not worthy of me; and whoever does not take up the cross and follow me is not worthy of me. Those who find their life will lose it, and those who lose their life for my sake will find it.

Matthew 10: 34-39

To those suffering from a broken relationship: Give yourself something you always wanted, not what you need. Indulge yourself in some way — it helps restore your self esteem.

Dr. Lee Salk

CODEPENDENCE & INDEPENDENCE

TOOL 10

Imagine what it would be like if God were a car dealer. Do you think He would own a small lot located in the low-rent district? Or do you think God would have a multi-dealership automotive plaza? Now let's pretend that you work for God as one of His lot personnel. One day you are detailing cars when God calls you into His office. God is going to give you a car from the lot so you can enter it in a car show. You are really excited about this once-in-a-lifetime opportunity. On the day of the show God's transport truck pulls up with the oldest junker on the face of the planet. You think to yourself, "This is terrible." The car is in really bad shape and you're embarrassed even to be associated with it. But what can you do? You're stuck with the assignment.

On the floor of the show all the other car owners are standing next to their prized vehicles. How do you think people are going to be looking at you as you stand next to your entry? You are representing a worthless, valueless car in the midst of priceless automobiles! Do you want to hang out next to this junker all weekend? Or would you rather hang out next to someone else's valuable show car? Do you feel good about yourself, focusing your attention on a terrible display? Or does it make you feel better to focus your attention on the other entries in the show?

After a few minutes of standing next to your junker, you can't stand it any longer. You want to get away from it so bad that you run right over to your neighbor's display. At first they are glad to see you, but because of your compulsive drive to get away from your own car, you start crowding their space. You might not realize it, but you are stuck to their car like glue. After a while your neighbor's display needs some space, so they ask you to leave. What are you going to do? You don't want to go back to the junker, so you attach yourself to anything other than the car God gave you to show the world.

Now let's pretend that no one in the coliseum wants you stuck to their priceless show car like glue. So you call God up at the dealership and start to protest. God is cool about the whole situation and knows of another assignment for you on the other side of town. "Thank God," you say as you arrive at another car show assignment. This time you're representing an extremely nice vehicle.

As you pull your car on to the show floor, you realize everyone else there is displaying a bunch of worthless junkers. Your car is the only nice one on the floor. To make things worse, the other people start crowding your display space in an attempt to make themselves feel better. You think to yourself that your car would be safer and look better if you could just get it away from all these worthless neighbors hanging around you.

What are you going to do? How can you isolate yourself and your display from these valueless junkers crowding your space? Surely something can be done! Are you going to make friends with the other car owners, who pose a serious threat to your display? Or is it better to avoid them and minimize the amount of potential damage they are capable of causing?

Finally, after making a decision, you fight everyone off and move your display to an isolated and desolate part of the coliseum. But now it's too lonely, and you are so far removed that no one even knows your display exists. How long can you remain isolated and still feel good about yourself or your display?

What a nightmare! First you were stuck displaying a valueless car and then you were stuck being surrounded by valueless cars. After arriving back at the dealership, God calls you into His office to check on your progress. You tell Him your story and God starts laughing. Apparently God has a great sense of humor and thinks your story is very funny. God gently explains to you that He created all the cars in the world and they are all valuable and priceless. God doesn't create worthless cars!

What does this story have to do with codependent and independent relationships? It's simple. The car show representative in the first assignment is similar to a person with codependent tendencies. The show car representative in the second assignment is similar to a person with independent tendencies.

People with codependent tendencies fail to recognize the value in their own life (or car), and end up classifying it as a junker. They think of themselves as junkers and would much rather hang around other more valuable people and situations in an attempt to make themselves feel better. Codependent people do not like themselves very much, and are embarrassed and ashamed of their own displays. So they attach themselves to other people's displays in an attempt to make themselves feel better. Codependency is almost like an addiction to people, problems and relationships that is fueled by a lack of self-value and self-worth.

Independent people, on the other hand, are those who fail to recognize the value and worth in other people's cars. They classify other people as junkers. No one wants to hang around junkers all day, so independent people spend a lot of time isolating themselves.

Codependency is the inability to recognize your own self-worth and self-value. Independence is the inability to recognize the value and worth in others. God, being the master creator of all cars, asks us to find equal value and worth in ourselves and in others. Both codependent and independent tendencies can cause serious harm to every aspect of our lives and relationships. It's difficult to love someone who devalues themselves, just as it's difficult to love someone who devalues others.

Unfortunately, no one is perfect. We all could be more loving toward ourselves and others. We all have codependent and independent tendencies in us. Take a look at the following characteristics of codependent and independent people to see on which side of the line your attitudes and behaviors fall:

CODEPENDENT	INDEPENDENT
I need other people.	I don't need anyone.
I can't stand to be alone.	I can't stand to be crowded.
I am driven by the need for the approval of others.	I don't care about others or their approval.
All my decisions are based on how they will affect others.	All my decisions are based on how they will affect me.
I don't allow myself to get angry, because it might hurt others.	I express my anger openly and freely. If others get hurt, it's their problem.
I have a hard time saying "No" when people ask me to do something I don't want to do.	I intentionally keep people away so they won't ask me to do anything.

CODEPENDENT (CONT'D)	INDEPENDENT (CONT'D)
I usually find myself fulfilling the needs of my relationship partner first, and never seeming to get my own needs met.	I am capable of fulfilling my own needs, and I make sure they get fulfilled first.
I fear being alone for life.	I fear being committed to someone for life.
I fear intimacy because I don't want anyone to find out who I really am.	I fear intimacy because I don't want anyone getting too close.
It really hurts me when other people let me down.	I alienate myself from people who let me down to prevent myself from getting hurt.

We know that codependent and independent tendencies are caused by the lack of value and worth. But if you are wondering what would cause people to devalue themselves and others, it's simple: Codependent people usually learn to devalue themselves from their childhood experiences. As children, codependent people never received the important messages of dignity, value and self-worth from their parents. Codependent people usually suffered a lot of traumatic events, abuse or neglect in the past, which imprinted a message of valuelessness on their subconscious. Maybe their parents' actions (like name-calling, substance abuse, divorce, criticism and abandonment) caused them to feel worthless as a child. Or maybe their parents' lack of loving actions (like never saying anything nice or saying the words "I love you") caused them to feel worthless as a child.

Codependent programming can also be learned through role modeling. If you are a woman and your mother displayed codependent tendencies, you probably would learn to value others before yourself. If your father treated your mother like she was worthless, you might assume that worthless role as well.

The more unhealed hurt you have suffered in your past, the more worthless and valueless you will feel in the present. People who feel worthless act just like the car show attendant who had to display a worthless car to the world. The only way to break your codependent tendencies is by finding a way to love and value those hurt parts of yourself. The best way to do that is by working your way through the healing process.

Independent tendencies also are learned from the same role modeling. If your father was the strong, silent type who didn't need anyone else, he probably didn't find much value and worth in other people. If your father couldn't find value and worth in other people, he probably didn't find much value and worth in his children. Children who were raised under these conditions might grow up not needing anyone else's love either, especially that of their father.

Independent tendencies can also be learned from negative past experiences. Usually, when people hurt us, we learn not to trust them. It's hard to find value and worth in other people who hurt us and can't be trusted. If every time you tried to be loving toward your father, mother, friends or relationship partner, they rejected and hurt you somehow, you would eventually learn to isolate yourself from those types of people as a form of self-protection. The more unhealed hurt you have suffered in the past, the less value and worth you will be able to recognize in others.

People who fail to recognize value and worth in others act just like the car show attendant surrounded by junkers. The only way to break your independent tendencies is to find value and worth in other people regardless of their hurtful actions. The best way to do that is by going back into the past and forgiving the people, situations and events where your independent tendencies were learned.

Both codependent and independent tendencies are equally harmful, to yourself and to your relationships, and are callings for healing work. Being completely independent without the ability to connect, depend on or share an intimate part of yourself with others is just as destructive as any codependent relationship where an individual cannot function without the approval of or connection with another.

The ideal condition is called inter-independence (see the Inter-Independence chapter for more information). The inter-independent condition is where we have developed every aspect of our lives (physical, mental, emotional and spiritual) into a completely independent state, maintaining a true sense of self that is strong enough to be shared with others in a loving, vulnerable and connected relationship.

The following steps are designed to help you overcome codependent or independent tendencies that might be preventing you from becoming truly inter-independent. They have been divided into two categories: overcoming codependent tendencies and overcoming independent tendencies.

Steps to Overcoming Codependent Tendencies

Step 1: Get in Touch With Your True Self

Knowing yourself and being comfortable with who you are is essential to breaking the cycle of codependency. Usually codependent people are terrified to be alone. They go from one relationship to the next, living a life full of constant distractions and things they're required to do. They use relationships with other people as a form of addiction to avoid being alone with themselves. It's necessary to begin a process of gradual withdrawal from this. If you find yourself obsessively involved with someone or their problems, it's necessary to completely detach yourself from the situation. Start small at first by scheduling a half-hour a day to be alone. Get to know yourself. Start a journal to explore any negative feelings and fears that will inevitably arise. Some journal topics might be:

* A positive and negative characteristics list about yourself.
* Your beliefs, definitions and purposes in life, happiness and love.
* Why is the approval of others so important? Whose approval do you seek daily?
* What are the most important things in your life that you could be accomplishing today?

Writing in the journal will help you to get to know yourself better so that in time you can increase the time spent alone from a half-hour to an hour a day. It will also be helpful to practice some meditation techniques. Then try a full day alone and eventually a weekend alone. Spend this time developing your relationship with yourself.

Step 2: Confront Your Fears

As you begin spending time alone, you may need to confront any fears that may arise. Codependent people usually fear being alone, isolated or detached from others on whom they are dependent. They fear never getting married, being unhappy, abandoned or left behind. Make a list of everything that you might fear regarding every aspect of an independent lifestyle. After you have identified these fears, transform them using the steps located in the Fear chapter.

Step 3: Reprogram and Heal Your Past

Reprogramming and healing any past issues where your codependent tendencies were learned is a key step. Usually codependent people were hurt repeatedly by people in their past. These negative past experiences were likely taken personally, causing that person to lose their sense of internal value and worth. Because codependent tendencies can result from any number of negative past experiences, events or role modeling, it's helpful to list all the ways in which you have been hurt in the past. Then list all the ways your parents, role models or guardians could have been more loving toward you. List all the ways your personal value and respect was lost or damaged. Look at any unhealthy behavior in the way family members treated one another. Try to identify any times in your past when you were not permitted, encouraged or taught through role modeling to maintain a healthy sense of inter-independence.

In order for a child to grow up without codependent tendencies, they would need two inter-independent role models or parents who respected the child's rights as a person. These parents would need to protect the child from ever getting hurt and feeling devalued or worthless. They would have to accept the child's strengths and weaknesses, allow the child to form their own identity, and at the same time encourage participation in an intimately connected family system. Unfortunately, no one has perfect parents, childhoods or behavior role models. But the good news is we all have the power and opportunity to go back today and heal any unhealthy experiences.

The best way to do this is through the imagination techniques described in the Healing chapter. Simply go back in your mind and revisit any childhood situations when you witnessed or were treated in a codependent, valueless or worthless manner. Have your adult self stand up for your child self and offer the necessary suggestions, advice, defense, support, proper role modeling, love and a place to vent any negative emotions that arise. Try working on your childhood codependent issues for an hour a day. It might take several weeks. Keep working through them until they are all resolved.

Step 4: Develop a Healthy Adult-Parent Relationship

In many cases codependent people never developed an adult relationship with their parents. It will be helpful to establish a new relationship with your parents if you find yourself participating in the following behavior:

❖ Allowing yourself to be treated like a child.

❖ Allowing your parents to criticize and judge your behavior and actions.

❖ Feeling obligated to call, visit or do things for your parents when you don't want to.

❖ Remaining dependent on your parents for financial or emotional support.

❖ Feeling as though you are not loved, respected or accepted by your parents.

❖ Keeping secrets from or editing your conversations with your parents.

The relationship we maintain with our parents says a lot about how we act or react in all of our other relationships. It will be helpful to establish an inter-independent relationship with your parents before you attempt one with your partner. Start this process by making a list of everything you want to change in your adult-parent relationship. Then write your parents a letter that expresses how you feel and what you want. Ask for their help and participation in rebuilding the relationship. If it's necessary, give your parents the proper ultimatums by letting them know how you plan to protect yourself.

It will also be powerful to help your parents heal any negative past experiences where your family system suffered injustices together. Remember, your parents were probably conditioned in the same manner as you were. A good way to help your parents heal is by writing the two-part healing letters described in the Healing chapter. If it's possible, get your whole family together for a healing session and work through your problems and issues together in an attempt to restore a healthy, inter-independent reality.

Step 5: Work With Your Relationship Partner

The next step is working with your relationship partner in an effort to become more independent. Many times opposites attract for the purpose of growth. Codependent people are usually attracted to self-confident, independent people. Independent people are usually attracted to the nurturing, supportive dependent people. If you find yourself in this type of relationship, take advantage of it by working with your partner. You are probably both experts at your own extremes. All you have to do is show each other your trade secrets and methods of operation. Share with your partner some positive ways to view the opposite extremes of their codependent or independent tendencies. Be supportive of one another. Make up exercises for each other. Help your partner grow toward their own inter- independence.

Step 6: Make Daily Efforts

Breaking codependent tendencies will require daily efforts on your part. Try to avoid any impulses to control, fix or manipulate other people. Maintain healthy communication with your partner at all times. Get in touch with your needs, wants, desires and feelings so they can be expressed in a healthy manner. Work on your self-acceptance, self-concept and self-awareness. Stop looking for happiness outside of yourself and develop your ability to create it from within. Don't do things you don't want to do. Participate in some hobbies or activities that require time alone, like painting, gardening and meditating. Develop a healthy set of boundaries and check them on a regular basis. Develop a strong relationship with God. It will serve as a great wealth of security in life.

Steps to Overcoming Independent Tendencies

Step 1: Get in Touch With Your Needs

Independent people usually spend a lot of time alone and have a hard time fulfilling their social and emotional needs. We all have the same needs, such as the need to be understood, the need for connection and unity with others, and the need to be loved. If you often find yourself alone, you may be filling your time with all kinds of distractions that prevent you from getting to know your true self. If that's the case, work on removing the distractions from your life so you can get in touch with your deepest needs, wants and desires. Try the exercises in the Primary Humans Needs chapter for help in this area. Concentrate on the social, emotional and spiritual needs, and how they are currently being fulfilled in your life.

Step 2: Confront Your Fears

Independent people usually fear being vulnerable, being hurt by others, being smothered, appearing weak or having needs. Maybe in your past you opened up, becoming completely vulnerable to your first boyfriend or girl-friend. If the relationship didn't work out, you were probably deeply hurt. Maybe you expressed your needs to people who couldn't be there for you, and eventually you learned not to trust. Maybe people from your past promised things that were never fulfilled and you were disappointed. As a form of self-protection, you might have developed the fear of depending on others. You may fear losing a part of yourself to another. You may fear trusting another person with the vulnerable, fragile part of yourself that can get hurt. Start by making a list of everything you fear, including your needs, vulnerabilities, inse-curities, jealousies and dependencies. It will be necessary to transform these fears by following the steps in the Fear chapter.

Step 3: Reprogram and Heal Your Past

Reprogramming and healing any past issues where your independent ten-dencies were learned is a key step. Usually independent people have been hurt many times in their past by people who have broken their trust and respect. This lack of respect and value toward others is usually carried into the present as a form of self-protection.

Because independent tendencies can result from any number or combi-nation of negative past experiences, events or role modeling, it's helpful to make a list of items regarding the ways you have been hurt in the past. Then make a list of all the ways your parents, role models or guardians could have been more loving toward you. List all the ways you lost the respect and trust toward others in your past. List all the experiences you still hold against other people in a resentful manner. Look at any unhealthy behaviors regarding the ways family members treated one another. Try to identify any times in your past when you were not permitted, encouraged or taught through role mod-eling to maintain a healthy sense of inter- independence.

Once you have completed your list, go back into your past and heal any situations where you learned to disrespect, devalue or mistrust others because of their harmful, abusive actions or behaviors. Work through your entire past using the information located in the Healing chapter.

Step 4: Develop a Healthy Adult-Parent Relationship

Independent people usually don't maintain a close relationship with their parents. It's beneficial to establish an inter-independent relationship with them before you attempt one with your partner. Begin by making a list of everything you would like from your parents or family. Then write your parents a letter that expresses how you feel and what you want. Ask for their help and participation in rebuilding the relationship. Express your needs, concerns, desires and feelings in this letter. If it's possible, work with your parents or family members to create a closer, tighter group. Try scheduling a family healing session or some group activities or outings where everyone can participate. Make it a priority to call or write letters on a regular basis.

Step 5: Work With Your Relationship Partner

The next step in the process is working with your relationship partner to become more dependent and less independent. Usually opposites attract for the purpose of growth. Independent people are usually attracted to the nurturing, supportive dependent people, whereas codependent people are usually attracted to self-confident, independent people. If you find yourself in this type of relationship, take advantage of it by working with your partner. You are probably both experts at your own extremes. All you have to do is show each other your trade secrets and methods of operation. Share with your partner some positive ways to view the opposite extremes of their codependent or independent tendencies. Be supportive of one another. Make up exercises for each other. Help your partner grow toward their own inter- independence.

Step 6: Make Daily Efforts

Breaking independent tendencies will require daily efforts on your part. It will be helpful to learn how to trust yourself and others. Spend some time daily getting to know and understand yourself better by practicing meditations and the self-awareness exercise. Participate in some activities or sports that require group efforts and participation. Find a need in the community and fulfill it. Be more compassionate and loving toward yourself, and your ability to give to others will increase. Develop a stronger relationship with God, and ask Him for help in finding the value and worth present in all of us.

Visions of Inspiration

O Lord, our Sovereign, how majestic is your name in all the earth! You have set your glory above the heavens. When I look at your heavens, the work of your fingers, the moon and the stars that you have established; what are human beings that you are mindful of them, mortals that you care for them? Yet you have made them a little lower than God, and crowned them with glory and honor. You have given them dominion over the works of your hands; you have put all things under their feet.

Psalm 8: 1, 3-6

You have to work constantly at rejuvenating a relationship. You can't just count on its being O.K.; or it will tend toward a hollow commitment, devoid of passion and intimacy. People need to put the kind of energy into it that they put into their children or career.

Dr. Robert Sternberg

COMMITMENT

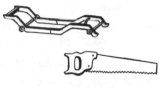

*E*very car and truck has a frame that ensures the structural integrity of the vehicle. If you were to build a car from scratch, you would start with the frame and attach the rest of the parts to it. Frames are generally made of steel because they need to be strong enough to handle the stress load of the vehicle's weight, not to mention our driving habits. Every time we drive our car through potholes and mud puddles and over speed bumps, the vehicle's frame is right there holding everything together. Knowing how important the frame is to your car's structural integrity, would you take a metal saw and slowly cut away at it every day? Would you drive around in a car that had most of its frame cut away? What do you think would happen if you were driving and your car's frame broke into many pieces?

In our relationships commitment serves the same purpose as the vehicle's frame. Commitment is the structural integrity and foundation on which all relationships are built. Commitment is what holds the different pieces of your relationship together as you and your partner travel through life.

Usually in a relationship one party offers some type of commitment and the other party offers a form of trust. For example, let's look at the relationship between you and your bank. The bank offers you a commitment of service and professionalism and you place your trust in the bank whenever money is deposited. You offer a commitment of collateral and the bank trusts you with a loan. In a personal relationship you might offer your partner a commitment of sexual monogamy and they trust you to not sleep around. If your partner offered you a marriage commitment, you would probably trust them to maintain it for life.

Commitments can be spoken, written or assumed in good faith. When we go to a bank for a new account, we automatically assume the bank is committed to honesty, and in return we offer our trust. As soon as we open an account, the bank backs up its commitment in writing, through the papers we sign. If both parties continue to maintain this commitment and trust (the basic frame work), the relationship will theoretically last forever. Now, if the bank broke its commitment, or if we just believed they did when they actually didn't, we would be forced to remove our trust and the relationship would be damaged. Commitment and trust go hand-in-hand and both are necessary building blocks in every relationship. If we fail to maintain either commitment or trust, our relationships will suffer damage.

In a personal relationship you have the choice to honor the commitment as agreed or destroy it through your own thoughts and actions. The marriage, engagement or boyfriend/girlfriend commitment is just like the steel frame of your car. When it is new, it is strong, serious and supportive. You maintain this commitment by honoring your partner in your thoughts and actions, or you destroy it by dishonoring them in your thoughts and actions. For example, every time you think lustful thoughts and sexually desire someone other than your committed relationship partner, you destroy a little piece of your sacred commitment, just like cutting away a little piece of your car's steel frame. Every time you dishonor your spouse by wishing you never married them or by thinking you missed out on someone better, you cut away at the foundation of your relationship. Every time you think negative thoughts about your partner, you are destroying the commitment you made in your head and heart. Having an affair is like taking a cutting torch to your relationship framework and burning the metal into tiny molten pieces.

To maintain a relationship commitment, you need to designate a special place in your heart for that person. God usually reserves the first-place spot in your heart for Himself, and then allows a second-place position for that very special committed relationship or marriage partner. A relationship commitment is honored and maintained by keeping your partner's spot safe in your heart. If you were married in a church, you likely asked God to bless your union. God will help you watch over that sacred space in your heart that was designated for your partner. So don't let any negativity in there to dishonor your partner, because in doing so you destroy the invisible framework and bond that you promised to uphold for your partner. If you keep your partner's honor upheld in your heart, you will be maintaining your end of the commitment. If you dishonor your partner in any manner, with any kind of negativity, your commitment will slowly erode away, a piece at a time.

If your car's frame is strong, you will be able to safely drive down life's roughest roads. The same is true of your commitments because all relationships will have their ups and downs. When you and your partner get into an argument and one of you leaves the house angry and hurt, there's no need to worry if you have a strong commitment in place, because your partner will be back to work things out. If one of you goes out of town on business or just needs some space, there's no need to worry if you have a strong foundation that supports your relationship. If your foundation is weak, disrespected and destroyed by your own thoughts, it won't last.

The following are designed to help you and your partner clarify your existing relationship commitment and resolve any past issues that may have a destructive effect on your abilities to make a commitment.

Strengthening Your Relationship Commitment

Understand Your Partner's Perspective

Have you ever wondered what your partner bases trust on? One person offers a commitment and the other person trust, and vice versa. It might be interesting to hear your partner's description of what their trust is based on. To find out, sit down with your partner and write out exactly what your partner is offering to you to place your trust in.

What have they agreed to provide you with in the future? Have they committed themselves to love you unconditionally? To be sexually monogamous? To uphold an honorable place for you in their heart, right below God? What do you expect from your partner? What have they committed to do for your relationship in which you place your trust? Look at all the internal aspects, like the thoughts they agree to hold toward you, and the external aspects, like the actions they agree to perform.

When you have completed these individual lists, exchange them with your partner and talk about the information in a non-judgmental and supportive manner.

Clarify Your Own Commitment

Next, it will be helpful to clarify the commitment that you offer to your partner. Write down the internal and external aspects of your commitment. How do you plan to internally hold them in your heart? If you make a commitment to love your partner for better or worse, describe the overall feelings, thoughts, perceptions and attitudes that you agree to uphold and maintain for them. Then describe all the external aspects of your commitment. What responsibilities, obligations and requirements do you agree to fulfill? Do you plan to take care of their financial, emotional, sexual, physical or spiritual needs? If so, which ones? After you have both finished your proposed commitments to one another, exchange copies and talk about the results in a non-judgmental and supportive manner.

Practice Forgiveness and Flexibility

As humans we all make mistakes. Neither you nor your relationship partner is perfect, so it's necessary to practice forgiveness and flexibility during the times they fail in their internal and external commitments. It might be helpful to write a two-part list that describes all the times your partner has failed on their commitments in the past and all the times you have failed on your commitments. Exchange lists with your partner, and if you come up with any items that cause angry, resentful or negative feelings, some healing work will be necessary. It's important to forgive your partner for their shortcomings so your hurt feelings won't interfere with the rest of your interactions. Follow the steps in the Forgiveness chapter if you or your partner still feel hurt after completing the lists.

Match Internal and External Realities

Many times our internal realities match those of our external realities. If we dishonor our partner in our heart, it won't be long before that is demonstrated externally by our words and actions, because our internal and external realities mirror and reflect each other.

It might be helpful for you and your partner to create an external symbol that represents your internal commitment to each other. This could be something like your wedding rings or a picture of a heart where you each draw half. Then every time you dishonor your partner internally in your thoughts, tear off a little piece of the external symbol. If you have designated your wedding rings as that symbol and you lustfully desire someone other than your partner, take your gold band and run it down the rough edge of a brick so that in time both your wedding ring and the commitment for which it stands accurately represent one another.

Promote the Positive

In life there are positive and negative aspects to everything. Usually people who have a problem maintaining and honoring a commitment view more negative disadvantages in it than they do positive advantages. A negative way to view commitment is to focus your attention on being trapped, burdened and tied down. A positive way to view commitment is to focus your attention on the advantages: a lifetime partner who is on your side; someone who will be there for you in your time of need; someone to help you, love you and offer their assistance; someone to trust, share things with and add meaning to everything you put your heart into.

It might be helpful to make a list of disadvantages that accompany your current relationship commitment. Study these issues, find the positive advantages and focus your attention on the positives instead of the negatives. Every coin has two sides, and you can find the positive advantages by flipping the negative side of the coin over. See the Criticism chapter for more information on finding the positive side of the disadvantages on your list.

Do Some Past Healing Work

A lot of our fears and problems concerning relationship commitments stem from negative past experiences. If you faithfully gave everything you had to a past relationship and through no fault of your own it didn't last, you probably experienced a lot of pain and hurt. This type of negative experience has the power to develop into a fear of commitments as a form of self-protection. Something else that might cause you to fear commitment is negative role modeling from your parents. If your parents had a very destructive relationship and remained committed to each other, you might have been subconsciously programmed into believing committed relationships are destructive. If you're a male who grew up with an overbearing mother and you haven't healed those issues with her, you might not commit yourself to any woman, because you fear she might turn out overbearing just like your mom. The same example would also apply to controlling or overly protective fathers.

The best way to overcome these fears is to do some healing work. It might be helpful to look at all your past relationships to see if you had any negative experiences concerning commitments. Look at how long you stayed committed to your jobs. Look at why your past relationships or marriages have ended. How long did they last? Look at your parents' relationship. What type of role modeling did they provide for you? Did your parents divorce or have affairs? If you fear rejection, abandonment, looking inadequate, stagnation, failure, entrapment or the loss of opportunity, chances are you developed these fears as a way of protecting yourself from those times when you were hurt. With your partner's assistance, take a close look at your life and trace any present-day commitment problems or fears back to their underlying sources in the past. Find out how and why you were hurt, and heal those experiences using the techniques described in the Healing chapter. By doing so, you will be reprogramming the subconscious tendencies that cause your fear of commitment.

Visions of Inspiration

No good tree bears bad fruit, nor again does a bad tree bear good fruit; for each tree is known by its own fruit. Figs are not gathered from thorns, nor are grapes picked from a bramble bush. The good person out of the good treasure of the heart produces good, and the evil person out of evil treasure produces evil; for it is out of the abundance of the heart that the mouth speaks.

Luke 6: 43-45

The fear of making permanent commitments can change the mutual love of husband and wife into two loves of self — two loves existing side by side, until they end in separation.

Pope John Paul II

Always remember the distinction between contribution and commitment. Take the matter of bacon and eggs. The chicken makes a contribution. The pig makes a commitment.

John Mack Carter

COMMUNICATION

TOOL 12

*C*ommunication is a lot like your car's tires because depth relates to quality. In our relationships there are five levels by which we can gauge the depth and quality of our communication. The first level is comparable to a tire worn down past the cords. This type of communication is social surface talk. We say it all the time: "Hi, how are you?" If we get an answer at all, it is usually the same old response of, "Fine." The second level of communication is comparable to a bald tire. That's where we talk about nonpersonal facts and information: "How has the weather been on the East Coast?" or "Did you see the game last night?" The next level of communication is comparable to a tire with the warning strips showing. That's where we talk about other people's actions and thoughts, and maybe a little bit of our own: "Hey, what does Bob think about this idea?" or "Well, do you have any ideas on this subject?" The fourth level of communication is a tire with about half of its tread intact. That's where we talk about our own feelings and emotions, or where we discuss the deeper effects and meanings behind the facts and figures. The fifth level of communication is comparable to a brand new tire with all of its tread pattern intact. Here we freely discuss our plans, hopes, dreams, feelings, emotions and ideas without the fear of being judged. In the fifth level we have the full freedom to say anything we want, knowing that whatever is said will be accepted and respected by our partner. That doesn't mean everyone will agree with us, only that they will accept and honor us regardless of the words spoken.

The quality, depth and operability of any relationship is directly related to the quality, depth and operability of its communication. If your relationship lacks depth, it's safe to say your communication also lacks depth. If you're experiencing relationship problems, chances are you're also experiencing communication problems. Look at the methods, amount and quality of communication between you and your partner. Have you already experienced a lot of blowouts? Is your vehicle heading for the ditch? Many times the inability to properly communicate causes severe problems in our marriages and relationships. When you or your partner experience a lack of intimacy, never-ending arguments, misunderstandings, blame, negative criticism, lecturing sessions, name calling, the silent treatment, unspoken expectations, pouting, door slamming, temper tantrums, the victim or martyr act, sarcasm, rudeness or negative body language in your relationship, it usually stems from some form of communication problem.

The following will help you understand the sources of poor communication and will discuss ways to improve your current ability through some powerful exercises.

Contributing Factors to Poor Communication

Fear

One of the most paralyzing factors in the inability to properly communicate is fear. It can take many forms. The fear of rejection can prevent you from being completely honest about your feelings and thoughts. The fear of being used and the fear of being taken advantage of can prevent you from expressing your vulnerability. The fear of hurting others may prevent you from truly speaking your mind. The fear of causing conflicts or arguments in the relationship may prevent you from speaking your concerns. The fear of abandonment may prevent you from revealing intimate parts of yourself. The fear of intimacy, the fear of mistrust, the fear of angry people and the fear of humiliation can all prevent good communication in your relationships.

Anger

When expressed in an unhealthy manner, anger can cause a lot of problems with your ability to properly communicate. During times of anger our ability to compassionately listen to our partner's point of view can become temporarily distorted. Instead of sharing our true feelings, we might use our anger in an unhealthy manner by bottling it up inside us, displaying the silent treatment, pouting or using guilt trips. Anger can also be misdirected into rage, verbal abuse or worse, instead of constructively expressing our hurt or threatened feelings in the communication process.

Problem Solving

Good communication does not require problem-solving ability, just the mutual exchange of thoughts and feelings. Helping others with their problems is a profound act when it is asked for. Unfortunately unwanted advice can leave your partner feeling disrespected, powerless over their own ability and annoyed — especially when all your partner needed was someone to listen to what they had to say. Usually when we make "helpful suggestions" or tell someone what they should do, they will keep complaining. The conversation will go around in circles, as one partner tries to openly express their feelings and the other partner attempts to fix the problems. When this happens eventually both parties end up frustrated. If your partner does not ask for your advice, it usually means that they just want to be listened to, heard and understood.

Blame

When we become consumed with being right, the other person automatically becomes wrong. When we focus our attention on proving our own point of view, we can't possibly recognize that of another. Blame becomes destructive to our communication when we view a problem from a one-sided perspective. By blaming others, we limit our ability to recognize our mutual involvement and responsibilities in the matter. Good communication requires both parties to completely acknowledge and understand the topic at hand.

Self-Doubt

Self-doubt is another powerful force that can contribute to poor communication. It also can take on many forms, like when doubting the improvement of our relationships makes us give up trying to effectively speak our concerns. By perceiving yourself in a self-doubting manner, you might become consumed with negativity instead of verbalizing a specific problem. By doubting your own emotions, you may fail to effectively express your angry, depressed or jealous emotions. Any time you doubt your ability, or your right to have needs, feelings or concerns, it will limit your ability to speak or interact effectively.

Passive Behavior

Another barrier to good communication is passive behavior. When we are too timid to speak our concerns, we can't effectively communicate. Passive behaviors can take on many forms. When we become excessively sensitive and fall prey to controlling and domineering influences, it becomes difficult to carry on a meaningful conversation. When we repress our feelings, close down, isolate ourselves and fail to speak our rights in a direct and assertive manner, we limit our partner's ability to reach us. When passive behavior is present in your relationship, there is a good chance you are not properly expressing yourself assertively.

Aggressive Behavior

Aggressive behavior is also a major problem when it comes to good communication. When we are too demanding, defensive, controlling and selfish we limit our own ability to effectively communicate. Aggressive behavior can take on many forms. If you are extremely defensive, it's not possible to hear any form of criticism or advice from others. If you don't allow yourself to hear anything disagreeable, you may constantly argue to defend your own point of view. If your aggressive behavior always demands better treatment from others ,you will have a hard time acknowledging your partner's point of view. If the tone of your voice relates messages of tension, hostility and aggression, it's possible the other party will not hear what you have to say. When aggressive behavior is present in your relationship, there is a good chance your partner will close down the communication process.

False Assumptions

Good communication is a process of verifying a mutual exchange of assumptions. When we make false assumptions regarding what our partner is thinking or feeling without actually inquiring, we fail to recognize the need to verify our predictions in words. Unfortunately, mind reading is dangerous because it leaves us with many distorted perceptions.

False assumptions can work against us several different ways. Sometimes we expect others to know what we are feeling and thinking because "if they were really close and cared about us, they would know these things." Other times we just know or assume what our partner is feeling and thinking based on their body language or past performances. When we assume instead of verifying, we are participating in poor communication.

Emotional Security

Establishing an atmosphere of emotional security is an important aspect of effective communication. Without it people will not feel safe enough or comfortable enough to freely express themselves. There are many different ways emotional security, atmosphere and trust can be violated in our relationships. By preaching, lecturing and telling others what they should and shouldn't be doing, we produce an atmosphere of defensiveness. When this happens ,your partner might close down communication because they do not feel trusted for their own decisions and judgments. When we give direct orders and commands, we produce an atmosphere of resentment that may imply disrespect toward our partner's needs and feelings. Offering unwanted advice, suggestions or solutions often creates an atmosphere of inferiority because your partner is not being credited with the ability to work out their own problems. Blaming, criticizing and making negative judgments often creates an atmosphere of inadequacy, leaving the other person feeling stupid, inferior or unworthy. Minimizing your partner's problems or attempting to distract attention from them in an effort to cheer them up often creates an atmosphere of disrespect. Indicating to the other party that you are not taking them seriously or are not interested in what they are saying will harm the emotional security that's necessary for good communication. Creating a secure emotional atmosphere can only be developed through genuine sincerity and concern.

Improving Your Communication Skills

Effective Listening

The biggest challenge to good communication is being able to effectively understand and listen to others. When people talk to us, they want to be understood. It takes effort and practice to put your own concerns and ideas aside for those of another. Try to see inside your partner and look at things from their point of view. Try to feel the same emotions your partner might be experiencing. Try to avoid comparing your partner's experiences and feelings to your own. Everyone will experience the same situation differently.

A good example of this might be when a young girl's pet goldfish dies. If you do not take the time to carefully listen and understand her feelings, you might say something like, "It's OK, we'll get a new one." But after viewing the situation from the young girl's point of view, you might realize that the death of her pet fish has affected her in the same manner as would the death of a close friend. The only way to effectively communicate is by listening carefully. See the Empathy chapter for more information on listening techniques.

"I" Statements

When expressing your feelings, it's important to use "I" statements, like "I feel angry," "I feel sad," or "I would like more attention." With these kinds of statements you take responsibility for your own feelings and speak for yourself. There is no right or wrong way to feel, so your partner will not have any reason to disagree with you when "I" statements are used. Try to avoid "You" statements, like "You caused me to be sad," "You're making me angry," or "You always do that." Statements like these only cause fights, arguments and defensiveness. "You" statements sound critical and judgmental, and your partner will usually respond in a defensive manner. Try speaking from the first person using "I" statements for an entire day and see how it feels.

Communication Content

Another area of communication concern is the context in which the information is presented. Effective communication usually contains three parts: your feelings, an explanation and a request. For example: "I feel frightened because you're exceeding the speed limit, and I would like for you to slow down." This three-part process will work better than saying something to your partner like, "You're driving like a dangerous jerk again."

Other more elaborate communication can include five parts:
1) Introducing the topic of conversation.
2) Presenting your mental thoughts, ideas or beliefs.
3) Presenting your emotional feelings.
4) Expressing your intentions concerning the other party.
5) Expressing your intentions or motivations regarding yourself.

For example: (1) I would like to discuss a problem regarding our relationship; (2) I think this would be a good solution; (3) I feel excited about the potential changes; (4) I am presenting this to you because I would like your assistance; and (5) I hope to reduce conflicts and increase our love for one another.

Try listening carefully to yourself and others in your interactions. If you recognize in your conversations that you or your partner are missing one or more of the five parts, simply ask them to elaborate on their beliefs, feelings, requests, explanations or motivations.

"Can/Will" Statements

Another communication problem is our inability to directly ask people for what we want. A good example of this is the "Can/Will" statement.

If I asked you, "Can you take out the trash?" what exactly am I asking you? If you say "Yes," should I expect you to remove the trash in the future? Or am I evaluating your physical capability to accomplish the task? Of course, we all know this statement was a request to have the trash removed. But asking the question in this way doesn't respect a person's right to say "No." Besides, using "Can" statements doesn't offer your partner the opportunity to take credit for helping out around the house. By saying "Will you please take out the trash?" you will be showing your partner respect and offering the freedom to refuse the request.

Try to monitor your "Can/Will" statements for a full day to see the results.

Communicating With Parables

Using parables is a powerful way to relay important and difficult messages to your partner. Parables are effective because they influence both right and left hemispheres of the brain. They work by tying a message together with an emotional and logical response in a way that is almost impossible to forget.

For example: Try to remember two specific events from your past. The first event can be a time when someone communicated important logical facts to you, such as the lessons taught at school when you were in the ninth grade on November 13. The second can be a time when important logical facts were communicated to you that had a great emotional effect as well, such as when you and your first boyfriend or girlfriend broke up. Out of these two events, the information that affected both brain hemispheres (logical and emotional) will be easier to remember, be clearer and sometimes be unforgettable.

Try using this emotional and logical method of communicating when you have something very important to state to your partner. Begin by taking some time beforehand to create a parable that will represent the lesson you are trying to get across. Pick a subject that is emotionally close to your partner, like sports, nature, animals, business or something they value highly. Then create a story in that subject setting that reenacts how you are feeling and what you are trying to explain. If you want to communicate how certain actions from your partner are hurting you, create a sad story where the main character is violated without mercy. If you want to communicate encouragement, create a brave story where the main character has to fight countless battles before reaching the kingdom. Make your story interesting enough to get the other party emotionally involved and stimulated. Then at the end, tell your partner how this story represents your life, relationship, feelings, desires, fears or concerns. Communicating in parables can be a very powerful way to make a lasting impact if they are presented at the right time and with a proper approach.

Communicating in Writing

If you are experiencing communication problems in your relationship, it can be helpful to restore the verbal flow through a written process. The intimacy journal is a very effective way to communicate daily in a nonverbal method. See the Intimacy chapter for more information. It might be helpful to address some of these topics to start:

❖ What I like the most and least about the ways we communicate with each other.
❖ When and why I intentionally avoid communicating with you.
❖ How we can improve the quality of our communication in the future.

Communicating by Mirroring

When we fail to understand what our partner is trying to explain to us, we are not effectively communicating. A good exercise to prevent misunderstandings and misinterpretation is to sit down facing your partner. Have one person start off expressing themselves on a particular subject. The other person's sole purpose is to listen without interrupting. After a while have the listening party repeat whatever the speaking party was trying to convey. Then the speaker either affirms, denies or modifies what they actually intended to imply. After about five minutes reverse roles with your partner and start the process over again. By practicing this exercise, you will strengthen your ability to eliminate any potentially misconstrued meanings in your conversations.

Visions of Inspiration

There is only one rule for being a good talker — learn how to listen.

Christopher Morley

If you are willing, my child, you can be disciplined, and if you apply yourself you will become clever. If you love to listen you will gain knowledge, and if you pay attention you will become wise. Stand in the company of the elders. Who is wise? Attach yourself to such a one. Be ready to listen to every godly discourse, and let no wise proverbs escape you. If you see an intelligent person, rise early to visit him; let your foot wear out his doorstep.

Sirach 6: 32-36

Put it before them briefly so they will read it, clearly so they will appreciate it, picturesquely so they will remember it, and above all, accurately so they will be guided by its light.

Joseph Pulitzer

COMPASSION

TOOL 13

*I*magine for a minute that when you bought a new car it came with a tiny, invisible genie. The sole purpose of this genie would be to reflect the car's overall mechanical and emotional well-being. The genie would serve as an interactive connection between the car's owner and the car itself. When the car was running well, this magical person would be happy and joyful, bouncing around on the back seat. When the car was having mechanical problems, the genie would be sad and depressed, hiding inside the dark trunk. The only way you can communicate with this magical little being is through compassionate interactions because the genie just doesn't respond to anything else. You can try yelling, screaming, threatening, tricking, criticizing, abusing, sweet talking and bribing the genie, but nothing works.

Now let's imagine the car is broken down and you need to know what's wrong before you can fix it. Since the genie automatically reflects the same conditions as the car, the genie is probably hiding inside the trunk and won't come out. What would you say to this little person in a compassionate manner that would get them to tell you what was wrong? At first you might call out thier name, then sit down beside your genie to put your arm around them. Next, ask your genie what's wrong — and remember, you can only communicate with them in a childlike, compassionate approach. Pretend your genie sounds just like a hurt four-year-old. If the genie said, "I'm really hurt," or "I'm really, really sad," what would your response be? How are you going to find out what's hurting and making your genie sad? If you can't be compassionate with this imaginary genie right now in your imagination, how are you going to be compassionate with yourself or your relationship partner?

Compassion starts internally. If you can't be compassionate with that hurt little person inside yourself, you can't be truly compassionate with others. The genie in this story represents the little inner childlike person inside every one of us. When you're feeling excited, your inner child (or genie) is probably bouncing around inside of you, just like the genie in the back seat of the car. When you're sad or hurt, your inner child is probably hiding in a dark corner. Being compassionate with yourself means finding a way to comfort and support that hurt childlike part of yourself long enough to figure out what is wrong so you can fix the problem.

The next time you don't like how you're feeling, try talking to that hurt little inner child the same way you would comfort and support any four-year-old you love very much. All you need to do is close your eyes and imagine what your inner child is doing. Next, put your arm around him or her and ask, "What's wrong?" Allow that hurt part to speak just like a four-year-old. Four-year-olds' sentences are short and uncensored. They speak exactly what's on their mind. They don't have problems demanding what they want, either. Just remember their requests are always valid. If you can honor your inner child's requests, they will be instantly happy. If it isn't possible or practical to honor their requests, simply explain why, in a gentle and caring manner. Try making some compromises with your inner child or offering them something else in return. Just remember the most important part of comforting any four-year-old is interacting with them in a loving manner.

By performing this imagination technique every time you are hurt or sad, you will be able to make yourself feel better. It will make you a more compassionate person, which in turn will strengthen your ability to be more compassionate with others.

Take a look at your life and relationships. Does it seem like your car is always breaking down and there is no one around to help you get it fixed? What about your relationship partner — could they be more compassionate with you when your genie is hiding in the trunk? Do you try to force other people's genies out of hiding with military-type force? Remember, the inner childlike genie only responds to genuine compassion.

Steps to Creating More Compassion

Step 1: Be Compassionate With Yourself

Giving and receiving compassion begins with you. When you learn how to be more compassionate with yourself, you will be able to be more compassionate with your partner. When you are more compassionate with your partner, you enable yourself to receive more compassion from them. But before you can be more compassionate with yourself, you first need to love yourself. To develop stronger ability in self-love, see the Self-Acceptance chapter.

Step 2: Listen to Your Feelings

The most important part of self-compassion is listening to your feelings. It's important to acknowledge, accept and appropriately manage all your emotions. When you cut yourself off from your emotional side by repressing negative emotions with denial, addictions or another type of obsessive or compulsive behavior, you eliminate the opportunity to comfort that hurt childlike part of yourself. The exercises located in the Self-Awareness chapter will help you get in touch with and listen to your inner voice on a regular basis.

Step 3: Transform Criticism

It's difficult to be compassionate with yourself and others when you fail to transform your own inner criticism. By acknowledging and confronting your inner criticism, which appears negative on the outside, you will discover that it can be a very loving and compassionate part of your being. If your inner child needs to have its mouth washed out with soap, see the chapters on Criticism and Affirmations for more information.

Step 4: Practice a Compassion Exercise

The next step is practicing this compassion exercise when you're feeling upset, self-destructive, unhappy, emotionally numb, worried, fearful, sad or angry. Any time you don't like the way you're feeling, you can practice the genie's imagination technique that was described in the first part of this chapter. Or if that doesn't work for your situation, you can practice it on a more cognitive level. The process is very simple — just ask yourself a series of questions and take appropriate actions. The basic formula for any compassion exercise is this: I think, I feel, I want, I need, I choose. For example, when you're not feeling very good about something, simply ask yourself what you are thinking, feeling, wanting and needing, and what course of action you can take. "I think I have the flu, I feel terrible, I want to feel better, I need some rest, I choose to go home early." Spend the necessary time working with yourself in this exercise, and before long your ability to be self-compassionate will spread into the lives of others.

Visions of Inspiration

The compassion of human beings is for their neighbors, but the compassion of the Lord is for every living thing. He rebukes and trains and teaches them, and turns them back, as a shepherd his flock. He has compassion on those who accept his discipline and who are eager for his precepts.

Sirach 18: 13-14

How often do the clinging hands, though weak, clasp round strong hearts that otherwise would break.

Mary Elizabeth Crouse

COMPROMISE

TOOL 14

*C*ars are a lot like relationships because they both function best when all of their parts work together in harmony. Relationships function best when both parties come together on beneficial ground in mutual unity. Cars function best when all the mechanical components work together in unity.

When your car develops a mechanical problem, there are usually a lot of parts that stop working together in harmony, and parts out of harmony are parts in conflict. The job of a good mechanic is to use his tools to fix those parts that aren't in harmony. Your relationship works a lot like the car in this analogy because you are your own relationship mechanic.

If you lived in total isolation, your decisions and actions would have little effect on anyone else. But when you're involved in any type of a relationship, your behavior has a great effect on others. Making decisions for yourself is like making sure parts on the shelf are in good mechanical condition. Making decisions in your relationship is like making sure all the parts in your car are in good condition and functioning in harmony. Your car has thousands of parts designed to operate together in harmony and we know how much mechanical maintenance they need. Just imagine how much more mainte-nance a good relationship requires, knowing that our lives consist of thou-sands of parts that are not designed to work together.

As your own relationship mechanic, one of your best tools is your ability to create win/win situations through compromise. Those old-fashioned com-promises from the past are not enough unless you incorporate a win/win sit-uation into the deal.

For example, let's say you and your relationship partner both wanted to eat an entire cake by yourselves. The standard compromise would be to share the cake equally. One person would cut the cake and the other party would choose the half they felt was the biggest. This agreement might seem fair to an outside mediator because the person cutting would try to create two equal pieces knowing they would receive the last piece. Unfortunately, this method of compromising usually leaves both parties feeling resentful. If both parties wanted to eat a whole cake and only received part of a cake, they might feel very unsatisfied.

If you are always giving in to your partner for the sake of the relationship, you and your partner are not functioning in harmony. When you're not functioning in harmony, you're usually functioning in conflict. Compromise where one or both parties give in or give something up usually don't work very well, because they create resentment, hurt feelings, jealousy and stagnation in the relationship.

The best way to successfully maintain a fulfilling, long-term, lasting relationship is to create a win/win agreement where both sides work together to create a situation that is better for everyone involved instead of simply splitting the cake. This requires both parties to communicate deeply and empathically and to understand one another's point of view. Usually this process begins by brain storming ideas and creating five, 10 or 15 options that are all better than simply splitting the cake and feeling resentful. You might sell the cake and buy two pies. You might trade the cake in for a winning lottery ticket and open your own cake factory. The possibilities are endless because by working with another person through a win/win agreement, you will open new doors and new ideas will start to flow. You will be creating a greater deal for yourself and for your relationship, just like the sum of the car parts totals a greater whole when they are all working together in harmony.

Solving our problems and conflicts in life through win/win agreements has the potential to create situations that are 100 times more beneficial than eating the entire cake yourself. That's because the creativity you share when working with your partner is a function of your Inner Self. God is also a part of your Inner Self and God will be right there with you, offering His suggestions and ideas, helping you create a situation that serves the greater purpose of all. God wants the whole world to eat cake, not fight over who gets the last piece.

If you and your relationship partner are not enjoying cake every day from your own cake factory, try increasing the amount of harmony between parts by practicing the win/win agreement every time a conflict arises.

Steps to Creating Win/Win Situations Through Compromise

Step 1: Make a Commitment

First it will be necessary to get all the involved parties to diligently work together to resolve the conflict in everyone's best interest. Many times it's not easy to talk about a cake factory when all you want to do is keep your partner from eating your fair share. Creating a win/win situation might take a while, depending on how important the issues are to everyone. Make a promise with your relationship partner to never leave them feeling cheated, used or taken advantage of through an unfair deal.

Step 2: Release Your Anger

Before you can create a win/win situation through compromise, it's necessary to release anger or resentment that may be present. Anger is released when we express why we feel hurt or threatened. (See the Anger chapter for more information.) Resentment is released when we forgive the person who hurt us in the past. (See the Resentment/Revenge chapter for more information.)

Step 3: Pinpoint the Exact Problem

Many times people see the same situation differently. Everyone has different backgrounds, beliefs, attitudes, thought patterns and mentalities. Before you can create a win/win situation, it's necessary for all the parties involved to first agree on an exact problem. To achieve a mutual opinion, try repeating your perceptions of the problem back and forth until you and your partner can agree on it. Use your listening skills and apply effort and attention to one another. Work together until both parties agree on a mutual problem.

Step 4: Understand the Other Party's Point of View

Before a true win/win agreement can be reached, it's necessary to see the problem from the other person's point of view. Try to understand your partner's needs, concerns and perceptions better than they do themselves. Ask the questions necessary to achieve a complete understanding. When possible, write down in advance a detailed description of how the other may view the situation. Ask yourself what your partner may be feeling. How does your partner view the situation? What are they concerned about or afraid of? What does your partner want? And why? Are there any situations from your partner's past that may be contributing to this mutual problem? How would you feel and what would you do if the situation were reversed?

Step 5: Agree on the Main Issues

Many times problems involve personal feelings, fears and compounded issues. Try to break down problems into specific issues that can be agreed on. Try to find the most important concerns that lie at the root of the problem. Try repeating your perceptions of the main issues back and forth until they are agreed on.

Step 6: Agree on the Desired Results

When anyone is consumed with what they want, they fail to recognize the other party's position. Try to determine what results you would be happy with and what results the other party desires. Try repeating your perceptions of the desired results back and forth until they are agreed on. Once you both know what you want, you only need to find a way to make it happen.

Step 7: Create Options That Achieve the Desired Results

The next step is to create ideas, possibilities and options that fulfill both parties' mutually desired results. Work together as a team using your creativity and imagination. Brainstorm to create feasible solutions. Once you start working together as a team, the possibilities are endless. What kind of deal can you and your partner create that will produce a bigger and better reality for both of you? Who else can be involved in this powerful opportunity? How can both of you get what you want in an equal and ethical manner? If the solutions and compromises don't come immediately, pray to God for guidance, justice and knowledge. Seek outside support systems, additional partnerships or more information when necessary. Once a solution has been reached, make sure you and your partner maintain the same perceptions of your mutually beneficial win/win agreement.

Visions of Inspiration

Whoever pursues righteousness and kindness will find life and honor.
Proverbs 21: 21

Be careful that victories do not carry the seeds of future defeats.
Ralph W. Sockman

Come to terms quickly with your accuser while you are on the way to court with him, or your accuser may hand you over to the judge, and the judge to the guard, and you will be thrown into prison. Truly I tell you, you will never get out until you have paid the past penny.
Matthew 5: 25-26

If you want to persuade people, show the immediate relevance and value of what you're saying in terms of meeting their needs and desires....Successful collaborative negotiation lies in finding out what the other side really wants and showing them a way to get it, while you get what you want.
Herb Cohen

COURAGE

*I*magine being trapped in your car during an extremely destructive earthquake. There's disaster and confusion everywhere. The ground is trembling, buildings are falling down all around you, gas lines are breaking and flames are igniting. It's incredibly traumatic and you're scared to death. Luckily for you the street ahead of your car is clear enough to safely escape. You're almost out of danger when you notice a small group of women and children trapped in the middle of a dead-end street, surrounded by a wall of flames. If someone doesn't do something immediately, it will be to late for them.

Let's imagine you would like to rescue these people, but for some reason your fear prevents you from pursuing this courageous endeavor. Sitting inside your car, you have three choices: you can sit there paralyzed and continue to put yourself in further danger; you can drive your car through the flames, load up the endangered women and children and rush back to safety; or you can simply leave the women and children behind to meet a cruel and painful fate. What are you going to do?

Things are really starting to heat up now, so let's look at the underlying forces that are paralyzing you so you can begin acting courageously. We know the car will respond to the driver's commands, just as your body will respond to your brain's commands. If you sit in the car with your foot on the brakes, the car isn't going anywhere. In the same way, if you think only self-centered thoughts about your own safety and well-being, you will remain paralyzed. The only way to get your foot off the brake and onto the gas pedal is to start thinking loving thoughts of others.

If you want to act courageously in this situation, you will need to start thinking more positive, loving, caring and compassionate thoughts about those trapped people and stop thinking fearful, endangering thoughts about your own well-being. Once you do so, the paralyzing fear will disappear. You will be free to hit the gas, crash through the wall of flames, save the women and children and drive off to safety.

If you're wondering about the moral of this story, it's simple: Courage is acting in a loving manner regardless of your fears. In the Fear chapter we compared fear to the brake pedal in your car, so it only makes sense to compare courage to the gas pedal. Fear works like the brakes on your car because it's designed to protect us from danger. A healthy use of fear would be to apply the brakes when a deer runs in front of your car. Fear can also be used in an unhealthy manner if you only assume a situation to be dangerous when it really isn't. If you were driving along and just imagined something running out in front of your vehicle when nothing was actually there, that would be an unhealthy use of fear. Unhealthy and imagined forms of fear can cause a lot of damage and destruction to your life, just like hitting the brakes for no apparent reason can cause a lot of damage to other motorists who run into the back of your vehicle.

When we are consumed by fear, our focus of attention is on ourselves. Our thoughts are primarily concerned with our own safety and well-being. Courage, on the other hand, is just the opposite. When we are acting in a courageous manner, our thoughts are primarily concerned with others and their well-being and safety. Courage is placing the safety and well-being of others above your own. Before you can act courageously in situations, you need to first take your foot off the brake pedal by controlling and evaluating your own fears and personal safety. Then, once your foot is off the fearful brakes, you can focus your attention on other people's safety and well-being. The more loving intentions you can create for others, the more gas you will be able to give the car in your courageous endeavors.

Fear can cause a lot of problems in our lives and relationships. Courage is a powerful way of overcoming unhealthy forms of fear. If you or your relationship partner could use some more courage in your daily life, the following steps may be of great assistance.

Steps to Discovering and Increasing Your Courage

Step 1: Make a List of Activities

First it will be helpful to create a list of activities where you desire more courage in your life. Write down as many situations as you are willing to work on. For example: I want more courage in confronting my employer, asking for a date, discussing finances with my spouse and skydiving.

Step 2: Make a List of Advantages

Now write down ten reasons, loving intentions or positive advantages that will benefit you or others concerning your activity list. Ask yourself, who will benefit from my courageous actions? How will I be a stronger person? What greater purpose will be served? Write down ten reasons for every item on your activity list. For example: "My family's standard of living would increase and my coworkers would be more productive if I were more courageous with my employer," or "My social life would improve if I had more courage to ask people out on dates." Try to create as many positive, loving reasons as possible to support your courageous endeavors.

Step 3: Evaluate the Situation

It's important to evaluate the possible consequences of your proposed courageous attempts because the lack of courage in dangerous situations without loving intentions to justify your actions is probably very wise. It is important to evaluate your fears and transform any unhealthy forms of fear. See the Fear chapter for more information. But accept healthy forms of fear as your own personal safety requires. Courage is only called for when the loving intentions outweigh the worst possible scenario your healthy fears are trying to warn you about. If you can't find loving intentions to go skydiving, it might be wise to listen to the message your healthy fears are trying to communicate. If you are having a hard time evaluating the situation and finding enough loving interactions on which to base your actions, ask yourself what the best choice is for everyone involved. It might also be helpful to look at some different alternatives to minimize your risks and still accomplish your same objectives.

Step 4: Practice Visualization Techniques

Once you have evaluated the situation and have determined that more courageous actions would benefit the lives of others, you can increase your courage by practicing visualization techniques. Begin this exercise with a relaxed, meditative state of mind. Then imagine yourself in the situation that requires more courage. Take this process step-by-step and imagine yourself successfully completing whatever it is you desire to do. In your mind everything works out great. Allow yourself to feel those successful feelings. In your mental picture you are safe, happy, courageous and confident. Feel the approval and admiration of the other people involved in your mental picture. Try to keep this process as accurate and vivid as possible. Talk to yourself, ask questions and look at the situation from different points of view. Spend as much time as necessary working with this exercise, allowing yourself to feel the positive feelings being generated by your courageous actions. By practicing this exercise over and over in your mind, you will slowly begin the process of changing your subconscious tendencies. In time the imagined courage will become a natural part of your everyday behavior.

Visions of Inspiration

The Lord is my light and my salvation; whom shall I fear? The Lord is the stronghold of my life; of whom shall I be afraid? When evildoers assail me to devour my flesh — my adversaries and foes — they shall stumble and fall. Though an army encamp against me, my heart shall not fear; though war rise up against me, yet I will be confident.

Psalm 27: 1-3

Have courage for the great sorrows of life and patience for the small ones; and when you have laboriously accomplished your daily task, go to sleep in peace. God is awake.

Victor Hugo

There is no fear in love, but perfect love casts out fear; for fear has to do with punishment, and whoever fears has not reached perfection in love.

1 John 4: 18

CREATIVITY

*I*magine driving your car down a peaceful, quiet country road, passing farm after farm. You are totally in tune with the rhythm of the road as it radiates throughout your vehicle. Your body and mind are quiet and relaxed, yet at the same time you're fully alert — almost like being at one with your car and the surrounding environment.

Then when you least expect it, something strikes you like a bolt of lightning. Looking over at the passenger seat, you see God. He has just appeared in physical form, and you are very happy to see Him. It seems God has dropped by to bring you a gift. It's wrapped in a small box with brightly colored wrapping paper. But before you can open it, God tells you a little something about your present.

It's a powerful tool that can solve almost any type of problem. It can be used anywhere in almost any situation. You need only turn it on and ask the appropriate questions. When the time is right, solutions appear almost automatically. This tool is connected directly to God's vast storehouse of knowledge. It will help you advance year after year, while the competition stays in the same place. It will help you invent new ways of getting better results for practically every application. It's unbelievable, God says, because this tool is a million times more powerful and useful than Mr. Spock's computer. In fact, this tool was used to create the entire Starship Enterprise.

By now you're really excited and can hardly wait to open the box. But before you do, what are you going to use it on first? Are there any problems in your life that need solving? Is there something in your environment, workplace, job site, relationship or home life that could be improved on somehow? Do you think your relationship partner could benefit from this useful gift as well? Well, surprise! You open the box and God bestows on you the gift of creativity and imagination.

Both creativity and imagination stem from your Inner Self. The only difference between creativity and imagination is that creative power is limited to reality and imaginative power is unlimited. Because creativity is a function of your Inner Self and your Inner Self is connected to God, your ability to co-create comes from God as a gift. God gave us this gift a long time ago, which is why humanity keeps advancing year after year and the rest of life on this planet keeps acting according to its natural programming and conditioning.

If you or your relationship partner are missing out on this wonderful tool, the following may be of assistance in using this powerful gift. It has been divided into two parts. The first part will help you get more in tune with the creative part of yourself, and the second part consists of various exercises that will help increase your creative capability.

Developing Your Creative Abilities

Recognize the Flow

Our creative abilities are at their best during a state commonly known as "the flow." The flow of creativity might be compared to water in a stream. It flows along until encountering a rock, and even then it simply continues to flow downstream around it. When we place water in a container, it conforms to the container's boundaries. In the same way, our creative ability works best when we are flowing effortlessly like water.

To find your own state of flow, you will need to perfectly align your mind, body and talents with the current activities in which you are participating. During the state of flow everything seems effortless, unified and in harmony. Time seems to fly as you are completely absorbed in your environment and work. When the activities we participate in are below our talents, we usually become bored. If the activities we participate in are above our talents, we usually become anxious. A good example of this is your average high school student who might experience anxiety taking a college-level exam and might get bored with a second-grade lesson. The student would probably find creative flow the easiest when working on a high school science project that is interesting and exciting. When we are in touch with our Inner Selves and in harmony with our current activities, we can find the state of flow that produces those good ideas known as creativity.

Let Go

To enhance the state of flow and creativity, you will find it helpful to quiet the part of your mind that produces the chatter-type thinking. It's necessary to release and let go of any predetermined thoughts, concerns and distractions which interfere with your state of flow. Sometimes people experience their most creative insights while showering, driving, waking up, walking in nature, watching sand run through their fingers at the beach, playing an instrument, dancing, vacationing or engaging in contemplative prayer. The Meditation chapter will help strengthen your ability to quiet your mind and let go of any unwanted distractions.

Convert Any Self-Criticism

One of the biggest blocks to creativity is self-criticism. When we doubt ourselves, our creative ability or ideas, we usually fail to follow through on them. Our inner critic might say things like, "If it were a good idea, someone would already have thought of it." Then six months later you see your idea come out in the market place. Maybe your inner critic says things like, "You're no good. What a stupid idea," "They'll think you're crazy," "You'll mess it up and never get another chance," "Nobody will care," or "They'll laugh at you." By confronting your inner negative voice and discovering its true intentions, you will be better prepared to use your creative ability. See the Criticism chapter for more information on converting any negativity you might be hearing from your inner voice.

Free Yourself From Predetermined Perceptions

Another big block to creativity is predetermined ideas of how things should be, will be or must be. Any time we convince ourselves mentally to expect a certain predetermined outcome, we cut ourselves off from creative possibilities. Anything that keeps you from recognizing and opening yourself up to new and improved ideas, challenges and ways of looking at or perceiving things will minimize your creative ability. Try to free yourself from pressures, competition, expectations, restricted choices, evaluation from others, supervision, repression, rigid thinking patterns and predetermined perceptions.

EXERCISES FOR INCREASING YOUR CREATIVE CAPABILITY

Inquiry Exercise:

A powerful way to increase your creative ideas is through the inquiry exercise of asking yourself one question each day. Focus your questions on important areas or issues in your life. Asking questions is an important part of the creative process. Almost everything that is manmade today started out with a question: "How can I make this product better? Why can't this be done differently? What would happen if...? What are my options to this problem? I wonder how my partner can accomplish this?" Ask yourself one powerful question a day and let your Inner Self work on the solution. Usually the answer will come to you when you least expect it.

Ritual Exercises:

Another powerful way to increase your creative ability is through the ritual exercise. It works by experiencing something different every day. Trying new, different and unusual things on a regular basis will strengthen your creative capability and soften rigid, controlling conforming patterns. By practicing the ritual exercise, you can hold on to the familiar without getting trapped in a stagnant daily routine. You can begin by taking a different route to work, listening to a different radio station, taking a different lunch partner out, doing a different nightly activity, saying a different prayer, viewing the world differently, or trying a different way to treat others for the day. By becoming familiar with new and unknown experiences on a regular basis, you will be better prepared to create new and unknown realities for your life.

Observation Exercise:

This mental exercise will help you strengthen your memory and creative attentiveness. Begin by closing your eyes for 15 seconds. Then open and close your eyes as fast as you can, like the shutter on a camera. Take the brief picture of whatever you are looking at and recreate it in your mind. (This works best with things that you're not very familiar with.) Try to recreate the exact shapes, sizes, colors, brightness and details in the picture. Try to hold this picture in your mind for as long as you can. Use your creativity to fill in any unknown or forgotten areas. Use your creativity to paint any fading colors. By maintaining the image of the picture for as long as you can, you will be strengthening your creative ability.

Visions of Inspiration

And if people were amazed at their power and working, let them perceive from them how much more powerful is the one who formed them. For from the greatness and beauty of created things comes a corresponding perception of their Creator.

The Wisdom of Solomon 13: 4-5

Be brave enough to live life creatively. The creative is the place where no one else has ever been. You have to leave the city of your comfort and go into the wilderness of your intuition. You can't get there by bus, only by hard work and risk and by not quite knowing what you're doing. What you'll discover will be wonderful. What you'll discover will be yourself.

Alan Alda

Imagination is more important than knowledge.

Albert Einstein

CRITICISM

TOOL 17

The hubcaps on your car are usually shiny and beautiful on one side, and dirty and brown on the other side. Hubcaps are a lot like coins because every coin also has two sides. The head side of a coin has a face that speaks nice things to us. If we were to compare the head side of a coin to a hub cap, it would be the beautiful and shiny side because it represents the positive aspects of things. As for the tail side of the coin — well, you know what comes from that end. It's usually dirty and brown and smells real bad because it represents the negative aspects of things.

Everything in life also has two sides, just like the hubcap and the coin. There are advantages and disadvantages to everything. You can focus your time, energy and attention on the positive side of things or the negative. It's your choice.

Knowing this about the coin and hubcap, let's look at how it applies to negative criticism or sarcasm that you and your relationship partner might be experiencing. The tail side of the coin represents negative forms of criticism, and the head side of the coin represents the loving intentions behind that criticism. Love is what flips the coin from negative to positive. If your relationship partner flips you a negative critical remark like, "You're getting fat," you can let the statement hurt your feelings and affect your relationship, or you can simply flip the coin over by searching for the loving intentions located on the other side. If "You're getting fat" represents the negative side of the coin, the positive side would be, "It sounds like you love me a lot and care about my looks, health and diet. Would you be happier if I lost some weight?" Both of these realities reflect the same coin, and both sides of the coin represent the truth. The only difference is that one side will cause harm and destruction and the other side will promote love and well-being.

Usually when we flip the coin in a toss for competition, we are bound by its determining factor. But life is not as strict, because God gives everyone the unconditional right to flip the coin over as many times as they like. If your relationship partner is critical and flips you the tail side of the coin, it's your God-given right (if not your duty) to flip the coin over to the positive side.

The best part about this coin trick is that it works on three different kinds of criticism: self-criticism, criticism from others and criticism toward others. Let's look at how this coin technique works on all these areas before we get into the actual flipping process that is described later.

- **Self-criticism.** The coin trick works especially well on any forms of self-criticism that you may be experiencing. Self-criticism is that negative voice or dialogue that takes place inside of our minds. For example, imagine you're walking down the street minding your own business when your internal dialogue starts saying things like, "You're going nowhere in life," "No one likes you very much," or "Give it up, loser." Have you ever heard your inner voice saying things like that inside of your head? Well, that's your inner dialogue speaking, and it will provide you with valuable messages if you flip the coin over from the negative side to the positive side.
  So the next time your inner voice brings you a message with the tail sign on top, stop yourself immediately, recognize and acknowledge the negative and flip the coin over so you can get to the positive side as soon as possible. If you fail to discover the positive intentions behind your negative self-criticism, it will mentally and emotionally tear you down. If you call yourself loser enough times, pretty soon you will begin to believe it and become that loser. By flipping the coin over, you will discover the positive messages and consequences your Inner Self is trying to warn you about.
- **Criticism From Others.** The coin technique also applies to other forms of negativity you may be experiencing from others. It works on criticism, sarcasm and almost any kind of negative projection.
  Take fear for example: Let's say your mother loves you very much (the positive side of the coin) and doesn't want you to get robbed, raped, assaulted or harmed (the negative side of the coin). If she always expressed herself from the tail side of the coin, you might hear things like, "Watch out for dangerous people; they're everywhere," "It's dangerous to live alone," or "I'm so worried something bad will happen to you." Pretty soon she might have you scared to death, afraid to ever leave your house. So the next time your mother tries to project a negative message by giving you the tail side of the coin, flip it over right in front of her: "Mom, it sounds like you love me a lot and don't want anything bad to happen to me. Is that correct?"

❖ **Criticism Toward Others.** Before you harm another person with negative criticism, stop yourself and flip the coin over so you can present that person with the positive side. For example, let's say your relationship partner decided to grow a goatee that you didn't like. You could use negative criticism like, "That circle of facial hair makes you look stupid." Or you could flip the coin over and say, "I think clean-shaven men are extremely sexy and attractive." By using the positive, you will be motivating and empowering your partner to change at least 100 times faster than by giving them the tail. It's almost impossible to effectively motivate anyone using negative methods. The positive side works so much better.

The following steps will help you transform your own inner criticism into its loving intentions. Then once you can effectively flip your own internal coin over, you will be better prepared to flip your partner's coin over. Then with a little practice, you will be able to flip all forms of negativity over to the positive side.

Steps to Converting Criticism Into Loving Intentions

Step 1: Recognize the Opportunities

The first step is to recognize your own inner voice or dialogue. Many times it says things like: "You're no good." "You can't do that." "You're fat." "You're stupid." "You're not good enough." Have you ever heard this little nasty voice inside your head? Some of us might not even be aware of this voice and just start feeling bad about ourselves when it's speaking. Other times we may hear our internal voice speaking and try to redirect the negativity toward other people, places, situations and events around us. If you are unable to recognize your own inner voice, make a daily log of every time you criticize others. Many times our negative criticism toward others represents messages that we refuse to hear about ourselves. Before you will be able to benefit from your Inner Self's message, it's necessary to first recognize the voice when it's speaking. By practicing self-awareness, listening to yourself and questioning your feelings, you will be better prepared to recognize your own inner dialogue.

Step 2: Question Your Inner Voice

Try to determine what your inner voice is trying to say. Every time you recognize negative self talk ask yourself, "Why am I saying this to myself?" For example, let's say you're sitting in a chair thinking about an upcoming meeting when your inner voice says, "You're not good enough. Those people won't like your ideas." Simply ask yourself the question, "Why am I saying this?" Look deep inside yourself and find the answer: "Because this meeting is really important to me, and I want them to like me a lot."

Step 3: Understanding Your Inner Voice

Once you have discovered the subject matter or what your inner voice is trying to say, you can discover the loving intentions behind the message by asking yourself this question: "What loving statements should I be saying to myself?" Then look deep inside for the answer: "I am very smart, and I have some great ideas for this meeting. I'll spend a little more time preparing for it because I want these other people to appreciate my efforts."

Step 4: Receive Criticism From Others

Negative criticism, before it is converted into its loving intentions, is very destructive. It often hurts others, kills love and breaks up relationships. No one can ever accomplish a positive intention using negative methods. After you have learned to transform and convert your own self-criticism (from Steps 2 and 3), it's important to flip the coin over in the same manner before accepting another person's criticism.

For example, let's say you and your partner are getting ready for a big night on the town. You have carefully selected your wardrobe, and just when you're about to walk out the door, your partner says, "That tie is very ugly." This type of negative criticism would probably hurt your feelings and could even be classified as a form of emotional abuse. But once you know how to flip your own coin, you can easily flip the negative message that your partner is trying to present you with. Simply ask yourself, "Why is my partner saying this to me?" Then answer your own question. "It sounds like she's concerned with my appearance." Then flip the coin over and get into the positive side of your partner's message by asking yourself the second question, "What loving statements should my partner be saying to me?" Then answer your own question:

"It sounds like because you love me a lot and want me to look my best tonight, you would like to see me wearing a different tie. Is that correct?"

Both of these statements are true and they both represent the same coin. The only difference is, one side of the coin will harm your relationships and the other side will empower and enhance them.

Step 5: Be Careful Criticizing Others

Converting negative criticism directed toward others works the same way as converting negative criticism directed toward yourself. Before you say anything negative to another person, flip the coin over and speak to them from a loving point of view. Maybe your partner's tie, hair or dress is ugly. But by giving them the negative side of the coin, you will only hurt their feelings, make them angry, ruin the evening and eventually destroy your relationship. By giving them the positive side, you will empower them to be a better dresser, strengthen your relationship and motivate them to change a lot faster.

Step 6: Make Daily Efforts

Converting criticism is hard work, especially if you have suffered a lifetime of negative criticism from your childhood role models or parents. If your parents were very critical, it will be very helpful to go back into your past and heal those times when you were verbally abused. Follow the exercises in the Healing chapter so you can break those subconscious tendencies of verbally abusing others in the same manner you were verbally abused. Practicing affirmations is another important requirement in converting your self-criticism. After you have discovered the true intentions behind your self-criticism, it's important to back up the underlying messages with some positive or special affirmations. Please refer to the Affirmations chapter for more information.

Visions of Inspiration

"Do not judge, so that you may not be judged. For with the judgment you make you will be judged, and the measure you give will be the measure you get. Why do you see the speck in your neighbor's eye, but do not notice the log in your own eye? Or how can you say to your neighbor, 'Let me take the speck out of your eye,' while the log is in your own eye? You hypocrite, first take the log out of your own eye, and then you will see clearly to take the speck out of your neighbor's eye.

Matthew 7: 1-5

The good critic is he who narrates the adventures of his soul among masterpieces.

Anatole France

Criticism should not be querulous and wasting, all knife and root-puller, but guiding, instructive, inspiring, a south wind, not an east wind.

Ralph Waldo Emerson

DEATH

TOOL 18

*A*ny time you sell your old car or trade it for a newer model, you can expect to do a lot of preparation work. There's physical work to do like washing and detailing. There's mental work like figuring out how to finance the new purchase. But even more important is the emotional work of saying good-bye to your old car and welcoming the new one.

If your old car was a dependable and faithful friend, you might have a hard time coming to terms with its departure. This process of emotionally releasing the old in preparation for the new is a lot easier when it happens over a longer period of time. If your old car had been giving you mechanical problems, you might have been resentful when it broke down. You would probably value it less and less every time it left you stranded. But if your car has always been there for you and one day it was stolen from the parking garage, never to be seen again, you would still have the same amount of emotional and mental releasing work to perform. But when the loss is unexpected, it will be a lot harder to deal with because of the shortage of preparation time.

When our cars get outdated by modern technology, acquire high miles and develop mechanical problems, we usually make a decision to move up to a newer and better model. We trade our old car at the dealership because it has served its purpose as far as we are concerned. The same is true in death because when we have served our final purpose here on earth, God trades our existence in for something different.

If God had recalled your number, you wouldn't be reading this right now. If God recalls the number of a person you don't know, you likely wouldn't even know it happened. If that were the case, there wouldn't be a need to perform any type of emotional, mental or physical preparation work. But if God recalls the number of a person who is close to you, it will be necessary to do a lot of work before you can come to peace with their passing.

If you recently suffered the death of a loved one, you are probably experiencing a tremendous amount of emotional pain. The best way to recover from this loss is to slowly work your way through the grieving process so you can get your life back into a loving, happy and peaceful state of existence. It may be helpful to refer to the Grieving/Loss chapter, in addition to the steps outlined in this chapter.

If you suffered the loss of a loved one when you were younger and have not worked your way through the emotional releasing and grieving process, it might be possible for this negative past experience to become trapped in your subconscious. For example, let's say a young child's mother or father died when he or she was five years old. That little boy or girl would have been severely traumatized and experienced a lot of pain and grief. This little person, who lacks the knowledge and tools to deal with the pain, would probably turn to the surviving parent for comfort and assistance. Unfortunately, many times the surviving parent is too consumed with their own grief, and the child fails to receive the love and support he or she needs to heal this traumatic experience. When this happens, the child will hurt for a short period of time before repressing these painful memories in their subconscious.

When a negative past experience is repressed, it usually comes out later in the form of transference or projection. For example, a little girl might take her mother's passing personally and say to herself, "If my mom really loved me, she wouldn't have left me. I must be unlovable, because my mom did leave me forever." If it goes unhealed, this unhealthy message could seriously affect this child's self-concept for the rest of her life. It's also possible for her to grow up with severe abandonment issues. If her father died, she might grow up seeking men who regularly abandon her emotionally, mentally and physically. If a little boy's mother died, he might grow up afraid to make another emotional investment of time, love and energy in a woman, since any woman he loves could leave him at any time, causing him to hurt like when his mother left. If people have failed to work their way through anger at God for recalling a loved one, it could seriously affect their relationship with Him, which will seriously affect the rest of their lives.

Take a look at your past. Have you suffered the death of a loved one? Are there unspoken words you didn't get a chance to express? Did their passing seal your opportunity to make amends and speak your final words of forgiveness and love to one another? If you look back on the situation, does it bring positive, happy feelings or negative, uncomfortable feelings? Have you attempted to work your way through the grieving process, or did you lack the tools and knowledge at the time to embrace your own pain? If you look back on the death of a loved one in your past and experience negative, uncomfortable feelings, you will need to perform some more past healing work to prevent this experience from resurfacing and interfering with your present interactions and relationships.

The healing process is different for everyone. The pain you are experiencing from the recent loss of a loved one is probably the worst experience you will ever go through. Whether you have recently suffered the death of someone close or if it was a long time ago, the following steps will help you through the grieving and healing processes. Take your time working through this process. It may take weeks or even months to complete. But by moving through these steps, you can transform your suffering and loss into peace and wholeness.

Steps to Healing After the Death of a Loved One

Step 1: Be Sympathetic to Yourself

It's important to be compassionate, nurturing and sympathetic to yourself. Usually when the news of death arrives, we first experience shock and disbelief. During this time it's important to comfort yourself and fulfill your own current needs, as long as it's done in a healthy and safe manner, such as:

- Crying, screaming, and venting in a safe environment.
- Endurance-related events until the point of exhaustion.
- Walking in nature or being around animals.
- Surrounding yourself with close friends, family or other activities.

If you are unable to be nurturing, sympathetic and compassionate to yourself, it is important to reach out to others who can be.

Step 2: Write a Letter of Feelings

It can be helpful to write a three-part letter that expresses your hurt, threatened, fearful or guilty feelings. Start this letter by expressing all your reasons, feelings and facts regarding the hurt you are experiencing. For example: "I feel hurt because you were a close friend and I will miss that friendship in my life," "I feel hurt because I really enjoyed sharing experiences in my life with you and I'll miss that in the future," or "I feel hurt because I loved you so much and now there's a terrible emptiness in my life."

In the second part of this letter express all your feelings of being afraid or being threatened. For example: "I feel afraid because now that you are gone, I am all alone," "I feel threatened because you provided all the finances and now I'm unsure about the family's future," or "I feel afraid that I may never remarry or find a new love in my life."

In the third part of the letter express all your feelings of guilt or inadequacy. For example: "I feel rotten because I never got a chance to make amends and now it's too late," "I feel accountable because I knew you were drunk and I didn't try to prevent you from driving," or "I feel guilty because anger, resentment and stubbornness have prevented us from speaking all these years."

Try to vent as many negative feelings and emotions as possible. Many times during this healing process additional feelings will arise. Feel free to add them to this letter as they surface.

Step 3: Write a Letter of Loss

Now write a letter describing your loss. In this letter list all the physical, mental, emotional and spiritual forms of your loss. Include in your descriptions the seriousness, consequences and all aspects of the loss you are experiencing. Describe in detail what this relationship meant to you, and all the ways you were loved and cared for by your departed. Describe how you will miss their conversations, guidance, interaction, assistance, caring and support. For example: "I feel a great loss because the children will miss their father's role modeling and guidance," "I feel a tremendous loss because I will never again feel your touch or hear the sound of your voice," or "I feel a painful loss because I will miss all the ways that you showed your love to me."

This letter can be many pages in length, describing as many losses and reasons as possible. Many times during this healing process additional items will surface in your memory. As this happens, feel free to add them.

Step 4: Write a Letter to Your Departed Loved One

The next step is to write a letter to your loved one. Before you begin, envision them in Heaven walking hand-in-hand with God. They are healthy, happy, peaceful and full of God's unconditional love, joy and happiness. Start by addressing the letter to your loved one. Tell them how much you miss them. Explain how you feel about everything. Tell them how you felt when you heard about their death. Express all your unspoken, unfulfilled dreams. Talk about precious moments and memories where you grew together and shared past events. Say all the unspoken words you never had a chance to share. Tell them everything that is going on in your life. Conclude the letter by acknowledging their happiness in the Kingdom of God. Let them know you are looking forward to reuniting with them someday. Close your letter with warm, loving statements.

Step 5: Write and Receive a Letter From God

Writing a two-part letter, to and from God, can be very healing. The first part of the letter is written to God and the second part is an imaginary response from God. Begin the first part of the letter by telling God your true feelings and concerns regarding the loss of your loved one. Explain the reasons behind the way you're feeling. Acknowledge God's divine forgiveness and unconditional love. Ask Him questions you have regarding the death. Fill the body of the letter with anything you would like to say. Close the letter with some words that confirm your willingness to trust and accept, and to remain faithful in your hope and love.

Begin the imaginary response portion of the letter by addressing it to yourself. Pretend God is speaking to you and you are writing down His words. Start with God confirming his divine unconditional love, wisdom, insight, understanding, forgiveness and compassion. Next, write anything you would like to hear from God. Address all the items that were written in the first part of the letter. Then conclude with a personal blessing from God.

Step 6: Write a Letter of Growth

In every situation we encounter, there are positive and negative attributes, advantages and disadvantages. It will further your healing process to write a letter describing all the positive aspects and gifts that are present regarding this experience. An example of some positive aspects might be your own personal growth, lessons learned, the release of any physical suffering, experiencing family closeness and turning to God, or anticipating the new life that follows after death. Try to find a positive and loving way to reflect on and look back on the experience. Try to find the good side of this situation by converting negative aspects into positives. What can you be thankful for or happy about? How would God or your loved one want you to view the situation? Many times this is the hardest letter to write. If you are unable to realize many of these experiences or attributes, give your loss some time. The Transformation/Transcendence chapter might help change your perceptions and rise above the situation. Hopefully this letter will provide you with some alternative ways to view your situation.

Step 7: Write a Letter of Acceptance

Begin this letter by listing all the ways the deceased person continues on in spirit and in memory. Describe how their memories continue on in our physical world through the friends and family who love them. Describe all your memories that bring you happiness regarding the past experiences you shared with them. Write about how the deceased person would want you to continue on with your life. It might be helpful to make a written history of events, recorded times, dates, places, situations or anything that will help your loved one live on in your memory. Conclude this letter with any special words that you would like to hear from your loved one.

Step 8: Create a Personalized Memorial

Almost everyone who is close to the loved one attends the common or public memorial and funeral services. Usually there are very few personal moments in these public services where we can personally and individually conclude our loss in solitude. You might find it healing to create and commemorate your own personalized services or memorial. This can be done by writing a poem, painting a picture, erecting a cross in the mountains, sealing and burying these healing letters, planting a tree or maybe just dedicating a special place in your heart for them. Anything that seems appropriate to you at the time will work well. Sometimes it is helpful to receive an object of sentimental value in exchange when we give up and release a part of ourselves. Try to find something that you would like to receive as a symbol of releasing your love.

Visions of Inspiration

Very truly, I tell you, the hour is coming, and is now here, when the dead will hear the voice of the Son of God, and those who hear will live. For just as the Father has life in himself, so he has granted the Son also to have life in himself; and he has given him authority to execute judgment, because he is the Son of Man. Do not be astonished at this; for the hour is coming when all who are in their graves will hear his voice and will come out — those who have done good, to the resurrection of life, and those who have done evil, to the resurrection of condemnation.

John 5: 25-29

Those who have the strength and the love to sit with a dying patient in *the silence that goes beyond words* will know that this moment is neither frightening nor painful, but a peaceful cessation of the functioning of the body.

Dr. Elisabeth Kubler-Ross

DENIAL

TOOL 19

*I*magine driving along with the wind in your hair, sun on your face and the radio playing your favorite song. Everything is going great because you're on the way out of town to get away from your problems for a few days. The weekend has finally arrived and a long overdue trip to the country is exactly what you need. Then suddenly the oil light starts flashing on your car's dashboard. What are you going to do? You think to yourself, "This is just great! Here I am trying to get away from my problems and more of them arise."

You realize there are two options available: You can pull over and deal with the situation directly. That will require inner strength and courage because it's not fun to deal with mechanical problems when you're on vacation. Or you can continue driving and use some form of denial or a defense mechanism to avoid the problem altogether.

Let's weigh the matter to see which option would be the easiest way out. Option one requires you to pull over, find a store, buy some oil and put it in the car. Option two only requires you to change your thoughts somehow and deny the whole situation. Option two is a whole lot easier and convenient, right? And besides, who wants to deal with problems anyway?

If you chose the second option, you might be interested in studying some defense mechanisms that will help you avoid the problem of the low oil light indicator. There are about 40 different defense mechanisms you can choose from, so let's look at a few.

* **Distraction** — At first you might try to distract yourself by turning up the radio to keep your thoughts away from the low oil situation.
* **Repression** — After driving a little farther, you will have to repress uncomfortable thoughts and feelings about the problem that keep popping up in your mind. Your subconscious knows the car is low on oil, so it will keep

sending those disturbing warning messages to your conscious mind. By repressing, you simply force those unpleasant thoughts and feelings back to where they came from.

❖ **Suppression** — Now you tell yourself, "I don't have time to deal with this situation right now; it's too inconvenient," or "I'll put oil in the car next month." Unfortunately, next month the same excuses will offer you another extension of time.

❖ **Intellectualization** — You can try to use your academic or philosophical knowledge to cover up the problem. You might try to think of logical reasons that explain how the wiring system and faulty oil warning light sensors might be generating a false reading.

❖ **Reaction formation** — Maybe you could replace the really bad situation going on inside the engine with a really good situation, like driving extra carefully. You might tell yourself, "Look at what a good driver I am. Surely nothing could be wrong here." Or you might drive really fast, proving to yourself, "The car couldn't be low on oil, because the engine wouldn't be able to handle this high-RPM stress load if the oil wasn't at the proper level."

❖ **Denial** — After driving a little farther, you keep getting warnings from your subconscious, and they are becoming more and more insistent. So now you need to use stronger defense mechanisms. Denial is like breaking the oil warning light bulb behind the dash board so it no longer blinks in your face.

❖ **Displacement** — If you can't deny the problem, you can try to displace it from its original source to another, safer source. You might say things like, "It's okay. Those lights go on and off all the time in other people's cars," or "Besides, look how those other motorists are driving. They shouldn't even be allowed on the road."

❖ **Distortion** — Pretty soon the engine starts smoking because of all the internal friction caused by the lack of oil. Distortion can help you come up with grandiose delusions and hallucinations, such as hearing voices or imagining that the spirit guides are instructing you to keep on driving.

❖ **Rationalization** — After a while your engine starts making a lot of noise and eventually throws a rod. Rationalization will keep you from experiencing this distasteful situation by changing your mental viewpoint. You might say things like, "I didn't want to go to the country anyway," or "I didn't like this car in the first place. I'm glad it blew up."

❖ **Addiction** — A good way to keep yourself from noticing engine parts scattered all over the highway is through addiction. If you abuse enough drugs or alcohol, you won't know what happened, much less know what oil has to do with a car in the first place.

When we use denial to avoid our problems they don't go away, they just get worse. God gave us the gift of denial to use only in emergencies and only for a short period of time. To a certain degree, denial in traumatic situations is healthy because it works like a "time out" during a football game. When something traumatic happens in life, like the loss of a loved one, we suffer with the painful news as long as we can. Then for our own well-being our brain calls for a "time out." We go into denial by saying things like, "This can't be happening. There must be some kind of mistake." Using one of the common defense mechanisms, we create for ourselves a short period of time to regroup and prepare for an upcoming crisis. Depending on the situation, using denial as a temporary break from your problems is healthy. But if you deny your problems altogether, they will only get worse until your personal engine parts scatter themselves all over the road of life.

In your own life, what types of actions and thoughts do you and your relationship partner generate as soon as you notice the warning lights going off? If your partner is using defense mechanisms to cover up their problems, chances are you will be able to see them clearly. But because your partner is expending a lot of energy to avoid these problems, they will not be so easily convinced. Who wants to openly acknowledge what they refuse to recognize? If this is the case, the following steps will help you and your relationship partner together work through any unhealthy defense mechanisms.

Steps to Confronting Denial

Step 1: Recognize Denial in Your Life

To make changes, you will first need to recognize areas of your life where denial is present. Unhealthy denial can be defined as the failure to recognize or the active avoidance of important issues that cause harm to yourself or others. There are several ways to discover unhealthy defense mechanisms.

❖ **Watch for blaming.** You can discover issues in your life you are denying by paying close attention to the amount of blame you place on other people and situations. Usually when negative problems arise, we try to deny our involvement by blaming other people. Blame is a calling for forgiveness work and personal responsibility. When we blame other people or situations in life, we surrender our own personal power to the other party, regardless of whether they are liable. If the problem is affecting your life, it's your problem. The only way to avoid the trap of blame and denial is to assume full responsibility for anything that is in your direct influence of control. An easy way to uncover important issues that are being denied in your life is by keeping a daily log. Simply make an entry every time other people or situations cause you problems.

❖ **Do a self-evaluation.** It's possible to ask yourself what issues in life you find very uncomfortable to talk about or think about. What is currently going on in your life that you are intentionally trying to avoid? What situations in life are causing you the most pain? If you say your life is great and you don't have any problems or pain, try rating five events in your life as the most pleasurable and five events as the most unpleasant. Then take a close look at the unpleasant list.

❖ **Ask a friend.** The easiest way to uncover situations in your life where you are in denial is to ask a trusted friend. This can be your marriage or relationship partner, a good friend or even a counselor. Ask this person if they recognize any unhealthy situations in your life that you might be denying. Usually we are totally blind to our own issues, especially when we spend a lot of time and energy trying to hide them. Usually we can see our partner's issues as clear as day, and in the same way that is how everyone else views your issues. Not only can your partner see your issues clearly, but also the time and energy you're expending to cover them up. It will be very beneficial to give the people in your life permission to help you grow through those areas.

Step 2: Face Underlying Fears

After you have recognized some potential problem areas of your life, the next step is to confront any underlying fears. Many times we avoid our problems and painful situations because of the underlying fears involved. It's possible to be in denial about the oil level in your car because of fear that your car will need expensive engine work. Or you may fear getting lost after leaving the highway or that the car won't start again after you shut it off. Once you recognize the problems you are avoiding, get in touch with the underlying fears that fuel your denial. It's important to confront them directly by following the steps and information located in the Fear or Courage chapters.

Step 3: Find the Greater Meaning

Many times when we deny important issues in our lives, we get trapped in dualistic thinking patterns. For example, we might view the lack of problems as good and the presence of problems as bad — or going to the country as good but stopping for oil as bad. By thinking in dualistic ways, we train and condition ourselves to avoid the bad and go for the good. Eventually, through the thoughts we think, our perceptions become distorted. We can correct our distorted thinking patterns by viewing problems from a larger perspective in a non-judgmental manner. Begin by finding positive and negative qualities of all aspects of your problems. For example, it's good to stop for oil because it will give you a chance to rest from driving. It's good to get to the country a little later because it won't be so hot outside. Positive and negative aspects exist in all problems and situations we experience in life.

Many times our problems — which we so desperately try to avoid through defense mechanisms and denial — are our only motivations for spiritual and personal growth. If problems never came up in life, we wouldn't have much motivation to develop our ability to be more loving, forgiving, stronger, more courageous people. It is only by overcoming our problems that we grow personally and spiritually.

God will help you find the greater meaning in your life and problems. Ask Him for assistance in discovering unhealthy defense mechanisms and forms of denial. He will also help you confront underlying fears and change your perceptions in life so you can find the positive aspects that exist in everything. Pray for the strength to grow personally and spiritually from the problems in life we all face.

Visions of Inspiration

Bread gained by deceit is sweet, but afterward the mouth will be full of gravel.

Proverbs 20: 17

Falsehoods not only disagree with truths, but usually quarrel among themselves.

Daniel Webster

Do not show partiality, to your own harm, or deference, to your downfall. Do not refrain from speaking at the proper moment, and do not hide your wisdom. For wisdom becomes known through speech, and education through the words of the tongue. Never speak against the truth, but be ashamed of your ignorance. Do not be ashamed to confess your sins, and do not try to stop the current of a river. Do not subject yourself to a fool, or show partiality to a ruler. Fight to the death for truth, and the Lord God will fight for you.

Sirach 4: 22-28

Truth, like surgery, may hurt, but it cures.

Han Suyin

DEPRESSION

TOOL 20

*I*magine driving to the beach for a day of sun and fun. As you get closer to the ocean, you start looking for a parking place. There's a public parking area several blocks from the beach, but you decide to find a spot closer by checking out some side streets. Pretty soon the pavement ends and the road turns to gravel. As you get closer to the beach, the gravel road turns to sand, and before long your car is stuck. The more gas you give the car, the more your tires spin, digging the car in deeper and deeper. The more your vehicle sinks into the sand, the harder it will be to get out. What would you do in this situation? Would you keep giving the car gas, or would you take your foot off the accelerator, jump out to study the situation and make the necessary changes? Would you call a tow truck? Get your shovel out? Or try to get a group of people together so that they could push you out?

Depression is an early warning signal for our lives and relationships, just like sand is an early warning signal for our cars. When we drive our vehicles too far out onto the beach, they start sinking instead of moving forward. It's usually an early warning signal that we have taken a wrong turn. The same is true with depression. When our life starts sinking lower and lower into a constant state of depression, it is a good signal that we have taken a wrong turn. Just as it's important to make the necessary corrections when your car sinks into sand, it's also important to stop whatever you're doing and make the necessary corrections at the first signs of depression. If you don't, you will only dig yourself in deeper and deeper.

Depression, and the underlying situations that cause it, can bring about a lot of damage to your life and relationships. Depressed people lose enthusiasm for life, and become consumed with negative emotions like sadness, hopelessness, uselessness, unhappiness, worthlessness, bitterness and discouragement. They may experience a lack of energy, motivation and willingness to accomplish goals, projects and responsibilities. Many times depressed people feel isolated, unsupported and unconnected to others. They may find themselves withdrawing from social environments, activities, friends, family or other relationships.

Depression can have two underlying causes: biochemical and psychological. Biochemical depression can start from a medical or chemical condition. It can be caused by imbalances or disturbances in our body's hormones or nervous system, like those a woman experiences after childbirth when her body is dealing with rampant hormonal changes, or from the effects of substance abuse or low blood sugar levels. It also can be caused by infections like influenza or diseases like cancer.

The other type of depression is psychological in nature and usually stems from an inability to cope in a healthy manner with our Inner Self or life. It is usually brought on by the failure to deal with problems concerning our emotional, mental and spiritual lives. Most depressions usually start out from a psychological perspective and, if prolonged for any period of time, have the ability to cause imbalances in brain chemistry. This is the beginning of a downward spiral as the biochemical and psychological forces begin to fuel and reinforce each other.

Depression can be treated from a biochemical perspective with antidepressant medications like Prozac. This treatment is helpful in the same way a tow truck is helpful in pulling your car out of the sand. The problem with this method of treatment is that if you don't deal with the psychological factors that cause or contribute to the depression, it's like driving your car back into the sand after the tow truck has pulled you out. Eventually your body will build up a tolerance to the medication and you will require several tow trucks to temporarily make yourself feel better. Antidepressant medication is helpful to get your life back on solid ground, but only if you deal with the underlying psychological causes.

There are many factors that can contribute to psychological depression: not dealing with anger, but turning it inward instead; not forgiving yourself; failing to grieve losses, like the death of a loved one, the loss of a job, the loss of your health, a financial loss, the loss of your spirituality, or a permanent disability caused by an accident; denying or repressing your feelings and emotions; allowing your self-concept to be damaged or lowered; losing hope, purpose or direction in your life and future; long-term conditioning in a depressive environment; or not dealing with guilt, anxiety, stress or fear in a healthy way.

The next time your car of life starts sinking into a place you don't want to be, stop what you're doing and figure out how to get back to the beach. Depression is a calling for growth, action and change. Depression calls our attention inward so we can deal with the real issues and restore ourselves to a state of happiness, contentment and peace. The following are designed to help you overcome and prevent depression from ruining your day at the beach.

Overcoming Depression

Seek Professional Help

Depending on the severity and length of your depression, it might be necessary to seek professional help. It might be impossible or impractical to free your car from the sand by yourself. Antidepressant medication and psychological assistance from professionals can be life-saving, just like a tow truck on a dark, rainy night.

Identify Your Type of Loss

Most forms of psychological depression are caused by an inability to deal with losses in a healthy manner. It's important to first identify your type of loss before you can effectively deal with it. There are many forms of loss:

* **Physical losses** — These are tangible and concrete losses, like loved ones, personal relationships, divorce, health, physical mobility, abortion, investments, job promotions, friends, material possessions, or losses caused by natural disasters, fires or floods.
* **Emotional losses** — These are intangible or abstract losses, like youth, love, freedom, dreams, ambition, self-respect, hope, control, direction in life, self-esteem, self-confidence, self-acceptance, integrity, friendship and trust. Emotional losses are just as powerful and devastating as physical losses.
* **Spiritual losses** — These are losses that involve your spirituality or the connection with your Inner Self. These losses include things like the loss of a greater meaning and purpose in life, or the loss of your connection, closeness and relationship with God from guilt over sin, or anything else that cuts you off from your spiritual source.

❖ **Imaginary losses** — These are losses we imagine to be real but that aren't necessarily so. They are created from distorted perceptions of the truth, like when we believe a friend cheated or betrayed us somehow, or when we think people don't like us or we assume our spouse is having an affair. In these cases the threat of a loss might be there, but it may never occur. Distorted perceptions of the truth can cause feelings of depression just as fast as if the loss actually did occur. You can eliminate these losses by searching for the truth. See the Perception chapter for more information.

Confront Your Losses

Once you have identified your losses, it's necessary to do something about them. Physical losses need to be mourned by working through the grieving process. See the Death and Grieving/Loss chapters for more information. Emotional or spiritual losses need to be rebuilt or replaced. Imaginary losses need to be confronted and the truth needs to be brought out into the open. You will start feeling better about yourself once you confront, grieve and replace your losses.

Deal With Anger

Anger is a powerful emotion that is designed to help and protect us. Many times depression is caused by anger that is turned inward. When we fail to express our anger in a healthy manner, it builds up inside of us and causes a lot of emotional and spiritual damage that can lead to depression. Other times we may become depressed when we fail to express anger at people who exhibit violating behavior toward us. Or we might violate others with our anger and later become depressed because of the damage we caused. Usually the same things that make you angry are the things that cause your depression. Find out what they are, come to terms with them by expressing yourself in a healthy manner and start setting the necessary boundaries if necessary. See the Anger, Boundaries and Behavior chapters for more information.

Practice Positive Mental Thoughts

A factor contributing to depression is self-defeating thinking patterns. When we focus on the negative, we cannot stop ourselves from feeling depressed. Everyone has the ability to control their own thoughts and minds.

Practicing meditation can help you develop your ability to focus your attention and control your thoughts. Practice positive affirmations on a regular basis, and converting self-criticism will help you maintain a positive mental attitude. Try monitoring your mental thoughts on a regular basis. If you catch yourself participating in self-defeating or negative thinking patterns, simply stop yourself, convert the criticism and reinforce it with a positive affirmation.

Try to add positive intentions to all your activities. For example, if you are going to eat an apple for lunch, pretend it's the last apple you will ever eat. Look at it with wonder, study its unique shape, smell it and try to get as much joy from it as possible. Use the same appreciation for everything you do. Try to remove yourself from negativity like gossip, pettiness, vulgar language, pornography and violent or depressing television news reports that focus on crime and destruction. See the Meditation, Affirmations, Criticism and Perceptions chapters for more information.

Change Your Behavior

Your behavior has a lot to do with the way you feel. If you position your body in a depressed position — bent over, shallow breathing, sad face, thinking sad thoughts — you will send certain signals to your brain causing feelings of depression. If instead you smile, sit up straight, breathe deeply, open your eyes wide and think positive thoughts, you will feel happier. Try it right now. Stop reading and take a happy vacation at the beach in your mind right now. Don't let one negative thought enter your consciousness for the next five minutes.

Just as your behavior affects the way you feel, the same is true for your actions. If you are depressed because the romance is missing from your relationship, change your behavior by buying flowers, writing affectionate notes and planning a romantic evening. Make it a priority to laugh at something at least three times a day; it's okay if you need to force yourself at first. Laughter is a natural healer and it releases chemicals in your brain that help prevent depression. Set aside some time every day to laugh at a joke book, rent a funny video or even attend a comedy show. By changing your behavior, you will be changing your feelings.

Schedule a Balanced Life

A good way to trap yourself in a depressing life style is to schedule a rigid, conforming routine. It's important to maintain a balanced life with a lot of flexibility. Don't mentally or physically overwork yourself. Try some relaxation techniques or meditation, or take a spiritual break when you find yourself getting overwhelmed. Work on your social schedule and make sure you have something to look forward to every day of the week. Set aside the time necessary for a good exercise program. When you are out of shape, it drains your emotional energy and enthusiasm.

Schedule some time for enjoyable adventures like entertainment, hobbies, interests, sporting events and fun things. Set aside personal time for prayer, meditation, relaxation, self-contemplation and planning. Make time in your relationships to work out problems and for mutual activities, sex, intimacy and play. Create a balanced life mentally, physically, emotionally and spiritually.

Set some goals to work on things you are depressed about. Begin by making a list of everything that makes you sad and depressed. Then decide what changes you would like to make happen. Next, make a plan you can work on daily, where every step you take gets you closer to your goals and desired results. See the Goals chapter for more information.

Express Your Gratitude and Appreciation

It's hard to feel depressed when you're expressing gratitude and appreciation. A good place to start is by telling God how grateful you are for everything and everyone in your life. Making a habit of worship is a great way to start the morning because it sets a grateful attitude for the rest of the day. Remember to ask God for assistance in dealing with your depression. Pray for the wisdom to identify the underlying causes of your depression, the strength to overcome the problems and the appreciation to recognize how good God's creation really is. See the Prayer chapter for more information.

Visions of Inspiration

Despair is better treated with hope, not dope.

Richard Asher

Make me to know your ways, O Lord; teach me your paths. Lead me in your truth, and teach me, for you are the God of my salvation; for you I wait all day long. Good and upright is the Lord; therefore he instructs sinners in the way. He leads the humble in what is right, and teaches the humble his way. All the paths of the Lord are steadfast love and faithfulness, for those who keep his covenant and his decrees. Turn to me and be gracious to me, for I am lonely and afflicted. Relieve the troubles of my heart, and bring me out of my distress.

Psalms 25: 4,5,8,9,10,16,17

Life has, indeed, many ills, but the mind that views every object in its most cheering aspect, and every doubtful dispensation as replete with latent good, bears within itself a powerful and perpetual antidote. The gloomy soul aggravates misfortune, while a cheerful smile often dispels those mists that portend a storm.

Lydia H. Sigourney

DIRECTION & POTENTIAL

TOOL 21

*E*very truck on the road has a steering wheel because it would be impossible to operate a vehicle without some type of steering device. Can you imagine driving a two-ton truck at 60 miles an hour and having the steering wheel pop off in your lap? Would you try to put it back on and regain control of the vehicle? Or would you throw it out the window and trust the truck to navigate itself?

In the same way, the direction of our lives needs a strong form of guidance, just like the truck needs a steering wheel. Without a strong form of guidance it's impossible to accurately navigate down the road of life. Throwing the steering wheel out the window is the same as living a life without a clearly defined purpose or direction. If you maintain vague mental purposes, future plans and dreams, it probably feels like you're driving around in a two-ton truck without any power steering. By the time you begin cranking the wheel of that beast, you may find the opportunities and turns have passed you by.

God, being the "Master Car Builder," designed each of us to navigate, perform and corner through life like an Indy race car. We are all given unlimited high-output potential, uniquely contained in our different makes and models. If you have been spending your life driving around town in what feels like that old truck and you would rather be performing like a race car, there are three things you can do: First, maintain your vehicle according to manufacturer's specifications. If you're driving a race car that requires race car tires, then make sure it is equipped with a good set of race car tires. Second, it will be necessary to discover your vehicle's unique qualities, potential and special talents and select a road specifically designed to meet those attributes. If your vehicle was designed to travel at a high rate of speed, don't try to use it as a moving van. The third item is providing daily supervision. You will need some type of steering device to make sure your daily road always lines up with the first two items.

By maintaining your vehicle according to the manufacturer's specifications and using it in a manner that brings out its full potential, you automatically create the road on which your vehicle was designed to operate. It isn't possible to select the wrong road and maintain your vehicle improperly and expect anything other than difficulties. So let's look at these three requirements in more detail before the steps are introduced that will help you get behind the steering wheel of that Indy race car.

❖ **Maintain your vehicle.** Maintaining your vehicle according to our manufacturer's specifications is very important. Race cars are designed to operate on race car tires and large trucks are designed to operate on large truck tires. God designed you to operate on love. If you placed different-sized truck tires on a race car, it would be dangerous, and the same is true in our own lives. God designed us to operate on love, and our ethics, morals and values need to be based on that love. When you act in a loving manner toward God, your neighbor and yourself, you are operating true to your nature and design. If your design specifications call for love and you act in a selfish, abusive, revengeful and unloving manner, you can expect conflicts and problems, just like a race car with truck tires.

If you live true to your loving nature and choose the road of a firefighter, you will be a successful, happy firefighter. An unloving, hateful, vindictive firefighter can't be happy or successful, no matter how much they enjoy putting out fires. The same is true of whatever road you choose in life.

❖ **Discover your vehicle's unique qualities.** Next, you will need to determine what unique qualities and special talents your vehicle has and select a road specially designed to meet those attributes. If you are a loving truck driver competing against race cars, you will probably be contented and fulfilled in your profession and never win a race. It's important to effectively match your vehicle's ability to the challenges and roads that are most compatible. God gave each of us our own unique talents, abilities and gifts. It's our job to discover, use, build on, develop and apply them in life to situations where they are best used. If God gave you natural fire-fighting abilities, the best road for your life might be the fire-fighting profession.

❖ **Supervision.** Once you have established a set of loving guidelines for your life that are represented in your everyday ethics, values and morals, and have discovered your unique talents and abilities to put out fires, then the right road for your vehicle would probably be as a loving firefighter. But since there is more to life than putting out fires, it's helpful to carry the same set of ethics, values, morals, gifts, qualities and attributes into everything you do.

Roads have many corners, just as we have many roles. In one afternoon we might play the role of mother, spouse, fire chief, neighbor and friend. If you want to perform like an Indy car in all of your roles, you need to carry the same set of loving principles wherever you go. If you do this mentally, you are operating your vehicle with manual steering. If you take the time to think about, redefine, study, write down and contemplate your principles daily, you are operating your vehicle with power steering.

Take a look at the guidance system you are using to navigate your own life. Is it clearly written down on paper, or is it something you hope will just happen by itself? Are you driving around in a two-ton truck without a steering wheel, hoping your future destination will be to your liking? Would you like to be driving around in an Indy race car, knowing exactly where you want to go and accurately ensuring your own destination?

Steps to Discovering Your Purpose in Life and Fulfilling Your Potential

Step 1: Create a Personal Value Statement

The first step on this road is to create a Personal Value Statement. Take your time preparing this statement because it will help guide the future direction of your life. Start by listing your ethics, guiding principles, virtues and positive intentions. To do this, you need to get in touch with the loving intentions that reside in your heart. Then make a list of guiding principles that will bring these loving intentions into your everyday life. A good place to start might be with your ethics, values and morals. They can come from several different sources, like God's laws, natural laws, personal laws and society's laws. See the Ethics, Values and Morals chapters for more information.

You can also use imagining techniques to get in touch with your true inner principles. From a relaxed, meditative state of mind imagine your own funeral service. Picture the faces of everyone you have ever meet in your life, all of whom are attending the service. Then imagine everyone giving a short speech that describes your life. What would you like them to say? Do you want these people to express their love and appreciation for your life? Do you want them to praise the difference you made in the lives of others? What would you want your family members, work associates, friends and local community to say about your personality and interactions? Would you like them to say how much money you acquired in a lifetime at the expense of others? Or would you like to hear how much love, care and compassion you brought into the lives of others? Practice this technique as often as necessary to get in touch with what's really important.

Another method you can use is to look at the different roles in your life. Begin by making a list of those roles, including husband or wife, relationship partner, best friend, father or mother, son or daughter, relative, neighbor, work associate, learner, teacher, role model, mentor and advisor. After studying all the different roles, create a list that represents the loving intentions behind your desired future interactions.

It might also help to start a collection of inspirational quotations, spiritual passages or other references you feel represent your ethics, values, morals and loving principles. When you have collected this information, combine it all together into your Personal Value Statement.

Step 2: Create a Personal Direction Statement

With your Personal Value Statement in hand you are ready to create a Personal Direction Statement. Start by listing all your qualities, talents, priorities and goals in life. Include the gifts and special abilities from all areas of your mental, physical, emotional and spiritual life. List your natural talents and abilities (such as physical size or endurance), your character strengths and abilities (such as your ability to work with other people) and your educational background (such as training, classes or degrees).

Next, list your current priorities in life. What's most important to you? Include all areas of your life, like family priorities, social relationship priorities, work and career-related priorities, personal plans and proposed achievements, retirement priorities and your priorities in relationship to God and the afterlife.

Now list your long-term and short-term goals in life. What do you want to accomplish this year, next year, in five years, 10 years and 20 years? Sometimes long-term goals are difficult to envision. It may be necessary to experiment with different stages and aspects of your life before you gain a clear perspective. Try asking yourself the following questions: What would I do with my life if there were no financial, time or personal constraints to hold me back? What did I love to do as a child? During my childhood years, what did I envision myself doing as an adult? How can I make a contribution to society in a loving manner? What can I do to bring out my best qualities, self-respect and self-fulfillment? What types of work-related activities would I participate in if success were guaranteed? What would I do with my time if I had only three years to live? What if I won the lottery; what would I be doing? After some serious contemplation, create a list that represents your Personal Direction Statement.

Step 3: Balance and Combine Your Statements

Now you are ready to combine your Personal Value Statement and Personal Direction Statement into one written form. This final statement will represent who you are, what you stand for and where you're going in life. It will represent the basic principles against which you measure everything in life. When combining the statements, you may find it helps to shorten or lengthen the final version. Try mixing the sentences and meanings together, or convert them into different subsections — whatever works best for your own situation. It's important to make sure items from the Personal Value Statement list don't conflict with items from the Personal Direction Statement list. If they do, you need to rework the direction of your life until it aligns with your ethics, values and morals.

Step 4: Create a Personal Value and Direction Prayer

Your Personal Value and Direction Statement will only be effective when it's incorporated into your daily life, efforts and contemplation. By regularly reviewing, reflecting on and basing your decisions on this statement, you will be better prepared to navigate your vehicle accurately down your chosen road of life. A powerful method of integrating your new Personal Value and Direction Statement in your life is through God and prayer. It helps to create your own personal prayer using your final statement. You can use the entire contents or just parts and sections from it.

Step 5: Make Additional Statements

Life is constantly changing, and as we grow, the direction and purpose of our life will also change. It's a good idea to review and update your statements regularly or when necessary. Post the final statement in an honorable and noticeable place in your environment. Read it every day and take a copy of it with you wherever you go so you can base your decisions on its integrity and principles.

These statements can be used by families, marriages, businesses and organizations. Some of the most successful companies in the world use similar mission statements. It helps the owners, managers and employees pull together in one unified force.

Creating a mutual Personal Value and Direction Statement for your relationship is similar to creating one for yourself, except that you need to use a list of ethics, values and morals common to both of you. And instead of focusing on your individual talents and abilities, you can focus on the purpose of your relationship and your commitment to each other. When creating a mutual statement,all the members who will be involved in its benefits should take a mutual and equal part in its creation. Those who fail to participate in its creation have little incentive to participate in its proposed objectives.

Visions of Inspiration

Better is a little with righteousness than large income with injustice. The human mind plans the way, but the Lord directs the steps.

Proverbs 16: 8-9

And heed the counsel of your own heart, for no one is more faithful to you than it is. For our own mind sometimes keeps us better informed than seven sentinels sitting high on a watchtower. But above all pray to the Most High that he may direct your way in truth.

Sirach 37: 13-15

Ultimately, man should not ask what the meaning of his life is, but rather he must recognize that it (is) he who is asked.

Dr. Viktor E. Frankl

DIVORCE

TOOL 22

*H*ave you ever dreamed of owning a classic car in mint condition? Take a minute right now and imagine your favorite type of car. Vividly picture its color, year, make, model and style. Now imagine that same vehicle, but this time imagine it in need of maintenance. Maybe the paint's faded, the tires are worn, the interior's rough and the drive train is broken. Can you still find value in both vehicles? Which car is more lovable — the one in need of some compassionate restoration work, or the one in excellent condition? How much personal satisfaction would you receive from rebuilding and restoring the second vehicle? Maybe you don't own the necessary tools or have the technical knowledge to restore a classic car. If not, would you drive it to the nearest salvage yard and pay a large sum of money to send the vehicle through the car crushing machine?

When you first got married, your relationship represented that perfect car in excellent condition. If you are considering a divorce, over the years your relationship has experienced neglect just like the second car. It's probably in need of some serious maintenance. Divorce causes the same amount of destruction to your relationship as the car crusher. The only difference is that most couples forget to take their kids out of the back seat when they drop the car off at the salvage yard.

Divorce is only a temporary solution to a much deeper problem. When divorce becomes a way to solve marital problems, everyone involved will suffer, especially the children. Tragically, the children usually get caught up in the trauma and experience extensive emotional damage. Kids instinctively know when they are not safe, loved, nurtured or cared for. In divorce, children are often scared, confused and angry because the family that symbolized love and security is now being destroyed, all because the marriage is in need of maintenance and restoration work.

Rebuilding a car and rebuilding a marriage are similar: both require hard work, but one is easier than the other. Rebuilding the car takes time, physical effort, knowledge, labor, materials, tools and a lot of parts. Your marriage is easier to rebuild because 99 percent of the work is mental and emotional. It doesn't require hard physical labor, parts or materials, and you're already holding the tool box. If you are now experiencing the pain and damage of divorce, see the Closure chapter for healing information. If you are considering a divorce and want to avoid the expense and damage of the car crusher, keep reading.

Usually, everyone enters marriage with great expectations. There are promises of everlasting love, hope, trust and commitment. In the beginning things are usually great. There's passion, intimacy, support, caring and consideration. But without maintenance the beauty can slowly turn to hurt feelings and unfulfilled expectations. Problems and conflicts inevitably arise in any relationship, and if they go unresolved, resentment and anger will grow. Unhealed past experiences may resurface in the form of transference and emotional baggage. Financial pressures that require more of our time may result in our spouse's needs being neglected. Some people spend more time maintaining their landscape than they spend on their marriages. Eventually someone is bound to scream for divorce.

Divorce doesn't solve the underlying problems that contribute to the breakdown of your marriage. If you run right out and get a new relationship, the same problems will follow you wherever you go. Some people run from one broken relationship to the next in an never-ending cycle of destruction, only to find their problems have compounded due to the extensive emotional damage to their children's shattered lives. The only way to solve your problems and save your marriage is to go back and do the maintenance work that's been neglected over the years. By working through the following steps, you and your partner can help each other restore your vehicles to show room condition.

Steps to Preventing Divorce

Step 1: Confront Your Spouse

The first step to healing your marriage is to confront your spouse regarding the breakdown of your relationship and talk about how you propose to restore it. Many times couples who are borderline divorce candidates will run hot and cold. Some days they want a divorce and some days they don't. Any marriage is savable as long as both parties are willing to work together on the issues. The challenge lies in getting both parties interested at the same time in saving the marriage. If you want to save the marriage and your spouse doesn't, there are some things you can do.

You need to motivate your partner to give the marriage another try. Some people are motivated by negative means — what they will miss out on, or what bad things will happen to them. Other people are motivated by positive means — what they will gain, or what's in it for them. Use your imagination and creativity to design a plan that will motivate your spouse to work on the marriage. One method of motivation that uses positive and negative means is to write your spouse a letter expressing your concerns and feelings. You can use ideas from or parts of the following sample letter. It focuses on the importance of healing work in your relationship and includes a list of advantages and disadvantages to divorce.

Dear Spouse:

I am writing you this letter today regarding our marriage. It has been mutually unfulfilling and frustrating for a long time. As I see it, we have two options:

Option 1: We can do some healing work and restore our marriage to the fulfilling way it was when we were first married.
Option 2: We can still get divorced, but do some healing work so we can move on to another relationship without bringing along emotional baggage.

Healing work is necessary in both cases because it will help resolve a lot of the underlying problems, resentment, anger and hurt feelings, which is necessary to restore our marriage. But if we get divorced, doing healing work now will help our interactions in the future. We will interact less vindictively toward each other if we resolve our anger and resentment now instead of airing our dirty laundry in divorce court. And if we work together now on our issues it will help us in the future as parents, when we will be faced with child support, visitation and custody issues.

Whichever option we choose, healing work will be mutually beneficial. I am willing to work with you on our relationship. Are you willing to work on our relationship with me?

I have also considered the following advantages and disadvantages to a divorce and I would like to share my findings with you. Please let me know if there are any items you see differently or think are missing.

ADVANTAGES TO TERMINATING OUR MARRIAGE AND SEEKING A NEW RELATIONSHIP	ADVANTAGES TO WORKING ON OUR MARRIAGE AND SAVING OUR EXISTING RELATIONSHIP
1. Our existing marriage is not fulfilling my needs.	1. We can learn to mutually fulfill each other's needs in the future. It will be easier to fulfill each other's needs because of our shared history and deeper sense of knowing each other.
2. Problems and issues seem too hard to work on and resolve. It's easier to get a divorce.	2. Both of us are equally responsible for everything that happens in our marriage. By working on our problems together, we can strengthen our marriage and become better, stronger and deeper individuals. If we don't work on our problems and continue to blame each other, we will lack problem-solving skills in our new relationship where the same issues will inevitably arise. If we don't work on our own issues, we will continue to experience them for the rest of our lives.
3. I don't love you anymore.	3. Love is thought and action that produces a feeling. We need to think loving thoughts and produce loving actions toward each other before we will experience a loving feeling. Love is not found, it is created. We all have a choice to be loving or not.

4. I hope to find a fulfilling relationship with someone else.

4. The same issues that prevented our marriage from being fulfilling will eventually surface in our future relationships. By working on our existing marriage, we can restore greater passion and deeper love for each other because of our shared history. We can experience a greater sense of connection, feeling, love and devotion for each other that is stronger than ever because of the hard times we endured.

5. I'm unsure of any advantages concerning divorce.

5. "Guilt of broken promises before God. Whoever divorces (except of unchastity) and remarries another commits adultery. Whoever commits adultery will not inherit the kingdom of God." (Matthew 19: 3-9, I Corinthians 6: 9-10).

6. I can't think of a case where divorce will help our children.

6. Divorce is extremely destructive for everyone, especially the children. We will be acting as a role model for their own possible future divorces and hardships. Problems are not resolved by avoiding them or running away. Our children will be mentally, physically, emotionally and spiritually harmed as they are torn between us: who gets what visitation rights, custody, attention, support and love?

7. I can't think of any financial advantage here either.

7. Divorce is financially devastating: we will lose half of our assets to the other; a forced sale of our house will bring a lower price; one of us will have to pay child support, and maybe alimony; and we will each have to pay attorney fees averaging $100-200 per hour while marriage counselors cost half that and work twice as fast.

I would like us to begin working on our relationship immediately. I am willing to commit myself to ____ hours per day for the next 30 days. (Include some dates here.) Are you willing to do the same? Please consider this letter seriously. I love you very much. Let's please work together.

Love, (your name)

Step 2: Establish a Healing Journal

After opening the subject of divorce with your spouse, you will find it helpful to start a healing journal. Most of the steps that follow are designed to be completed as written letters. The purpose of the healing journal is to be a place for your joint written agreements, amendments and healing letters. A three-ring binder works well for this. Next, establish a sacred place for your journal to be kept so you and your partner can reread any of the previously entered items.

Step 3: Write a Letter of Commitment

The first entry in the journal is a letter of commitment. Make a written agreement with each other regarding your proposed commitment. Start by committing yourself to a specific amount of time each day that you will set aside to work on the relationship. Usually one to three hours per day is helpful. Next, commit yourself to a certain number of days you will work through this process together. Describe what you hope to achieve. What are your reasons behind this proposed work? What problems or issues do you want to resolve? Describe your willingness and the amount of effort you will expend on these endeavors. Are you willing to do what it takes? Describe your sincerity, confidence and the willpower that will be necessary to complete the healing process. What will happen to your commitment if things get uncomfortable, difficult and hard? It might be appropriate to commit to remaining sexually monogamous to your partner during the course of the healing agreement. Add other applicable commitments you would like to make to each other. Sign your letter of commitment and enter it in the journal.

Step 4: Consider a Temporary Separation

You might consider temporarily separating from your partner for a specific time, although depending on your situation, this might cause more harm than good. In other cases it might be too late because your partner is already gone. There are many advantages to couples spending some time away from each other:

❖ It may prevent further destruction of your relationship if you are constantly fighting, arguing, upsetting or abusing each other.
❖ It gives your partner some time alone to work on their own issues.
❖ By temporarily stepping away from the situation, you have a clearer picture of the negative behaviors in which you have been participating.
❖ It allows couples the time necessary for their true feelings to surface.
❖ You and your partner may start to miss each other and may be able to use these positive feelings to expedite your healing process.
❖ It acts as a symbol or constant reminder of what will eventually happen to your marriage if you and your partner fail to do the necessary healing and forgiveness work.

If you and your partner need a temporary break from each other and feel it will do more good than harm, you should create a temporary separation agreement. In it describe your proposed living arrangements: Will the other spouse live at a nearby hotel, apartment, friend's or parents' house? Should you and your spouse take turns living in the home? Who, when, where and at what times will your partner spend time with the children? How are the bills going to be handled? How long should your temporary separation agreement last? Will you be having sex with each other during this time?

Make sure all your concerns are mutually agreed on before completing this step. When you finish the agreement, enter it in your journal.

Step 5: Heal Harmful Actions

Make a list describing all the ways your partner has hurt you in the past. Try to come up with at least 40 but no more than 100 major items. Include all serious incidents but leave out minor events that no longer bother you. Include for each item a brief description of the facts, events and circumstances surrounding the past incident. Ask yourself how many times your partner has betrayed your trust. When have they let you down? How did they hurt you? What did they do to violate or abuse you?

After you have finished your list, write a two-part healing letter for each incident. Instructions on how to do this can be found in the Healing chapter. You will know when these items are healed when you can look back at the situation and feel positive feelings instead of negative feelings. Take your time on these letters and complete them to the best of your ability. Enter all your letters in the journal as they are completed.

Step 6: Write Letters Identifying Problems

There are several ways to uncover and identify problems your relationship is experiencing. You can make individual lists of problems of which you are both aware or you can list your partner's specific issues and then list your own. After you have combined these items into one list, start working on solutions. Come up with goals you can both work toward. How can you help your partner with their issues? How can you improve your own?

Work together on these issues to see if it is possible to create a win/win compromise. Other issues might need to be eliminated altogether. Listen to and trust each other when working through the problems. Address the types of behaviors that need to be changed, the compromises that need to be made and the future agreements that will bring about the results you want. Make step-by-step plans to eliminate all the problems. Then record your letters in the journal.

Step 7: Write a Primary Human Needs Letter

Look at your primary human needs to make sure they are being fulfilled in a healthy manner. We all have similar needs, and when they are not being met, we usually blame our partners. Maybe there was a time in the relationship when your partner fulfilled all of your needs, but over the years they became neglected. If so, it will be helpful to complete the exercise in the Primary Human Needs chapter. Once you both have completed the exercise, discuss your results. Express your needs, hurts and feelings in a non-judgmental and vulnerable manner. Talk about ways these needs could be better fulfilled in the future. Keep working everything out until both parties are satisfied with the future fulfillment of their needs. Write separate letters describing how your partner's needs were neglected in the past. Describe how your partner has been hurt because of the neglect and how you plan to fulfill your partner's needs in the future. Enter both letters in the journal.

Step 8: Heal Past Experiences

It will also be helpful to heal your traumatic childhood experiences at this time. Many times our negative past experiences can cause severe damage to our present relationships in the form of transference or projection. It's necessary to heal these past experiences to prevent their negative influences from resurfacing in your everyday behavior.

You can begin this process by writing down 50 to 100 items concerning the worst situations that you have experienced in your past. Maybe you were the child of an alcoholic parent and experienced a lot of emotional neglect and abuse. Maybe your mother or father died or left you at an early age. Maybe you were criticized a lot, shamed, disrespected or raped in the past. Analyze your life, including childhood items and past relationship or marriage experiences. Are you experiencing any similar problems in your current marriage? If so, add them to the list. Include every major event or situation in your past when you were badly hurt and never received the love and support you deserved. How were you treated as a child? How did your parents treat each other? Are you treating your spouse in the same manner as your parents treated each other? Were your parents divorced? Take a look at the items on your list from Step 6 and try to figure out how these issues were developed in your past. Trace them back to a time when you were treated in a similar manner. Then add that negative past experience to your list.

Once you and your partner have completed your individual lists, you can start your healing work. Look at your items and see if there are any corresponding or similar issues that can be grouped together. Then follow the instructions in the Healing chapter and reprogram these events in your subconscious. Usually the visualization technique works best for our early childhood issues and the letter technique works best for more recent events. Working together with your partner is empowering and bonding. Take turns helping each other through the imagining technique by guiding and asking questions. Help each other vent negative emotions and replace them with positive emotions. Work through both lists until every item can be looked back on from a positive point of view. Then after you have completed the healing work, enter a letter in the journal that explains how you can be more sensitive regarding your partner's past issues.

Step 9: Write a Letter of Responsibility

The next step in the process is to write a letter assuming responsibility for any actions that caused harm to your marriage or partner in the past. This letter will probably need to be many pages in length. Include all the situations where you abused or neglected each other in any manner, or when you have been selfish or let your own insecurities harm each other. List all your partner's primary human needs that you knew about yet neglected: when your partner needed your love and support but was criticized instead, or when you manipulated your partner to do something that wasn't in their best interest but your own. List all of the specific times, places and events when you failed to live up to the promises you made in your wedding vows.

Usually the most damage occurs by negative mental perceptions we place on our partners. By placing an honorable mental perception on your mate, you uphold the love and respect necessary to maintain the relationship. By placing a devaluing mental perception on that person, you destroy them in your own thoughts. List all the times you devalued your partner in your mind, causing the breakdown of your relationship. Once both parties have finished their letters of responsibility, you need to forgive each other. Follow the procedures in the Forgiveness chapter and create letters that can be entered in the journal.

Step 10: Write a Letter of Love

Now you can write a letter that describes the love you feel for your partner. Make a list of at least 100 reasons why you love your spouse. Start with some physical attributes like their personal appearance, the things they do and their personality. Then list mental attributes like the way they think, their sense of humor and intelligence. Next, list emotional attributes like their ability to be loving, compassionate and understanding. Finally, list spiritual aspects like their integrity, honor, values and morals.

This may be a hard letter to write. Maybe you don't feel very loving toward them right now. If not, try to force yourself. Maybe it will help to look at the things you used to love about your partner. Start writing and allow yourself to find and feel those loving feelings that used to be so strong. When we think loving thoughts and follow them with loving actions, we usually reap the results of loving feelings. Once you receive your partner's letter, you may feel more loving toward them.

If your mind keeps producing negative thoughts about your partner, use the techniques in the Criticism chapter to convert those thoughts into loving intentions, and write the items down. If these unloving thoughts are related to a negative past experience where a healing letter was written, you need to go back and rework that issue. Once you have both finished your letters, read them aloud to each other, exchange copies and enter them in the journal.

Step 11: Redefine and Maintain Your Marriage

At this point you can redefine and maintain your marriage. Begin by redefining your marriage vows. Everyone has certain expectations regarding what marriage should be like. Many times when these expectations are not met, we are disappointed. It will be helpful to redefine exactly what marriage means and symbolizes. Begin by writing down your own ideas and expectations regarding the purpose and function of your marriage. Then consider your partner's perspectives. Work together to create a new set of wedding vows. The Direction/Potential chapter can help in this effort, since creating a new set of wedding vows is similar to creating a Personal Value and Direction Statement.

Marriage requires daily maintenance. It is a never-ending challenge for personal and mutual growth. If you grow along with your partne,r your marriage will provide you with a lifetime of companionship, love, joy and happiness. If you don't continue to grow with your partner, your relationship will stagnate and eventually end up in divorce.

Step 12: Seek Outside Support

Saving your marriage from divorce may require the assistance of others. If so, it's crucial to turn to others for help in your time of need. Friends, family, counselors, therapists, and church or other support groups can be of life-saving assistance. You also need to turn to the ultimate support system: God. Many couples get married in God's house but fail to include God in their relationship. God has already blessed your marriage and He will be there to help you rebuild it. All you have to do is ask. Pray for assistance daily. Ask for guidance, patience, support, strength, wisdom, knowledge and understanding every step of the way. It is from God that we learn love, the foundation of every lasting relationship.

Visions of Inspiration

The divorced person is like a man with a black patch over one eye: he looks rather dashing but the fact is that he has been through a maiming experience.

Jo Coudert

You cover the Lord's altar with tears, with weeping and groaning because he no longer regards the offering or accepts it with favor at your hand. You ask, "Why does he not?" Because the Lord was a witness between you and the wife of your youth, to whom you have been faithless, though she is your companion and your wife by covenant. Did not one God make her? Both flesh and spirit are his. And what does the one God desire? Godly offspring. So look to yourselves, and do not let anyone be faithless to the wife of his youth. For I hate divorce, says the Lord, the God Israel.

Malachi 2: 13.5-16.5

A divorce is like an amputation. You survive, but there's less of you.

Margaret Atwood

Some Pharisees came to him, and to test him they asked, "Is it lawful for a man to divorce his wife for any cause?" He answered, "Have you not read that the one who made them at the beginning 'made them male and female,' and said, 'For this reason a man shall leave his father and mother and be joined to his wife, and the two shall become one flesh'? So they are no longer two, but one flesh. Therefore what God has joined together, let no one separate." They said to him, "Why then did Moses command us to give a certificate of dismissal and to divorce her?" He said to them, "It was because you were so hardhearted that Moses allowed you to divorce your wives, but from the beginning it was not so. And I say to you, whoever divorces his wife, except for unchastity, and marries another commits adultery."

Matthew 19: 3-9

EMPATHY

TOOL 23

*I*magine for a minute that you are looking for a partner to join your automotive repair business. You place a "partner wanted" ad in the newspaper, but only two mechanics are interested enough to show up for an interview. They both have similar training, references and abilities, but one owns a very special tool called Empathy. It enables him to focus his full attention on the project he's working on. By using this tool, the mechanic can connect with a car on an emotional and logical level. Empathy allows this person to listen to the engine run and know exactly how it's been driven, how it's been maintained and what repairs are needed. It's almost like he thinks and feels what the car would think and feel if it were alive.

The other mechanic who applied for the interview lacks this unique and powerful tool. He seems to be more focused on his own interests and concerns than on the projects and customers in your shop. Because he is self-occupied, he lacks the ability to truly connect with a vehicle. He fixes problems and addresses issues based solely on his own point of reference. Sometimes the mechanical challenges he faces line up with his own point of view and other times his point of view is limited, leaving him frustrated and at a disadvantage when he encounters an unknown situation on the job.

Of these two mechanics, which would you want as your partner? Would you be a more valuable partner if you owned this special empathetic tool? Can you think of other situations in life where this valuable tool could be used? What about in customer service — could these empathetic qualities be used to connect with clients and better understand what they are willing to pay for compared to what you are offering to sell? What about in business negotiations — could these empathetic qualities be used to gain negotiating insights on your banker, landlord, attorney and investors? Could this powerful tool be useful in your family and personal relationships, particularly when others are in need of your comfort and support? With the powerful tool called empathy you can improve many aspects of your life and relationships.

When we develop our ability to get close to the feelings and thoughts of others, we gain the power of understanding. By using this power of understanding — empathy — we can increase intimacy in our relationships, create compromises for problems that were previously unsolvable and help others in need.

Empathy can take time to learn and develop. Many times we are so consumed with our own ideas, opinions, points of view, needs, concerns, problems and feelings that we fail to take time to acknowledge or understand those of another. When this happens, the people with whom we interact might perceive us as self-centered, shallow, selfish, uncaring, unconcerned and distant. When you empathetically listen to your partner without interruption, understand every aspect from their point of view, feel what they feel and think what they think, you have already helped and empowered them. They will automatically feel loved, cared for and understood because you have taken the time to make them the center of your focus.

You will also empower yourself in your ability to deal with your partner on important issues. After you know where they are coming from, you will be better prepared to help them with exactly the right form of assistance and service. So many times we want to help our partners feel better, take away their pain and provide them with answers, but we can't. It's their pain and they need to work through it themselves. Our answers might not be the right answers for their unique situation, especially when we don't understand their state of mind. The best way you can help your partner through their pain, suffering and negative emotions is by being there to empathize — to understand, listen and experience their situation the best you can.

Developing Empathy

Develop Physical Empathy

When we try to fully and deeply understand a person, it's helpful to use physical empathy. It works by copying or mirroring another person's body language. When we use or position our bodies in a certain manner, it sends specific signals to our minds. When we use our bodies to copy or mirror another person's body, we can send some of the same messages to our minds that they are sending to their mind. By copying another person's body language, we can better understand what they are feeling and experiencing. For example, picture a depressed person. Their posture is probably slumped forward, head held down, and their voice is probably saddened and slow. Their facial expression might be gloomy and their breathing pattern shallow. If you copied that type of body language with your own body, you would be better able to know, without speaking a word, what they are feeling.

To increase your empathetic ability, copy the facial expressions, body posture, tone of voice, muscle tension or relaxation and breathing rate of another person. Repeat the key words they use frequently, and the tempo and rhythm with which they speak and form their sentences. Use the same amount of eye contact and same amount of touching and hand gestures.

Once you have connected and understand the other person's position, you can begin to help change the way they are feeling by slowly changing your own body language, and hopefully theirs will follow. For example, if they are cold, hurt and distant and have their arms crossed, you can begin to open up your arms in an attempt to reach out to them. You can increase eye contact to let them know just how much they are accepted, or soften the tone of your voice and begin to smile as you reassure them that everything will work out.

Develop Mental Empathy

Mental empathy works by trying to fully understand what another person is thinking, perceiving and believing — in other words, trying to see the world the same way they do. This isn't always easy, since everyone perceives and relates to the world in a different way.

Some examples:

❖ Some people see a glass of water as half empty and others see it as half full.
❖ Other people relate to the world by noticing similarities first, while others notice differences first. One person may see two coins in your hand while another person will see a dime and a penny.
❖ Some people are motivated by possibilities, like how they will benefit from a business deal, while others are motivated by concern about how they might lose if they get involved in a business deal.
❖ Some people need only their own approval to know they have completed a good job. Others know they have completed a good job when they receive external approval and compliments.

We all relate to the world at one time or another by using all of these methods, but people's actions are usually dominated more by certain patterns than others. By using mental empathy, we can easily see the world from someone else's point of view and relate to them more effectively. To do this, find and acknowledge some form of truth in whatever the other person is saying, even if you feel what they are saying is irrational, unfair, unreasonable or totally wrong.

As an example, consider an argument with your partner where you were trying to comfort them and understand their point of view. Perhaps your partner started an argument with a statement like, "It's all your fault that we're late. You should have stopped for directions." In an attempt to mentally connect with your partner, ask yourself, "How can I find truth in this statement?" An empathetic response might be, "Yes, it is true that we will be arriving late." Next, after listening carefully to everything they are saying, try to view the situation from their perspective. Once you have enough information, try to repeat their mental perspective using your own words to determine if you have fully understood their point of view. If your partner said something like, "The whole night is ruined. We're going to be the last ones there," your empathetic response might be, "It sounds like you're concerned about what others might think of us for arriving late." If you are unsure of your partner's thoughts, concerns or beliefs, ask some questions. Keep checking your interpretations with your partner until they are completely understood.

Develop Emotional Empathy

Emotional empathy is when we try to understand how another person is feeling based on our interpretation of what they are saying, how they are acting and the circumstances surrounding the events. Begin the process of emotional empathy by studying the other person's situation, their body language and what they are saying. After you have collected some information, it's important to ask questions. Use statements like, "I can imagine you might be feeling (angry, sad, disappointed). Is this correct?" Try to keep your emotional empathy in question form. It helps to imagine a similar situation from your own life and compare it with theirs. But try not to verbalize this comparison to the other person, since everyone experiences situations differently.

Develop Spiritual Empathy

With spiritual empathy we try to connect with the another person on a much deeper level. Spiritual empathy works when we try to understand another person's mission or purpose in life. We all have a drive to choose for ourselves a purpose in life and a higher power. Some people are God-centered and their mission or purpose in life might be driven by God's law or their religious beliefs. Other people might be more self-centered and their mission might be to do whatever feeds their ego or makes them feel good. A money-centered individual might base their decisions and actions on their financial goals and bottom line.

There are many types of centers that we can choose for ourselves: prestige, fame, knowledge, family, government, power, influence, fashion, pleasure and more. By understanding a person's center, you are better equipped to understand on what they base their decisions, motivations and ethics. Try asking the other person to tell you the most important thing in their life or the purpose of their life. If they say, "Life is a sport. Drink it up," you might be dealing with someone who likes to compete, win at sports — or maybe they've just been watching too much television. If they don't know their life's missions or purpose, you may be dealing with someone who is confused and searching.

By knowing another person's life's mission and center, you will have deeper insight into what method they are currently using to deal with their issues. If you are trying to help another person out of a painful place, you can use spiritual empathy to connect with them in prayer. Take their hands and pray to God in a mutual request for help. Ask God for assistance, guidance, courage, wisdom, insight or anything they may need.

AN EMPATHY EXERCISE

A good way to develop your ability to empathetically understand others is by practicing this empathy exercise: Begin with a partner, facing one another. Have one person talk nonstop for ten minutes as the other person listens carefully and practices their empathetic ability. Now reverse roles. After this twenty-minute exercise, complete strangers can feel close — almost like they were lifelong friends. That's the power of understanding, and it all starts with a tool called empathy.

Visions of Inspiration

A fool takes no pleasure in understanding, but only in expressing personal opinion.

Proverbs 18: 2

If then there is any encouragement in Christ, any consolation from love, any sharing in the Spirit, any compassion and sympathy, make my joy complete: be of the same mind, having the same love, being in full accord and of one mind. Do nothing from selfish ambition or conceit, but in humility regard others as better than yourselves. Let each of you look not to your own interests, but to the interests of others.

Philippines 2: 1-4

If one does not understand a person, one tends to regard him as a fool.

Carl Jung

ENABLING

TOOL 24

*I*magine for a minute that you and your auto mechanic have a special relationship where every time your car breaks down, the mechanic fixes it for the standard going rate. In the beginning of this relationship each person was on their best behavior. Then as the relationship becomes more serious, things start to change. Over time the mechanic becomes more giving, submissive and fearful. When the car needs anything, the mechanic is right there sacrificing everything for the sake of the relationship. Every time the car needs gas, the mechanic fills the tank at no charge. When the car needs new tires, the mechanic is right there with a free set. Things are going so well you could take the car out and crash it into a brick wall and the mechanic would faithfully stay up all night fixing it so that the vehicle would be ready first thing in the morning. Some days when you're bored and want a little excitement, you drive around as fast as you can in first gear until the engine blows up, knowing your faithful, self-sacrificing partner will put up with anything just to keep the relationship functioning smoothly.

If you were the mechanic in this story, do you think you would be happy, satisfied and fulfilled? If you played the role of the driver, would you need to take personal responsibility for the maintenance and upkeep of the vehicle? Well, you're right. The mechanic is probably very unhappy with the relationship and the driver could care less about their driving habits.

But wait — the story continues. Over the years the mechanic grows more and more resentful toward the driver. Then one day the mechanic blows up and demands they both see a traffic school therapist to work out their problems. Do you think the driver wants to see a counselor? Do you think the driver has any reason or incentive to change? Do you think the driver even recognizes a problem with the relationship? Not likely. As far as the driver is concerned, everything is going great.

The mechanic and the driver fight about their issues off and on over time.

Then after several years of being consumed with resentment, the mechanic walks away from the relationship. Once the mechanic is gone, do you think the driver will treat the vehicle better? If the car's gas tank was always filled by the mechanic, do you think the driver will worry about buying fuel? But if the mechanic stopped filling the tank and one day the car ran out of gas, do you think the driver would need to take personal responsibility for the fuel consumption? Of course, and the same is true for the driver's other unhealthy behaviors.

It didn't take long before the driver realized just how valuable that mechanic was as a relationship partner. As you can imagine, the driver begs the mechanic to come back. The driver says they will do anything, even go to counseling and traffic school.

Now several weeks have gone by and both parties are in a lot of pain. The mechanic suffers from years of resentment, the lack of healthy boundaries and pain from the recent breakup. The driver suffers from their own unhealthy behaviors and driving habits, plus the loss of the partner. What do you think will happen next? How can these two people work through their problems and pain to get back to love and happiness? What would you do if this situation happened in your life?

Eventually the mechanic realizes that resentment stems from a lack of forgiveness and lack of forgiveness only hurts the person who has suffered the injuries. Knowing this, the mechanic decides to write several forgiveness letters that take away the pain. The mechanic realizes that even though they love the driver, there is some type of subconscious force that fueled all those years of enabling behavior. The mechanic takes a deep look inside and discovers underlying fears, codependent tendencies and a lack of self-value and self-love. After making these discoveries, the mechanic decides to do some past healing work to break the enabling behavior.

The driver also wants to be free of pain and realizes the need to change unhealthy behaviors. The driver looks at their behavior and realizes that the manner in which they treated the mechanic is the same manner in which the driver was treated by their parents or role models in the past. So the driver decides to do some past healing work as well. The driver goes back in the past, heals negative subconscious programming, breaks abusive behavior tendencies, learns new behaviors and is now a more loving person. The driver and the mechanic get back together, establish a healthy inter-independent relationship based on mutual love and respect and live happily ever after.

The moral of the story is this: If you want your partner to change thier unhealthy behavior, don't wait until you're totally consumed with hurt, pain and resentment before you decide to stop your enabling behavior. If you can identify with the mechanic in this story, the following items will help you influence your partner to change their unhealthy driving habits.

Counteracting Your Partner's Unhealthy Behavior

Confront Your Own Fears

Before you can influence your partner to change their unhealthy behavior you first need to work on your own. Usually one person takes on the enabling role and the other person acts the abuser, selfish, self-centered perpetrator role. Once the enabler stops allowing, accepting or putting up with the abusive behavior, the perpetrator is forced to deal with their own problems. Before the enabler can effectively stop accepting and promoting their partner's abusive behavior, they need to heal any underlying forces in themselves that allow the abuse to take place.

For example, in the case of the driver and the mechanic there was some kind of fear that drove the mechanic to put up with abuse year after year. It might have been fear of rejection, fear of losing the partner's love, fear of losing the partner's approval, fear of conflict, fear of abandonment or fear of divorce. It's necessary to get in touch with your fears and transform them by using the information in the Fear chapter. The enabler will not be able to break enabling behaviors as long as they are driven by fears that keep them stuck in the suffering, self-sacrificing enabler role.

Work on Your Codependent Tendencies

Another factor that can keep the mechanic trapped in the unhealthy enabling role is codependent tendency. Usually somewhere in every enabler's past, they didn't receive the love and support they needed from their parents or role models. Children raised by parents who failed to give them the love and respect they deserved usually grow up lacking self-value and self-love. Once this condition is imprinted on their subconscious, they will regularly create situations in life where they allow others to treat them with the same unloving and undervaluing behavior.

If you are unable to love and find value in yourself, you may find yourself putting up with abusive behavior from your partner in an attempt to gain their respect, approval and love. A codependent person may find themselves sacrificing and putting up with a lot of unfair treatment to gain their partner's love. They fear that if they don't, their partner will abandon them, taking away what little love they are receiving. If your partner stopped loving you and you were unable to love yourself, you would feel like that hurt, unlovable little child from the past. Knowing how terrible that sick feeling of being unloved is, a codependent person will do anything to prove their loveability. In order to break that cycle, you need to go into your past and love that hurt part of yourself. See the Self-Acceptance and Codependent/Independent chapters for more information.

Show Your Partner the Problems You Want Changed

Begin by telling your partner about the changes you would like to see made in your relationship. If you have already had a thousand verbal conversations with your partner on this subject, you may want to put your concerns in writing. If your partner denies there are problems or refuses to recognize them, chances are your partner is dealing with subconscious tendencies resulting from negative past experiences. If that's the case, it will be necessary to be more persistent in your request.

Communicate With Parables

When you talk with your partner about your concerns, it's helpful to use a parable to illustrate your point. By creating a personal story that represents your partner's unhealthy behavior, you can create an emotional impact that will be almost unforgettable. The instructions for this technique are described in the Communication chapter under the exercise entitled "Communicating With Parables." Take the necessary time to create a powerful story and present it to your partner at a well-planned opportunity.

Show Your Partner How You Feel

Once your partner is fully aware of the problems in your relationship, you can start motivating them to change by showing them how badly their behavior is hurting you. Tell them that you plan to treat them in the same manner as they have been treating you. If your partner is self-centered and selfish, show them how other people feel who are constantly being treated in a self-centered and selfish manner. If your partner is critical and emotionally abusive, let them experience the negative effects of that behavior first-hand. If you are uncomfortable motivating your partner in this way, try to find another method to show them the damage and pain their behavior is causing others.

Teach Your Partner to Change Their Behavior

After a week of experiencing the negative effects of unhealthy behavior first-hand, your partner will probably be a lot more motivated to change their ways. Unfortunately, this will not come naturally for your partner and they will need your help. If your partner is selfish, they were probably treated in the same manner by their own parents. Not only would they suffer with negative subconscious programming from their own hurt, but they probably lacked the necessary role models to teach them how to act in a loving manner. If your partner is critical, they probably don't know how to convert their criticism to loving intentions. If your partner is jealous, possessive and insecure, they probably don't know how to convert their fears to more loving intentions. It will probably be necessary to work with your partner and teach them new loving behaviors. Every time they act in an unhealthy manner, stop them and help them work through the negative and get back in the positive.

Turn Up the Heat

If your partner is still unwilling to change their behavior, you will need to be more persistent in your request. Most people usually take the course of least resistance in life. If it's easier for your partner to stay the same instead of changing unhealthy behavior, they will probably choose that course of least resistance and remain the same. If it's easier for your partner to experience the pain of personal growth than to stay stuck in unhealthy behavior, they will learn to change and take that course of least resistance. One of the most powerful ways you can motivate your partner to change unhealthy behavior is to allow them to experience the direct result of their own problems. That doesn't mean resorting to negative means of punishing your partner; it means to stop taking the abuse yourself and let them suffer the consequences of their unhealthy actions. Try to enforce, enlarge or expedite the natural consequences of your partner's behavior in any way possible as a tool to help them change.

Go on Strike

Another way to be more persistent in your request is to go on strike. All relationships work best with an equal amount of give-and-take. If one person always gives and the other person always takes, there are bound to be unfulfilled needs, problems and built-up resentment. If you always fulfill your partner's needs and they neglect yours, go on strike until they offer you fair treatment. Tell your partner you are sick of giving and not receiving and you plan to withhold all that you contribute to the relationship for a specific amount of time or until your partner shows a willingness to work on making changes.

Help Your Partner Heal Their Past

If your partner is still unwilling to make changes, try to make the road to personal growth and change easier for them. If your partner is acting out of a subconscious tendency that was developed in their childhood, they will need to do some past healing work before these tendencies can be broken. Most people will do anything to avoid those haunting, sick feelings and memories from their negative past experiences. You can help your partner change their present-day behavior by helping them heal their past traumatic experiences. Study the information listed in the Past Experience/Transference and Healing chapters. Work through your own issues if you have not already done so. Once you know how, you can help your partner through their own issues. Schedule an hour every day for a month to help your partner clean out their closet.

Set Protective Boundaries for Yourself

If your partner is unwilling to change unhealthy behaviors, you need to set up boundaries to protect yourself. Boundaries are personal laws we create to protect ourselves from violating or destructive behavior. Tell your partner in advance that you plan to remove yourself from their unhealthy behavior. Make the necessary plans and follow through with your intentions. See the Boundaries and Abuse chapters for more information.

Remove Yourself From the Situation

As a last resort, you may need to leave your partner temporarily. Tell them where you plan to stay, and that you will stay there until they get the professional help they need to change their unhealthy behavior. Don't be afraid to leave your partner once you have exhausted all of your resources. If your partner truly loves you, they will miss your presence and begin the slow, hard process of change. If they don't love you enough to make the changes necessary to save the relationship, you shouldn't waste any more of your life putting up with an unloving, abusive person.

Ask God for Assistance

God doesn't like to see unhealthy behavior in His children. God will help you and your partner change — just ask for that help in your daily prayers. Just remember: You don't own your partner; they belong to God. So ask God for help in changing your own enabling behavior so He will have an easier time changing your partner.

Visions of Inspiration

If another member of the church sins against you, go and point out the fault when the two of you are alone. If the member listens to you, you have regained that one. But if you are not listened to, take one or two others along with you, so that every word may be confirmed by the evidence of two or three witnesses. If the member refuses to listen to them, tell it to the church; and if the offender refuses to listen even to the church, let such a one be to you as a Gentile and a tax collector.

Matthew 18: 15-17

Jesus said to his disciples, "Occasions for stumbling are bound to come, but woe to anyone by whom they come! It would be better for you if a millstone were hung around your neck and you were thrown into the sea than for you to cause one of these little ones to stumble. Be on your guard! If another disciple sins, you must rebuke the offender, and if there is repentance, you must forgive. And if the same person sins against you seven times a day, and turns back to you seven times and says, 'I repent', you must forgive."

Luke 17: 1-4

Confront the dark parts of yourself, and work to banish them with illumination and forgiveness. Your willingness to wrestle with your demons will cause your angels to sing. Use the pain as fuel, as a reminder of your strength.

August Wilson

ETHICS, VALUES & MORALS

TOOL 25

*H*ave you ever driven a rental car at night in a strange city without using a map? If you have, you know how hard it is to effectively arrive at your destination on time without getting lost. Without a dependable source of guidance you can either explore the city until you find your destination or you can stop and ask directions every 15 minutes. Unfortunately, when you ask for directions along the way, some people you speak with won't have any clue where they are themselves! Other people may try to steal your car, wallet or luggage. Some people may try to help but won't know the street names. Using a map is the only effective way to navigate your vehicle through unfamiliar territory. A map lets you know where you are in relation to where you want to be and can guide every decision you make along the way. By following a map, you won't get lost or make mistakes that may lead you to a dangerous part of town.

So where are you in life in relation to where you want to be? What are you using to guide your decisions along the way?

Every day we make decisions and base our actions on those decisions. All of our actions come with their natural and appropriate consequences. If we base our decisions on other people's actions, group surveys or what other people do on television, we may end up lost and confused. If we base our decisions on a well-defined set of ethics, values, and morals, we are using a powerful road map that will protect us from getting lost in a dangerous part of town. The only effective way to navigate through life is by using our own internal map of ethics, morals and values.

If we maintain our ethics, values and morals on a written list, we can regularly reflect on them whenever making important decisions during the day. If we keep our ethics, values and morals only in our mind, it's like trying to memorize a map of an unfamiliar city just before our plane takes off. Without a clearly defined set of ethics, values and morals it's just too easy to be influenced by what other people are doing or by what we're feeling at the moment.

Who has the best set of ethics, values or morals? The answer is you! You are solely responsible for all your actions in life. You're the only one who can accurately create a road map on which to base your decisions.

If you don't have your own internal map and are tired of getting lost using other people's maps, there are four ways you can acquire your own set of ethics, values and morals. They are God's law, man's law, natural law and personal experiences to consider. God's law usually comes first on most people's list, since God is our creator, designer and divine law-giver. He knows exactly what type of behavior is appropriate for our design specifications. He knows and wants what's best for us and His laws are designed for our protection and well-being. God gave us a beautiful life and world to enjoy and His laws will not prevent us from experiencing that joy or beauty; they only protect us so that it can be experienced to the fullest.

So if you find yourself getting lost in New York trying to use someone else's map of Chicago, the following steps are designed to help you develop your own written set of ethics, values and morals. The process of creating this statement requires us to look at God's laws, man's laws, natural laws and personal laws. After we study and consider these four areas, we can create a balance by combining these principles into a written form known as the personal EVM statement.

Steps to Creating Your Own Road Map

Step 1: Consider God's Laws

The first set of ethics, values and morals to consider are those from God. It stands to reason that God, being our creator, designed us according to the type of life we are meant to live, and that God's laws would support that design. We can get to know that law through our Inner Self when God speaks to us through our conscience. We can also get to know God's law by reading about it in His written scripture.

God's law starts in the Old Testament with Exodus, Leviticus, Numbers and Deuteronomy. In Exodus 20: 1-17 God gives us the Ten Commandments. The first three Commandments protect our relationship with God and the next seven protect our relationships with others. After humankind adopted these universal rules of relationships, God further defined and extended their implications and meanings in the New Testament, beginning with Matthew.

The New Testament includes the Sermon on the Mount and the Beatitudes, where God's law is based on the love of God first and the love of our neighbor second. God's laws help ensure our best interests, design specifications and a safe passage around life's roughest neighborhoods.

Step 2: Consider Natural Laws

The second set of ethics, values and morals to consider are natural laws. These laws are not as clearly defined, but we know when we have violated them because of the outcomes of our actions. Natural laws run in accordance with our human nature, the environment and world we live in. When we violate ourselves, others or nature, we suffer the natural consequences. When we violate the environment with air, water and land pollution, we suffer the physical consequences. Natural laws require us to respect, maintain and honor many things in a responsible manner: our planet and environment, and neighboring plant and animal life forms; our personal talents, gifts and abilities; our sexuality; our health and diet; our desires and needs; our livelihoods and retirements; and our neighbors, families, parents, grandparents, children and relatives.

Step 3: Consider Society's Laws

The third set of ethics, values and morals to consider are man made laws. These laws are designed to protect and promote the general welfare of our society, government and the individual rights of its citizens. While it's difficult to maintain a clear direction in life based solely on manmade laws — because of the extensive number already in existence and the number of new ones created every year — it's important to abide by them as best as possible.

Step 4: Consider Personal and Individual Laws

The fourth set of ethics, values and morals to consider are our own personal and individual laws. These laws are designed and created to protect our physical, mental, emotional and spiritual well-being. They are usually established as the result of personal or painful past experiences. For example, a recovering alcoholic might make a personal law that says: "I will never drink again." Personal laws are healthy only if they are maintained out of love and not out of a lack of forgiveness. There are several ways we can get in touch with our own personal laws:

- ❖ Make a list of actions and mistakes that have hurt others in the past.
- ❖ Make a list of the actions and mistakes where you have hurt yourself in the past.
- ❖ Make a list of the ethics, values and morals that were lacking in your parents' or guardians' lives.
- ❖ Choose an influential person you know and make a list of the qualities, ethics and values that you respect and admire about them.

Step 5: Combine All Four Areas

After these four areas of ethics, values and morals are taken into careful consideration, combine parts of each of them to create your own personal EVM statement. In doing so, try to establish a balanced set of principles that will bring out your best qualities. Your final statement should inspire and lead the people in your life, and that most importantly will be a statement you can be proud to have as the guiding source of your life and destiny. Allow yourself some time to work on your personal EVM statement. It might be helpful to make a rough draft at first, and carry it around with you so you can make notes, additions, deletions and revisions before writing the final copy.

Visions of Inspiration

The law of the Lord is perfect, reviving the soul; the decrees of the Lord are sure, making wise the simple; the precepts of the Lord are right, rejoicing the heart; the commandment of the Lord is clear, enlightening the eyes; the fear of the Lord is pure, enduring forever; the ordinances of the Lord are true and righteous altogether.

Psalms 19: 7-9

"Teacher, which commandment in the law is the greatest?" He said to him, " 'You shall love the Lord your God with all your heart, and with all your soul, and with all your mind.' This is the greatest and first commandment. And a second is like it: 'You shall love your neighbor as yourself.' On these two commandments hang all the law and the prophets."

Matthew 22: 36-40

I believe that unarmed truth and unconditional love will have the final word in reality. This is why right, temporally defeated, is stronger than evil triumphant.

Martin Luther King Jr.

EXPECTATIONS

TOOL 26

*H*ave you ever loaned a friend the use of your car? What did you discuss with them before handing over the keys? You probably talked about insurance, how long the car would be used, when it would be returned and who would pay for the gas. Let's imagine for a minute, though, that you and your friend were participating in a nonverbal experiment and the car was going to be borrowed using hand signals. As you might imagine, your friend would probably point to himself and make silly hand signals as if he were actually driving. Next would come time for the important information like when the car would be returned. Your friend would point to the clock and signal the car's return at 11:00 a.m. That time frame works well for your schedule because it allows ample time for you to reach your noon appointment. You hand over the keys and don't give it another thought — until 11:50 a.m. rolls around and your car isn't back yet.

What thoughts are going through your mind? You were expecting the car to be returned at 11:00 a.m., and it's still not back. Are you worried for your friend's safety? How are you going to get to your appointment? Why did you loan the car in the first place? Do you call a cab or wait a little longer? What type of hand signals would you like to use this time when your friend returns?

When you loaned the car, you had certain expectations in your mind that said the car will be back at 11:00 a.m. Your friend also had certain expectations in his mind that said he needed to return the car at 4:00 p.m. Then once we turn that thought loose, our brain usually starts setting it in concrete. Soon we start basing our plans on that thought and adding other factors to it. Eventually these expectations will become very real to the person who created them in their thoughts. As you can see, unspoken expectations or assumptions can be very dangerous and damaging to your relationships. Not only could this situation cause a nasty fight on the car's return, but the trust on which the relationship was built can be damaged. If this situation really happened, would you ever loan that person your car again?

Now this simple car story probably would not go to such extremes in everyday life, because people don't generally loan their vehicles with hand signals. But people create unhealthy mental expectations in their minds every day. For example, if you married a physically active and attractive partner, you might expect them to maintain their beauty. You might expect your employees to work hard when you're not around. You might expect your partner to conserve money, pay a fair share of the expenses or even support you financially. Do you expect your relationship partner to make you happy? Should they be there for you in your time of need? Should they respect, love and care for you?

The number of expectations we place on other people is endless. Like most things in life these expectations can have either a positive effect or a negative effect on your relationships. Healthy expectations are mutually agreed on, committed to, accepted, recognized, verbally spoken and are flexible. For example, you both may verbally agree that the car will be back at 11:00 a.m. and then allow several hours for uncontrollable factors like a flat tire, traffic jams and road construction. Unhealthy expectations are not directly spoken but are assumed based on past histories of performance or fixed on rigid expectations.

The only way to convert unhealthy expectations to healthy expectations is to talk about them. Unfortunately, this isn't always easy, due to our fears. You might fear hurting your relationship partner if you bring up the physical beauty expectation, or fear looking greedy talking about your money expectations. You may fear looking weak, silly, inadequate or shallow with some of your other expectations. If fears can keep a person from getting on an elevator, they certainly have the power to keep you from expressing an unspoken expectation to your partner. If that's the case, the following expectations exercise will help you and your relationship partner convert unhealthy expectations into healthy ones.

THE EXPECTATION EXERCISE

Begin by sitting down with your relationship partner and write a list of everything you expect from the other person. You can each start with ten items each or compete with your partner item-for-item. The usual expectations will come up first, but as you continue, try to uncover unspoken and hidden expectations as well. It might be helpful to ask yourself: What could my relationship partner do that would cause me great pain and disappointment? In what areas of my life do I depend on my relationship partner the most?

After you have uncovered some of your unspoken expectations, talk with each other about your concerns, ideas or fears. Try to establish mutual agreements concerning any problems that arise. Other issues may be resolved by a deeper understanding of your partner's perspectives. Unresolved issues can be accepted without any future disappointments, or you can work together on those issues to create a win/win situation through compromise.

This exercise also works well on things you expect of yourself. During your daily activities when you're feeling frustrated, guilty or upset, ask yourself, "What things do I expect of myself?" Are you placing any rigid or controlling expectations on yourself? Do you have any subconscious expectations that are in conflict with your conscious expectations? Do your thoughts correspond with your emotional feelings in most of your activities during the day? Do you find yourself expecting certain levels of accomplishment concerning your performances or objectives that you are not currently prepared for? If you expect a new car or a promotion, do you have written plans and goals for these proposed accomplishments? If not, write down your expectations and then refer to the Goals chapter for more information.

Visions of Inspiration

Assumption is the mother of screw-up.

Angelo Donghia

It is not enemies who taunt me — I could bear that; it is not adversaries who deal insolently with me — I could hide from them. But it is you, my equal, my companion, my familiar friend, with whom I kept pleasant company; My companion laid hands on a friend and violated a covenant with me with speech smoother than butter, but with a heart set on war; with words that were softer than oil, but in fact were drawn swords.

Psalms 55: 12-14.5, 20-21

If you expect perfection from people, your whole life is a series of disappointments, grumblings and complaints. If, on the contrary, you pitch your expectations low, you are frequently surprised by having them perform better than you had hoped.

Bruce Barton

FEAR

TOOL 27

*F*ear serves a valuable purpose in our lives, just like the brakes on your car. Your vehicle's braking system was designed by the manufacturer for one purpose — protection. It protects you as well as the property and lives of others. Without brakes we would experience a lot of problems and accidents in life. Just imagine what would happen if you tried to drive across town without using the brakes. If someone cut you off and endangered your life, how would you prevent an accident from happening?

Every driver is responsible for the use and maintenance of their own brakes, just as we are each responsible for the proper use and maintenance of our fears. We can use our brakes in a healthy manner to prevent an accident or we can use our brakes in an unhealthy manner to cause people driving behind us to crash into the back of our car. Failing to pay attention to our driving habits is just as destructive as failing to pay attention to our fears. Both can cause a lot of damage and destruction to our lives and relationships.

The healthy use of our fears can protect us from danger and keep other people and things around us from being hurt. The unhealthy use of our fears can impair our ability to function and paralyze us for no particular reason. Any time you fail to stand up for your rights with an employer, you are experiencing fear. Any time you fail to ask someone out on a date, you are experiencing fear. Any time you cannot ask that important question in front of a group of people, you are experiencing fear.

Unhealthy fear causes unnecessary stress, sleeplessness, relationship problems, nausea, hot flashes, breathing and heart rate changes, anxiety, and impaired social and work performance. Unhealthy fear causes isolation, prevents us from accomplishing the things we want, and restricts and distorts our rational thinking patterns. Unhealthy fear promotes obsessive thoughts and compulsive behaviors, and prevents us from being vulnerable in our intimate relationships.

To avoid the unhealthy results of fear in our lives and relationships, we need to practice continued self-awareness and evaluate and confront our fears as they arise. Because fear is such a powerful force, many of us just react to our fears without ever testing their authenticity. If you are driving at night and a dog runs in front of your car, you would react with healthy fear by slamming on the brakes. If in your mind you only imagined a dog running out in front of the car (the same fear) and slammed on the brakes, it would be an unhealthy response because the threat or danger never really existed. The same is true of all aspects of our lives and relationships. Just because we fear something doesn't mean there's any real threat or danger.

Most of our fears stem from unhealed negative past experiences. Usually something from our past hurt or threatened us, and in an attempt to protect ourselves in the future, we subconsciously create a present-day fear. For example, small children are not inherently afraid of bees. If you are afraid of bees as an adult, somewhere in your past you were probably minding your own business when a bee attacked you and left a lot of pain and a big welt. Because of this negative past experience, you would subconsciously learn to fear bees in order to protect yourself from another attack. We can also program our subconscious by watching a killer bee movie on television and then obsessing on those thoughts. Or maybe you watched as your best friend was stung by a wasp and went through the painful situation with them. If you weren't born with your present-day fears, then it's safe to say they were learned somewhere in your past.

As an adult this fear of bees can be healthy if it protects you and doesn't affect anyone else in a negative manner. But if you are a carpenter working on a ladder with a power saw in your hand and you start "wigging out" when a bee flies past, it would be safe to say your fear is unhealthy — because you could fall off the ladder and drop the saw on your coworker's head. Healthy fears protect you and others; unhealthy fears violate, endanger, inconvenience, upset, limit personal growth, and cause harm to yourself and others.

There are a number of common fears that can seriously affect relationships: losing your partner's love, your partner cheating on you, being abandoned, being intimate, losing your sense of self to another, being emotionally hurt, looking weak, being vulnerable and losing control; or, the fear of God, fear of death, fear of conformity, fear of the unfamiliar, fear of success, fear of failure or the fear of fear itself.

A strong relationship with God is a powerful force for overcoming your fears. God teaches love, and when you are focused on being loving and trusting in God, it's impossible to be consumed with fear. Love focuses your attention on the positive aspects of other people and situations, and fear focuses your attention on protecting yourself from the negative. Love lives in the present, while fear worries about the future. Love is based on positive thoughts, actions and attitudes, while fear is based on negative emotions.

The following steps will help you transform fears you may be experiencing in your life or relationship. The procedure is described using written letters, but it can also be practiced through imagination techniques. Because fear is a powerful, overwhelming and paralyzing force, it might be more beneficial to practice the exercise in the written form first. Then once you become familiar with the principles, it can be practiced in your imagination when an unhealthy fear arises.

Steps to Transforming Fear

Step 1: Acknowledge Your Fear

First, it will be necessary to recognize and acknowledge your fears. What are you afraid of? What scares you and causes anxiety in your life? Make a list of several fearful events and pinpoint the exact cause of your fear. Start the written exercise by explaining your fears and any circumstances that accompany them. Write down the environmental conditions and events surrounding the fearful event.

Step 2: Create the Worst-Case Scenario

Now write a detailed description of the worst possible outcome concerning your fear. What would happen if this fear came true? What would you be most concerned about? What's the worst thing that could go wrong? Then write a step-by-step script of events and role-play them on paper.

Step 3: Experience Your Worst-Case Scenario Emotions

After you have described the worse thing that could happen as a result of your fear, experience and feel the emotions that would be related to this worst-case scenario. It's important to actually feel the true emotions behind your worst possible scenario. Connect the thoughts with their corresponding feelings and explore the situation. Are you experiencing feelings of embarrassment, shame, humiliation, pain, suffering, anger or sadness? How do you feel about yourself? Write a couple of paragraphs that describe the truest feelings, emotions and thoughts you would have if your worst possible scenario became a reality.

Step 4: Find and Heal a Similar Situation From Your Past

Many times fear is a learned response. You probably have experienced a similar situation in your past that endangered or hurt your well-being in some manner. It's important to locate that past experience and heal it. Once you are able to connect your present-day fear with its corresponding traumatic past experience, write a healing letter to free yourself from that negative subconscious tendency. Information on writing a healing letter can be found in the Healing chapter. This letter can be added in your current writings or completed separately. Address the healing letter to a person, place, thing or animal. For example, someone afraid of bees could remember back in time to when they were stung. Then they could write the healing letter to the bee colony and pretend the bees could write back an imaginary response letter. If you are more comfortable with the imagination technique than the written letter exercise, feel free to use it instead. Go back in your imagination and give yourself the love and support you need but didn't receive during the past bee attack.

Step 5: Create the Best Possible Scenario

The next step is to create a detailed description of the best possible outcome concerning your fears. What would you like to happen in the future? How would you like to be treated? The best possible scenario is usually the exact opposite of whatever your fearful thoughts are picturing. For example, if you are working with the bee issue, the worst possible scenario would be getting stung again. In the best possible scenario you might describe a friendly, respectful relationship between yourself and every bee in the world. After you have created the best possible scenario, write a step-by-step script of events and role-play them in your mind and on paper. In the last couple paragraphs describe the feelings that would accompany this scenario. Describe on paper your relieved, happy, peaceful, relaxed and contented feelings toward your new-found bee relationship. It is important to actually feel the emotions as well as writing out the thoughts so your subconscious can be reprogrammed with the new information.

Step 6: Make Daily Efforts

Transforming fears often requires daily effort. Many times our fears are built over a long period of time and it might be necessary to repeat this letter exercise several times. Every time you do it, the process will be easier and your fears will become smaller. There is an imagination technique in the Courage chapter that might also be helpful. Ask God for strength and courage on a daily basis. Pray for the replacement of your fears with faith, hope, love and guidance. These gifts are given by God frequently. All we have to do is learn the lesson that fear teaches and desire its gifts in our heart. You can even incorporate the following fear-reducing techniques in your daily efforts:

- ❖ **Gradual exposure.** Fear can be reduced by gradually exposing yourself to whatever you're afraid of. Start out small and safe. Every day increase your interaction until you feel confident and safe around that which you fear.
- ❖ **Modeling.** Fear can be reduced by observing others who respond to the similar situation in a healthy manner. Research and study information regarding the feared subject. Visit and familiarize yourself with others who interact with whatever is feared. Try to understand which points of view and perceptions they use to maintain a healthy perspective, then incorporate them as your own.
- ❖ **Operant conditioning.** Fear can be reduced by placing more importance on the results of the fearful actions than on the fear itself. During a fearful experience try to focus and place more importance on the loss of opportunity, disadvantages, inconveniences or negative consequences your fears are causing in your life than on the worst possible scenarios.
- ❖ **Anxiety journal.** Fear can be reduced by keeping a daily record of irrational thoughts and behaviors that contribute to fear. See the Anxiety chapter for more information.
- ❖ **Relaxation and breathing techniques.** When you experience a fearful situation, focus on your body's reaction. Loosen up any tightness and concentrate on your breathing by taking long, deep breaths. See the Stress chapter for other relaxation information. Try to verbalize your fears out loud. It might help to talk about them with others in an effort to seek support, encouragement or even humor.

❖ **Systematic desensitization.** Try to imagine the situation that causes the fear. Allow yourself to experience the feelings that these thoughts create. Next, imagine yourself reacting to the same situation in a relaxed and comfortable manner. Role-play it over and over in your mind until it feels comfortable.

Visions of Inspiration

But if God so clothes the grass of the field, which is alive today and tomorrow is thrown in the oven, will he not much more clothe you — you of little faith? Therefore do not worry, saying, 'What will we eat?' or 'What will we drink?' or 'What will we wear?' For it is the Gentiles who strive for all these things; and indeed your heavenly Father knows that you need all these things. But strive first for the kingdom of God and his righteousness, and all these things will be given to you as well. So do not worry about tomorrow, for tomorrow will bring worries of its own. Today's trouble is enough for today.

Matthew 6: 30-34

God is love, and those who abide in love abide in God, and God abides in them. Love has been perfected among us in this: that we may have boldness on the day of judgment, because as he is, so are we in this world. There is no fear in love, but perfect love casts out fear; for fear has to do with punishment, and whoever fears has not reached perfection in love.

1 John 4: 16.5-18

You gain strength, courage and confidence by every experience in which you really stop to look fear in the face. You are able to say to yourself, "I have lived through this horror. I can take the next thing that comes along." You must do the thing you think you cannot do.

Eleanor Roosevelt

FORGIVENESS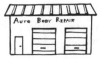

TOOL 28

*P*retend for a minute that you own the only auto body shop in town. Then one day, after parking your car at a local store, you notice a dent in the driver's door. It seems someone has carelessly backed into your car and left the scene without leaving a note. If the responsible party never came forward, how would you ever find out what had happened? Would you feel better about the situation if you knew who did it and why? Let's take a look at some questions regarding the accident to gain a better understanding of the experience.

Would you be angrier if the damage happened by accident, or if it were intentional? Do you think someone wasn't watching where they were going and didn't actually know they hit your car? Or do you think someone was trying to deliberately get even with you? Would it make a difference in the number of repairs your vehicle would require?

Because you own the auto body shop, would you fix the dent immediately and not hold anyone accountable? Or would you drive around town with the dent in your car, hoping that the responsible party would come forward and apologize? Would you fix it for your own satisfaction or would the repairs have anything to do with the unknown responsible party? If this happened to other cars in the same parking lot would you continue to park there in the future?

What does this little scenario have to do with forgiveness? It's simple. The auto body damage represents the emotional, mental, physical and spiritual damage that everyone is bound to experience in life. The unknown driver who caused the damage can be anyone who has hurt you in the past. The forgiveness process, just like the repairs, can take place immediately in your own shop. The repairs won't cost you a penny and you're already holding a toolbox of everything you may require.

Lack of forgiveness is extremely destructive, not only to yourself but to every single aspect of your life and relationships. Forgiving restores your emotional well-being. Lack of forgiveness only causes further destruction in your life. Your ability and reason to forgive have nothing to do with the responsible party. Forgiveness is fixing your own car for your own reasons. The damage has already been done; the dent has already been made. You can either heal it through forgiveness work or you can drive around town being angry and hurt every time you look at your car door.

Unfortunately, many people choose to be hurt and angry for years. First, they start to resent the parking lot and store where the accident happened, then the people who work and visit the store and whoever it was that they think might have intentionally caused the damage. Pretty soon the lack of forgiveness slowly eats away and destroys their entire peace of mind, happiness, life and relationships.

The choice is yours. You can add negative energy to your hurt and make it grow until it consumes everything in its path, or you can add positive energy to your hurt and heal yourself and possibly others.

Unfortunately, many people in life don't know how to forgive. They either lack the knowledge, fail to realize the importance or can't seem to forgive themselves first. Just as auto body work is more than spraying paint over a rusted dent, true forgiveness is more than just saying the words, "I forgive you." True forgiveness takes place in your entire being – physically, mentally, emotionally and spiritually.

* **Physically.** It might be necessary to repair the damage to your car or to another person's car before the healing process can be complete. Physical forgiveness can include material retribution, physical effort or some form of amends or confrontation.

* **Mentally.** This is where the entire forgiveness process starts. You may need to view the situation in a positive manner, recognize the gifts that are involved, work to convert your unhealthy thoughts and realize the importance of forgiveness.

* **Emotionally.** You will need to restore the person who hurt you to their proper, respectable and rightful place in your heart. Forgiveness is complete when you can emotionally view in a loving manner the person who caused you damage.

* **Spiritually.** You will need God's help in the forgiveness process. God makes our forgiveness contingent on forgiving others. God asks that we turn the wrongs of our fellow brothers and sisters over to His greater authority for judgment.

Take a close look at your life and relationships for signs of poor auto body work. Are you driving around in a car full of dents? What does your relationship partner's car look like? Usually when the vehicles we drive around in every day start looking like they have been through a demolition derby, we begin shopping for a trade-in. Let's look at some common expressions made by people in need of auto body work to see if anything sounds familiar:

- ❖ "I can't forgive my partner unless they say they're sorry." Forgiveness is a personal choice, just like fixing a dent in your car. It doesn't matter how the dent got there, who did it or for what reason. Forgiveness is something you do for your own well-being.
- ❖ "I don't want to appear weaker and forgive the responsible party because it's almost like I would be condoning their actions." Only strong people have the power to embrace their pain and restore their emotional well-being. People who possess that strength don't appear weaker at all. If you don't approve of or condone another's actions, the same strength can be used to let them know about it.
- ❖ "They don't deserve to be forgiven for what they did to me." Only God can read our hearts, intentions and conditions. Many times we lack the knowledge to fix our own dents, much less judge another. That's why God says judgment is His alone.
- ❖ "Forgive and forget." Yes, forgive by restoring your relationship, but don't forget the important lessons that are involved. If the parking lot is notorious for dents, don't park there in the future. Set some healthy boundaries for your self-protection when necessary, but don't let that interfere with your personal auto body repair work.
- ❖ "Time heals all wounds." Not if you don't do anything about them. Unforgiving items will become repressed, only to turn up later in the form of revenge or resentment.

If you have experienced a dent in the past, the following steps will help get your car in the body shop for repairs. If you have suffered a major loss, it may be necessary to first work through the grieving process before true forgiveness can take place. If that's the case, refer to the Grieving/Loss chapter for more information.

Steps to Forgiving

Step 1: Describe the Situation

Write a short description about the situation for which forgiveness is necessary. Explain what happened and why you are hurt. What are the events that led up to the incident? How were you emotionally, physically and mentally hurt, injured, abused or damaged?

Step 2: Re-create and Reexperience Your Feelings

Writing a description that explains how you are feeling will help resolve any negative feelings you may be experiencing. It's important to work through your emotions and experience the feelings behind them again. Don't try to avoid these negative feelings. It's necessary to embrace them and allow yourself to feel them. Start by describing why you are angry. What caused you to be hurt? List as many reasons as possible and then describe why you felt threatened. What was the worst possible scenario that could have happened? List as many reasons as possible and get in touch with your sadness. What did you want to happen that didn't? List as many reasons as possible and then describe anything you may feel sorry for. What did you regret doing? Try to vent all of your negative emotions in this step and get everything down on paper. If you don't vent, the negativity will stay trapped inside your subconscious only to come out later in the form of transference, projection or resentment.

Step 3: Understand the Views of Others

It helps to view and understand the events as they might be perceived by the party who hurt you. Try to find a logical reason behind their actions by putting yourself in their position. Imagine that the person who hurt you had no idea their actions would be harmful. If you think their actions were intentional, realize that everyone can be motivated to cause destruction, harm and injustice when they themselves are hurting. As humans we are all as loving as we can be all the time. People just don't inflict pain and suffering on others for no reason. The person who hurt you had to be in a lot of pain themselves to have participated in their destructive behavior. Try to understand the hurt and pain that motivated the person in need of your forgiveness. Study the situation from their point of view. Then write down the most loving explanation you can think of that would help explain the actions of the party who hurt you.

Step 4: Write an Imaginary Response Letter

After trying to gain an insight into the person who hurt you, write an imaginary letter from that person that states anything you would like to hear from them. Have them apologize for their behavior and ask for your forgiveness. Perhaps they offer to make amends or retribution for hurting you. It doesn't matter if they would actually say these things or not. It's your dent and you can imagine that this person is coming from a completely healed state where they are capable of saying anything you deserve to hear. Imagine they are actually speaking to you as you write down what you would like to hear them say. Once you have completed the letter, allow yourself to feel the emotions that would be involved if this person were actually strong enough to write this letter.

Step 5: Grant Forgiveness

Next, create a forgiveness letter in response to the imaginary letter you completed in Step 4. Address this letter to the person you plan to forgive. Explain to them why forgiveness is important for your well-being. Tell them why it's important to resolve the situation for everyone's personal, emotional and spiritual well-being. Write anything you want to say in response to the imaginary letter that was previously written. List anything you may be grateful for regarding this past event. Tell them in writing that they are forgiven. Talk about your desire to release all your negativity from this situation and restore the feelings of love, happiness, hope and peace to your life. In concluding the letter, express some loving intentions and wishes toward this person and let them know you have restored their rightful place in your heart.

Step 6: Take External Actions

The previous five steps will have completed the internal aspects of the forgiveness process. Depending on the situation, it might be important to perform some of the following external actions before the situation is completely resolved.

If the person who caused the damage is someone close to you, it will probably be necessary to express your feelings and let them know about your unconditional forgiveness. It's important to clarify any unresolved issues and empathetically understand their point of view. This will help your relationship grow and help prevent similar conflicts in the future. You may want to discuss and express your personal needs at this time and request better treatment and consideration in the future. Or you may want to make some compromises and win/win agreements. Other times it might be appropriate for the other party to make amends for the damage and harm you suffered, or for you to set some boundaries to protect yourself in the future.

If the person who has caused the damage is not someone close to you, it's still a good idea to confront them in a constructive manner. Be honest, open and direct as you state how their actions hurt you. Find out if they are aware of how their actions affected you. Many times you will find that this person has no idea how their actions affected you. In many cases talking with them can resolve the whole situation in a matter of minutes. If confronting the person would cause additional harm or damage or if it's not possible to confront them due to other circumstances, you may want to consider other options like praying to God for that individual's well-being and healing. Or you can share your story or previously written letters with other people, outside support groups, counselors, mentors or close friends.

Step 7: Practice Self-Forgiveness

By working through the previous steps, you hopefully have completed the internal and external forgiveness process necessary when another person causes damage to your vehicle. But what happens when you are the one responsible for putting the dent in your door? Self-forgiveness is just as important as forgiving others; in fact, it might not be possible to forgive another if you continue to punish yourself for mistakes you made in the past. People who can't forgive themselves are no different from people who intentionally pound dents in their own doors. The lack of self-forgiveness is just as destructive to your entire well-being as a sledge hammer is to your windshield. If you still feel guilty, remorseful and unforgiving, express those negative feelings on paper. Begin by writing what you regret doing, what you would like to come to peace with and what you feel sorry for. Then continue with the following steps to complete the self-forgiving process.

Step 8: Write a Letter to God

The next step is to write a letter to God and explain your sorrow. Tell God how you are feeling and ask for His unconditional love, mercy, forgiveness and guidance. Fill the letter with anything else you would like to ask or express to God. Conclude your letter with some loving statements.

Step 9: Receive an Imaginary Response Letter From God

Now you can create an imaginary letter from God in response to the letter written in Step 8. State everything you would like to hear from God. Start this letter by addressing it to yourself. It might be helpful to imagine yourself in God's presence, experiencing His unconditional love, forgiveness and compassion. In your imagination pretend God is speaking to you and you're writing down everything He says. In the body of the letter put anything you would like to hear God say about your situation. Conclude your letter with God's blessings and reconfirming statements of His unconditional forgiveness.

Step 10: Acknowledge Your Gifts

You are certain to have received some positive gifts from your experience. Write down all the lessons you learned. How have you grown closer to God from this process? Are you a stronger or better person because of this experience? Have you gained the wisdom to not repeat the same mistakes in the future? Has your ability to love and be compassionate grown because of the past mistakes? Positive aspects can be found in every situation. Ask yourself what you have learned from this experience so a similar situation can be avoided in the future.

Step 11: Have Internal Compassion

Now you need to find a compassionate way to view your own actions. You have acknowledged your actions in a regrettable manner, but take a look at your frame of mind before you made the mistakes. If you had known the future outcome of your actions, you probably wouldn't have followed through with what you now know was a mistake. If you didn't know any better in the past, there really isn't any reason to beat yourself up for it in the present. Try to find a compassionate way to view yourself. Pretend the past self who made the mistake is an innocent, unknowing little child. In your imagination try to find a compassionate way to speak to and comfort that child after the mistake was made. Now find a way to treat yourself in the same manner. Write down some loving words to yourself that are comforting, forgiving and understanding.

Step 12: Make Daily Efforts

Forgiveness is a daily process and event. The longer you withhold forgiveness, the more damage it will cause you and others. When you deal with problems and situations promptly, resentment and anger have little opportunity to grow. When another person puts a dent in your door, it's important to get your vehicle into the auto body shop as soon as possible. When you put a dent in your own door, it's important to learn the necessary lessons and find a compassionate way to forgive yourself. When you knowingly have injured another by putting a dent in their car, you need to make the necessary amends and promote understanding as soon as possible. Everyone involved will benefit from these noble actions.

Visions of Inspiration

For if you forgive others their trespasses, your heavenly Father will also forgive you; but if you do not forgive others, neither will your Father forgive your trespasses.

Matthew 6: 14-15

Put away from you all bitterness and wrath and anger and wrangling and slander, together with all malice, and be kind to one another, tenderhearted, forgiving one another, as God in Christ has forgiven you.

Ephesians 4: 31-32

 As God's chosen ones, holy and beloved, clothe yourselves with compassion, kindness, humility, meekness, and patience. Bear with one another and, if anyone has a complaint against another, forgive each other; just as the Lord has forgiven you, so you also must forgive. Above all, clothe yourselves with love, which binds everything together in perfect harmony.

Colossians 3: 12-14

To err is human, to forgive divine.

Alexander Pope

A wise man will make haste to forgive, because he knows the true value of time, and will not suffer it to pass away in unnecessary pain.

Samuel Johnson

GOALS

TOOL 29

*G*oals are a lot like cars: both have the potential to take you anywhere in the world. Goals and cars are tools that focus time and energy on a specific road in life. If you can look at a road map, pick out a location and drive there, you have already mastered the same techniques necessary to accomplish any objective you desire. Picking a location on a road map is the same as selecting a desired objective for your life.

Take a minute to think of a few things you want to accomplish or acquire in this lifetime. Would you like a new boat, a house, a new wardrobe, a business or a different career? Write down anything you would like to achieve in the future. What aspects of your life, economic situation, health, fitness, family, education, relationships or personal achievements would you like to improve?

Once you have selected your final destination – whether it's Miami on a road map or a boat for your family – you need to create a step-by-step plan to get there. To get to Miami, you need to drive down your street, turn on to another street and another, until eventually you arrive at your destination. Each mile in the right direction gets you one step closer to where you want to go. The same is true with your life goals – they're also completed one step at a time. If you don't create a step-by-step plan to follow in accomplishing your goals, you will have a hard time achieving them.

Accomplishing goals, just like driving a car, requires effort. God will help you in your attempts to achieve any worthy goals in your life. God is a part of your Inner Self, as is creativity, imagination and intuition. It is through your creative ability that God will help you come up with the steps necessary to reach your goal. Once you have a plan for where you want to go in life, you need only follow it. This requires a positive attitude, the ability to motivate yourself and some time-management skills.

Your car is a tool that focuses energy on one single objective: moving forward. A goal also works like a tool because it focuses your efforts, thoughts, time and energy on a single objective: moving forward. When you don't plan the use of your time and energy, they get consumed by other perhaps unimportant diversions like television, what seems urgent to other people, pleasurable activities or the minor inconveniences of life that constantly arise. Goals help you clearly define the most important use of your time, efforts and talents. When unimportant interruptions attempt to cut into your life and consume your valuable time and energy, you have your goals right there to help remind you of your previous commitment. When you set up for yourself a precise, step-by-step procedure, you can accomplish anything you set out to do.

The following steps are designed to help you evaluate, plan and follow through on your personal intentions. This process is described in written form so your goals won't get distorted, forgotten or sacrificed. When you write your goals on paper, they become a source of direction, inspiration and focus in your life and relationships.

Steps to Accomplishing Goals

Step 1: Evaluate Your Proposed Goals

Before you set your goals it's important to evaluate their consequences and options. Just as every action in life has a reaction and every problem in life has a solution, every goal in life has options and consequences to consider. Take the time necessary to think, contemplate, ask for advice, pray and consider all the possibilities that are feasible regarding your proposed goals. Make sure your goals are your own and are not derived, pressured or influenced by an outside motivation. Try to not compare your situation, plans or successes to another person's. Usually other people's situations have little to do with your own. Making comparisons will only leave you feeling unsuccessful or over-successful, neither of which will help you reach your full potential or proposed accomplishments.

Step 2: Make a Positives and Negatives List

After considering the consequences from Step 1, write a two-part list of positive and negative aspects for each of your proposed goals. Start by writing all the positive benefits and advantages you can gain by accomplishing a goal.

Then write the negative consequences, sacrifices or disadvantages you might exchange or experience if you don't pursue and accomplish this goal. For example, if your goal is to buy a house, your consideration might be rent payments vs. mortgage payments, homeowner responsibilities and commitments vs. short-term lease commitments and complete maintenance vs. limited maintenance. Include positive and negative consequences regarding your mental, physical, emotional and spiritual self, as well as the possible effects your goal will have on others.

The goals that provide you with the most motivation are those that promote the common good of other people in your life. Write down all the positive ways your goal will benefit other people in your life. Try to write down as many positive reasons as possible because if you have enough of them, you can motivate yourself to accomplish anything.

Step 3: Put Your Goal in Writing

Next, it will be necessary to commit yourself to accomplishing your goals. Begin by setting your goals in writing after your research has been done and you have made your decisions. Post your goals in a conspicuous and honorable place in your environment as a constant daily reminder. To gain support, encouragement and self-discipline from other people, tell them about your commitment. Be very specific about every detail of your proposed goals. A clear, specific description will help you visualize your goals and help you know when they have been accomplished.

Step 4: Develop the Right Attitude

It's important to maintain positive and optimistic attitudes and thoughts regarding your intentions. If you believe in yourself and your ability to accomplish your goals, you will accomplish them. If you think and believe thoughts of failure or discouragement, you probably won't succeed. It's important to stop worrying about the things you fear and can't accomplish and start working on the things you can accomplish.

Set aside a specific amount of time every day to practice imaginary techniques. Imagine yourself succeeding at what you want to accomplish and allow yourself to feel the emotions related to those thoughts. Developing your own personal affirmations to reinforce your positive mental attitude will also be helpful. Try using some affirmations like "I'm capable of accomplishing anything I set out to do," or "I will use any positive means necessary for the accomplishment of my intentions ..." Be prepared to confront any criticism from yourself or others at the first signs of hardship. See the Affirmation and Criticism chapters for more information.

Step 5: Make an Instruction List

Next, create a list of instructions or written plans you need to accomplish your goal. Make these plans detailed and include all the actions, procedures and steps needed to reach your desired accomplishments. Goals are not accomplished in one big step; they are accomplished by smaller steps, like climbing stairs. It's not realistic to jump from the bottom landing of a set of stairs to the top landing in one motion. By using small steps, you can climb anything one step at a time. When you create your instruction list for your goals, make sure each step is challenging but realistic. If you can't create a step-by-step process for your goal where every step builds on the next, your goal is probably unrealistic and out of your reach.

It's probably a good idea to avoid steps that depend heavily or solely on other people. Dependable outcomes are best achieved by yourself. If you have a hard time formulating the steps, let God help you in the process. He will speak to you through your intuition, imagination and creativity. See the Creativity and Inner Self chapters for more information.

Step 6: Set Timetables

Now make a timetable for every item on your instructions list from Step 5. Assign a calendar date as a deadline for completing each step from the instruction list. Schedule into your daily activities the necessary time to think, work and complete all of the steps from your instruction list. Using daily planners or personal organizers can help you schedule these steps.

Step 7: Establish Support Systems

It will be beneficial to list ten people who can help you accomplish your goals. This list might consist of people who can help you acquire knowledge, skills or information. Pick people who can inspire you, add to your experience, add to your contacts, offer practical helpful feedback, increase your influences through their referrals or serve as a good source of observation.

Other people to consider for this list might be your closest friend, harshest critic, mentors or your fieriest competitors. Add others to your list whose work is greatly respected in your profession or role models whom you admire and aspire to emulate. Make a list of requests describing how these people can help you accomplish your goals. Then in the future if their assistance and support is needed, proceed by asking these people for their help.

Step 8: Evaluate, Minimize and Accept Risks

Many times the fear of taking risks or the lack of planning for risks can severely set back your attempts. It's important to confront any fears you might have, such as fear of failure, fear of the unknown, fear of disappointment or fear of loss. See the Fear chapter to transform any fears that may arise. Next, it will be helpful to evaluate, minimize and accept the necessary risks involved in reaching your goal. Make plans to minimize risks, including setting limits that control a permissible loss; testing your theories to obtain feedback; trying certain aspects of the risky situation on test markets or in smaller situations; or even considering getting other people, partners or investors to share a mutual risk with you.

Step 9: Seek Additional Information

Accomplishing goals might take additional information or first fulfilling other needs with greater priorities. Most goals can be considered the same as needs because they both are desired objectives. Unfortunately when we are unable to fulfill our own primary human needs, we may be prevented from fulfilling other alternative needs and goals. Other times we might neglect some of our needs, hoping the proposed goal will fulfill what is missing in our lives. If you are looking for a boat to fulfill your spiritual needs, you might be disappointed when you reach your final destination.

Take some time each day to envision the type of person you will have to become to fulfill your goals. Look at what prevented you from accomplishing similar goals in the past. Ask yourself what's stopping you from achieving your goals right now. Once you know the answers, you can eliminate obstacles and move forward toward completion of your goals. Getting other information may be necessary to successfully reach your desired destination. Seminars, workshops, trade shows, libraries, the Internet and the Primary Human Needs chapter might be helpful in this process.

Step 10: Have Mental Discipline

Accomplishing goals requires mental discipline as obstacles and resistance arise. You will need to make a commitment and remain persistent in your intentions when the going gets tough. Strength, power, endurance and drive are powerful tools in accomplishing goals. Remain flexible and expect temporary setbacks, especially when others are involved in the accomplishment process. These setbacks are constructive tools that strengthen endurance and promote learning experiences. Learn from failed attempts and find new ways to turn obstacles into advantages. Incorporate the principles of flexibility and learning opportunities into every aspect of your goal process.

Step 11: Make Daily Efforts

Accomplishing goals requires hard work and daily efforts. It's important to designate some time every day for thinking. Contemplate where you are in relation to where you want to be. Think of better or different ways to overcome any obstacles that arise during the process. Pray to God for strength, courage and determination. Review your progress dates and instruction lists every day to keep your objectives fresh in your mind. Try to focus your attention on the positive aspects of your goals on a regular basis. It's important to write down your accomplishments as you achieve them so you can celebrate them with a sense of personal satisfaction. By rewarding yourself every step of the way, you will be better able to keep a positive attitude and sense of personal success.

Step 12: Practice Time Management

You may need to make more time in your life to pursue and accomplish your goals. If you need more time, the following tips may help.

❖ **Analyze how you spend your time each day.** Divide your days into 15-minute time slots and record what you did during that time period. When you have collected enough information, you can study the results and make necessary corrections to the way your time is currently being spent.

❖ **Make to-do lists.** Make a daily list of things to do, one day in advance or at least the night before, and a weekly list of things to do during the coming week. End your day by making a list of tomorrow's most important priorities. Record these events in your daily schedule, taking into consideration the activities that are most important.

❖ **Recognize and analyze your daily energy levels.** Take advantage of peak energy levels during the day by scheduling your most important projects and activities during the times when your body and mind function at their top levels. Schedule easier or less important tasks during your lower energy times of the day. When you take your peak energy levels into consideration, you can apply your best efforts to the greatest and most demanding priorities.

❖ **Focus your efforts.** Conserve time by focusing your attention on completing one project at a time. It takes time and energy to start and stop projects. Many times we handle correspondence, documents and memos several times, only to put them back in the same pile to be reread. Stopping short of a nearly completed project, only to begin work on it at a later date, also wastes valuable time.

Visions of Inspiration

For truly I tell you, if you have faith the size of a mustard seed, you will say to this mountain, 'Move from here to there,' and it will move; and nothing will be impossible for you.

Matthew 17: 20.5-21

Since the mind is a specific biocomputer, it needs specific instructions and directions. The reason most people never reach their goals is that they don't define them, learn about them, or ever seriously consider them as believable or achievable. Winners can tell you where they are going, what they plan to do along the way, and who will be sharing the adventure with them.

Denis Waitley

GOD

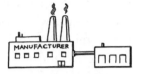

TOOL 30

We are all connected to God in exactly the same way a car manufacturer is connected to its product. A Ford car would not exist if Ford Motor Co. didn't build it. If we researched the design specifications, safety features and marketability of a Ford product, we would end up at the manufacturer's office. In the same way, if we researched our design specifications, difficulties or purpose in life, we would end up with our Heavenly Creator.

Let's take the example of a flashing temperature warning light in our car. On the surface the problem might appear to be the light itself. But almost all problems in life run deeper than the external conditions that bring them to our attention. If we researched the problem deeper, we might trace the warning light to the wiring behind the light, and from there to the temperature sensor. Looking further we might trace the problem to a low coolant level. If it's empty, we could fill it and consider the problem solved, or we could dig deeper to understand why the existing coolant leaked out in the first place. With much research we might find a small hole where antifreeze was dripping from the bottom of the radiator. We could get a new radiator, hoping the problem doesn't happen again; or we might dig deeper to discover the hole was caused by loose radiator brackets. If we installed a new radiator in loose brackets, wouldn't it wear away another hole causing another leak, causing our car to overheat, causing the indicator light to flash? After studying the bracket problem, what if we discovered a design problem? What if the car manufacturer designed a radiator that was too small for the brackets? Wouldn't the original problem lead us back to the car's designers?

The same is true of every aspect of our lives and relationships – except God doesn't make design errors. If we are experiencing a problem in life, it usually means we're not living according to our creator's design specifications. When we trace our problems in life as deeply as we can, the bottom line we end up with is our relationship with God. In fact, many of our problems and conflicts in life can be avoided if we maintain a close relationship with God because He is constantly there to help and guide us through them. When we are in touch with God through our Inner Self and prayer, God will help us overcome our problems and conflicts by guiding us through our intuition, conscience and self-awareness. If we fail to maintain a close relationship with God and our Inner Self, we will not be aware of His council and guidance when we vary from our factory-set specifications. It takes faith, dedication and time to develop this kind of relationship with God, but once it's established it's priceless.

Just because we have a close relationship with God doesn't mean all of our problems in life will magically disappear without any efforts on our part. If we complained to the manufacturer every time a warning light went off in our car, we probably would not get very favorable results. The same is true with God. If we complain to God and ask Him to solve all our problems without first doing our own personal work, we won't get very favorable results either. When we do personal work first, we can usually correct our own problems and realign ourselves in accordance with our factory-set specifications. By failing to do the necessary work and not researching our problems more deeply, we will probably experience a lifetime of radiator repairs.

But just because we can solve our own problems in life doesn't mean we don't need a relationship with God. Part of our subconscious programming requires us to choose a higher power for ourselves, just like a Ford car is designed to use Ford parts. We are all designed as spiritual beings with spiritual needs. We all have a drive to possess and be possessed by something greater than ourselves. Many of us spend several decades of our lives in futile attempts to search for answers before we realize nothing can ever fully satisfy us except a healthy relationship with God. Our failed attempts usually include items like money, knowledge, careers, power, fame, marriage and financial success. Without a relationship with God all of our earthly attempts to find fulfillment are in vain. Life is not worth living without God.

If you are constantly being confronted with problems, difficulties, disasters and crises, or constantly finding yourself feeling empty and unfulfilled, you may want to consider building a stronger relationship with God. A strong relationship with God will help you overcome anything life can throw your way because God will be there offering His protection, assistance and guidance. A close relationship empowers us with the ability to personally grow, love one another and find greater good in all of life's natural processes. When we neglect our relationship with God, we find ourselves consumed with frustration, lack of fulfillment and despair as we hit bottom with nowhere else to turn. When we put God first in our lives, we become empowered beyond belief. God desires a close relationship with all of us; all we have to do is maintain our fair share of it.

The following items will help you develop and maintain a closer, stronger relationship with your heavenly Father and Creator.

Steps to Increasing Your Relationship With God

Heal Your Past Relationship With God

Before you can begin to develop a stronger relationship with God, it might be necessary to do some inner healing work regarding any negative past experiences you may have suffered. Unfortunately, we all probably have experienced some negative situation during childhood that could be blamed on God. This could be a bad religious experience, unanswered prayers or the death of someone very close to us whom "God has taken." These types of negative past experiences will interfere with your present day relationship with God unless they are brought into the open and healed. Start by making a list of all the ways you felt violated or hurt regarding your religion, spirituality or relationship with God. Were you condemned as a sinner? Were you forced to attend church or synagogue services? Were you emotionally, physically, mentally, verbally, sexually or spiritually violated by a religious figure? Have certain members of a church treated you improperly in the past? Do you blame God for difficulties you have suffered in life? Which unanswered prayers do you blame God for neglecting? When were you angry, disappointed, frustrated, fearful or fighting for control with God? Try to make a list of ten different situations from your past and begin the healing process by following one of the exercises listed in the Healing chapter.

Maintain a Close Relationship With Your Inner Self

Your Inner Self is the spiritual part of your being that resides in and brings your physical body to life. By maintaining a closer relationship with your Inner Self, you will also have a stronger relationship with God. One of the functions of your Inner Self is intuition. This function is an inner knowing of things without any logical proof. When you maintain a strong connection with your Inner Self, God will talk to you through your intuition and bring greater wisdom, insight and knowledge to your life. By cutting off your awareness from that spiritual part of your being you will experience a lot more problems and difficulties. Without your intuition your only option to deal with situations in life is from a logical and physical perspective. The better connected you are to your Inner Self, the better interactions and relationship you will have with God. Refer to the Inner Self Chapter for more information.

Uphold a System of Ethics, Values and Morals

Another function of the Inner Self is your conscience. It lets you know with appropriate signals and feelings when your actions have helped or harmed other people. When you participate in destructive or harmful actions, your conscience lets you know with the appropriate emotional response of guilt. If you fail to listen to your conscience, you limit your ability to listen to God when He is talking to you. It's very important to maintain a connection to your Inner Self and carefully listen to your conscience because when you intentionally sin, you cut yourself off from God. You can't love God and maintain a close relationship with Him when you are intentionally harming His other children (our brothers and sisters) and ignoring His warnings. To increase your relationship with God, make a list of everyone you have ever harmed and go back when possible and make amends. Listening to your conscience, making amends, and confessing your sins to God and – if it's your practice – to a religious leader through confessional services will greatly strengthen your relationship with God.

Keep a Spiritual Journal

Another powerful method of increasing your relationship with God is through a spiritual journal. Its purpose is to record your daily reflections, intuitive insights, treasured experiences, special messages from God, significant events in your life, dreams and their interpretations, and your homemade prayers. Every day record the most significant events or thoughts that you had and your response to them. Be honest, and keep your journal private; its contents and dialogue will be between you and God. This is a great way to measure growth, protect your most precious spiritual memories and increase God's influence in your daily life.

Participate in Outside Activities

Your relationship with God can be increased through your service and interactions with others. Many times God speaks to us through other people. Participating in events like church or synagogue services, community projects, forgiving and loving your neighbors, self- or group-directed spiritual retreats, sacraments, charitable giving of yourself and your resources to others, small friendship group meetings, and bringing other people closer to God will all increase your personal relationship with your Heavenly Creator. Try participating in new and different events or activities regularly.

Use Imagination Techniques

Using the gifts of imagination and creativity that God has given us is important, since God's reality is so much larger than our preconceived notions and points of view. A good example of preconditioned points of view can be found in the words used to communicate with God. You might recite a prayer from memory and individual words like "Our Father" might not have much meaning. But by using your imagination, you can create profoundly greater depth and personalized meaning for every word. This will promote a greater understanding of God and create more meaningful, in-depth and unique conversation in your relationship.

Try taking a single word that you might use frequently in prayer and imagining every possible aspect of the word. For example, take the work "father." What does it mean to be God's child? What is God's fatherly pride in you like, or His fatherly guidance, love, care-taking or understanding? Or take the word "heaven." Turn your imagination loose and create a personalized picture for yourself. What is heaven like? How do you feel there? Try the word "Creator." Imagine the process necessary to create a small seed of grass that can lie dormant for years, but when planted will grow and produce in a continuous cycle. After creating your personalized images for each word, you will find they have significantly more meaning when you use them in prayer. These words and their personalized meanings can be endless, just like your relationship with God.

Prayer and Meditation

Prayer and meditation are your primary tools for communicating and maintaining a relationship with God. If you have a shallow prayer life, it's safe to say you have a shallow relationship with God. A good way to identify problems with your prayer life is to compare it to your everyday human interactions: If a friend never called, would you consider your friendship very close? If not, take a close look at the following scenarios and see how they apply to your primary method of interacting with God.

❖ Turning to God in prayer only during times of need – might seem like a friend who only uses you for favors, money or whatever else they want when tragedies and disasters strike.

❖ Asking God for assistance, guidance and direction without making yourself available to His responses – might seem like a friend who calls on the telephone and complains about their other problems without letting you enter into the conversation.

❖ Failing to express gratitude, praise and appreciation to God in prayer – might seem like an ungrateful friend who always wants more – someone who never finds anything good enough, or who never appreciates or never acknowledges your gifts, efforts or sacrifices in the relationship.

When you fail to maintain good communication, your friendships (human or divine) will suffer. To strengthen your communication ability, refer to the Prayer and Meditation chapters for more information.

Read God's Written Disclosure

One of the best ways to increase your relationship with God is to read about Him in His written disclosure statement and information package. God has to be very discreet regarding the ways that He discloses Himself to humankind. God gave everyone the gift of free will and if God made His presents indisputably known to humankind, He would be violating that gift of free will. So God decided to create a very discreet way to disclose information about Himself that will not violate anyone's free will. To work best, this method would have to be written down so it could be passed from one generation to the next. It would also need to be available in every language of the world and would include a list of God's laws. This book would contain information about our purpose in life, and information about our Creator and His relationship with all of humankind.

If you're wondering about the name of God's written disclosure statement, it's called the Holy Bible. The Holy Bible is the only written disclosure statement that fulfills all of these requirements. We know the Bible comes from God because of the general theme that runs through its entirety. God used about 40 unrelated authors over a period of 1,500 years to create the Bible. When we combine all the books of the Bible, they line up in perfect harmony with the same theme running through their entirety. Even more impressive, all the prophecies that are predicted in the Old Testament were fulfilled in the New Testament hundreds to thousands of years later. There are more than 60 major prophecies and 270 ramifications that were recorded in the past, and then re-recorded when they were fulfilled hundreds of years later.

We know the Bible is trustworthy because all the original manuscripts that have been discovered all state the same text. There are more than 5,000 original Greek manuscripts, 8,000 original Latin manuscripts and many others that state the same text after they have been translated. There are only 400 different words between all these original copies that are considered speculative, and none of them affect any concepts of the Bible's doctrine.

The best way to prove the Bible's authenticity and to increase your relationship with God is by reading the Bible daily. God will personally talk to you through this written disclosure statement. Try it for yourself by reading a few pages a day. If your copy contains an older-style text, try getting an updated version. It will be easier to read.

Get Baptized

Another powerful way – and quite possibly the only way – to begin an everlasting relationship with God is through baptism. It is a public sign and symbol of your agreement with God. A good analogy would be a written contract or business deal where both parties agree, sign their names before witnesses and make specific commitments. God has already presented humankind with His part of the deal. Getting baptized and accepting God into your life is where you sign and enter that deal yourself.

It is up to God alone to decide our eternal afterlife existence. It is up to each of us individually to establish our relationship with God. It makes sense that God would establish a common plan and agreement regarding our afterlife existence, as well as the conditions for us to enter into that relationship.

This plan would have to be available to everyone and we would be required to make our own decisions to enter our part of the agreement. Baptism represents our commitment to God by His written plan and agreement from the Bible. Let's look at what the Bible teaches us about baptism:

* No one can enter the kingdom of God without being born of water and the spirit. John 3: 5
* That every nation should be baptized. Matthew 28: 19
* That baptism represent salvation. Romans 6: 3-4
* That we should be immersed in water. Acts 8: 38
* After a conversion experience. Acts 8: 35
* Without any delay. Acts 16: 33
* That your sins may be forgiven and you will receive the gift of the Holy Spirit. Acts 2: 38

Many of us were baptized when we were small children. But, unfortunately, as infants we lacked the independent will to accept God into our lives. If you have not accepted God into your life, you have only fulfilled half of the agreement. If you have not been baptized or if you have not accepted God into your life as an adult, it might be a good idea to get baptized a second time or make some form of confirmation accepting God into your life. For more information refer to the New Covenant chapter and contact your local church.

Maintain a Healthy Perception of God

It's impossible to maintain a close, healthy and loving relationship with anyone when you are at the same time thinking unhealthy, negative or distorted thoughts about that person. The same is true with our relationship with God. If you logically or subconsciously believe God is punishing, controlling, unjust and untrustworthy, you will have a negative, fearful and shallow relationship with Him. If you believe God to be close, protective, caring and trustworthy, you will be better able to interact with Him in a loving manner.

The way we view God has a lot to do with the way we live and interact with the world. Many times our images of God are subconsciously formed in our early childhood. As dependent and vulnerable children we look up to our parents almost as though they were gods because to us they are our all-powerful caregivers, creators and only source of survival. People with unloving, distant parents tend to view God in a distant and unloving manner. If our parents were critical and judgmental, we might subconsciously view God as demanding, strict and stern. If our parents were abusive alcoholics, we might perceive God as being punishing, angry, untrustworthy and unpredictable. In the same way, children of caring, loving and protective parents grow up subconsciously perceiving God in a healthy, positive manner.

Logically, you can restore any unhealthy perceptions of God by reading about Him in His written scripture. Subconsciously, you can restore unhealthy perceptions of God by evaluating your early childhood relationship with your parents and working through the following exercise. If you discover any negative characteristics in your parents, you can evaluate your perception of God to make sure these same characteristics are not present. If you find yourself perceiving God in the same negative manner as you do your parents, you can transform these perceptions by using the information listed in the Perceptions chapter.

To begin this exercise, rate each of the following words on a scale of 1 to 5, with 1 being never and 5 being always. These words describe your childhood perceptions of your mother and father. For example if your mother was strict all the time, give her a rating of 5; if she was strict some of the time, give her a rating of 3; and if she was not strict at all, give her a rating of 1. Next, compare the results with your views on how God acts and interacts in your relationship with Him. If your parents were strict and punishing when you got into trouble, does God's personality represent the same characteristics? If your parents were strict and punishing when you were a child and you haven't healed those negative past experiences, do you find yourself to be strict and punishing also? Or do you find yourself at the other extreme, being irresponsible and rebellious? If so, you need to perform some past healing work to change your behavior. Start by forgiving your parents so you can change the negative perceptions of how God interacts with you in your relationship with Him.

CHARACTERISTICS	DURING MY CHILDHOOD MY MOTHER WAS	DURING MY CHILDHOOD MY FATHER WAS
Angry		
Appreciative		
Caring		
Close		
Compassionate		
Critical		
Demanding		
Disappointed		
Disruptive		
Distant		
Encouraging		
Forgiving		
Generous		
Gentle		
Gracious		
Holy		
Impatient		
Just		
Lenient		
Loving		
Passive		
Protective		
Providing		
Punishing		
Sensitive		
Stern		
Strict		
Strong		
Trustworthy		
Unpredictable		
Unreasonable		
Vindictive		
Wise		

Include God in Your Daily Life

The best way to increase your relationship with God is through your daily existence with him. You can include God in your work as you dedicate your service to society in an effort to greater glorify His kingdom. You can include God in your sleep by closing your day in prayer and asking Him to cleanse, empower and enlighten your Inner Self during the night. You can include God in all your daily activities, actions, words, behaviors, relationships and attitudes. The best way of incorporating God in your daily life is by surrendering your life to God. This act comes from your heart as your earthly existence is committed over to the will of your Heavenly Creator. Instead of being self-employed, you can become God-employed in every aspect of your life and relationships.

Visions of Inspiration

Then God spoke all these words: "You shall have no other gods before me. You shall not make for yourself an idol, whether in the form of anything that is in heaven above, or that is on the earth beneath, or that is in the water under the earth. You shall not bow down to them or worship them; for I the Lord your God am a jealous God, punishing children for the iniquity of parents, to the third and the fourth generation of those who reject me, but showing steadfast love to the thousandth generation of those who love me and keep my commandments."

Exodus 20: 1, 3-6

Jesus answered, "Very truly, I tell you, no one can enter the kingdom of God without being born of water and Spirit. What is born of the flesh is flesh, and what is born of the Spirit is spirit. Do not be astonished that I said to you, 'You must be born from above.' "

John 3: 5-7

Peter said to them, "Repent, and be baptized every one of you in the name of Jesus Christ so that your sins may be forgiven; and you will receive the gift of the Holy Spirit. For the promise is for you, for your children, and for all who are far away, everyone whom the Lord our God calls to him."

Acts 2: 38-39

Recounting of a life story, a mind thinking aloud...leads one inevitably to the consideration of problems which are no longer psychological but spiritual.

Dr. Paul Tournier

GOD'S EXISTENCE

TOOL 31

f I were to read to you an autobiography of your relationship partner before you ever met them, you would have logical facts and information concerning that person. This data might be forgotten over time if you didn't find it to be of any relevance. You would also have the choice to believe in the accuracy of the information or to doubt it somehow. Just because you memorized a bunch of logical information from an autobiography doesn't mean you have a relationship with that person. A relationship only becomes real through our interactions and experiences.

The same is true of our relationship with God. People who don't believe in God simply have never had a relationship with Him. People who do believe in God established a relationship with Him some time in their past. When we take the time to believe in the possibility of God and then seek a personal relationship with Him, we can't help but believe in His existence.

If you don't believe in God, you need to look deep inside yourself to confront any fears or beliefs that may be holding you back. Look at any harmful past religious experiences, parental conditioning or evolution teachings and ask yourself, If God were real, what's the worst possible thing that could happen to me? After you have confronted and healed any of these items, simply seek God with your whole heart and being. God will reveal Himself to anyone who honestly seeks a relationship with Him. Ask God to give you the gift of faith. Once the seed of faith has been planted in your being, it will develop and grow into a lifelong relationship if you are willing to maintain, respect and nurture your half of the partnership. The more you invest, the more you will receive.

The following exhibits are designed to prove God's existence. This proof is based on the principles that our lives and world could not possibly exist without an all-powerful, loving and intelligent Being and Creator – God. Once you believe in the possibility of God's existence, you can develop a deep and meaningful relationship with Him which will empower, enhance and add meaning to every aspect of your life.

Exhibits Proving God's Existence

Exhibit 1: Ontology Exhibit

Ontology is a branch of metaphysics dealing with the study of being and the essence of things. When we study cause and effect in relationship to the world around us, we can draw these conclusions:

❖ All actions create a reaction or result.

❖ All actions and reactions are brought about by something or someone else.

❖ Nothing in life just happens by itself. All reactions in life are caused by actions and all causes have their appropriate effects.

❖ Every cause, effect, action or reaction in life has a greater force, power or intelligence behind it.

For example, when we see a building, we know it is the result of the actions of builders, architects and engineers. The builders need a greater intelligence than the building they are creating. The same is true with the universe, world and all that happens and exists in it. Because life in this world holds power and intelligence, the creator would need to hold greater power and intelligence. Power and intelligence can't be created by something without power or intelligence. Nothing comes from nothing. Intelligent life, our world, our environment and our universe come from an all-powerful and intelligent creator known as God.

Exhibit 2: Cosmology Exhibit

Cosmology is a branch of metaphysics dealing with the study of the universe as a systematic order. As we study the existence of life in relationship to the world around us, we can draw these conclusions:

❖ All things in this world exist in a constant state of entropy.

❖ Everything in life that lives will eventually die: our bodies, cars, houses, sun, atmosphere and our very lives are in a constant state of decay, erosion and deterioration.

❖ Physical life forms limited to a constant state of entropy, death, erosion and deterioration can't possess the power to reproduce from themselves an everlasting cycle of life.

❖ Our world, universe and lives, which exist in a closed and limited system of power limited to a constant state of decay, erosion and deterioration, can't possess the power to have created themselves.

Because our world, environment and its life forms are in a constant state of entropy, death, erosion and deterioration, the world, and all the life in it, would have to be created and be maintained by something independent and outside of its limits. This independent and outside source would need to be everlasting, self-reliant, non-decaying, non-eroding and would need to possess a greater power than that which it supports and maintains. This eternal, unlimited, all-powerful source is God.

Exhibit 3: Chemistry Exhibit

Chemistry is the study of the chemical composition and characteristics of matter. When we study the properties of a chemical reaction, we can draw these conclusions:

❖ A chemical reaction is the result of two or more chemicals interacting in relation to their own limited properties.

❖ Chemicals have no control or choice over the way they act or react; they have no free will.

❖ Humanity and life is more than a mixture of chemicals and chemical reactions.

❖ Humans are capable of thoughts, feelings, free will, and the choice to act and react without being limited to the chemicals of which they are composed.

There is a force of life inside of us that is greater than and independent from the chemicals of which our earthly bodies are composed. This powerful force that we call life enables us to live and exercise our individual free will. This non-chemical source of life is present in every living being that has control over its own physical and chemical bodies. This life source that resides in

every one of us created humankind in the image and likeness of His own spirit. This non-chemical source of life that resides in all living things is God.

Exhibit 4: Philosophy Exhibit

Philosophy is the study of or search for basic principles and knowledge.
When we study ethics, values and morals in life and in relationship to the
world around us, we can draw these conclusions:

❖ Humans have an inherent moral code to distinguish between good and
  bad, right and wrong. We all have an inner knowing (our conscience) that
  is not part of our mind, body or independent free will.
❖ Mothers have an inherent desire to care for, love and protect their children. Humans have the inherent desire to make a difference in life, find
  meaning and purpose for their accomplishments and be a part of something greater than themselves.
❖ Humans prefers love to hate, truth to lies, peace to war, and happiness to
  sadness.
❖ This voice of conscience is evident in every race, from the most primitive
  tribal members who make sacrifices to their gods to the holiest of religious
  monks.

Our internal direction and guidance system (our conscience), which is
present in everyone, has to come from one universal source. This source
needs superior intellect, the ability to be all-knowing and possess the power to
enforce its desires and direction. This universal source of conscience has to be
equally connected to everyone, to determine the effects of our actions in
regard to the other people who might be affected. This universal, all-knowing,
all-powerful guiding source of all our lives is God. He is our supreme law giver,
higher power and always present loving Father.

Exhibit 5: Evolution Exhibit

Evolution is a science-based belief that humans evolved from a process of
random mutation in which the simplest forms of life developed into the most
complex forms by adapting to their environment over thousands of years. The
whole process started with the "Big Bang Theory," which theorizes that an
explosion occurred millions of years ago with enough force to create the uni-

verse and our solar system. When we study evolution, we can draw these conclusions:

❖ If heaven, earth, stars and universe were created from an explosion, everything would exist in a state of disorder. The planets and moons in our
   solar system would be jagged and not round. They would not orbit with
   the clock-like precision with which our entire solar system operates.

❖ There is no evidence, example or proof that any animal, especially apes,
   has ever evolved into a higher form of life such as a human. There have
   been horizontal changes in species that allow us to better adapt to our
   environment, but there has been no vertical upward movement where any
   species has become more complex in its design. There is no scientific evidence that one type of species has ever evolved into another type of
   species.

❖ Theoretically, if we evolved from the simplest forms of life like a single-
   celled organism, we would reproduce through binary fission by splitting
   off part of ourselves to create a new entity. In order for this type of organism to develop into the male and female species, in one lifetime two of
   these organisms would have to mutate perfectly – one with a male reproductive system and another with a female reproductive system – and mate
   successfully. If they didn't mate successfully, they could not reproduce at
   all. If these mutated organisms could not mate, they would not be able to
   pass along their genetic code. Knowing the complexity of the male and
   female reproductive systems, what do you think the chances are that two
   beings could mutate fully functional male and female reproductive systems? Scientifically it is not provable and theoretically it is not possible for
   an organism that reproduces through binary fission to mutate into male
   and female beings.

❖ If the whole process of life started from a big bang explosion in space and
   we evolved from plants, or a single-celled organism, how would we develop the complex system of eyes without the prior knowledge that vision
   actually existed, or the complex system of hearing without the prior
   knowledge that sound actually existed? That makes about as much sense
   as if your entire family, generation after generation, started growing
   antennae out of the top of their heads to take advantage of something in
   the future that we do not know existed today. If this process took thousands of years, all species would have to build on these unusable origins
   successfully, generation after generation, until they were complete.

If the process of evolution were believable, logical or scientifically provable, it could be said that God created the world, universe and our lives through evolution. But evolution is not an option because of the numerous inconsistencies and the improbability that are involved. When we eliminate evolution as an option, the only other alternative is God – our loving, all-powerful Heavenly Creator who created the heaven and earth in six days and rested on the seventh.

Exhibit 6: Logic Exhibit

Logic is defined as the science of pure reasoning, and in studying logic we can draw these conclusions:

❖ We all have free will to believe in God's existence or to refuse this belief by denying a relationship with Him.
❖ God, who gave us freedom of choice, will not violate it or interfere with our decision to use it any way we see fit.
❖ If God wanted to remain a secret, there would not be any proof or evidence of His existence.
❖ If God wanted to make Himself known to those who desire a relationship with Him, it would need to be in a manner that would not violate anyone else's freedom of choice.

The best way to prove to yourself the existence of God is by honestly pursuing a relationship with Him. God will not violate anyone's free will. He will not reveal Himself to anyone who doesn't honestly seek His presence. It logically stands to reason that God wants a personal relationship with everyone and the best way to offer this invitation without violating anyone's free will would be in written form. This written invitation would include stories about God's relationship with His people and would contain God's moral laws, standards and instructions to protect His beloved children. This written form or book would need to be printed in every language of the world and be available to everyone on request.

This written form exists and is known as the Holy Bible. In Genesis, the first chapter of the Bible, God explains His creation of the heavens and earth, and every living thing that resides in them.

Exhibit 7: Theology Exhibit

Theology is the science that studies God and all that relates to Him. When we study the positive effects of how God changes the lives of all those who seek Him, we can draw these conclusions:

❖ There are billions of individuals from every walk of life and economic class who all give witness to the same personal and powerful testimony of God's existence.

❖ There are billions of people who define their personal experience with God as being miraculous in nature, divine in experience and overwhelming in the nature of love, peace and power.

❖ From these experiences there originate stories of dramatically changed lives, answered prayers, healing from permanent disability, miraculous recoveries from diseases, overwhelming experiences of inner peace, the power to overcome addictions, fulfillment and security in life.

There are countless examples of personal testimony to God's existence. They start in the earliest known records of man's existence and continue to the present. The vast majority of humans would not believe in God if He did-not make Himself known to his beloved children in a very real manner.

All these exhibits have been written to establish the necessary logical proof of God's existence. Once you accept the fact that our world and your life could not exist without God, the next step is to begin the process of developing and maintaining your own personal relationship with Him. Begin by seeking God with your whole heart and being, and He will make Himself very real to you. Once God introduces Himself to you and you believe in His existence, you can increase your relationship with Him by using the information listed in the New Covenant and God chapters.

It can be a very frightening experience to seek God, but a life without God is much worse. Without a close relationship with God there is nothing in this world that can offer you complete fulfillment. You can be your own god, but a life of the self is still filled with loneliness and struggle. You can serve money as your god, but once you own all the finances in the world your life will still be empty and meaningless.

It's a good thing our God is the God of love, caring, compassion, forgiveness and understanding. He deeply desires a close and personal relationship with each one of us. Once you put some time and effort into your relationship God will begin working with you and your life. He might ask you to make some changes, but they will be for your overall best interests. In giving to God, you will be blessed beyond belief. In trusting God, you will be empowered and enlightened by Him beyond belief.

Visions of Inspiration

Ever since the creation of the world his eternal power and divine nature, invisible though they are, have been understood and seen through the things he has made. So they are without excuse; for though they knew God, they did not honor him as God or give thanks to him, but they became futile in their thinking, and their senseless minds were darkened. Claiming to be wise, they became fools; and they exchanged the glory of the immortal God for images resembling a mortal human being or birds or four footed animals or reptiles. Therefore God gave them up in the lusts of their hearts to impurity, to the degrading of their bodies among themselves, because they exchanged the truth about God for a lie and worshiped and served the creature rather than the Creator, who is blessed forever! Amen.

Romans 1: 20-25

GRIEVING & LOSS

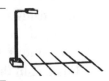

TOOL 32

*I*magine for a minute that you have driven an expensive car to the shopping mall. The lot is crowded so you choose to park in a spot on the outskirts of the property. You don't mind the walk because it's a nice day, and after several hours of shopping you head back to your car. As you get closer to where you thought you parked and don't see your car, you think to yourself, "Did I park here or is my car farther up?" After walking and searching for some time you realize your car has been stolen! Unfortunately, you have just experienced a loss, and now it's necessary to work your way through a grieving process if you want to emotionally, spiritually and psychologically recover.

Everyone experiences grieving differently because every loss, like the people it affects, is different. There are four main stages to the grieving process. By identifying these stages and understanding how they work, you will be better prepared to handle any losses experienced in life. The four stages are confrontation, confusion, change and contentment. Let's look at how each of these stages applies to the scenario of the stolen car:

* **Confrontation.** In the confrontation stage you will be confronted by the loss. This stage usually includes some form of shock and denial. For example, you might walk around the parking lot trying to convince yourself that you simply forgot where you parked the car. You might say things like, "This isn't real," "This can't be happening, " or "Maybe my car was towed by mistake." Your denial might go on for days as you call every impound lot in the city looking for your car. Eventually reality sets in and you accept the situation. The greater your loss, the more shock, denial and disbelief you will experience. Once you have accepted the facts, you will be able to move on to the second stage.
* **Confusion.** In the confusion stage you will experience emotional turmoil and confusion. At first you may be furious at whoever stole your car (anger

turned outward). In an extreme rage, people often direct their anger at the perpetrator, society, police, the mall owner or the store clerk who detained them in line. Next, you might experience depression (anger turned inward) as you blame yourself for parking where you did or for going to the mall in the first place. You may swing through a wide range of emotions, from rage to sadness, from guilt to anger, to depression.

❖ **Change.** In the change stage you need to start making changes and adjustments in your life. Physical changes might include a new form of transportation. Maybe at first you don't feel like going anywhere, but eventually your friends begin to drive you around. Later you will probably buy another vehicle. Emotional and spiritual changes might include forgiveness. For example, you may quickly realize that the angry emotions you experienced in the previous stage were not pleasant and that you would rather forgive the person than remain resentful for the rest of your life. This stage also includes reinvesting your time, energy and love. If you spent a lot of your time taking care of the car that was stolen, you will need to find another outlet for your time, energy and love – maybe taking care of someone else's car, or taking care of your new car.

❖ **Contentment.** The fourth stage in the grieving process is the contentment stage. You will know when you reach it because you will be able to look back on the situation in appreciation. Your pain will be gone and you will be able to recognize the gifts that were available from this growth process. You can look back on the loss of your car and realize it happened for a reason.

Everything in life happens for a greater reason and higher purpose. When you are in the middle of a loss, this might seem impossible to accept. But you probably realize now, looking back on times in the past when you have experienced losses and reached this stage, that you wouldn't trade those events for anything. That's because the lessons and growth experiences you gain from the four stages of your losses are priceless. The gift from your stolen car experience might be a large insurance check that enables you to buy a better car. Or the gifts might far exceed financial measures. You might not get an insurance check but receive lessons of humility, self-love and love for others who are also hurting. It is through our losses that we have the opportunity to become a stronger, more loving and compassionate individual.

The gifts that God bestows through losses are unlimited, but before you can receive them, it is necessary to work through the grieving process. When you fail to do the necessary healing work, it's possible to remain stuck, angry and bitter for the rest of your life. If you never dealt with the stolen car issue, you probably would experience fear every time you had to leave your new car unattended. You might be hateful toward tow truck drivers or teenage kids, who were indirectly blamed. You might never again buy or own an expensive car. The damage to your life when you fail to grieve your losses can be endless.

The grieving process is probably one of the greatest tools available for our lives and relationships. Life is full of losses and the only healthy way to deal with them is by working our way through the grieving process. If you have recently suffered a loss, you can begin by allowing yourself the necessary time and freedom to work through the following four stages of grieving.

Stages to the Grieving Process

Stage 1: Confrontation

The first stage everyone will need to work through is the confrontation stage. Here you will probably experience denial, disassociation, disbelief, shock or disorganization. It's important in this stage to reach out to other people who will just be there to listen. Genuine empathy is a very powerful healing source. If you are helping another in the grieving process, listen and try to feel what they are feeling and understand what they are saying. It can also help to seek out counselors, religious leaders, therapists, support groups, friends and family who will be there for you. During this time try to find a healthy, safe way to nurture yourself. Allow yourself the freedom to scream, cry, deplete your energy, take time off work, surround yourself with people, play with children, be around animals, walk in nature or participate in some type of loving, comforting and positive activity. Do what is best for you during the confrontation stage.

Stage 2: Confusion

During the confusion stage you will experience a lot of emotional instability. There might be anger, guilt, emptiness, hopelessness, despair, fear, depression or rage. It's very important in this stage to deal with your emotions in a healthy manner. Most of us don't like negative emotions and will do anything to avoid them. This is dangerous because when we avoid or deny emotions, they can become repressed and surface later in the form of transference. Repressed or denied negative past experiences can become a part of our subconscious programming and affect the way we interact with others.

One of the most efficient ways to work through and vent your negative feelings is by writing letters that describe your loss. Explain what actually happened. Describe in great detail how you feel. Describe all aspects of your losses, including physical losses and things that will be missed; mental losses like peace of mind, loss of dreams and goals; emotional losses like loss of confidence and happiness; and spiritual losses like loss of faith, hope, love and trust. Identify as many losses as possible and describe how and why you feel hurt, threatened, afraid, scared, angry, sad or guilty. Identifying all your losses on paper will help you move out of the confrontation stage and quicken your healing process.

In this stage it is important to face your pain. You will need to find the strength to face the situation, regardless of how unpleasant it may seem. It might be helpful to create a story regarding your loss, maybe with something symbolic using animals, to help express the tremendous emotions that you are experiencing. Tell your story over and over again to a good friend – someone who will be there to listen and comfort you in your time of suffering.

Stage 3: Changes

It is in the changes stage that you make the adjustments necessary to move on with your life. Here you accept the loss and begin the process of restoring your overall well-being. Forgiveness is an important part in this process. You need to forgive God, yourself and anyone else you blame for the loss. This is the hardest stage to work through. Many people find themselves trapped here because true forgiveness is difficult. See the Forgiveness chapter for assistance.

Writing a two-part forgiveness letter to God is very powerful. Many times major losses affect our relationship with God because we blame Him or believe He is punishing us for some reason. God does not punish and while He has the power to prevent losses, He probably did not do so because it was not in the best interest or for the greater good of everyone involved. Your loss might seem overwhelming to you at the time, but you can handle it because God is right there with you to encourage your personal growth and promote your ability to be a more loving, stronger person.

Start your two-part letter by addressing it to God and speaking your mind. Tell Him everything. Vent all your emotions, feelings, pain and suffering to

Him. Let your letter flow with whatever is on your mind and in your heart. God can handle it. Ask God any questions about your loss. Close the letter with words that confirm your willingness to trust, accept and remain faithful in your hope and love. Write the second part of this letter in the form of a response from God to anything you stated in your first letter. Start the second letter by addressing it to yourself. Pretend God is speaking to you and you are simply writing down His words. Have God reconfirm His unconditional and divine love for you. Next, write anything you would like to hear God tell you. Address all the items you mentioned in your first letter. Conclude the letter with God's blessing, encouragement and special words of faith, hope and love.

Now it can be helpful to write another letter that describes how your life will be different. Describe in detail how this loss will specifically change your life. How are you going to adjust to your new situation or environment? Include in this letter your new goals and plans for the future. To start the process of replacing this lost part of your life, you need to invest in something different. You will need to find a place, person or activity into which to pour your time, effort, love, concern and energy. The process of choosing those places, activities or persons will be different for everyone. Some possibilities might be self-love, remarriage, volunteer or charity work, a closer relationship with God, a new friend, family relationships, a job or career, college or other education, clubs, traveling, art, music or sports.

Stage 4: Contentment

The last stage in the grieving process is the contentment stage. To reach this stage, you will need to view your loss in a positive manner by looking back on it as a natural part of your learning and growth experience. Before this can happen, you need to find the positive aspects or gifts that are present in the situation. God is an important part of every aspect of your life, including your loss, grieving process and the way you view the world. God will help you understand and ultimately find true acceptance and appreciation for your experience. One gift that is present in all losses is the opportunity to be a more loving and compassionate person. If you are having a hard time finding the greater good in your loss, please refer to the Transformation and Transcendence chapters for more information.

Acceptance is also an important part of your healing process. It might be helpful to write down all the reasons why accepting your loss would be more beneficial than dwelling on it, like, "I can't truly live in the present if I spend my time consumed by the past," or "I choose to accept this loss because it is affecting my happiness and peace of mind." You can also give or receive an object or event that symbolizes the conclusion of your grieving process, like planting a tree or erecting a memorial or cross in nature, or anything else that seems appropriate at the time.

Visions of Inspiration

So Joseph went up to bury his father. With him went up all the servants of Pharaoh, the elders of his household, and all the elders of the land of Egypt. They held there a very great and sorrowful lamentation; and he observed a time of mourning for his father seven days.

Genesis 50: 7 & 10.5

Not only should we be unashamed of grief, confident that its expression will not permanently hurt us, but we should also possess the wisdom to talk about our loss and through that creative conversation with friends and companions begin to reconstruct the broken fragments of our lives...We should not resist the sympathy and stimulation of social interaction. We should learn not to grow impatient with the slow healing process of time... We should anticipate these stages in our emotional convalescence: unbearable pain, poignant grief, empty days, resistance to consolation, disinterestedness in life, gradually giving way under the healing sunlight of love, friendship, social challenge, to the new weaving of a pattern of action and the acceptance of the irresistible challenge of life.

Rabbi Joshua L. Liebman

GUILT

TOOL 33

When your car was new, it probably had a bright, shiny paint job. But weather and environmental conditions seldom let cars retain that finish for very long. Your car can be damaged by the heat of the sun baking away the shine and color, not to mention damage from salt water, pollution, hail, acid rain, snow and freezing temperatures. One of the best tools you can use to revitalize your car's finish is an electric buffer. It works by spinning a soft buffing pad against the painted surface to remove a very thin layer of faded paint, leaving behind a shiny new surface.

What does this analogy have to do with guilt? It's simple: Guilt works just like an electric buffer. Your life can either reflect the bright shine of a new car, or it can resemble a mess that has been left outside in the scorching heat to oxidize. Destructive weather conditions that can destroy the painted surface of your car are just like destructive actions that can destroy your life and relationships. Once you or your car are affected by destructive conditions, the shine will be lost. The buffing process generates a burning type of friction that eats away at your painted surface. This burning heat removes the old and brings out the new. Guilt works the same way because when you participate in harmful, destructive or sinful actions toward other people, you experience a burning type of internal friction known as guilt. The emotion of guilt can rob you of your happiness, honor, integrity and shine. The only way to restore your shine after it's faded is by getting out the buffer and making amends for your actions.

Guilt is a powerful tool given to us from God to be used as a calling for honorable actions. When you do something wrong and feel that electric buffer producing heat, it's important to make amends right away to bring back that great shine. If you delay or avoid making amends for your mistakes, that electric buffer will continue to burn away on your surface and destroy the paint job. So guilt is your personal notification from God to go back and make the necessary restitution, amends, apologies, settlements, compensation and retribution for your harmful words or actions.

Shame is another emotion that feels similar to guilt but burns ten times hotter. Shame is unhealthy and destructive to your life and relationships, because shame is like being guilty all the time for no apparent reason. Shame is like putting sandpaper on your buffer and eating right thorough the paint to the metal surface of your car. You can tell the difference between guilt and shame because guilt is produced when your actions have hurt another person directly or indirectly while shame comes from a lot of negative past childhood conditioning where you were constantly made to feel worthless and inadequate. See the Shame chapter for more information if you feel guilty all the time for no apparent reason.

God wants us all to display our cars in the Eternal Car Show with bright, shiny paint jobs. Take a look at the brightness and shine of your vehicle and that of your relationship partner. If the sander has cut into the metal, you are experiencing shame. If you see a lot of buffer marks and burns in the paint, you are not making your amends fast enough. If your car could use more shine, the following steps will help you transform guilty feelings into honorable actions.

Steps to Transforming Guilt

Step 1: Acknowledge Your Responsibility

When your Inner Self communicates a feeling of guilt, there are only two choices to make: You can grow spiritually by acknowledging your responsibilities, maintaining your relationships in an honorable manner and making the necessary amends for your inappropriate actions. Or you can cut yourself off from your spiritual source, deny and repress your guilty feelings, harm your relationships by blaming others and attempt to justify your inappropriate actions. Once you have recognized, accepted, acknowledged and incorporated the honorable choice in your life, you need to acknowledge your inappropriate actions as soon as possible, regardless of the behavior experienced from others. If you want to transform your guilty feelings into an honorable shine, you need to admit your mistakes and correct them as soon as possible.

Step 2: Identify the Parties Involved

You will usually find that at least three parties have been affected by your inappropriate actions: God, you and another person. But depending on the situation, many other people could have been affected in a negative manner.

Consider, for example, a couple of school boys who started fighting in the classroom. Regardless of circumstances both are at fault and both are guilty of inappropriate behavior. Each boy disrespected himself by his loss of control and his loss of education. Each boy disobeyed God by his intentional act of violence. And each boy violated the other boy by the fight and the events that led up to it. But, in addition, each boy affected the school's principal for the inconvenience and resulting disciplinary actions. Each boy inconvenienced his teacher and classmates for disrupting the learning experience. And each boy dishonored his parents by his violation of trust and reputation.

When you consider all the people you affected in a negative manner, it will be helpful to make a list of their names. Be sure to include God and yourself at the top of the list.

Step 3: Take Necessary Actions

Once you have identified the parties affected by your inappropriate actions, you can begin to make amends. There are an unlimited number of ways you can help restore the situation. Many times by looking to your Inner Self for answers, you will automatically know the best way. Here are some methods and ideas that might be helpful:

❖ **Apologies.** A good place to start is to apologize and acknowledge your errors. A good apology needs to be sincere and come from your heart: "I was wrong. I made a serious mistake. I failed to show you respect and I never should have done that. I'm deeply sorry." You can apologize in person, over the phone, by messenger, in a note or by sending a letter. Simply state any actions you regret and express your desire to restore the relationship to its best possible condition. Don't explain or defend your actions, because regardless of the circumstances, inappropriate behavior can't be justified.

❖ **Reimbursement.** If it calls for it, you can make amends through material or financial means. For example, a shoplifter can send the store an appropriate amount of money to compensate for the stolen item. A thief can return stolen possessions to their owners or anonymously to the police.

❖ **Compromise.** You can determine an appropriate and fair retribution by asking the injured party directly. After your apology it may be possible to work together and produce a mutually acceptable compromise. For example, if your child breaks a glass vase in a store, it might be possible to negotiate a settlement at the item's cost instead of paying full retail price. Other times, working together with the injured party might be the only way to make the appropriate amends.

❖ **Other methods.** Making amends is an important part of your healing and growth process. But sometimes making amends can cause more harm than good. Don't attempt to make amends when doing so would cause additional harm to others. If it's not possible to make amends without causing more harm than good to others, you can make amends indirectly by offering some form of retribution to an outside party by doing charity or volunteer work.

Step 4: Use Imagination Techniques

Making sincere apologies and necessary amends takes a great deal of personal strength. It takes a deep level of personal security and sound fundamental principles to genuinely make amends. Without personal strength you may find yourself feeling vulnerable, fearing that others will perceive you as weak or take advantage of you. If you find yourself lacking the ability to make amends, it helps to use imagination techniques to strengthen your ability. Start from a relaxed, meditative state of mind. Envision yourself in a safe place and then invite the person you have harmed into that space. Talk to them in your imagination. Tell them what has happened, that you're sorry and that you want to reconcile the damage. Ask for their forgiveness and listen to their positive response. Allow yourself to experience the feelings that are derived from this positive encounter.

Step 5: Learn Necessary Lessons

Before this process can have a positive effect on your life, it's necessary to learn from your mistakes. Try to discover the root cause of the problem and work at correcting that area of your life. When you fail to learn from your inappropriate actions, nothing will prevent you from experiencing the same situation again in the future. Guilt is a calling for personal growth, and a calling to restore your shine. It's also a tool that can be used to develop your personal strength and a great way to learn valuable lessons in life.

Visions of Inspiration

When any of you sin and commit a trespass against the Lord by deceiving a neighbor in a matter of a deposit or a pledge, or by robbery, or if you have defrauded a neighbor, or have found something lost and lied about it – if you swear falsely regarding any of the various things that one may do and sin thereby – when you have sinned and realize your guilt, and would restore what you took by robbery or by fraud or the deposit that was committed to you, or the lost thing that you found, or anything else about which you have sworn falsely, you shall repay the principal amount and shall add one-fifth to it. You shall pay it to its owner when you realize your guilt.

Leviticus 6: 2-5

"And why do you not judge for yourselves what is right? Thus, when you go with your accuser before a magistrate, on the way make an effort to settle the case, or you may be dragged before the judge, and the judge hand you over to the officer, and the officer throw you in prison. I tell you, you will never get out until you have paid the very last penny."

Luke 12: 57-59

Suspicion always haunts the guilty mind; The thief doth fear each bush an officer.

Shakespeare

HAPPINESS

TOOL 34

The next time you're out driving and come to a stop light, take a look around for someone driving an expensive luxury automobile and see if the driver looks happy.

Chances are they will have a very serious look on their face. Now look around for the oldest, most beat up, rusted sedan you can find – maybe one filled with teenagers and loud music – to see if that driver looks happy. Chances are you will find more happy people in old beaters than you will in expensive imports.

Let's imagine for a moment that your car has its own set of emotions. What do you think would make your car happy? Happiness can be found internally, so let's give your car a perfect interior with new upholstery and carpeting. And happiness can be found externally through entertainment and fun events, so let's give your car a great exterior with a perfect paint job and shine. Now do you think your car would be happy? What would happen if you locked your car away in a dark storage unit to protect its new interior and exterior from damage? If a car in excellent interior and exterior condition sat useless in dark isolation for years, do you think it would be happy? Of course not. Your car wants to be driven, appreciated and cruised until the tires fall off. Your car would only be happy serving others and fulfilling its purpose in life. But the more your car is driven, the more maintenance it requires, and after a while it will experience downtime in the mechanic's shop. Do you think your car would be happy experiencing downtime in the mechanic's shop? If you gave your car the choice between sitting in an isolated storage unit never needing maintenance, and receiving maintenance on a regular basis because it was used to cruise the highest mountains and the longest beaches, which do you think your car would choose? Do you think your car would learn to accept and appreciate the shop downtime as being necessary to enjoy the fun it had traveling?

Humans experience happiness in much the same way your car would if it had emotions. Just as the car needs a nice interior to be happy, you need to find happiness from within. The car also needs a great exterior, just as you need external activity and excitement in your life. But happiness consists of a lot more than these two components. Like the car, it's important for you to discover and fulfill your unique potential and learn to appreciate the downtime you experience in the auto shop of life. When you look at happiness in terms of the four basic components below, it's easier to understand how to find it in your life and relationships.

* **Internal aspects.** Self-acceptance, self-concept, self-confidence, self-love and personal peace are components of happiness that come from within. It's impossible to live a happy life when you don't know yourself or like yourself. Since happiness is an emotion that originates from within, it's essential that the rest of your internal emotions not be in conflict. When you lack personal peace and become consumed by your own greed, anger, jealousy, anxiety and fear, it's impossible to be happy.

* **External aspects.** Happiness comes partly from external situations, events and activities, and from the beauty in life. Happiness can be found in art, music, nature, play, food, pleasurable activities and thrilling sensations, as well as in the simple things like your environment, friends, family and relationships. But these activities in and of themselves can't sustain a true state of happiness.

* **Participation.** Happiness is more than the sum of the first two parts. It also comes from the anticipation of things to come and in the pursuit of or participation in things that bring personal fulfillment. Sometimes you experience more happiness by planning, preparing and anticipating an upcoming vacation or party than you do in actually participating in the event. Happiness comes from dreaming about that new car and working toward your plans, goals and things you desire. You can find happiness in the service of others, being the best you can be and in fulfilling your purpose and intention in life.

* **Maintenance.** Another important aspect to happiness can be found in a healthy respect for life's natural processes. When you respect and appreciate life's trials, tests, lessons and downtimes, you gain the ability to be happy in any situation. Many times the tragedies, injustices, crises, disasters or traumas that you experience in life bring the greatest lessons and growth opportunities. Life is a process of personal and spiritual growth toward God. When you fail to grow, you aren't living true to yourself. It's

the hard times that truly teach us to respect and appreciate the good times. Without struggles in life there would be nothing to compare the valuable gift of happiness against.

If your car needs some interior or exterior restoration work, you may be interested in the following items. They are designed to help you and your partner cruise the highest mountains and the longest beaches.

Creating Personal Happiness

Make Happiness a Priority in Your Life

We all make choices every day concerning our personal happiness. Happiness can be created by making a conscious effort to choose your responses based on the stimuli in your environment. For example, if you insulted a person (the stimulus), they would probably be offended (the response). If you complimented a person, they would probably choose to be pleased. If you fail to recognize these choices, you allow your personal happiness to be contingent on situations outside your control. If someone calls you insulting names, you can make a conscious decision to not take it personally. Recognize and try to increase the small gap between stimulus and response so you can make choices that will increase your happiness.

Develop a Stronger Relationship With Your Inner Self

It's impossible to be happy without being true to your Inner Self. Your Inner Self is the essence of your being that is connected to God. When everything is being properly maintained in your life, it's the nature of your Inner Self to function in a state of complete happiness and union with God. When you're in touch with your Inner Self, God will communicate with you and help you along the path that's in your best interests. Being true to yourself along this path allows you to experience the greatest amount of happiness possible.

When we fail to maintain a connection with our Inner Self, it's possible to get trapped living a life of self-willed ways based on ego. Many times when we don't like what our Inner Self is trying to say, we try to silence it with distractions, addictions or denial – all of which will lead to unhappiness, more problems and greater conflicts. The best way to get in touch with your Inner Self is by practicing quiet time, prayer and meditation every day. See the Inner Self, Prayer and Meditation chapters for more information.

Practice Self Love and Self-Acceptance

Once you are in touch with your Inner Self, you can begin the process of self-acceptance and self-love. It's impossible to be happy when you don't like who you truly are. Maintaining positive self-worth and self-concept is an essential requirement for happiness. See the Self-Concept and Self-Acceptance chapters for more information.

Take Personal Responsibility

Taking personal responsibility for your life is an essential requirement for personal happiness. When you blame other people and situations you make yourself the victim. It's hard to be happy living the life of a victim. Happiness can be found in actively setting goals, following through with plans and making changes in situations you don't like. You need to stop blaming other people, situations and events outside of your control. Happy people assume full responsibility for their own life, outcomes and well-being. See the Blame and Goals chapters for more information.

Fulfill Your Primary Human Needs

It's is hard to be happy when your primary human needs aren't being met. You can find happiness when you are functioning in a state of physical, mental, social, emotional and spiritual well-being. When you neglect one area, other areas will suffer. For example, if you neglect a physical need for food, you become mentally irritable, which affects your social relationships. Emotionally you start feeling grouchy and lose any happy feelings. Eventually the spiritual connections between God and your Inner Self suffer because your attention is focused solely on your physical need for food. You can find happiness by creating a balance among all five categories of primary human needs. If you depend on others to fill your own needs, you will many times find yourself let down. See the Primary Human Needs chapter for more information.

Heal the Past

We learn a lot about happiness from our past conditioning. If we had a happy childhood, we will have developed the skills necessary to be a happy adult. Children who grew up in a loving home where there was mutual support, encouragement and respect usually adjust to a life of happiness much easier than those who didn't. If you had an unhappy childhood, you likely learned a lot of unhealthy messages concerning your self-worth, problem-solving skills, trust, respect, relationships and life in general. If you have spent a good portion of your adult life learning unhealthy messages and lessons, you can increase your happiness by going back into your past and doing some healing work. Simply go back and revisit those negative experiences, venting negative emotions and replacing them with the love and support you never received as a child. See the Past Experiences/Transference and Healing chapters for more information.

Discover Your Unique Potential

God created each of us with unique talents, gifts and potentials. When you discover and use those qualities in the service of society, you can't keep yourself from experiencing true success and happiness. Many times people find themselves trapped in careers they hate, spending long hours at a job and receiving little personal satisfaction. Work is important to happiness because it serves as a creative outlet for your unique talents and gifts. When you get in touch with your God-given gifts and use them to serve others, you will be participating in work you love. Instead of asking what's in it for yourself, ask how you can help others. See the Direction/Potential chapter for more information.

Do the Right Things

It's impossible to experience lasting happiness when you fail to do the right things. If you don't maintain a clearly defined set of ethics, values and morals, you may find yourself taking the easy way out, compromising your integrity and participating in unhealthy behavior "because everyone else is doing it." Many times this will lead to problems, conflicts, troubles, destruction and unhappiness. Happiness is our reward from life when we think, act and live in the manner we know to be right. See the Ethics/Values/Morals chapter for more information.

Give to Others

Selfishness is a major stumbling block to happiness. Living a life solely for yourself will bring you nothing but sadness and misery. If you want more love in your life, develop your ability to be more loving and giving to others. If you want more respect and admiration, treat others as you would like to be treated. If you want more friends, be a better friend. Those who bring happiness to the lives of others can't keep it from themselves. True happiness comes from service to others, from making a positive difference in life and from putting other people before yourself.

Live a Life of Love

We are all designed to live a life of love. It is through loving yourself, others and God that a lifetime of happiness is created. When you fail to love, you aren't being true to yourself and you will be unhappy. True, genuine, unconditional love is what makes you feel good about yourself. Love is the secret to happiness and life is the process of developing your ability to love. See the Love chapter for more information.

Place God First in Your Life

Ultimate happiness can be found when we place God first in our lives. We are all responsible for and in charge of our own lives. We all have a psychological need to live for something greater than ourselves. We have all chosen for ourselves some type of higher power or governing force that we consciously choose to live for. If you have chosen over God other people, government, or the pursuit of money, power, knowledge, success, sports, fame or fortune, you can expect a lifetime of unfulfillment and unhappiness. When you place God first in your life, God will give you back a full life. See the God, God's Existence and Prayer chapters for more information.

Visions of Inspiration

You have no more right to consume happiness without producing it than to consume wealth without producing it.

Bernard Shaw

Blessed are the poor in spirit, for theirs is the kingdom of heaven. Blessed are those who mourn, for they will be comforted. Blessed are the meek, for they will inherit the earth. Blessed are those who hunger and thirst for righteousness, for they will be filled. Blessed are the merciful, for they will receive mercy. Blessed are the pure in heart, for they will see God. Blessed are the peacemakers, for they will be called children of God. Blessed are those who are persecuted for righteousness' sake, for theirs is the kingdom of heaven. Blessed are you when people revile you and persecute you and utter all kinds of evil against you falsely on my account. Rejoice and be glad, for your reward is great in heaven, for in the same way they persecuted the prophets who were before you.

Matthew 5: 3-11

Remember that happiness is a way of travel – not a destination.

Roy M. Goodman

HEALING

TOOL 35

*N*ewer model cars have an onboard computer system under the dashboard called the brain box that controls most of the car's electrical and operating functions. The brain box, like all computer systems, is composed of hardware and a set of operating instructions called software. If something happens to your vehicle's software, do you think the car will run properly? If your home computer's software develops a defect, do you think it will properly run programs and applications?

Like a computer, your body and mind make up the hardware and you are in charge of programming most of your own software. As a human you come with a basic operating system factory-set by God. It is part of your Inner Self and is unchangeable. The rest of your software can be changed, deleted or improved at any time.

The manner in which we program our own software can be broken down into two parts: past and present. The experiences, lessons, mistakes, hardships, conditioning and role modeling from our past will influence our thoughts and behaviors in the present. The thoughts, attitudes, perceptions and plans we create in the present will influence our future behavior. If you are unable to change your present and future behaviors by thinking different thoughts, it will probably be necessary to go back into your past and heal any negative experiences that have affected your natural subconscious programming.

The best way to reprogram negative software from your past is by doing healing work. Emotional healing work is one of the main principles of this book and many of the chapters refer to these procedures. It's probably one of the most powerful tools this book has to offer, and also one of the most rewarding experiences you will ever encounter. So let's take a look at how we were originally programmed and how our programming can become distorted. Then at the end of this chapter are two exercises that will help you and your partner reprogram negative past experiences.

When you buy a new computer, it usually comes with a basic operating system installed by the manufacturer. In the same way, God gives us natural software that is almost identical in every child. God only installs the best software because the programming that is evident in young children allows them to use about 90 percent of their creative ability. As small children we learn new things at an amazing rate of speed. We hold on to what is safe and at the same time experiment with new things. Young children work through their negative emotions very efficiently. One minute they're happy, but if the next minute something upsets them, they work through their anger and quickly they're happy once again. Talk about courage! Are you brave enough to tell a 20-foot-tall giant weighing nearly a ton, "NO! I won't do what you say!" as he picks you up off the ground and lifts you nearly two stories in the air? Compared to the size of an adult, two-year-olds do it all the time. With their natural programming children are very loving, naturally happy, and fearless, and they don't have a problem assertively asking for their needs.

But as children we start to develop mentally and soon gain the ability to change our own programming. It's the thoughts and negative situations that we experience as children that influence and change our God-given natural programming. For example, if as children we watched our fathers abuse our mothers, we might believe this was normal and accceptable behavior for men and women. We wouldn't know any better because there wouldn't be anything to compare it to. If our father abused us in the same manner, we would either take it personally, believing we were unlovable and deserving of this behavior, or we would believe that is how everyone else acts and grow up abusing other people in the same manner as we were abused. Children whose natural programming has been distorted by abusive thoughts and conditioning have two responses when it comes to their present and future behaviors: they will either seek abusive relationships thinking they deserve them, or they will abuse others in the same manner as they themselves were abused.

Any negative experience you or your relationship partner have suffered in the past carries with it the ability to affect your subconscious programming and software. Children are not born abusive; it is a learned response that comes from an abused person's past. If abusive people can't change their future behavior by thinking different thoughts in the present, then they need to go into the past and heal the negative experiences that imprinted that type of conditioning on their subconscious programming.

These harmful experiences from our past can be one of the most powerful methods available for us to develop our ability to grow and love. Everything that happens to us has a greater meaning and purpose. People who have suffered a horrible childhood are actually very blessed because if they do their healing work and learn to embrace their own hurt and pain, they will become deeper, more loving individuals. That's because people who have the power to embrace their own pain can embrace the pain of others.

Even if you claim a great childhood, there are still many situations in life that have the power to affect your subconscious programming. If you are afraid of bees, somewhere in your past your subconscious programming was changed – probably when you were stung. This bee experience can be positive if it keeps you away from dangerous beehives. But if this conditioned method of responding to bees is causing problems in your relationships, then even people with "great childhoods" have the opportunity to benefit from some past healing work.

If you or your partner are experiencing or have experienced any of the following, it will be beneficial to do some past healing work:

❖ A situation, event, or circumstance from your past that causes you to experience negative feelings, thoughts or emotions when you look back on it.
❖ Recurring unpleasant memories from your past. Usually our first response is to stuff these memories back down, but they are coming up for a good reason – to be reprogrammed.
❖ Anything your parents, family, guardians or role models did to you or to each other that was harmful, unhealthy, inappropriate, unsafe, unethical, immoral or improper.
❖ Any time you were violated or you violated another. This could be almost anything, like abuse in all its forms, harm, neglect, criticism, shaming, threats, assault, abandonment, rape, incest, or anything that was physically, mentally, emotionally or spiritually violating in any manner.

There are three effective ways to reprogram negative past experiences that have affected your subconscious programming. You can heal them verbally with the help of a professional therapist; you can work them out in a written letter form; or you can reprogram them through imagination techniques. The written and imagination exercises are included in this chapter. Both of these methods are easy to use, efficient, extremely powerful and – unlike a professional therapist – neither will cost you a penny.

It might be best to start out with the written system until you have enough experience loving and reprogramming those hurt parts of yourself, and before you attempt the imagination technique. The written exercise is more grounded and focused, while the imagination technique is more free flowing and it's easier to be distracted. Try both and use the one that works best for your own situation. The letter system works well for more recent experiences and the imagination technique works well for earlier childhood experiences. Sometimes for extremely serious past tragedies and injuries it might be necessary to use both methods. Use the written one first, and then go back and enforce it using your imagination.

THE WRITTEN HEALING EXERCISE

Introduction

This exercise is designed to heal or reprogram your past experiences by writing a two-part letter system. In the first part of the letter you vent your emotions and express all the negativity that surrounded the original incident. The second part of the letter reprograms the destructive messages by replacing the negative software with positive messages and loving ways of viewing yourself and the situation.

It's necessary to actually feel and experience all of the original emotions that were involved with the negative past experience. If you try to avoid the emotions or fail to go deep enough, the healing procedure will not work. When this situation was originally programmed into your software, the experiences hurt you emotionally and some events were logically recorded in your mind. If you go back and logically attempt to reprogram the experience, it will affect only half of the program. The software was created both logically and emotionally and it's necessary to reprogram the same file using both logic and emotion.

It helps to start your healing work from a relaxed, meditative state of mind. Do some breathing exercises beforehand, or perform your favorite meditation or relaxation techniques. Make sure you have a private environment where you won't be interrupted. Include lots of tissues because a good emotional healing experience will touch you in the form of tears. Pray to God first for His assistance. God is our ultimate healing source. Ask Him for help in your attempts to reprogram and heal the negative past experiences.

Instructions

Part One A. Begin by addressing your letter to the person or persons who hurt you in the past. Who was to blame? Who caused the injustices?

Part One B. Start your letter by explaining the events surrounding the situation. What happened? How were you violated, abused or wronged? Try to vividly imagine the situation, recall every detail and write them down.

Part One C. Now re-create and vent your anger. At the time of the event you had every right to be angry. If you don't feel anger now, try to bring it back and re-create your feelings. Imagine that it just happened again or that you are standing by helplessly watching the same situation happen to another innocent person. How would you feel then? Force yourself to get angry on paper. Keep the logical side of your brain out of the situation and find that hurt, angry, violated, abused inner part of yourself, that childlike self who is not afraid to get really mad and upset. Get in touch with that two-year-old who will throw a temper tantrum anywhere. Don't worry about sentence structure – just scratch it all out. Call names if necessary and let the person who hurt you know what you think.

Part One D. After venting all your anger, change emotional gears to feelings of fear. Get in touch with that vulnerable, scared or threatened part of yourself. At the time you were probably terrified because something or someone was threatening your well-being. Try to imagine the worst possible scenario. How much more damage and suffering could have been caused to you? Everything could always be worse than what it was. Describe how you felt scared, fearful or threatened. What were you worried about? What might have happened? Vent these emotions and experience all those feelings and thoughts on paper until they are all gone.

Part One E. In the next part of the letter get in touch with your guilty feelings. What do you blame yourself for? Are you experiencing feelings of inadequacy or shame? Are you sorry for being there? Have you made any mistakes? Do you feel weak and vulnerable? Pretend that the hurt little childlike part of you is writing the letter. Allow yourself to feel the feelings and describe them on paper. Vent until they are all released.

Part One F. Next, get in touch with your sadness. Allow yourself to feel sorrow. Ask yourself what you wanted to happen that didn't. Usually all we want is to be loved and accepted, but that is probably not what you received. Describe your feelings when you did not get what you wanted. Experience those feelings and vent them on paper until they're released.

Part One G. Before you conclude the first half of your letter, make sure all your negativity is vented. Write down anything else that seems appropriate. It is important to get everything unpleasant out now. Check your emotions of anger, frustration, sadness, disappointment, fear, concerns, guilt and inadequacy, and make sure there is nothing more you need to say.

Part One H. Conclude your letter with some closing words or loving statements. Just because this person's actions were lacking love doesn't mean you have to bring yourself down to their level. You can choose to be loving regardless of the circumstances. Try to write down some loving, caring and supportive things about the person who hurt you.

After you have thoroughly revisited the negative past experience and vented the emotions surrounding it, it's time to start the second part of the letter. The first half of this letter was addressed to the person who caused you harm. The second half is an imaginary response letter addressed back to you from that person.

Part Two A. Begin by addressing the second half of your letter to yourself. Pretend the person you wrote to in the first half of the letter is responding to you with a reply. Try to vividly imagine this person speaking to you as you write down their words.

Part Two B. Next, write down everything you would like to hear this person say. It doesn't matter whether you think they would actually say these words or not. This is your imaginary response letter and you need to write down the words you deserve to hear. You can imagine this person is in a completely healed state of being and is capable of being very loving. In reality the person who hurt you was very unloving – in fact, they were probably very violating. They didn't say or give you the love and respect you deserved at the time, or you wouldn't be writing about this past incident. But just because they didn't speak healing words of love and forgiveness doesn't mean you don't deserve to hear them. If that person was incapable of loving and respecting you in the manner you deserve, you can give yourself that love and respect now. You need only pretend this person is coming from a completely healed state of sorrow, love and regret. Begin by having this person from your past start their letter with an apology. Have them apologize for their actions with the kindest, most sincere words possible. Have them state that they never knew how badly their actions hurt you.

Part Two C. Next, have this person acknowledge and validate every one of your feelings. Have them state that you have the right to feel the way you do, and that you are justified in your feelings and thoughts.

Part Two D. You may want to hear this person ask for your forgiveness. After they do, it will be helpful to understand how they viewed the situation. Write an explanation that would explain the ways they perceived things. Write their excuses, how they misunderstood, how they were treated in the same manner by their parents. Maybe they were trying to help or teach you a lesson. Maybe they did the best they could or maybe they were just plain careless or mentally impaired. Try to walk a mile in their shoes and come to a deeper understanding of their perspective.

Part Two E. In the next part of the letter, have this person express more sorrow and their loving feelings for you. Have them state how much they care, how much they respect you and how much they appreciate you. Allow yourself to feel the love and respect they hold for you. List all reasons for the love and respect you deserved and never received.

Part Two F. To conclude your letter, you need to find a positive and loving way to look back on the whole situation. Ask yourself, "What has this past experience taught me? How am I a better, stronger person because of it? How can I carry its lessons into my everyday life? How has it allowed me to be more compassionate to other people who experienced similar situations?" Find a positive way to look back on this event from your past.

It's important to feel the positive and loving feelings the second letter was designed to generate. It will be very powerful to read it out-loud to yourself after it's written, or even a few days or weeks later. If you have successfully worked your way through the written healing process, you can look on the negative past experience a few days later in a positive or neutral manner. If it still feels negative, you will need to go deeper into your feelings.

Don't send these letters unless the receiving party knows what they're for and is strong enough to help you embrace your pain. The person who hurt you in the past doesn't have anything to do with your present day healing and forgiveness process.

Before you read any further, get out some paper and heal those negative past experiences right now. If you don't, they will affect your subconscious programming for the rest of your life. Not only will they keep popping up in your mind, they'll continue to cause serious problems in your everyday relationships in the form of emotional baggage.

THE IMAGINATION TECHNIQUE EXERCISE

Introduction

The other procedure to heal or reprogram your negative past experiences works through imagination. It is similar to the written exercise but is more flexible because everything is re-created in your imagination. Many times it is faster and easier than the written procedure, but it requires a lot more mental focus and experience with forgiveness. In this exercise it's necessary to control your thoughts and mental pictures for an extended period of time, almost like meditating. Once you get into a scene from your past, you will need to remain there until it is reprogrammed. If you lack the mental discipline to keep yourself focused, this exercise will not be very effective. If you need them, there are some exercises in the Meditation chapter that will help you develop your ability to focus your attention.

This exercise works the same as the two-part letter system. First, you need to experience and vent your negative emotions. Work through your anger, frustration, fear, concern, guilt, inadequacy, sadness and disappointment. Then replace the negative with the positive by giving yourself the love and support you deserved but never received. Just as in the letter exercise, it's necessary to feel and experience all your original emotions. If you avoid your emotions, this exercise won't work. The original experience was recorded on your software using both emotional and logical data, and it will need to be reprogrammed using both.

Once you have opened up a past experience in your imagination to be healed, it's important to stay with the experience until you can end the session on a positive note. Try not to leave a situation unresolved or in a negative state. After successfully healing one situation, allow yourself to stay with the positive and loving feelings for as long as possible before exiting the situation in your mind.

It may also be helpful and rewarding to work through this procedure with a close friend or relationship partner. By narrating the mental picture that's going on in your imagination, your partner can help guide you through your negative experiences by asking questions, keeping you from getting stuck and reinforcing the positive with encouraging and supportive words. If practiced with respect and love, it can forge a strong connection and bond of intimacy between couples. You might want to try this exercise individually at first and then, once you feel comfortable with it, try it together. If you experienced traumatic incidents in the past, like incest, rape or extensive physical abuse, and find yourself getting stuck and unable to resolve these issues with your partner's help, you might want to seek assistance from a professional therapist. Some situations might take several sessions before they can be fully resolved. With every encounter the situation will become easier to confront.

Finally, before you begin, it's necessary to start from a relaxed, meditative state of mind. Practice some relaxing meditation and breathing techniques and make sure you're in a comfortable, safe environment with no interruptions. If you begin crying, don't bother with tissues – just let the tears roll off your face. Any form of physical distraction will detract you from your work. Pray to God for strength, courage and assistance. If you are working with your partner, pray for them as they heal their past. God is the ultimate healing source and He will help free you from your emotional baggage.

Sample Exercises

There are many ways to revisit your past in your imagination. Most of your healing experiences will need to include two main characters who are always present, as well as many other minor characters who come and go. The two main characters are your adult self as you are today and your past or child self as you were when you experienced the event. For example, an early childhood scene could include you, the adult who looks like you today and your past self, who looked as you were when you were five years old. Other characters might be family members, parents, other people who hurt you or even God.

A good way to understand how this works is to imagine that God has given you a time machine. You can go back anywhere in your past and no one can see your adult self except for your child self. You can move in and out of situations and give your past self all the love, support, encouragement, hugs, advise, courage and compassion they never received but always deserved.

For example, if your father was an alcoholic who physically and emotionally abused you, it's possible to go back to any painful experience and revisit the situation in your imagination. Simply go back in the time machine to a situation when you were five years old and your father was hitting the young child. Imagine that scared, frightened and paralyzed five-year-old in your imagination. Next, picture your father sending the little child to their room and your adult self has just witnessed the whole scene. You know how the little person is feeling because you are experiencing the same sick feelings. Have your adult self go to the child's room and sit down beside them. In your imagination have your adult self help the child self verbally express their anger, fears, wants, needs, feelings, insecurities, vulnerability, sadness and desires. The adult self can ask questions and offer loving support. Tell the child it's not their fault, they're okay and that you love them very much. Find a way to give your child self all the love, comfort, support and respect that they deserve. Have your adult self hold your child self until they feel better.

It's necessary to find a positive way to look back on the situation before you leave the scene. Find the gifts or lessons that can be gained from it. Ask yourself how the lessons from this past experience benefit your present life? How has the past made you a stronger person? Are you more loving or compassionate toward other people who have suffered through similar situations? Keep working with the scene in your imagination until you can actually feel the positive feelings it is generating. Once your child self is feeling loved and respected, tell them it's time for you to go. Then get back into your time machine and return to the present.

Every time you revisit that scene, your adult self and your past self will feel better about your life. If you don't have the courage or strength to comfort the hurt child, you can bring along in your imagination a friend who can. Or you can take the child's hand, leave the situation and walk down the street to God's house, where God is always glad to see you. Because the scene is taking place in your imagination, you can do anything you want as long as you continue to experience the feelings and reprogram them in a positive manner.

Other variations on this scene might include having the father come into the little child's room to apologize, having the child forgive the father, and having the child and the father talk about the father's abusive, alcoholic behavior. Or maybe your child self felt guilty for doing something wrong. If so, you can go back and make amends for that behavior. The number of ways you can reprogram your negative past experiences is unlimited as long as you learn to love the victim (your past self), the one who has caused your past self the harm and your adult self.

If you have successfully worked your way through this imagination technique, the negative experience from your past can be looked back on a few days later in a positive or neutral manner.

Variations on the Exercise

Usually there are many events from the past in need of healing and many ways of healing them. As you work through some of your past issues, other previously forgotten situations may arise. Your Inner Self will try to reject these negative situations from your software until they are gone. Try not to get overwhelmed, and work with one issue at a time. Many times this type of healing work drains a lot of energy, so pace yourself and reprogram only one or two situations a day. If memories of forgotten experiences start to emerge, make a list of these experiences so you can come back to them later. You can start with some of your smaller issues and work your way up to the larger, traumatic experiences. This will give you some practice and make the larger episodes seem less intimidating.

After all your major crises are reprogrammed, you may want to float around in your past and address whatever pops up. Other times you may want to locate specific problems in your present day interactions and trace them back to your past where they were learned. Unfortunately, this is more difficult than it sounds because your software can be the result of many combinations of events. The best way to reprogram your software is to start from your birth and work forward. But regardless of the way you work through your past experiences, the following items are some specific areas that you may want to consider:

❖ **From your birth.** A good place to start is at the hospital when you were born. Sometimes our parents lead us to believe we were unwanted as children. You may have heard your parents say things like, "I wish you were never born," "I wish you were a boy," "I wanted a girl instead," "I never wanted to get pregnant," "You ruined my life," or "I wanted a career, but instead I got a child to take care of." These words can almost destroy a young child's self-concept. If you heard this, you need to go back to your birth and welcome yourself to the world just as you are. Have your adult self show your child self how much they are loved and appreciated by the way they are spoken to, touched and held. Be there for the child self until their little person feels welcome. Have the doctors, nurses, visitors, religious leader, friends and even God welcome your child self to the world.

❖ **Moving forward in time.** If you can't remember much of your early childhood, re-create what you want in an attempt to fill in the pieces. Try to remember: Where did you play? What was it like to explore new things? What did your first home look like? Was it an apartment, house or trailer? What does your room look like? What color is it? Is it brightly lit and decorated? If not, have your adult self bring in some flowers, balloons, decorations and toys. Find out what your child self needs that he or she isn't getting. Figure out how your adult self can compensate, and perform those actions in your imagination. Then allow your adult self to feel the joy, happiness and love that your child self is experiencing.

❖ **Specific harmful incidents.** It won't be long before you remember a negative situation from your past. When that happens, simply experience the situation again and allow your adult self to feel the emotions. Try to work through your negative emotions of anger, fear, sadness and insecurity. After your adult self has worked through and felt the negative emotions, start expressing positive, loving and comforting statements to the child self. If it's hard at first, just hold each other and let your feelings of understanding and acceptance speak to each other. After a while tell your child self it's going to be okay. Tell your child self how much they are loved. Make your child self feel it's okay to ask questions when they don't understand. Try to free your child self from guilt and shame because it wasn't their fault. When the little person feels ashamed, frightened or scared about things, comfort them any way you can.

❖ **School situations.** Often the school environment is very competitive and hostile. You may want to be sure there aren't unresolved school situations, like kids bullying you on the playground, kids teasing you, or other role models shaming you. Maybe your child self gets called to the front of a classroom, doesn't know the answer and all the other kids laugh, and from that time forward you have had a hard time speaking in front of a group. If so, simply have your adult self take your child self out in the hall after the incident and give them the love and support they need. Tell your child self the other kids didn't mean to hurt you, they really like you and thought you were just being silly. Everything's okay! When the child self feels better, take them back into the classroom. Maybe you can run through the experience differently, get the wrong answer and still feel accepted and valuable. The possibilities are endless.

❖ **Separating from parents.** Sometimes we may get consumed by our parents' problems and find ourselves taking on their identities. Your creative and unique child self might have assumed an unhealthy role to help keep the family together. The child self might feel responsible for your parents' happiness, sadness, pain, problems, divorce or alcoholism. Maybe your parents told you, "You're the reason I drink," "It's your fault I'm unhappy," or "If you were good, this wouldn't have happened." If your parents hurt you in this manner, vent the pain and replace it with positive and loving reassurances. Try to find out what your child self truly desires. What does that little innocent person wish things were like? It might be necessary to help the child self pack up their belongings and tell their parents it's time for the child self to live their own life. Tell the parents it's time to give them back their shame, guilt, problems, emptiness, anger and their own unresolved issues. Then take the hand of your child self and walk out the front door, down the road and out of the situation.

❖ **Introducing other characters.** At first you might want to work through a specific issue using your adult self as the main caregiver and supporter. After you have addressed and worked through the situation, you can bring other role models into the healing action. For example, if your father hit you and sent you to your room, you might want to comfort the child self using your adult self first. Then when it feels safe, you can bring in the father. Imagine him making the necessary amends, apologizing and offering the much-needed support and loving statements. Just because your father didn't give you the love and support that you needed and deserved in the past doesn't mean you can't give it to yourself right now. Have the father act in the most loving manner possible. How would he act if he were in a completely healed state and could function without the influence of his own problems?

❖ **Playing and experimenting.** Many times your child self was prevented from doing many things. You might not feel that you deserve anything good or that there is never enough. For example, if your mother reprimanded you for touching things in a store, take your adult self and your child self into a store and touch everything you want as often as you want. Go back and do the childhood things you missed out on. After you have worked through a difficult situation, have fun with your child by going out for ice cream. After all, you deserve it and there is more than enough to go around.

❖ **Inappropriate role modeling.** Other times you may have experienced inappropriate role modeling from your parents. Maybe your father didn't treat your mother with the love or respect she deserved. Maybe he put her down as a form of control to compensate for his own insecurities. Maybe your mother took the abuse year after year. If you witnessed this type of role modeling, you may have grown up with a defect in your present day relationship software. A boy conditioned this way might seek out passive women and treat them the same way, and a girl might seek out abusive men just like her father. It's helpful to go back into your past and re-create scenes where the whole family treats one another with the love and respect everyone deserves.

❖ **God.** The most powerful healing takes place when you ask for God's assistance. If you are helping another, at the crucial healing moments ask for God's touch. Ask God to remove the negative and replace it with the positive. God is the ultimate source of love and support, and he offers an infinite supply. Don't hesitate to take your child self out of any harmful situation and down the road to the big white church. Go up the stairs, open the doors and remain in His presence. If necessary, leave your child there until you are able to revisit the situation and promote further healing.

Visions of Inspiration

And he gave skill to human beings that he might be glorified in his marvelous works. By them the physician heals and takes away pain; the pharmacist makes a mixture from them. God's works will never be finished; and from him health spreads over all the earth. My child, when you are ill, do not delay, but pray to the Lord, and he will heal you.

Sirach 38: 6 - 9

We are healed of a suffering only by experiencing it to the full.

Marcel Proust

INNER SELF

TOOL 36

Imagine driving down an unfamiliar road and losing your sense of direction, just as if someone had tied a blindfold over your eyes. Do you think you would experience severe problems and difficulties almost instantly? If you compare your life to a car, does it feel like you are driving with a blindfold tied over your eyes most of the time? Do you feel lost in a car that is going nowhere? If you want to remove the blindfold and get back on the road of life, you need to get in touch with your Inner Self.

People refer to the Inner Self with many different names: true self, soul, subconscious mind, id, psyche. People who are well-connected to their Inner Self are spiritual, soulful individuals who know, like and accept themselves. Your Inner Self is the very core, essence and vitality of your being.

To better understand your Inner Self, you will find it helpful to look at your entity in two parts. The first part, your physical existence, consists of your body, ego and logical mind. The second part is your spiritual existence, and is referred to in this book as your Inner Self. To better understand the Inner Self, we can break its functions down into the following parts:

❖ Spirituality – your connection to God.
❖ Intuition – your inner knowing.
❖ Conscience – your ability to determine right from wrong.
❖ Independent Will – your freedom of choice.
❖ Creativity and imagination – your ability to create.
❖ Self-Awareness – your ability to evaluate yourself.
❖ Retention – your storage of past experiences.

It's through these seven parts of your Inner Self that you're separated from the rest of life on the planet. These functions allow you to advance year after year, while animals continue to act and react according to their environmental conditioning.

It is through the Inner Self that you have a spiritual connection to God. Your Inner Self is the eternal part of your being created in the image and likeness of God. People who are well-connected to their Inner Self can listen to God speak to them through their intuition and conscience. They can use a combination of emotions, intuition, creativity and conscience, along with their logical minds, to guide their existence down life's highways. People who are well-connected to their Inner Self know and feel their tremendous value and worth because they know and feel their spiritual connection to God.

People who lack a connection to their Inner Self have only their ego or false sense of self for support. They rely on their logical thoughts to tell them who they want to be or who they want others to think they are. People who lack a connection to their Inner Self seem to wander through life emotionless, lost, confused, frustrated, unhappy and lacking spiritual direction. They stumble around blindfolded, trying to use their logical minds in an effort to guide every aspect of their lives. Many times they forget things, make serious mistakes and crash through the rocky hillside of life without any direction.

You can either live true to yourself by maintaining a strong connection with your Inner Self or you can avoid, deny and reject your Inner Self and live in a false state of self. The choice is yours. What type of driving habits do you have? What about your relationship partner – are they well-connected to their Inner Self? Or are they crashing through rocky terrain blindfolded?

Why would anyone choose to reject a relationship with who they really are and try to live according to who they are not? There can be many reasons, the first of which is fear. If God guides you down the road of life through your Inner Self, and if a close relationship with your Inner Self will keep your vehicle on that road, then by fearing God you might fear where that road will take you and instead choose your own road. But considering humans' limited view of things, which choice would appear to be more scary?

Another reason for avoiding a close connection with your Inner Self is lack of discipline. It is not always easy to do the things your Inner Self asks of you. Often your false sense of self is conditioned by the ways of the world. If God's ways conflict with the world's ways, your Inner Self will let you know about it through your conscience, in the form of negative feelings. To satisfy your conscience, your Inner Self might require you to make amends or ask you to perform some other necessary action. Listening to and following the advice of your Inner Self is not always an easy thing to do.

Another reason you might avoid a relationship with your Inner Self is uncomfortable negative feelings. Emotions are a part of your Inner Self, and by avoiding or repressing your negative emotions, you aren't being true to yourself. When you're experiencing negative feelings, your Inner Self is trying to communicate an important message of growth and change. For example, if you're driving down the road and a negative thought and feeling pops into your head, your Inner Self may be trying to communicate with you. Maybe it's calling for some past healing work. Or maybe it's trying to warn you of an upcoming danger. If you try to shake the feeling, you cut yourself off from your subconscious spiritual guidance system, otherwise known as your Inner Self.

The only way to guarantee safe passage down the road of life is to take off that blindfold, listen to your Inner Self and stay on the road God has chosen for your life. God wants what's best for you and He will guide you down the right road if you listen to and follow the advice of your Inner Self.

Strengthening the Connection With Your Inner Self

The following items have been designed to help you discover, interact and increase the connection with your Inner Self. These areas are divided into seven parts and can be studied and worked on as needed. Developing a closer connection with your Inner Self is not an easy thing to do but by working on these individual areas your connection will be greatly strengthened and your life greatly empowered.

Part 1: Spirituality

The most important part of your Inner Self is your spirituality. This is your connection to and relationship with God. Without spirituality or God in your life you will probably experience great suffering and find little meaning in life. Some other aspects of your Inner Self also may not be available for your use, such as intuition or conscience, because God talks to us through these areas. If you don't maintain a close relationship with God, it will be hard for you to accept God's counsel, guidance and direction in your life.

Beginning a relationship with God requires effort on your part. God is part of your Inner Self, but without intentional efforts on your behalf, a relationship is impossible. Consider the doors in adjoining hotel rooms. God is always present in us and the door to His room is always open. It is your responsibility to open the door from your own room. Both doors need to be open to maintain any kind of meaningful relationship. The stronger your relationship with God, the more powerful the rest of your Inner Self functions will be. To increase your relationship with God and the spiritual aspect in your Inner Self, refer to the God, New Covenant and Prayer chapters.

Part 2: Intuition

Intuition is the inner knowing of something without proof. A small portion of the information you take in is stored in your conscious mind and the rest is stored in your unconscious mind. If you take a test without knowing the answer in your conscious mind and choose the first answer that seems right using your intuition, you will probably do better than by trying to rationally work through a system of pros and cons. When your conscious mind doesn't have the answer, you can turn to your intuition and tap into the wisdom of your universal mind. The stronger your connection is with God, the more accurate and dependable your inner knowing will be.

To develop your intuitive ability, you need to recognize and listen to your inner voice. Avoid anything that cuts off your conscious self from your Inner Self, like getting high, addictions, sin or denial. Make a committed decision to seek the truth no matter how painful, fearful or difficult it may be.

To practice your intuitive ability, look deep inside yourself and find both sides of the situation. Usually there will be a positive voice and negative voice. After finding both sides in yourself, determine which force is more dominant. Usually the direction of that voice is the right choice and the underlying force is usually incorrect. For example, if someone offered you a job and your acceptance of that job required a significant lifestyle change, what would you do? You could use your logical brain to evaluate the pros and cons and hope everything works out, or you could tap into your intuitive ability. If you have a good connection and relationship with your Inner Self, simply look in and find out what voice or force in you is the strongest. A positive voice or feeling might be stronger, saying, "Take it. I'm excited. How wonderful." The negative voice might be on the bottom and less dominant saying, "Don't do it, you'll get hurt like last time." The voice from the strongest side usually works best.

It's necessary to locate both sides before they can be accurately compared with each other. Usually when you go against the guidance of your Inner Self, the deal doesn't work out as you thought. For more information on strengthening your intuitive ability, see the Contemplative Prayer section in the Prayer chapter.

Part 3: Conscience

Your conscience is that deep inner knowing of right and wrong that lets you know when your actions have promoted the positive or the harmful negative. This inner knowing comes from the supreme law giver – God. Your conscience is another method by which God speaks to you. It is a powerful tool you can use to analyze your actions before or after they have been taken. Harmful or destructive actions will cause you to feel guilt and negative feelings, while loving and helpful actions will cause you to feel good about yourself. Unfortunately, this part of your Inner Self can become repressed. Over time, through constant negative influences or conditioning, you can begin to disassociate from your conscience. You can nurture and maintain a healthy conscience by doing the following:

❖ Making amends for your harmful past and present actions.
❖ Doing what is right, not what is best.
❖ Establishing a written direction and potential statement to help guide your life.
❖ Seeing the Guilt, and Ethics, Values, and Morals chapters.

Part 4: Independent Will

No one can limit your ability to think, act, perceive or behave in any manner unless you allow them to. You have the power to choose how your daily and past events will affect the rest of your life. Animals don't have an independent will or the freedom of choice like humans do. They act according to their instincts, conditioning and environment. In a sense they were programmed to function in a certain manner by nature, their environment and God. You can train or reprogram a dog to act differently from what its natural instincts call for, but the dog can't choose to act differently. Through the ability of your Inner Self and independent will you are aware of your own programming and can change it any time you want.

Part 5: Creativity and Imagination

Your creativity and imagination are gifts that can be used in many different ways. For example, try to form a picture of yourself reading this book. Maybe you're floating up in the air looking down at yourself. Now notice in the picture how you could improve or change your posture or the amount of lighting to be more comfortable. By using these functions of your Inner Self in this way, you can improve almost every aspect of your life.

Imagination can be used to help reprogram your perceptions, actions, thoughts and behaviors. You can begin this process by imagining certain events or situations you wish to improve in the future. Next, picture yourself acting through the desired results in your mind allowing yourself to feel the corresponding emotions. Eventually this technique will help reprogram your thought processes and open up alternative methods of behavior.

You can use this technique in every aspect of your life, like achieving goals, preparing for a big office presentation, getting closer to God, dealing with relationship problems and confronting fears. Let's say you want to modify a form of negative behavior like anger. You need only picture a situation that's causing problems in your life. Maybe the kids are misbehaving and you don't want to lose control and blow up anymore. Next, imagine the situation as it would normally happen. Then picture all those events, words, action, sights and sounds as if you were viewing them on a movie film, one frame at a time. Start the film over, but this time change your words and actions. If you want to be more loving and understanding, find that place in your heart and introduce it into your actions on the film. Feel the feelings as you are watching the film. By watching this loving film in your mind on a daily basis, you will find new power to change your old methods of interacting with your children.

Part 6: Self-Awareness

Self-awareness is the ability to determine and evaluate how you are thinking, feeling and behaving. For example, you can look at your life and understand that you are addicted to drugs. You can even notice a different perception of time as it seems to pass quickly when you are high. The feelings and emotions that stem from your Inner Self contain important messages. By listening to your internal conditions through self-awareness, you can learn, grow and make changes necessary in your life.

Positive emotions are the reward for being true to your Inner Self.

Negative emotions are warning signs from the Inner Self to change your actions immediately. Unfortunately, many people only want to experience positive feelings and will do anything to avoid negative feelings. This often leads to greater problems. In fact, the number one reason behind most psychological disorders is the avoidance of pain and problems in life. When you listen to your Inner Self, you will experience both positive and negative feelings. When negative emotions arise, it's best to handle the situation quickly by making the necessary corrections so you can get back to those positive feelings. Things will only get worse when your negative feelings are ignored through the lack of self-awareness. Some ways to increase your self-awareness might include:

❖ Spending time focusing on your feelings from a meditative state of mind.
❖ Accepting your feelings and emotional responses as part of your Inner Self.
❖ Asking yourself questions and exploring your negative feelings – What is this all about? What's led up to this experience? What was I thinking beforehand? What do I need right now? What can I do right now to feel better? What is my Inner Self trying to say?
❖ Following your inner knowing wherever it leads you. It might take you back to the original cause of the negative emotions. It might take you into the past where old memories and unforgiving events need healing. It might lead you into the physical, to the tension, stress or anxiety that you are experiencing.
❖ Making needed corrections and adjustments to your life.
❖ Seeing the Self-awareness, Self-Acceptance and Meditation chapters.

Part 7: Retention

Another aspect of the Inner Self is your retention capability. This is where harmful and unpleasant memories from your past are stored that affect the way you view and interact with others in the present. If you were abused as a child and didn't heal, forgive and grow stronger from the situation, those unpleasant memories will get trapped and remain in your retention area and become a permanent part of your subconscious programming. Young children are not born with abusive tendencies. But if a young child is put in an abusive home environment that child will either grow up abusing other people in the same manner they were abused or grow up believing they deserve to be abused. Anything you don't forgive becomes trapped in your subconscious retention area in the form of emotional baggage. Not only will those painful memories from the past keep you from maintaining a close connection with your Inner Self, they will continue to affect the future way you interact and view the world.

You have the ability to perceive situations as either positive or negative. What you choose in your retention is what you will produce in your realities. A way to convert negative retention into positive retention is with this exercise:

❖ Imagine yourself as a young child who experienced lack of love, support and understanding.

❖ In your imagination or on paper, express and feel your feelings of anger, fear, insecurity and sadness.

❖ Find a way to give your inner child the love and support they never received but always deserved.

❖ Find a positive way to view the situation from now on, by looking at the gifts or lessons learned from the experience.

❖ See the Healing, Past Experiences/Transference and Forgiveness chapters.

Visions of Inspiration

Do not fear those who kill the body but cannot kill the soul; rather fear him who can destroy both soul and body in hell. Are not two sparrows sold for a penny? Yet not one of them will fall to the ground apart from your Father. And even the hairs of your head are all counted. So do not be afraid; you are of more value than many sparrows.

Matthew 10: 28-31

One might compare the relation of the ego to the id with that between a rider and his horse. The horse provides the locomotor energy, and the rider has the prerogative of determining the goal and of guiding the movements of his powerful mount toward it. But all too often in the relations between the ego and the id we find a picture of the less ideal situation in which the rider is obliged to guide his horse in the direction in which it itself wants to go.

Sigmund Freud

INSECURITY

*T*ry to imagine for a minute what it would be like if our cars were responsible for fulfilling their own needs. When the fuel level was low on your car, it would automatically sense that need and drive itself to the gas station. If your car, failed to fulfill its own needs and ran out of gas all the time, do you think it would start to doubt itself? If your car always ran on fumes and noticed other cars with their tanks full of gas, do you think it would wonder what was wrong with it? Do you think it would fear not being good enough? Would this fear help your car get to the gas station more often, or would this fear cause your car to hide in the garage hoping no one found out about its little problem? If your car hides in the garage all the time and acts in a self-doubting manner, would you consider it insecure?

This analogy applies to every aspect of our lives and relationships because we are all responsible for fulfilling our own needs. Everyone has higher needs and wants in life, just like our cars have a need to run on gas. If we fail to recognize or fulfill our own needs, we will hurt inside just like a car would hurt running on fumes. If we hurt inside from unfulfilled needs and see other people who are not hurting inside, we might develop some type of fear that says, "You must not be good enough," "You can't fulfill your own needs," or "You will never get what you really want and need in life." When combined with our existing hurt, this fear will produce insecurity. Everyone has needs and everyone experiences fear, so it's safe to say that everyone experiences insecurity in their lives and relationships.

Insecurity is a great gift if it's immediately recognized and transformed into the fulfillment or expression of our unmet needs and higher wants. If we deny or fail to acknowledge our unmet needs, fears and insecurities, they will come to the surface and negatively affect our self-concept, attitude and behaviors. If we acknowledge that insecure part of ourselves, those negative feelings can be transformed into the fulfillment of our needs. If we regularly fulfill our own needs over a period of time, we will develop inner confidence and courage. Insecurity is a calling for us to use self-confidence and courage in the fulfillment of our needs.

Let's pretend you're at a party feeling very insecure. You're standing by yourself and the only other person you know there is your relationship partner, who is socializing with the other guests. What would you do in this situation? Would you acknowledge your fears, higher needs and wants and do something about them? Or would you take these insecure feelings personally and stand around feeling inadequate? Would you blame your insecure feelings on your partner for leaving you all alone? Before you answer, let's look a little closer at the three available options:

❖ **Option 1:** If you acknowledge your uncomfortable and insecure feelings but fail to recognize your higher wants and needs and fears, your only option is to stand around consumed by those terrible self-doubting, insecure feelings.

❖ **Option 2:** If you deny and repress your insecure feelings, they will eventually resurface in ways that are unhealthy or destructive to your relationship. For example, after the party a big fight might break out in the car because you blamed your partner for leaving you alone. You might use the silent treatment and try to hurt your partner the same way you were hurt. You might try to control future situations by saying you won't go to any more parties. You might tell your partner they can't have any friendships outside your relationship because you don't know how to deal with your hurtful, insecure feelings.

❖ **Option 3:** You can get in touch with your higher wants and needs and deal with them in a healthy manner. Your higher wants and needs may be wanting to be accepted and liked by the people at the party, or wanting to be social and have a good time interacting with the other guests. You will also need to get in touch with your fears and deal with them in a healthy manner. You may be scared other people at the party won't like you very much or won't accept you for who you are. You may be scared your partner likes the other guests more than you. Once you know your fears, you can transform them into courageous actions and fulfill your needs in a confident manner.

God gave us the beautiful gift of insecurity so we can be stronger, more courageous guests in the ballroom of life. God wants you to be happy and confident, and He wants you to fulfill your every want, wish, desire and need. But that's not possible if you don't RSVP the invitation known as insecurity. Take a look at your life. When was the last time you felt insecure? Did you stand there in self-doubt, take it out on your partner, or did you deal with it in a courageous manner? How does your partner deal with their insecure feelings?

Steps to Transforming Your Feelings of Insecurity

Step 1: Recognize Your Insecure Feelings

It will be helpful to make a list of events, situations or activities that bring about your insecure feelings. Write down as many items as possible, like trying new things, meeting people, working with your hands, speaking in front of a group or watching your partner socialize with other people. Try to identify as many things as possible that produce those insecure feelings.

Step 2: Discover the Underlying Messages

Once you know what causes your feelings of insecurity, you can discover the underlying messages your insecure feelings are trying to present and explore them. When you feel insecure, stop what you're doing and ask yourself, "What are these feelings trying to say to me?" Take a close look at what you're doing when these feelings arise. What are you trying to accomplish? What would you like to happen that might not? Get in touch with your higher source of wants, needs, desires and intentions. Maybe you feel insecure when meeting new people, and your higher want might be to be accepted and liked by others. If you experience insecure feelings when speaking in front of a group, your higher want might be to be respected and appreciated for your efforts. Write a paragraph for every item in Step 1 that identifies and explains your higher wants and needs.

Step 3: Discover and Heal Underlying Fears

All forms of insecurity are based on some type of fear. Usually we learn these fears in our past as a form of self-protection. The next step is to discover and heal any underlying fears that might prevent your higher wants and needs from being fulfilled. For example, if you feel insecure when speaking in front of a group, you might have made a mistake in front of your class in school years ago and your classmates laughed at you in a cruel manner. This could have really hurt you and you developed a fear of speaking in front of groups as a form of self-protection. To correct this situation, it's first necessary to identify the fears that enforce your insecure feelings and find when in your past you learned this fearful attitude. Heal that experience by venting your negative emotions and replacing them with positive and loving reassurances. You can do this by following the procedures in the Healing or Fear chapters. By working through and healing negative past experiences, you will experience less pain, fear and insecure feelings in the present.

Step 4: Make Daily Efforts

The next time you experience insecure feelings, acknowledge your higher wants and needs and openly express them to your relationship partner. If your partner is unable to help fulfill your higher wants and needs, try to fulfill them yourself or seek other healthy ways of fulfilling them. Then reassure yourself that everything will work out for the best. A strong relationship with God is also very helpful. Try to avoid distorted thinking patterns (see the Perceptions chapter) and place your trust and confidence in God. God promises to provide for us everything we need.

Visions of Inspiration

Though an army encamp against me, my heart shall not fear; though war rise up against me, yet I will be confident. One thing I asked of the Lord, that will I seek after: to live in the house of the Lord all the days of my life, to behold the beauty of the Lord, and to inquire in his temple. For he will hide me in his shelter in the day of trouble; he will conceal me under the cover of his tent; he will set me high on a rock.

Psalm 27: 3-5

No one can make you feel inferior without your consent.

Eleanor Roosevelt

The fearful unbelief is unbelief in yourself.

Thomas Carlyle

INTER-
INDEPENDENCE

TOOL 38

*P*retend for a minute you're the personnel manager for a large automotive repair shop. It's your job to hire and fire the mechanics and shop assistants. Your company is opening several new locations and you need to put together a group of people to operate the new facilities. After running a help wanted ad in the newspaper, you sort the applicants who responded into four categories. Let's take a closer look at these types of mechanics to find out from which group you would want to hire:

❖ **Group 1 – Dependent mechanics.** These people are completely dependent on other people for almost everything. They are physically dependent on someone else to drive them to work, mentally dependent on someone to tell them what to do, and emotionally dependent on other people to help them find value in themselves and the projects they are working on.

❖ **Group 2 – Codependent Mechanics.** These people are not as dependent as the first group, but their work performance is greatly affected by their emotional and mental conditioning. Emotionally they lack the ability to recognize their own worth and value. They don't feel very good about themselves, so they attach themselves to other people, situations and addictions in an attempt to make themselves feel better. They fear changes, risks, letting go, abandonment and rejection. They look for things outside of themselves to make themselves feel complete. They recreate negative situations in the present so they can experience the same old familiar negative feelings of the past.

❖ **Group 3 – Independent mechanics.** These people are almost the exact opposite of the second group because they don't need anyone. They don't interact well with others, because in their eyes other people are useless and worthless. Because they don't recognize the value of other people, an independent person doesn't feel much need to interact with anyone. Usually they have been deeply hurt by people in their past, so now they alienate and isolate themselves from others as a form of emotional protection. Independent people at the same time desire and fear closeness and intimacy. They either abuse or refuse commitments. They are loners who experience very little individual growth because they live in their own world most of the time.

❖ **Group 4 – Inter-Independent Mechanics.** These people are able to connect, bond, interact with and depend on others, and at the same time have a strong enough sense of self to stand on their own. They have a balance between their own sense of self-worth and the sense of worth in other people. They have developed every aspect of their physical, emotional, mental and spiritual lives into an independent state strong enough to be shared with others in a loving, vulnerable and dependent manner.

After looking over your four choices, which group of auto mechanics would you choose to build the most successful organization? Which type of person would you like to work with side-by-side, day-in and day-out? Which type of person would make the best relationship partner? Can you imagine a shop full of Group 1 people? It would be like a giant day care center, only with bigger and more dangerous toys to play with. Group 2 people would bond together as an inseparable team, which would be great if you could find some way to make them recognize their own internal value and worth. Unfortunately, if one person in the shop were having a bad day, you would have to close down the business because they would all be having a bad day together. Group 3 people wouldn't have the emotional problems to deal with like Group 2, but they wouldn't work together at all. Everyone would be off in their corner doing their own things. Group 4 people appear to be the best choice. They can combine their efforts, talents, ideas and knowledge into a powerful team and have the emotional maturity to carry out specific tasks and assignments independently.

What does all this have to do with your life and relationships?

The auto mechanics in Group 1 are dependent on other people in the shop, just as children are dependent on their parents. Young children depend on their parents to feed and take care of them. Without their parents' care they wouldn't survive their childhood years. Children depend on their parents for emotional support and love, and to help establish their emotional identities. If children learn unhealthy, negative messages about themselves, they grow up failing to recognize their self-worth and value. Adults who subconsciously fail to recognize their self-worth and value struggle through life with codependent tendencies, just like the auto mechanics in Group 2.

On the other hand, independent tendencies can be just as destructive as codependent tendencies. It's a necessary part of a child's growth process to establish independence. Slowly children become less dependent on their parents and more independent as they learn to take care of themselves. But independent adults who can't trust, connect with or recognize value in others probably struggle through life just like the auto mechanics in Group 3. Independent tendencies are subconsciously formed when people are deeply hurt in their past and learn to alienate and isolate themselves from others as a form of self-protection.

Usually independent people can only accomplish so much on their own, which is why inter-independence is so important. The group of mechanics in Group 4 symbolizes mature individuals. They are strong enough to do everything independently, yet at the same time are strong enough to depend on a relationship partner to create things they can't do themselves. Two inter-independent people working together can produce greater realities than two independent people working by themselves because of the combined efforts, knowledge and teamwork. When two inter-independent relationship partners get together they can:

❖ Experience closeness, intimacy and a strong bond with each other, while at the same time experiencing and appreciating their own identities and uniqueness.
❖ Promote personal growth and bring out their partner's best qualities.
❖ Experience true intimacy and allow for each other's individualities.
❖ Respect and accept commitments.
❖ Feel free to be themselves and openly express their needs in a vulnerable manner.
❖ Not feel the need to control one another.
❖ Accept their partner's limitations and disadvantages.
❖ Welcome closeness and risk vulnerability.
❖ Care for each other and at the same time detach from each other.
❖ Create an equal balance between giving and taking.

God asks that we value ourselves as much as we value others. He asks that we recognize our own self-worth as much as we recognize the worth of others.

We all have been hurt in the past, and unless we do some healing work, it isn't possible to find value or worth in that hurt part of ourselves or others. Take a look at your life. Are you codependent, independent or inter-independent? What about your relationship partner? Successful auto repair shops, marriages or relationships can't be built on anything other than true inter-independent relationships. If you are experiencing a shop full of codependent mechanics or independent mechanics, the following steps might help you and your partner develop stronger inter-independent realities in your relationship. But first it's necessary to overcome any codependent or independent tendencies. See the Codependent/Independent chapter for more information. After these tendencies are overcome, it will be possible to start building inter-independence into your relationship using the following steps.

Steps to Developing a Stronger Inter-Independent Relationship

Step 1: Identify Problem Areas

First, identify problem areas in your relationship. Consider the following issues and try to pinpoint some areas where stronger inter-independence would be beneficial:

* Sexual issues: the ability to experience and express closeness before, during and after sex.
* Emotional support: the ability to empathetically listen without offering unwanted advice.
* Communication: the ability to effectively communicate and express your needs, feelings, wants, and desires to one another.
* Intellectual: the ability to express your ideas and have your partner accept your differences.
* Recreational: the ability to play and have fun together as well as apart.
* Work: the ability to accomplish common goals and share mutual tasks and assignments.
* Creation: the ability to create together.
* Community: the ability to maintain outside friendships, connections and unity with others.

❖ Crisis: the ability to face difficult situations in life together, and cope with pain and tragedy.

❖ Conflicts: the ability to compromise and create win/win situations, and overcome any differences.

❖ Commitment: the ability to trust and remain honorable in every aspect of your commitments.

❖ Spiritual: the ability to worship, pray and support each other and share ultimate meanings and concerns.

After studying how these areas apply to your relationship, make a list of individual problems and the general areas from which they stem. What areas of your life would you like to improve on individually and together?

Step 2: Commit to Greater Closeness

To have a strong inter-independent relationship, it's important to work on creating greater closeness and intimacy. A good way to create this is through the exercises listed in the Intimacy chapter. Use the intimacy journal to try to uncover any fears or problems you use to block closeness. Use the intimacy log to chart your closeness patterns. Try to discover any root causes or recurring sources that interfere with your closeness. Make a commitment to disclose everything to your relationship partner. The things we try to deny, hide and conceal eventually consume us and harm our relationships. Schedule some time every day to develop a stronger bond together.

Step 3: Commit to Greater Individuality

When a couple spends too much time together, each partner begins to lose his or her sense of individuality. Growing more and more alike, a couple's ability to compromise and develop intimacy may increase, but as this happens, each person may begin to conform to please the other. In the beginning of a relationship each partner is usually attracted to the other person's sense of self – who they are and what they represent. When partners spend too much time together, each may change the person their partner was attracted to in the first place. When two people become exactly alike, the passion in the relationship will slowly fade away. That's why it's important to spend time alone and participate in individual friendships, hobbies, activities and meditations. Take time to develop a healthy sense of self. See the Self-Awareness, Self-

Acceptance and Self-Concept chapters for more information. Make sure you both develop and maintain outside friendships. Regularly renew your individual connection to the world, nature, God and yourself. Then when you reconnect with your relationship partner, you will experience a greater sense of passion and closeness. Allow yourself the time to miss your partner and pull back together in an exciting, passionate cycle. Schedule some time every day to develop a stronger individuality and sense of self.

Step 4: Create a Relationship Direction Statement

You may find it helpful to create a relationship direction statement. Sit down with your partner over several days and define every aspect of your relationship. Determine what you want from it, what it stands for, what it represents, how you want to be treated and what is most important to each of you. See the Direction/Potential chapter for more information on this process. When you have completed your mutual statement, it will need to represent everything you are committed to and desire from the relationship. It will stand for your higher wants and what is really most important in your life. Because it is based on your ethics, values and morals, it will help promote a stronger sense of self, happiness and prosperity in your interactions. Some issues that you may want to consider while creating your statement might be establishing an equal balance of power and decision-making methods; discussing money and financial issues; revision or incorporation of your marriage vows; a commitment to empower and support each other in your individual issues; a mutual system of give and take; setting a priority and importance for the expression and fulfillment of individual needs; future problem and conflict solving methods; a commitment to keep agreements and promises; mutual acceptance of responsibility when problems arise; breaking blaming or victim cycles; being yourself, and enjoying life and each other.

Step 5: Create Personal Bylaws

You might consider creating personal bylaws for your relationship. These are items or issues that each partner agrees to work on. Once you have created your relationship direction statement from Step 4, you can easily determine if your or your partner's actions are in conflict with the statement's principles. Usually the direction statement contains idealized situations and conditions for a great relationship, but because no one is perfect, it is helpful to have a written set of bylaws.

For example, maybe your partner has some trust issues from their childhood. Maybe they grew up in an alcoholic family where promises were regularly broken. These issues will usually surface indirectly in your relationship in the form of hurt feelings, insecurities, fears or problems. If your direction statement contains clauses like, "To honestly express all of our negative concerns and confront all problems immediately," and your partner is unable to follow that clause because trust issues keep surfacing, your partner's bylaws might state something like, "To automatically extend trust and do healing work necessary to overcome these tendencies." Your bylaws might state, "To be sensitive to my partner's trust issues and make my intentions known through constant communication and reassurance."

Another way to discover underlying issues to be addressed by your bylaws is through the conflict resolution exercise in the Problems/Conflict chapter. Fill out the forms and save them every time a conflict arises. After a while you will have enough information to create the bylaws that will hopefully prevent those problems that seem to keep occurring.

Visions of Inspiration

Finally, all of you, have unity of spirit, sympathy, love for one another, a tender heart, and a humble mind. Do not repay evil for evil or abuse for abuse; but, on the contrary, repay with a blessing. It is for this that you were called – that you might inherit a blessing.

1 Peter 3: 8-9

The goal of our life should not be to find joy in marriage, but to bring more love and truth into the world. We marry to assist each other in this task. The most selfish and hateful life of all is that of two beings who unite in order to enjoy life. The highest calling is that of the man who has dedicated his life to serving God and doing good, and who unites with a woman in order to further that purpose.

Leo Tolstoy (from a letter to his son)

INTIMACY

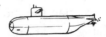

*B*efore anyone can effectively work on a car, they will need to know how it works. A mechanic who lacks insight into a car he is working on will be limited in his ability to properly fix, maintain and care for that vehicle. If a car mechanic knows how to take care of cars, he probably knows how often to change the engine oil. But do you think a car's mechanic is qualified to work on a nuclear submarine? How often should the oil be changed in a nuclear reactor? Or maybe a better question to ask is, "Does a submarine even have engine oil that needs to be changed like a car's does?" Is it possible for the car mechanic to fix problems on a nuclear reactor when he doesn't understand how it works?

The same is true of your personal relationship because you and your partner are your own relationship mechanics. The only difference is that while most cars operate on similar mechanical principles, each person was created different from every other person on the planet. Internally you are as different from your relationship partner as a submarine is different from an automobile. The only way your partner is going to know anything about the real you is through deep communicated insight and understanding, known as Intimacy. If your partner doesn't know anything about you, they will be limited in their ability to love, help and care for you, just as an automobile mechanic is limited when working on a nuclear reactor he doesn't understand.

Before it's possible to love someone on a deep level, you need to know a lot about that person on a very deep level. Your partner can love you only as much as you let them, and only as much as they understand who you are. If your partner doesn't know you very well, they won't be able to love you very well. If you don't know your partner very well, your love for them will be limited.

Before you can share who you are with your partner, you first need to know yourself. True intimacy requires that you first get in touch with your true self, or your Inner Self, find out who you are and then share that information with your partner in a mutual exchange. It is almost impossible to maintain a deep and meaningful relationship without intimacy. You are far more complex than the most advanced nuclear submarine that was ever built. No one can get to know you if you don't first get to know yourself and then share who you are with your loved one. If you are experiencing a lack of intimacy, shallow forms of love in your relationships or your nuclear reactor is about to blow up, the following items may be of some assistance.

Techniques for Creating Greater Intimacy

Get to Know Your True Self

We all have two selves: the false self, or ego, which is who we want to be or who we want others to think we are, and our true self or Inner Self, which is the eternal and spiritual part of our being that's connected to God. The first step in creating greater relationship intimacy is getting to know your true self better. Your Inner Self has many functions, and there are many ways to develop a closer relationship with that part of your being, as well as many ways to avoid getting in touch with that part of your being. If you spell intimacy using five words, it says In-to-me-you-see. It is impossible to allow another person to see into the real you if you are hiding that real you from yourself. See the Inner Self chapter for more information on getting to know your true self better.

Keep a Mutual Intimacy Journal

A very powerful way to create more intimacy in your life is to keep a journal together. This technique will help you express your deepest feelings, keep in touch when schedules conflict, improve communication and develop greater intimacy. Begin your intimacy journal by agreeing that each day you will write in it and read your partner's last entry. Establish and agree on some of the following guidelines:

❖ Keep the contents of the journal secret from others outside of the relationship.

❖ Honor the journal because everyone's deepest feelings are sacred. Never bring the contents up during an argument.

❖ Be totally honest with yourself and remember to respect your partner's feelings, thoughts and ideas – especially when you don't agree.

❖ Agree on how and when you will talk about the subjects that are discussed in your journal.

❖ Agree on the approximate maximum or minimum lengths you will write during each entry.

Begin your journal by picking a subject and flowing with it anywhere it takes you. Once the subject is concluded, change it to anything you like. Some subjects to start out with might be: My favorite childhood memories are... The purpose of my life is... My life has the most meaning when... I feel angry, happy, loved when... How do you feel about this?... This is what happened to me today... What I have always wanted is... These are my wishes... What attracted me to you when we first met was... What is your ideal vacation like?... These are my dreams... These are the things I love about you... These are the things I greatly appreciate about you...

You will never run out of things to talk about. Make sure to record the month and years in your volumes so you can look back over time on your enduring and honest love.

Keep an Intimacy Log

Another powerful way to create more intimacy in your relationship is to keep an intimacy log. This technique will help you and your partner keep track of and improve on closeness cycles. Begin this process by recording daily how distant or close you feel to each other. Include a brief description of any events or circumstances that might be contributing to a lack of intimacy in your relationship. Keep separate records and review them weekly or monthly. After you have established enough past history, try to resolve any problem areas and improve on your mutual closeness times. For example, one partner might need extra space after completing a difficult project at work, and both of you might feel very close to each other on Saturday and Sunday nights. Once you have a history of your intimacy cycles, you can increase the time you spend together on days of mutual closeness and take advantage of other times when your partner needs space. It might also be helpful to keep a mutual calendar of commitments, dates and special events to look forward to. By using a mutual calendar, you can plan accordingly for work deadlines or other events that might eliminate some of your closeness times together.

Intimate Family Activities to Share Together

Another way to increase the amount of intimacy in your relationship is through external activities. Take a look at the following family activities to see if any sound interesting. Make a family memories scrap book. While eating dinner, play a game of trading places, where mother and daughter, father and son trade places and try to act like one another. Family camping trips can be very bonding. Invite relatives or neighbors over for dinner, movies or visits on a weekly basis. Do outdoor or indoor picnics. Sing songs or make up songs. Play family charades. Visit a local park. Take evening drives in search of different ice cream spots. Tell your children "When I was little stories." While traveling in the car, invent creative games using the alphabet. Play board games instead of watching television. Work on jigsaw puzzles. Take family and individual photos. Pray special prayers before meals that acknowledge your family's uniqueness. Celebrate birthdays by playing King or Queen for the day, where the rest of the family makes all of the King's or Queen's wishes for the day come true. Take unexpected walks at night. Exchange lots of hugs and warm expressions of your love for each other. Visit the local zoo and museum. Establish mystery meal times, where leftover foods are disguised in aluminum foil and what each family member chooses becomes that person's meal. Read children's Bible stories aloud before bedtime. Go ice skating. Roast hot dogs and marshmallows in the fireplace. Go roller skating, bowling or set up a family basketball team. Spend twice as much time apologizing and making amends than you spend fighting and arguing. Go fishing or on nature walks. Play hide-and-seek around nightfall. Sing lullabies before bedtime. Celebrate the holidays by caroling in the neighborhood and by making decorations, wreaths, ornaments, candles, music and cookies. Rent mountain bikes. Make a tree house. Read bedtime stories. Take turns saying grace before meal times. Plan extended family reunions. Find the humor in things when everything goes wrong. Start a family art show and gallery. Draw names to establish the daily routine of chores, keep a rotating list of jobs and set up family cleaning nights. Encourage individual interests like music lessons, hobbies and sports. Make a family banner and logo. Study and read together. Set up Saturday morning rituals like serving everyone's favorite food, wearing pajamas until noon or making pancakes shaped like animals. Show frequent signs, gestures and actions of love, respect and support for one another. Share Sunday brunch after church. Establish an allowance system for family projects, tithing, clothing allowances, budgeting and living within one's means. Take turns at meal times describing one good and one bad thing that happened that day. Take time to laugh, play and enjoy your daily events. Vote on and celebrate a "Family Member of the Week" award. Focus on and give individual attention to each other. Document your family history with videos, pictures and audio recordings. Take family time-outs when emotions run high, but never let a family member leave home or go to bed angry or hurt without resolving the issue. Establish guidelines and limits on television watching, or remove the television from your home completely.

Intimate Couple Activities to Share Together

Another way to increase the amount of intimacy in your relationships is through external couple activities. Take a look at the following items to see if anything sounds interesting. Create pleasant surprises for each other. Cultivate a garden that symbolizes your relationship. Go camping in the back yard. Read a bedtime story. Buy flowers for each other. Bake bread. Buy a joke book and humor each other. Play Frisbee at the park. Play strip poker. Visit a playground on a summer's night. Make a scrap book of the life of someone who's close to you. Browse at your local book store. Take a bike ride through a secluded wilderness area. Look for pictures in the clouds. Give and receive hot oil massages. Go sledding. Visit an antique store. Write a love letter to each other. Play chess. Take a moonlight walk. Climb a tree. Leave love notes in unexpected places. Look through your old photo albums. Relive childhood activities. Change your television-watching routine. Visit a record store and pick out selections for each other. Go skinny dipping. Make a surprise visit to someone close to you. Take turns sharing your fantasies. Watch for falling stars. Take a drive to the country, mountains or beach. Give yourself permission to do nothing at all. Take a twilight horse-and-carriage ride. Surprise each other with concert, theater or ball park tickets. Go on a picnic. Make choices from a restaurant guide and randomly choose one when you are undecided. Play cute jokes on each other. Build a snowman. Bake cookies. Take bubble baths together. Enroll in classes that are mutually interesting. Share late night desserts by candlelight. Eat breakfast in bed. Re-create and continue holiday traditions. Decorate your home for all the holidays. Visit nature. Experiment doing different activities blindfolded. Share soft music and candlelight.

Exchange routine chores with your partner for a week. Plant a tree. Take turns sharing your dreams, fantasies and desires.

Visions of Inspiration

Happy is the one who finds a friend, and the one who speaks to attentive listeners.

Sirach 25: 9

Whoever betrays secrets destroys confidence, and will never find a congenial friend. Love your friend and keep faith with him; but if you betray his secrets, do not follow after him.

Sirach 27: 16-17

One must learn to love, and go through a good deal of suffering to get to it, like any knight of the grail, and the journey is always toward the other soul, not away from it.... To love you have to learn to understand the other, more than she understands herself, and to submit to her understanding of you. It is damnably difficult and painful, but it is the only thing which endures.

D. H. Lawrence

JEALOUSY

*P*icture yourself making a long-distance road trip through the desert. The nearest town is at least 300 miles away and your car is low on gas. What would happen if your car ran out of gas in the next few miles? What would you do if another motorist didn't happen by for several days? As you pass through this barren part of the country under these conditions, would you be worried about your own well-being?

Trying to forget about the possible dangers for a while, you keep driving and hope something turns up. Then to your surprise, about 50 miles later you come upon a small gas station. There are two cars in line ahead of you waiting for fuel. The owner of the station comes out and informs everyone that he doesn't have enough gas to go around. As you watch, the two cars ahead of you fill their tanks, using up all the gas, and drive away. How would you feel? Would you be angry at the station for running out of fuel? Would you be anxious and afraid, not knowing how you are going to arrive safely at your destination? Or would you be jealous because the other motorists were in line ahead of your car?

You sit in your car so consumed by anxiety, anger and jealousy that you don't notice the station attendant bringing out a reserve tank of gas. He walks up to the driver's door and sees that you are about to emotionally blow up. He tells you he will give you all the gas you need if you can give him the correct answer to a riddle, but that if you can't come up with the correct answer, you'll be out of luck.

What would you do?

You only have three options. Let's study them closely. First, you can drive away emotionally hurt, angry and jealous, and hope to find another gas station farther down the road. Second, you can strike out in anger at the owner of the station for playing games with you. You could find a way to punish him and inflict on him the same hurt you are experiencing. Or third, you can comfort and reassure that hurt part of yourself so you can think clearly enough to answer his riddle and get the fuel you so desperately need.

What are you going to do? What kind of decision would your relationship partner make here? Would they turn their hurt on themselves and drive off? Would they turn their hurt on others? Or would they embrace that hurting part of themselves in a loving manner and make the situation work to their advantage? The wise decision, of course, is to choose the third option of internal reassurance work, since the other two options will only make matters worse. After making this decision, you ask the station attendant to explain the riddle, and he says, *"Through what process are feelings of jealousy created in you, and how can you work your way back through that process?"* After the station attendant gives you the riddle, he says that he will check back with you in fifteen minutes. Great, you think. This will be easy because I was just feeling jealous when those other people in line ahead of me took all the fuel. All I need to do is understand why I got jealous in the first place and then reverse the process.

So you think through the process: I needed gas and I had a hard time getting my needs met because of the desert environment. The inconvenience of this unmet physical need caused some of my emotional needs to surface. I don't feel a lot of love for myself right now because I should not have gotten myself into this kind of situation in the first place. I don't feel very loved by those other people in line who took all the gas without sharing. To make matters worse, the pain of these unmet needs is being intensified by the negative emotions of fear. I am afraid of being stranded out here all alone. There is a big risk and danger involved if I run out of gas, so I believe my fears are justified. I am sitting here burning up inside with all this emotional turmoil, which I find myself blaming on sources outside of myself – namely, the people who took all the gas. So to reverse the process, I would probably need to confront my fears and deal with my higher wants and needs in a healthy manner.

You're thinking to yourself, Wow, that was easy, when the station attendant returns to hear your answer to the riddle. You give him this answer: Jealousy is an ugly internal emotion being blamed or focused on an outside source. It stems from a lack of loving intentions, unfulfilled needs and fear. If you want to reverse the process, you need to work your way through the fear, get in touch with your higher wants and needs, and express them in a healthy manner.

The gas station attendant is shocked to hear your answer. He says you are absolutely correct. It seems he has been asking that same question of couples for more than 20 years. Every time three cars pull up to the pump, someone always drives off and inflicts hurt on themselves or drives off and inflicts hurt on their relationship partner. But it seems you're the first person who is strong enough and brave enough to embrace your own hurt. Congratulations, he says, but how did you know the answer to the riddle? It was easy, you say. Your car needs gas just like people need love. Running out of gas in the desert represents a serious threat to your well-being, just like the lack of self-love and love from others represents a serious threat to your emotional well-being. Something that threatens your well-being, like getting stranded in the desert, will cause fear and the combination of the two will produce jealousy. Besides that, you say, I have already taken a look at the following steps and found that they're an excellent way to transform jealousy into loving intentions.

Steps to Transforming Jealousy

Step 1: List Your Past Jealous Experiences

Try to think back over the factors that contributed to your jealous experiences in the past. Then write down several items that could make you jealous in the future. When was the last time you experienced those sick, envious, anxiety-related fearful emotions? Look at your personal and professional relationships. What does your relationship partner do that causes you to feel jealous? Maybe you're competing for a promotion at work and a coworker is getting credit for the company's efforts instead of you. Maybe you desire attention from another person and find yourself being ignored. Are you jealous over another person's achievements, friendships or assets? Try to imagine situations in which your relationship partner could make you jealous. Write down as many items as possible.

Step 2: Identify the Underlying Reasons

Now try to identify the underlying reasons behind your jealous feelings identified in Step 1. Once you have identified the reasons, write down an explanation for your feelings. Try to keep your explanation focused on yourself. How does it make you feel? How does it affect your needs and desires? How does it affect your life and your participation in the relationship? For example, if your partner is dancing with another person at an office party, you might start your paragraph off like this: I would like my partner to be dancing with me instead. I feel hurt because I want to be out there having fun. I feel disrespected – how dare they treat me like this. I want my partner to be interested in me. I want my partner to love me. I feel like hurting my partner because they are hurting me with their disrespectful actions.

Step 3: Transform and Confront Your Fears

Usually some form of fear is responsible for jealousy, and its explanation will usually surface in the paragraph you wrote in Step 2. If not, it might be necessary to dig a little deeper to discover the underlying insecurities, worries, potential loss, lack of control and worst possible outcomes. Once you identify and transform these fears, you can confront them. For example, if your relationship partner is dancing with someone else, you might assume they are romantically or sexually involved, or that they don't love you, or that they love someone else more, or that your relationship will come to an end. Once you have identified the underlying fears, proceed by following the healing steps in the Fear chapter.

Step 4: Discover Your Loving Intentions

After you have confronted and transformed your fears, you can discover the loving intentions underlying your jealousy. Usually there are good intentions behind jealous feelings. To get in touch with those intentions, try asking yourself what would you like to have happen. Once you know the answer, verbalize it to the other person. For example, you might say to your relationship partner after the dance, "I really value our relationship and you mean a lot to me. Can I please have the next dance?" Or if a neighbor buys a new car you have always wanted, you might say, "I really like this car. I'd like to own one myself someday." By verbally expressing your loving intentions, you release a lot of the inner tension that produces insecure jealous feelings.

Step 5: Seek Self-Reassurance

The next step to transforming your jealousy is to seek self-reassurance. Usually when we feel insecure over our external realities, it stems from our internal realities. If you feel insecure over an external issue like your partner's dance, you might be wondering if you're good enough or if your partner is looking for a better person. If your neighbor has the ability to acquire that new car, you might be insecure about your own ability to acquire one. Jealousy is a calling for more self-love, self-worth and self-assurance. When you experience insecure jealous feelings, it's necessary to stop yourself and recognize your own self-worth and value. One way you can help reassure yourself is by doing affirmations. For example, when your partner is dancing, you can mentally reassure yourself by saying, "I love myself, there is a lot of love in our relationship and everything is great." Or you can mentally reassure your own value by saying, "I am good enough and can work hard enough to acquire that new car just like my neighbor did." For more information and other methods of developing more inner self-worth, value and love, follow the instructions, healing steps and exercises in the Self-Concept, Self-Acceptance and Affirmations chapters.

Step 6: Seek Reassurance and Assistance From Others

After you have provided your own reassurance, you can ask for assistance from others when possible. If you're feeling insecure about your partner's commitment to your relationship, ask them about it. If your relationship partner is socially active and you go to parties often, you might ask them to show you some attention and reassurance every so often. Maybe they could give you a hug every 15 minutes or talk about the value of your relationship with other people at the party. Try working together with your partner to create some methods of reassurance that will help you overcome your jealous feelings.

God is also a constant source of reassurance and assistance. Ask for guidance, strength and courage in every aspect of your life, especially when jealous feelings are involved. After you are familiar working your way through this process in written form, it can be mentally used to transform any jealous feelings the next time the opportunity arises.

Visions of Inspiration

O, beware, my lord, of jealousy; it is the green-eyed monster which doth mock the meat it feeds on. Trifles light as air are to the jealous confirmation strong as proofs of holy writ.

Shakespeare

Now the works of the flesh are obvious: fornication, impurity, licentiousness, idolatry, sorcery, enmities, strife, jealousy, anger, quarrels, dissension's, factions, envy, drunkenness, carousing, and things like these. I am warning you, as I warned you before: those who do such things will not inherit the kingdom of God. By contrast, the fruit of the Spirit is love, joy, peace, patience, kindness, generosity, faithfulness, gentleness, and self-control. If we live by the Spirit, let us also be guided by the Spirit. Let us not become conceited, competing against one another, envying one another.

Galations 5:19-23.5 25-26

To cure jealousy is to see it for what it is, a dissatisfaction with self, an impossible claim that one should be at once Rose Bowl princess, medieval scholar, Saint Joan, Milly Theale, Temple Drake, Eleanor of Aquitaine, one's sister and a stranger in a pink hat seen once and admired on the corner of 55th and Madison-as well as oneself, mysteriously improved.

Joan Didion

LONELINESS & ISOLATION

TOOL 41

*H*ave you ever saved up a lot of money to have a brand new coat of paint put on your car? Those who have are so excited about their accomplishment all they want to do is drive around town and show it off. The same is true when you buy a new car or paint a work of art on canvas. When you're proud of something, you have a natural desire to share it with others. You wouldn't paint a beautiful work of art and bury it in the back yard, or buy a new car and lock it away in storage forever. If you did, you would probably experience some pretty sick feelings of waste, disrespect, regret and lack of connection.

The same is true of your personal relationships. God created each of us with tremendous internal value and worth, and when we hide that internal value and worth from other people, we experience the sick feelings of loneliness and isolation. God, being the Master Artist, is very proud of His creations. He doesn't want His beautiful artwork hidden underground, so He designed a fail-safe mechanism for us. When we have an overabundance of internal value that isn't being shared with other people, the fail-safe mechanism produces negative feelings of loneliness and isolation. Loneliness is a calling for deeper social interaction so your God-given internal value and worth can be shared with others.

Just because you interact with people, though, doesn't mean it's not possible to feel lonely and isolated. Many people work all day surrounded by customers and coworkers yet still feel lonely and isolated because they fail to share their internal value, worth and gifts with others on a deep and meaningful level. The more internal value and worth you have in your life, the greater your need will be to share it with others. Your car may have a beautiful paint job, but why would other people care if they didn't know you on a personal level? There could be thousands of other cars around you, but if no one has the opportunity to connect with your internal beauty, you will still feel very alone. In the same way, your internal beauty can only be shared with other people through deep and meaningful friendships and relationships. It's not enough for people to just see or know about your internal beauty; it needs to be shared, given away as a gift and experienced by others in a meaningful manner to prevent that fail-safe mechanism from creating the uncomfortable feelings of loneliness.

If you are in touch with your internal value and worth, there's a good chance you may experience loneliness and isolation at some point during your life. People move away, close friends get married, spouses die, children go off to college, more people are working out of their homes, everyone is working longer and harder hours. Technology is taking away more of our avenues of social interaction. Without ever leaving your home, you can bank through the Internet, shop by phone and order movies through the television.

Are you having a hard time finding someone to share your internal value with? What about your relationship partner? It's possible to be married and surrounded by children all day and still feel isolated. If you feel like your art-work is being buried underground, it's time to take action. The following items will help you meet new people and develop new friendships so your internal beauty can be displayed for the whole world to appreciate.

Part 1: The Opening Statement

There are several approaches you can use to start conversations when meeting new people. By better understanding these approaches and practicing them, you will become more confident and empowered in creating new friendships so your internal beauty can be shared with others. Some of these approaches are:

- ❖ **Direct approach.** In the direct approach you state your intentions directly. By getting right to the point, you can simply express your request and intentions in an honest and confident manner. For example, you might say to someone you're interested in meeting and getting to know better, "Hi, I'd like to introduce myself. My name is _____. I find you very attractive and would like to get to know you better. I was wondering if you were available to go out sometime?" The direct approach is based on honesty: it's direct, simple and gets right to the point.
- ❖ **Imaginative approach.** In the imaginative approach you create an indirect

statement or question designed to start a conversation. For example, if you're at the beach, you might say something like, "What a beautiful sunset," "This is really exciting. Did you see that parasailer go by?" "Isn't the ocean beautiful?" or "I've been watching your serve and I think it's great. Would you be willing to give me some pointers?" A good question might be, "What do you think of the band tonight?" or "Are you taking a foreign language this year?" Try to pick a topic, event, situation or environmental condition of mutual interest so the other person can easily join the conversation. Listen closely to this person's response so that you can reply in a manner that will open up and keep the conversation going.

❖ **Humor approach.** The humor approach works by creating a joke or a funny description about a shared event in an attempt to open up a conversation. For example, if you're at a party, you could make a joke about something that noticeably stands out. If it's a theme party, maybe the decorations look funny. This approach usually works best for those with a natural ability to make other people laugh. If you are not naturally funny, be careful not to offend the other person. By using this approach, you can easily begin a conversation after sharing some pleasant, fun humor and laughter.

Part 2: Creating and Maintaining Conversations

After you've successfully introduced yourself with a favorite approach, try to keep the conversation flowing and alive by using some of the following items:

❖ **Eye contact.** After you make an opening statement, it's important to maintain eye contact. If you look away or let your eyes drift across the room, the other person might not take your approach seriously. By maintaining eye contact, you're telling the other person you consider them important and are interested in interacting with them.

❖ **Flowing statements.** It's important to keep the conversation flowing by using statements that lead deeper into the topic. Try to avoid using a one-word response to the other person's questions. When they answer with a one-word response, acknowledge it with a flowing statement and lead them deeper into the conversation. For example, you might say, "What a beautiful sunset." If they respond, "Yes, it is," you can flow deeper with, "Yes, it sure feels good to be here. I don't get to visit here very often. How about you?" Also try to ask questions that require a more detailed response, like, "What do you think this world would be like if there weren't sunsets?" or "Sometimes I get so busy with my job I miss out on the opportunity to witness such a beautiful sunset. When was the last time you watched a sunset like this?" Once the person responds to your sunset question, they have the opportunity to come back and talk more about your job. If they don't pick up on the job lead, you can always talk about it yourself or pick up on one of their lead words by asking questions to continue the conversation.

❖ **Backup topics.** A good conversationalist is well-prepared with plenty of backup topics. Try to keep current on a variety of interesting subjects like hobbies, current events, movies, books, sports and jokes. Talk about things that interest the other person. Ask questions that you feel the other person will enjoy answering.

❖ **Listen carefully.** It is important to be a good listener. Many times in our conversations the other person will throw out cues and lead words for us to follow. If you are too consumed with your own thoughts or thinking about what to say next, you may miss the other person's lead.

❖ **Body language**. Much of our communication is nonverbal and you can pick up on a lot by watching body language during a conversation. Try to keep an approachable distance. If the other person is backing up, you're too close. By facing them and comfortably leaning toward them, you can promote a sense of interest. Touching indicates warmth and interest. If you find yourself acting nervously, try to verbalize your feelings. If the other person appears nervous, fidgeting or is using other distracting methods, try to put them at ease with some reassuring statements.

❖ **Attitude.** The right attitude is important in meeting new people. If you truly believe that "everyone is beautiful in their own way," others will naturally be attracted to you. If you believe "people are typically bad and should not be trusted," you will naturally further your own isolation. What we maintain internally in our attitudes will surface externally in our reality.

❖ **Compliments and appreciation.** In your conversation try to look for opportunities to offer some form of personal praise. Everyone likes to feel good about themselves. Offering honest forms of personal praise is a very powerful tool in your conversations and relationships. Ask yourself, "What qualities in this person can I truly admire and respect?" Let them know how you feel. Try to create situations for the other person to feel important and good about themselves. Offer them credit for new ideas or express your approval and admiration when you can. Remember to show appreciation, especially for little things that are often overlooked. Try not to take anything for granted.

❖ **Concluding a conversation.** It's important to conclude a conversation properly if you want to promote good rapport for the future. If you leave abruptly and don't express how much you enjoyed talking with this person, they may get the impression that you're not very interested in them. If you tell someone you're late for an appointment immediately after they share with you something deep and intimate, they might assume you don't really care about what they just said. Try to wind down your conversation with some form of concluding statement that lets the other person know where you stand. Are you interested in seeing or talking with them again? Did you enjoy meeting them? Share with them some of your deeper desires, needs and wishes at the conclusion of your talk.

Part 3: Activities and Events for Meeting People

Once you're comfortable with starting conversations and keeping them flowing, you'll probably be ready to participate in some social activities. If that's the case, the following items, activities and events might help you share your internal beauty with the rest of the world:

❖ Join a church group. Many churches have small groups, group ministries, Bible studies, support groups and friendship groups. They usually meet socially once a week and are committed to being open, accepting and eager to befriend new members. They pray for one another and express the love that God holds for everyone. If your local church doesn't offer these types of groups, call one that does.

❖ Consider enrolling in night classes. They will enrich your education and your social horizons.

❖ Join a bowling league. It's a fun and easy way to meet other people.

❖ Find an exercise partner at the gym.

❖ Work out during prime-time hours. Start up a conversation while waiting for classes or in line for the machines.

- Ask someone from your church out to lunch.
- Go out regardless of whether anyone else wants to go along.
- Ask your friends to introduce you to other people.
- Become well-informed on subjects that create stimulating conversation.
- Get a total makeover. Update your wardrobe, get a new look and try a new hairstyle. Not only is it a great self-concept boost, but it's a great excuse to visit stores and shopping malls.
- Make a point of meeting and getting to know your neighbors.
- Visit a comedy club. You will usually be seated with groups of people you don't know.
- Become a member of a professional organization that represents your field of business. This is a great chance to advance your professional and personal interests.
- If you are a man, consider joining an aerobics or cooking class. They are generally filled with women.
- If you are a woman, consider joining an automotive or martial arts class. They are generally filled with men.
- Don't forget to smile and work on making yourself more approachable.
- Get involved with your local political party or organization.
- Attend a bachelor auction.
- Participate in charity work. Donate your time to a hospital, soup line, shelter or church.
- Take western dance classes. They're a great place to meet new people.
- Take acting, sailing, rock climbing, self-improvement, massage therapy, golf or tennis classes, courses or lessons. They're a great place to enrich your life and relationships.
- If you're a parent, coach a little league, soccer, baseball or basketball team. Become a Boy Scout leader or join the PTA.
- Invite everyone you know to a potluck party and require that everyone bring a great dish and a new friend.
- Hang out at the local coffee/espresso bar.
- Confront and transform any forms of fear that might be holding you back from interacting socially. See the Fear chapter for more information.
- Visit your local museums, art galleries and theaters regularly.
- Start a social group of friends from work. Set up a meeting once a week, even if it's only to share an after-hour drink.
- Set a goal to initiate a conversation with one new person every day.

- ❖ Rent space for a weekend at a local swap meet or flea market. It's fun to unload your unwanted items and talk to everyone who stops by your booth.
- ❖ Turn off the television.
- ❖ Develop a close relationship with God.

Visions of Inspiration

Faithful friends are a sturdy shelter: whoever finds one has found a treasure. Faithful friends are beyond price; no amount can balance their worth. Faithful friends are life-saving medicine; and those who fear the Lord will find them. Those who fear the Lord direct their friendship aright, for as they are, so are their neighbors also.

Sirach 6: 14-17

A friend is not known in prosperity, nor is an enemy hidden in adversity. One's enemies are friendly when one prospers, but in adversity even one's friend disappears.

Sirach 12: 8-9

Pray that your loneliness may spur you into finding something to live for, great enough to die for.

Dag Hammarskjold

What then is the lonely person to do? ... He must not be passive, waiting on the sidelines for someone to rescue him. Nor must he allow himself to be absorbed by the crowd. He should not count on being carried along in singles bars, group sex, political demonstrations or on following the current trends and opinions of others... A lonely person cannot, then, wait for friends to assemble around and take care of him. Friendship, for each of us, begins with reaching out... It always hurts to try to be a friend to man. It wears us down and wears us out, but it is still more rewarding and healthier to choose the active role rather than the passive one... When a person asks that age-old question, "What can I do about my terrible loneliness?" The best answer is still, "Do something for somebody else."

Ann Landers

LOVE

TOOL 42

*E*nergy and love are a lot alike. In fact, love is a form of spiritual energy that can be generated and received in mental, physical or emotional forms. Just like energy, love can come from many sources and can be used in many ways. For example, your car generates kinetic energy when it is moving. The headlights use electrical energy to produce radiant energy when they shine. A compressed spring stores energy, and there's even energy in your car's heated and air-conditioned air. Your car's energy can be used in positive ways like driving a friend to the airport, or in negative, destructive ways like crashing through a wall into someone's living room. Your car can even give energy to and receive energy from another vehicle, like when a truck pulls a trailer.

Energy can mean different things, depending on how it is used. Have you ever heard the expression, "I energy you!"? What does that mean? Who knows – it could mean anything, just like the expression, "I love you!" What does it mean to you when someone says, "I love you"? What does this expression imply when you say it to your child? What about your relationship partner? Do you love your child the same way you love your spouse? What about people who say they love their cars? What does that mean? Are they referring to a feeling, a thought, an action or an energy? Like energy, love can mean different things to different people. So let's look at how love applies to your personal relationships and how you can use it in a healthy or unhealthy manner.

The value of love: Love is the most valuable commodity in the world. We all need love just like a fish needs water. Without love, life would not be worth living. With love in our lives we are empowered beyond belief. Without love in our lives we will shrivel up and die a slow, painful and lonely death. Love is the very essence and core of our being. It is the energy that sustains who and what we are. Everyone in life has a deep-rooted desire to love and be loved.

The different forms of love: Many times people only recognize love in its emotional form. We might hear people on television say things like, "I don't love you anymore," as they express their emotional feelings. But love is a lot more than what we feel. Love is a spiritual form of energy that can be given or received in physical, emotional or mental forms. Love usually starts in our thoughts, then spreads to the physical world through our actions, and then it will produce the emotional feelings. If you want to experience those powerful emotional feelings of love, it's necessary to think loving thoughts and produce some loving actions. If you think angry, vindictive thoughts, there is no way you will experience loving feelings or produce any loving actions. It's possible to be angry with our spouse and force ourselves to do something nice for them in our actions, like buying flowers. Pretty soon our minds kick in and after we see how happy our partner is upon receiving the gift, our emotions will follow. Love is a spiritual gift from God that starts mentally and finds its way to physical expression. But the emotional feelings we call love have very little to do with what love really is all about.

Healthy and unhealthy forms of love: Love is an energy that can be used in a positive, healthy manner or a negative, unhealthy manner. There is unconditional love, which is very accepting, supportive and forgiving. There is tough love, which is disciplined, authoritative and conforming. If your son were using drugs, you could unconditionally love him and accept his destructive behavior, hoping that he doesn't overdose and die, or you could use tough love and put him in a rehabilitation hospital in an attempt to save his life. Too much tough love can be unhealthy, just like too much unconditional love can be unhealthy.

Authentic love: God is our role model and divine teacher for authentic love. Sometimes God uses tough love when necessary and other times He uses unconditional love. He loves each of us exactly as we are. He also loves each of us enough not to leave us as we are today. God's love for us is designed for our well-being and spiritual growth. Authentic love promotes the good that is within that person. It protects, uplifts, reinforces and builds on the positive while minimizing and protecting from the negative. God is love and we are all called to love others in the same way God loves us.

The three parts of love: Relationship love consists of agape, a spiritual type of unconditional love; phileo, a brotherly type of friendship love; and eros, a romantic type of passionate love. Another way to view these three types is from the spiritual plane of agape, the physical plane of phileo and the emotional plane of eros. We experience these different types of love in different amounts and at different stages of our relationships. Many times in the beginning of our relationships we are drawn to our partner with a lot of eros (emotional love), and over time eros develops into a deeper form of phileo (brotherly love) and agape (spiritual love).

False forms of love: Love is not the infatuation stage or the sex act. Many times we feel a lot of powerful, passionate and positive emotions when we first start dating. This is called the infatuation stage, and it slowly fades in every new relationship. The infatuation stage is a calling to develop a deeper relationship with that person and to increase your ability for phileo and agape love. The infatuation stage is almost like a little carrot that God teases us with to let us know what is possible when we deepen our brotherly and unconditional forms of love. Some people think the infatuation stage should last forever. They go from one relationship to the next chasing those feelings, hoping once they find the right partner, they will experience the infatuation stage for the rest of their lives. Unfortunately, that won't happen, because the infatuation stage affects our brain chemistry almost like a form of anxiety. Our bodies can't sustain that chemical condition for very long and eventually the high wears off and the honeymoon is over. If deeper forms of spiritual and brotherly love are not developed during this time, many people simply move on to another relationship. After a lifetime of chasing infatuation, it's possible to end up lonely and isolated. The same applies to the sex act, sometimes referred to as "making love." Sex binds two people in a very deep and intimate manner. But those close feelings after sex have very little to do with the agape and phileo forms of love.

The acceptance of love: Many times we give love to our partner the same way we would like to receive it. But loving a person this way might not be in their best interests. If our gift of love fails to promote the good in the other person, they might not like it and reject it. Other times we might expect to be loved by our partners in the same way we were loved as children by our parents. For example, if your parents made you feel loved by buying you things, you might associate loving actions only in the form of gifts, jewelry, clothes and expensive toys. Your partner could be the most loving, supportive, compassionate, understanding and caring person in the world and it's possible you could overlook their loving intentions if they didn't come from a store.

If you and your partner would like to experience each other's love on a deeper level, give the following love exercise a try.

STEPS TO THE LOVE EXERCISE

The following exercise will help you and your partner strengthen and increase the amount of love in your life and relationships. The exercise is designed to be filled out by the person who desires to be more loving. But it will be very helpful the first time you try it for you and your partner to fill the form out for each other. Simply have your partner answer the questions in columns (2) through (5) by inserting a different word for every situation. By filling out the form for your partner, you will be showing them how to be more loving. After you exchange completed forms with your partner, make a commitment to follow through with these actions. Try to complete every item on the form in a few weeks' time using the checklist located in column (6). Once you have completed these items, fill out the form yourself and follow through with your loving intentions. Once the exercise is completed, start over again with different ideas. Over time it will become easier because the more love you give, the more love you receive.

If you or your partner are having a hard time filling out the form, try meditating on or praying for the answers that appear difficult. It might also be helpful to look into your past at the ways your parents expressed their love for one another. If your parents or role models were not very compassionate, you might have a hard time being compassionate to your partner. The list in column (5) contains self-love items, because if we lack self-love and self-compassion, we won't be able to be compassionate with others.

Column 1 Answer each question in columns 2 through 5, by inserting a different word from this column into each question.	Column 2 How can you be more (fill in word) with your partner?	Column 3 How can you be more (fill in word) with your children or family?	Column 4 How can you be more (fill in word) with your friends, or assicuates?	Column 5 How can you be more (fill in word) with yourself? (if applicable)	Column 6 Make a commitment to fulfill each effort in every column at least once a week. Use this space as a checklist as items are completed.
Loving Actions	Partner	Family	Others	Self	Checklist
Accepting					
Caring					
Compassionate					
Confronting					
Considerate					
Committed					
Encouraging					
Empathetic					
Forgiving					
Honest					
Interested					

Column 1 Answer each question in columns 2 through 5, by inserting a different word from this column into each question.	Column 2 How can you be more (fill in word) with your partner?	Column 3 How can you be more (fill in word) with your children or family?	Column 4 How can you be more (fill in word) with your friends, or assicuates?	Column 5 How can you be more (fill in word) with yourself? (if applicable)	Column 6 Make a commitment to fulfill each effort in every column at least once a week. Use this space as a checklist as items are completed.
Loving Actions	Partner	Family	Others	Self	Checklist
Intimate					
Motivating					
Patient					
Polite					
Positive					
Respectful					
Supportive					
Trusting					
Understanding					
Validating					

Visions of Inspiration

"Teacher, which commandment in the law is the greatest?" He said to him,
" 'You shall love the Lord your God with all your heart, and with all your
soul, and with all your mind.' This is the greatest and first commandment.
And a second is like it: 'You shall love your neighbor as yourself.' On these
two commandments hang all the law and the prophets."

Matthew 22: 36-40

Beloved, let us love one another, because love is from God; everyone
who loves is born of God and knows God. Whoever does not love does
not know God, for God is love.

1 John 4: 7-8

Love is swift, sincere, pious, pleasant, gentle, strong, patient, faithful, pru-
dent, long-suffering, and never seeking her own; for wheresoever a man
seeketh his own, there he falleth from love.

Thomas A Kempis

LUST

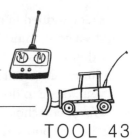

TOOL 43

Imagine driving back home late in the day and you begin to notice you're hungry. You don't have any money to buy food, but that's okay because you're only a couple of blocks from your house where your partner is preparing a home-cooked meal. As you come to a stop light, you notice a fast-food restaurant across the street. As you wait for the light to turn green, it seems your Hunger and your Logical Reasoning start having a conflict.

- ❖ The hungry part of you says, "Pull over and feed me some of that fast food."
- ❖ The logical part of you says, "No way. We're only a couple of blocks away from a home-cooked meal."
- ❖ Your hunger responds, "I will eat anything, I don't care what type of food it is. I want it right now!"
- ❖ Your logic responds, "But we don't have the money or the opportunity to buy that fast food."
- ❖ Your hunger says, "Shut up. I'm hungry. Pull over and let's pork out."
- ❖ Your reasoning says, "Never. It's impossible. We'll lose our appetites and hurt our partner because they have worked hard all day to prepare a quality home-cooked dinner."
- ❖ Your hunger replies, "I don't care who gets hurt as long as I eat right now."
- ❖ Your brain says, "What do you care about?"
- ❖ Your hunger says, "I don't care about money, time, ethics, values, morals, life, death, God, the wife, the kids or the car. There's only one thing that matters to me and that's to satisfy my cravings at any cost. The only thing I care about is food. Now pull the car over before I explode."

Your Logical Reasoning makes a good argument, but your Hungry Desire is very persistent. Both of these voices represent a part of your being and both sides feel justified in representing their own point of view. As the driver of the car, it's a good thing you have the final say. You know neither side is going to back down and you know it's not possible to choose one side over the other without causing even more problems. After listening to this internal war, what will you decide to do?

Wow, good choice. It's good to see you decided to make some kind of compromise and both sides get what they want in a healthy and safe manner. That was good thinking because it's the only way to stop your internal war from consuming your life and relationships. But what kind of compromise do you think would be acceptable in this situation? Let's look at both sides a little closer before making that decision.

God created your desires, just like a bulldozer. Your desires are easy to persuade and redirect but are impossible to stop. Your brain's logical reasoning, on the other hand, holds the bulldozer's controls and has the knowledge and decision-making power. Your brain can easily redirect your desires, just like you can redirect a bulldozer by steering it in a different direction. But your brain is not strong enough to hold that bulldozer back for very long without getting crushed into the pavement.

The best way to handle this situation would appear to be to compromise: Let your desires stop at the restaurant but only to look at the menu for a second, then redirect their attention to that home-cooked meal waiting a block away. Once your hunger starts looking at the menu, it will want to order, but it wouldn't be appropriate to order, especially since you have no money. So your brain needs to be in control during this entire process. If your brain fails to take control, those powerful bulldozer-like desires will make you order everything on the menu, attempt to eat without paying, get caught and be thrown in jail.

This little story about hunger and logical reasoning also applies to sexual desires. The hunger for food and the hunger for sex are both God-given natural desires. All of our desires are designed to serve a positive purpose in life or God wouldn't have given them to us. But just because we desire something doesn't mean it's good for us or good for our well-being and relationships. Any time we feed into our internal desires without maintaining a strong form of positive mental control, those desires have the power to consume our lives, well-being and relationships. If we surrender our logical reasoning to our drive for hunger, it will consume us in a gluttonous way. If we allow our sex drive to override our logical reasoning, it will consume us in a lustful manner. When we mix our natural desires with positive and healthy thoughts, we get positive and healthy results; when we mix negative, devaluing, harmful or destructive thoughts with our desires, we get negative and unhealthy results. God has given us all the gifts of desire; with that gift comes the responsibility of using it wisely.

The following steps may help you transform unhealthy forms of lust into powerful and healthy methods of strengthening and building your relationships.

Steps to Transforming Lust Into Healthy Forms of Desire

Step 1: Recognize Unhealthy Forms of Lust

The first step is to recognize unhealthy forms of lust that might be present in your life. Lust or sexual desire can be considered unhealthy when you:

❖ View another person as a sex object without genuine loving intentions or considerations for their spiritual, emotional, ethical or intellectual well-being.
❖ Dwell on sexual desires for another person who is outside your committed relationship or marriage.
❖ Desire another person sexually that you know is married or in a committed relationship.
❖ Allow your natural desires to override and consume your ability to reason and think in a positive and loving manner.

If your sexual desires include any of these items, it is lust and will cause damage and destruction to your relationship.

Step 2: Recognize the Damage

The next step is to recognize the damage lust causes to you, your relationships and others. The damage is usually different for married couples and single people.

Marriages and committed relationships. When you lust after another person outside your committed relationship, you lose a part of yourself, your sexual energy and your sexual attraction, all of which have been committed to your partner. As this lust continues, your partner becomes less desirable and exciting while other people outside the relationship become more attractive and desirable. These actions will undermine the passion, trust and commitment on which the relationship is built and will eventually destroy the love you hold for your partner.

Singles or in general. When you lust after another single person, you destroy your inner peace and limit your opportunities. By dwelling on lustful thoughts, you reduce the object of your attention to nothing more than a sex object. These thoughts are very destructive and inappropriate, and limit your opportunity to meet new people. By wasting time, energy and desire lusting after other people, you miss out on the opportunity to develop a healthy and satisfying relationship with them. The next time you feel aroused and attracted to a member of the opposite sex, focus your attention on meeting and getting acquainted with them in an attempt to develop a fulfilling relationship. When you decide to lust after them, you limit your growth and opportunities in a disrespectful manner.

Step 3: Make a Decision Regarding Unhealthy Thoughts

The next step is to make a decision regarding the direction of your bulldozer when you find yourself participating in lustful thoughts. This process starts when someone attracts your attention. You might find yourself experiencing feelings of sexual desire or excitement for that individual. These are normal reactions and shouldn't be denied. When you deny or repress a natural part of yoursel,f it will surface later in an indirect and unhealthy manner. It's okay to look at another person and admire their beauty, just as it's okay to look at the menu in the restaurant. It's even healthy to acknowledge their beauty mentally or verbally, but after your desires have seen the menu, they are going to want to place an order unless your mind takes control by changing the course of your bulldozer. At this point, after acknowledging your desires, your mind has several options:

❖ You can choose to change your thoughts and actions to a different subject and continue along your way.
❖ You can choose to feed into your negative lustful thoughts, eventually causing destruction and devaluation to yourself and others.
❖ Or you can choose to think positive thoughts, which will transform your desires toward your committed relationship partner and increase passion

in your existing relationship. If you're single, you can transform these thoughts into a powerful incentive to meet new people.

Step 4: Convert Desires Into Positive and Beneficial Situations

If you chose the last option, the next step is to create positive and beneficial situations from your natural desires. God created these natural desires for a good reason. When you use them in a positive and healthy manner, they will produce positive and healthy results in your life. These results will be different for married and single people.

Marriages or committed relationships. When you are attracted to a person outside your committed relationship, it's helpful to mentally focus and transform that sexual energy and desire back to your partner. You can do this with imagination techniques as you replace the person outside your relationship with your committed sexual partner. For example, if you're walking down the street and see a sexy, attractive individual, you can acknowledge their beauty and allow yourself to think sexy, passionate thoughts about your partner instead of the stranger. When you are committed to this process, you program and condition yourself to the images of your partner and create stronger passion, desire, love and commitment in your marriage.

Singles or in general. When you are attracted to single members of the opposite sex, it's helpful to mentally focus and transfer your sexual energy to the following:

❖ Admiration of the total person – mentally, spiritually, physically and emotionally.
❖ Thoughts and actions leading to compliments and verbal appreciation.
❖ Thoughts and actions leading to introductions that will allow both people to get to know and learn more about each other.

By committing yourself to this practice, you will feel better about your own sexuality, be better able to maintain an attitude of respect and honor for yourself and others, and be able to create more friendships and meaningful relationships.

Visions of Inspiration

O Lord, Father and God of my life, do not give me haughty eyes, and remove evil desire from me. Let neither gluttony nor lust overcome me, and do not give me over to shameless passion.

Sirach 23: 4-6

For this is the will of God, your sanctification: that you abstain from fornication; that each one of you know how to control your own body in holiness and honor, not with lustful passion.

1 Thessalonians 4: 3-5.5

It is easier to exclude harmful passions than to rule them, and to deny them admittance than to control them after they have been admitted.

Seneca

MAINTENANCE

TOOL 44

*H*ave you ever drained the antifreeze from your car to see how far you could drive it before the motor blows up? Your relationships might last a little longer than your car in that respect, but not by much. When it comes to maintaining your vehicle, you have two choices: You can provide excellent maintenance on a regular basis so your car will provide a lifetime of faithful service, or you can neglect the necessary maintenance work and see how long it will last. Which choice seems best to you? Would you milk your car for everything you could and then abandon it on the side of the road when the motor seized up? Or would you take the necessary time and effort to properly care for the vehicle?

With both cars and relationships comes the responsibility of maintenance. If we don't maintain our vehicles or relationships properly, they will leave us stranded on the road of life. If we provide regular, excellent maintenance for our vehicles and relationships, they will produce a lifetime of faithful service. It's that simple. Unfortunately, some people spend more time maintaining their landscape than they do their marriages and personal relationships. If you or your relationship partner are driving around in a vehicle that has never had its oil changed, the following items may be of some assistance.

When you buy a new car, it's hard to know exactly what kinds of oil, belts, filters and fluids it will need. Every make and model of car is different, just as every person is different. Your car usually comes with an owner's manual that lists its needs, but with your relationship it's not that easy. As you and your relationship partner change, so will your needs. The only way to determine what kinds of oils, belts, filters and fluids your relationship will need is through constant communication.

Every car owner has a give-and-take relationship with their vehicle. Your car gives you reliable transportation and you give it oil, gas and regular check-ups. If you fail to provide your car with gas, it will fail to provide you with reliable transportation. The same is true in your personal relationship. If one partner always takes too much, there is bound to be as much resentment as if your car were constantly in the shop charging up expensive repair bills. You might be somewhat understanding when your car is in need and extend it extra maintenance in good faith. But if you are always overextending yourself, you will eventually feel used and find more reliable transportation. In the same way, it's necessary to establish a fair give-and-take deal with your relationship partner to make sure no one feels taken advantage of or used. The only way to establish a mutual give-and-take situation is to sit down with your partner and clarify your expectations.

Once you know that your car needs to have its oil changed every 4,000 miles, it's necessary to make those trips to the garage a priority in your busy schedule. Usually when you're running from one high-pressure appointment to the next, it's hard to take the time to service your vehicle. Many times you know your car needs an oil change, but you just keep putting it off for another day. This lack of maintenance only increases the amount of stress and wear on your engine. If maintenance is neglected over a period of time, your engine will lose its performance and could blow out on you when you need it most.

The same is true in your relationship. Your partner needs regular maintenance and it's necessary to make them a high priority in your busy schedule. By keeping your equipment – and your relationship – in excellent condition, they will both be there for you in peak performance when they're needed the most.

Look at your relationship. Is it in excellent condition? Or are you experiencing a lot of expensive downtime because maintenance has been neglected? It's very expensive and painful to milk a car until it blows up. It's a lot more economical and wise to take excellent care of your vehicle so that it can provide a lifetime of faithful, fulfilling and reliable service. If you find your vehicle is in need of service, the following steps will be of assistance.

Steps to Maintaining Your Relationship

Step 1: Define Your Assumptions

It's important to clarify your expectations regarding a fair give-and-take situation. Usually relationships work best when partners share equally. When one partner regularly gives more than they receive, there's bound to be resentment. Everyone has different needs and every relationship will have a different type of give-and-take situation. The only unhealthy arrangements are ones that are not clearly defined and mutually accepted and agreed upon. It's necessary for both partners to get in touch with their own ideas, assumptions and expectations regarding what is to be given and what is to be received in the relationship. It might be helpful for you and your partner to make separate lists and begin by clearly defining what you feel comfortable giving and what you would like to receive. Make sure you include all aspects of your lives, money, finances, retirement, child care, emotional support, household duties, cleaning, cooking, quality time, leisure time, love, sex, auto maintenance, paperwork, yard work, shopping, education and employment. Address every area of your physical, mental, social, emotional and spiritual lives, opportunities, activities and interests. Take your time making the list in an effort to address everything. If you come up with more items that you give than you receive, you might be experiencing resentment and frustration from the past. It's healthy to get this out in the open.

Step 2: List Proposed Changes

The next step is to make a list of proposed changes you would like to see in your relationship. Begin by listing all the things you would like to receive but aren't receiving now. Describe how your give-and-take situation could be more fair. What would make your marriage or relationship more fulfilling? Are you giving too much overall or in any specific areas? Try to address any negative feelings or issues that surfaced from the previous step. It will probably be helpful to complete the exercise located in the Primary Human Needs chapter at this point. It contains a list of all physical, mental, social, emotional and spiritual needs. After working through the exercise, take a close look at how these needs are being fulfilled in your relationship. Take your time on these lists to make sure every aspect of your life is addressed.

Step 3: Create a Balance

The next step is to create a balanced win/win agreement. Begin by empathetically listening to and understanding your partner's concerns regarding their lists of needs and proposed changes from Steps 1 and 2. Work together to create and define an arrangement that fulfills both partners' needs.

Compromises where one person agrees to surrender something in exchange for another rarely work out over time. By working together with your partner, you can create a win/win give-and-take agreement that makes both of you happy and satisfied. See the Compromise chapter for more information.

Step 4: Perform Daily Maintenance

The next step is to maintain your relationship on a daily basis. Now that you and your partner have clearly defined ideals and goals for a mutual give-and-take situation, it's necessary to set aside the proper amount of time to fulfill them. Unfortunately, lack of time, inability to schedule or overcommitting yourself can cause major problems in your relationship. Spending quality time to experience the good times and work through the bad times is essential. Try not to get trapped by today's pressures and neglect the ones you love or take them for granted. We are all given the same amount of time every day and it's up to us how we schedule it.

Visions of Inspiration

Husbands, love your wives, just as Christ loved the church and gave himself up for her, in order to make her holy by cleansing her with the washing of water by the word, so as to present the church to himself in splendor, without a spot or wrinkle or anything of the kind – yes, so that she may be holy and without blemish. In the same way, husbands should love their wives as they do their own bodies. He who loves his wife loves himself. For no one ever hates his own body, but he nourishes and tenderly cares for it, just as Christ does for the church, because we are members of his body. "For this reason a man will leave his father and mother and be joined to his wife, and the two will become one flesh." This is a great mystery, and I am applying it to Christ and the church. Each of you, however, should love his wife as himself, and a wife should respect her husband.

Ephesians 5: 25-33

For those who want a relationship to continue: Communicate. Negotiate. Compromise. You must be able and willing to change. You must be able to consider another person's needs. You must talk with each other, not just guess what your partner is thinking. What else are words for?

Dr. Hanna Kapit

MALE & FEMALE DIFFERENCES

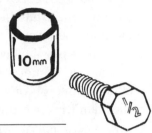

TOOL 45

Picture what it would be like if you were an auto mechanic who worked in a small town. Half the people in your town owned domestic cars and the other half owned foreign cars. Knowing that domestic cars use standard-sized nuts and bolts and foreign cars use metric sizes, what kinds of tools would you want in your tool box? Would you want to own a complete set of wrenches and sockets that fit both foreign and domestic cars, or would you use a large hammer to beat a 10mm socket onto a 1/2-inch bolt? Would a good auto mechanic appreciate the differences between standard and metric sizes, or would they overlook, disrespect and force the issues?

In the same way, the differences between men and women are just as crucial as those between foreign and domestic cars. Men and women share many similarities, just like both vehicles, but problems will arise if the differences are overlooked, disrespected or forced. Being aware of these differences is like owning both sets of tools, and creating a balance in your relationships is like using your tools.

Trying to change your partner's differences would be like trying to replace all the metric-sized bolts in your car with standard sizes. Even if that possibility existed, you would probably end up ruining a perfectly good automobile and destroying your relationship.

If you and your partner are experiencing foreign-domestic conflicts, it will be helpful to first understand more about these differences and then find a way to support, appreciate and validate each other's differences. By doing so, you will be expanding yourself through personal growth and acquiring more tools for your tool box.

There are many factors contributing to the differences between men and women. They include gender conditioning by our parents, learned behaviors through role modeling and the biochemical differences between testosterone and estrogen. But one of the major differences happens to children before they are born. Both boy and girl babies are identical during the first few weeks after conception, but then the boy babies receive an acid bath that washes over their brain, eating away the corpus colosum. This natural process in boys causes a smaller passageway between their left and right brain hemispheres. It allows men to be more unilateral in their thinking patterns and helps them to remain focused on one thing at a time, separating logic from emotion. Girl babies don't receive this chemical bath and they generally have wider passageways between the right and left brain hemispheres. This allows women to think in patterns that are more bilateral in nature. They have easier simultaneous access to the left brain's logic and the right brain's intuition, imagination and emotions.

Unilateral thinking patterns in men are usually more logical and direct, progressing in a structured order like a straight line. Bilateral thinking patterns in women usually fluctuate back and forth between logic, emotion, facts and feelings, scanning and receiving all at the same time in an almost circular manner: If a man thinks like a calculator where $(5 \times 2=10)$, a woman would think like a computer where $Z=10$ because $5 \times (5 \times .4)=Z$.

These psychological differences help explain why men are generally more comfortable communicating facts, solutions and purposes. Women, on the other hand, are generally more comfortable flowing from topic to topic and communicating in deeper emotional manners. But don't worry if you are more logical by nature – it's possible to develop your ability to be more connecting, creative, interactive and emotional. If you're more emotional by nature, it's possible to develop your ability to think logically, directly and sequentially. Neither form of thinking is better than the other, because God created both men and women perfect in their own way.

THE BALANCE EXERCISE

The following items describe some common differences between men and women. Try to determine where you and your partner stand on these issues by placing a check mark in the appropriate boxes. Then work together to create a balance that will benefit and empower your relationship.

Partner A	Partner B	
❏	❏	I tend to solve problems using an external focus, by looking outside of myself, relying on facts and past experience for guidance.
❏	❏	I tend to solve problems using an internal focus, by looking inside myself for the answers, using self-contemplation and my inner knowing as a guide.

BALANCE - We will try to look at situations from all points of view. Problems are best solved through logical facts as well as intuition and creativity.

Partner A	Partner B	
❏	❏	When I feel overwhelmed and consumed by a problem, I prefer to be by myself and work through the situation in solitude. I usually feel worse talking about a problem that is not solvable at the current time.
❏	❏	When I feel overwhelmed and consumed with a problem, I prefer to talk about it. It helps me clarify my thoughts and feel connected and supported, even if the problem is not solvable at the present time.

BALANCE - If my partner works out problems in solitude, I will give them the necessary space and time. I will try not to bother or interrupt them and trust in their ability to resolve it themselves unless they specifically ask for help. If my partner needs someone to listen and support them, I will make sure I am there to listen. I will trust in their ability to resolve it themselves unless they specifically ask for advice. I will recognize that offering unwanted advice will usually upset my partner further, regardless of the way they work through their problems.

Partner A	Partner B	
❏	❏	When something is bothering me and someone asks, "What's wrong?" and I answer, "Nothing," it means, "I

❏ ❏ don't want to talk about it now because it won't help me feel better and will only cause further frustration."

❏ ❏ When something is bothering me and someone asks, "What's wrong?" and I answer, "Nothing," it means, "If you really care about me, you would help me feel safe enough to discuss it."

BALANCE - We will try to be alert to one another's needs, respecting our partner's wishes when something is bothering one of us.

Partner A   **Partner B**

❏ ❏ I feel our relationship is going great when my partner is happy and contented with me.

❏ ❏ I feel our relationship is going great when we are mutually sharing the good times as well as the bad times.

BALANCE - By expressing our needs, feelings, wants, desires, satisfactions and dissatisfactions in a healthy manner, we can diligently confront and resolve our mutual problems in an attempt to maintain the fullest amount of peace, happiness and contentment in our relationship.

Partner A   **Partner B**

❏ ❏ I assume our relationship is a 50/50 proposition. As long as my partner is giving, I assume everything is functioning great in our relationship. I don't expect my partner to give past the point of equality. If my partner stops giving, I assume there's a problem.

❏ ❏ I assume our relationship is a 50/50 proposition. But sometimes I find myself being overly self-sacrificing. I will give of myself almost to the point of complete self-depletion, under the assumption that my partner will give back to me in my own time of need.

BALANCE - We will make the equality of our relationship a top priority. We will attempt to fulfill one another's needs to the best of our ability. To avoid resentment from overgiving, we will monitor our relationship closely and not give past the point of burnout or unfairness.

Partner
A

Partner
B

❏   ❏   I don't like anyone telling me how I should behave.

❏   ❏   I don't like anyone telling me how I should feel.

BALANCE - We will try to support and validate one another's feelings and actions by recognizing the positive intentions that underlie them.

Partner
A

Partner
B

❏   ❏   My greatest relationship needs are receiving appreciation for all that I do, being accepted just as I am and being trusted to do the right things.

❏   ❏   My greatest relationship needs are being respected for all that I do, being cared about in all that happens to me and being understood in how I am feeling.

BALANCE - Many times we give to others in the same manner we ourselves wish to receive. Instead, I will identify and give to my partner in ways they would like to receive.

Partner
A

Partner
B

❏   ❏   A lot of my identity is based on my accomplishments, occupation and career.

❏   ❏   A lot of my identity is based on my relationships and sense of connection with others.

BALANCE - We will maintain a high level of respect for our careers and relationships. We will also realize that our own personal self-worth and identity comes from inside us in who we are, not what we do.

Partner   Partner
  A   B

❏   ❏   In an argument I will defend my actions and judgments because I believe I have a good reason for all that I do.

❏   ❏   In an argument I will defend my right to feel any way I want to because I have a good reason for the emotions that I am experiencing.

BALANCE - When we argue to defend our own point of view, we make each other wrong. When my partner is made to feel wrong, they usually start to defend their own point of view with much more force. Many times our actions will offend the other partner's feelings, creating a situation where both of us are arguing to defend our own points of views. We can neutralize the situation and create a balance by listening to one another and recognizing the good intentions behind our partner's actions and feelings.

Partner   Partner
  A   B

❏   ❏   I have a greater need for independence than intimacy. I find myself pulling closer to my partner to fulfill my need for connection and closeness. When it's satisfied, I find myself pulling away to protect my sense of self-identity. When I am in need of intimacy again, I draw closer in a continuous back and forth vertical cycle.

❏   ❏   I have a greater need for intimacy than independence. I find myself reaching great highs where I feel very loving, giving and close. Other times I experience great lows where I am in need of a lot of love, support and closeness. This cycle seems to repeat itself in an up and down pattern.

BALANCE - I will try to be aware of my own cycles and those of my partner. I will try to support my partner in their downtimes, anticipating greater rewards and repayment in the uptimes. I will allow my partner their time, freedom and space to pull away when necessary. I will trust in my partner's return, anticipating stronger passion and connection when their cycle comes back around.

Visions of Inspiration

So God created humankind in his Image, in the image of God he created them; male and female he created them.

Genesis 1 : 27

Nevertheless, in the Lord woman is not independent of man or man independent of woman. For just as woman came from man, so man comes through woman; but all things come from God.

1 Corinthians 11: 11-12

The woman is increasingly aware that love alone can give her full stature, just as the man begins to discern that spirit alone can endow his life with its highest meaning. Fundamentally, therefore, both seek a psychic relation one to the other, because love needs the spirit, and the spirit love, for their fulfillment.

Carl Jung

What counts in making a happy marriage is not so much how compatible you are, but how you deal with incompatibility.

George Levinger

MANIPULATION & CONTROL

TOOL 46

*H*ave you ever observed another motorist dangerously swerving all over the road? Did you wish you could somehow control that person's car to prevent an accident? Unfortunately, the only form of control we have on the road of life is over our own driving habits. It isn't possible to control another person, because God has given everyone the gift of free will. We can try to make our roads safer by locking dangerous people in jail, but that won't limit their free will.

Take the drunk driver, for example. If they're behind the wheel of a car, that person is the only one responsible for controlling their actions. Because drunk drivers are a danger to themselves and other people on the road, society can make laws to control that type of unhealthy behavior. We can take away a drunk driver's license, car and money, but it won't stop them from getting drunk and stealing someone else's car. If that's what a drunk driver wants to do with their free will, there isn't anything anyone can do about it.

What does this have to do with your relationships? You can't control your relationship partner's driving habits, behaviors or actions and they can't control yours. You could try to get your partner thrown in jail, but even then you would only be limiting their actions, not changing their free will. Do you think the inmates and convicts in jail have a very healthy or positive relationship with the judges, police and legal system who are trying to control their behavior? Do you think you would have a very healthy relationship with your partner when they start rebelling against your attempts to control them?

Control can be healthy and necessary in dependent relationships, but it is unhealthy in independent and inter-independent relationships. Control in the form of guidance, discipline and tough love is necessary in a dependent relationship like that between a child and parent. It is healthy in society, where the drunk driver is dependent on the police, legal system and detox center to control their unhealthy and dangerous actions. It can even be healthy in the workplace where an employee is dependent on their employer for direction, job site responsibilities and training. But control in personal relationships and marriages is unhealthy because it destroys the inter-independent reality necessary to produce trust, acceptance, personal growth, genuine love and freedom. By attempting to control your partner, you are limiting their personal growth, interfering with their freedom, undermining their trust and failing to give your partner the unconditional love and acceptance they need.

Control not only harms our partners, but it usually robs us of our own personal freedom. Take for example a wife who tries to control her husband's smoking habits. Regardless of the methods she attempts, she ultimately doesn't posses the power to control another person's actions. The more she tries, the more consumed she will become in her efforts. More and more of her time, thought and energy will become consumed as she looks for clues, hides the matches and worries and wonders what her husband is doing behind her back. Eventually she will end up frustrated and hurt as her husband begins smoking more and more.

Usually we have positive and loving intentions behind our attempts to control another person. The wife who tries to control her husband doesn't want him to get lung cancer. Society has good intentions regarding the drunk driver – to prevent destruction on the roads. When a parent doesn't allow their child to play in the street, the loving intention would be for the child's safety. The loving intention behind an employer's control is probably for the company's profitability and productivity.

Any attempt you make to control or manipulate your relationship partner is simply a calling for you to express your loving intention directly and let your partner assume responsibility for their own actions, behaviors and driving habits. Ultimate control in life belongs to God; no one has the right to manipulate or control another.

Look at your partner's driving habits. Do you find yourself wanting to grab the wheel, or do you allow your partner to drive the car themselves? What about the way you are treated by your partner? Do you feel controlled, manipulated or detained in jail? It's not easy to express your loving intentions and sit back and accept your partner's decisions. It will take a great deal of internal strength, courage and self-control to allow your partner their own personal freedom.

We have all been given an equal amount of personal power by God. When a situation arises outside of our control, we can use our power in a healthy manner by expressing our loving intentions and allowing others their own personal freedom. Or we can use our personal power in an unhealthy manner by attempting to control their actions in manipulative ways. If your loving intentions are valid, there really is no need to violate another through futile attempts to control and manipulate.

If you or your partner have been spending a lot of time in jail, the following steps will help you transform any manipulative or controlling desires into positive and loving intentions.

Steps to Transforming Manipulation and Control Into Positive Intentions

Step 1: Recognize Your Unhealthy Behavior

Any time we try to influence another person without directly expressing our intentions, we are participating in manipulation. Manipulative and controlling behaviors can take many forms. For example, anytime we play helpless, the cute little boy or girl act, use guilt trips, withhold our love and support, give unwanted advice or give the cold shoulder, we are participating in manipulative behaviors. Any time we belittle our partner with criticism, make threats, demand or use domineering force, we are participating in controlling behaviors. Try working with your partner to identify issues of control or any indirect methods of manipulative influence. Then make a list of items that you want to control in another person (like smoking) and what method you have chosen to use (like hiding the matches and guilt trips).

Step 2: Identify Your Underlying Intentions

Try to identify your positive and loving intentions behind every item on the list from Step 1. For example, in the smoking husband situation you might be deeply concerned for his health and don't want him to suffer heart and lung problems, or you might think he would feel and smell better if he quit. After you discover your loving and positive intentions, write them down because it's necessary to share these intentions with your partner in an upcoming step.

Step 3: Confront Your Fears

Beneath every controlling person is the fear that something will not work out or will go wrong. The common belief is that if you're not there to offer your assistance, nothing will get done and things won't be handled properly. If someone doesn't control your partner, a loss will be suffered or the worst possible situation will occur. Look at the explanations from the list of positive and loving intentions from Step 2. If you look closely at these items, you will discover your fears. For example, the wife who tries to control her husband's smoking probably perceives it as a threat to their relationship. The underlying fear would be losing her husband's health and her relationship with him. Look at the worst possible outcome or the most unfavorable results regarding the situation you are trying to control. After you have identified your underlying fears, it's necessary to transform them. See the Fear chapter for more information on how to do this.

Step 4: Heal the Past

The next step is healing any past childhood issues where your controlling or manipulative behaviors were learned. Usually people who are very controlling grew up in very controlling or very chaotic childhood environments. Maybe your over-protective parents didn't want you to experience harm, so they controlled your every move. As adults these people will treat others they love in the same way their parents treated them. Other times manipulative people were unable to get their childhood needs met in a direct manner so they learned to deal with the world indirectly through manipulation. For example, children usually ask for ice cream directly. If you didn't have your ice cream requests granted, you might have learned to fake an injury or throw a manipulative fit to receive your desires. Maybe you felt very unsafe and unloved growing up in a chaotic environment that lacked structure and control. If so, it's possible you developed your present day controlling behavior as a form of self-protection.

If your parents or childhood role models were overly controlling, non-controlling or didn't satisfy your wants and needs in a healthy manner, some healing work will help reprogram your negative subconscious tendencies. To break these subconscious control issues, you will need to go back in your imagination and reexperience the negative feelings, then give yourself the love and support you never received. Begin by following the information and directions listed in the Healing chapter. Have your adult self speak comforting and reassuring words of love and support to your child self when you have been hurt by another person's controlling behavior. Allow your child self to express their needs, make their own mistakes, learn from them and still have everything turn out for the best. Imagine your adult self and your parents offering support and encouragement, rather than controlling you with orders and directions.

Step 5: Make Daily Efforts

Once you have transformed your fears and healed your childhood experiences, you can work on your daily efforts and behaviors. Begin by stopping yourself before you try to control or manipulate your partner. Next, directly express your loving intentions (from Step 2) and allow yourself to fully accept your partner's decisions. Slowly this process will help you become a more loving person and your partner will have more motivation to change themselves. Some other daily efforts that will help you become more loving and less controlling are: Learn to appreciate your partner's imperfections by converting your negative criticism. Try to find the greater truth in everything because it's impossible for someone to have all the answers. Be more open-minded and try to empathetically listen to your partner's point of view. Practice being a true leader by inspiring and motivating your partner to follow your lead instead of telling them what to do. Give your partner the chance to make their own mistakes and grow from the lessons. Develop a greater trust in God to take care of things that lie outside your control.

Anti-Manipulation/Control Exercise

This exercise is designed to help prevent you from being manipulated or controlled by others. It works almost like a broken record. All you need to do is keep saying NO, by repeating the same response over and over again. It might be necessary to acknowledge some form of truth in what the other party has to say so you don't appear rude. For example, if a controlling friend calls you up and pressures you to go out when you don't want to, your response might be, "No thanks, I feel tired." If they don't respect your decision, they might respond with, "Come on. It's going to be lots of fun!" Your response: "It does sound fun (finding the truth), but I'm too tired to go out (repeating your original response using the broken record)." Their response: "You can sleep in tomorrow, it will be OK." Your response: "You're right. I could plan to sleep in tomorrow (finding the truth), but I'm too tired tonight (broken record)." Their response: "Come on, it won't be the same without you. I haven't seen you in a while." Your response: "Let's plan something later, but tonight I'm too tired to go out." Their response: "I would rather go this evening." Your response: "I realize that, but I'm too tired to go out tonight." This technique will quickly wear down even the most persistent manipulator. It usually doesn't take very long for the other party to acknowledge your free will and accept your decision.

Visions of Inspiration

You were taught to put away your former way of life, your old self, corrupt and deluded by its lusts, and to be renewed in the spirit of your minds, and to clothe yourselves with the new self, created according to the likeness of God in true righteousness and holiness. So then, putting away false-hood, let all of us speak the truth to our neighbors, for we are members of one another.

Ephesians 4: 22-25

You shouldn't go into a relationship expecting that he or she will change. If you pick your mate wisely, you will both make adjustments, but it's unfair to expect your future mate to make basic changes. Put yourself in his or her shoes. Would you want to be overhauled or would you expect your mate to love you as you are?

Dr. Zev Wanderer and Erika Fabian

MEDITATION

TOOL 47

*H*ave you ever heard the expression "A mechanic is only as good as their tools"? Some mechanics are judged by the quality and condition of their tools. If you needed to hire a mechanic for your own shop, would you choose a mechanic who owns a large tool box with over 5000 of the best automotive tools ever made, or a mechanic who owns a handful of worn household items they carried around in a paper bag? If you don't own good equipment and take care of it, you will have a hard time getting your work accomplished.

The same applies to your life and relationships, except that God has already given you all the mental, emotional and spiritual tools you will ever need. We are all given the biggest tool box available and it's completely loaded. Unfortunately, if our mental and spiritual tools are not used and maintained on a regular basis, they will get rusty, lost, stolen and dull. Our tools, just like anything else in life, need constant maintenance if we want to ensure their well-being. A great way to keep your tools in excellent condition is by practicing meditation on a regular basis. Meditation will sharpen every tool in your mental tool box, just like a file will sharpen a saw.

Let's take a few minutes to look at the condition of your everyday tools and evaluate their sharpness. Attention is one of the tools you use every day. If you couldn't focus your attention on a specific task, it would be impossible to get anything accomplished; it wouldn't even be possible to read this book if your attention were bouncing around like a bunch of monkeys. So to test how sharp your attention tool is, take this little test: For the next two minutes don't think about monkeys. Don't imagine what they look like, don't picture what they would do if they got into your house. Don't pay any attention to their silly behaviors. You're free to think about anything you want except for those furry creatures with long tails. Stop reading at the end of this sentence and count the number of monkey thoughts your mind is not supposed to think about for the next 120 seconds.

If during this exercise monkeys took control of your mind, then it's safe to say your tool of attention could use a little sharpening. It's easy to see how meditation can strengthen the tool of attention, but did you know it can be used for many things like reducing the amount of stress and anxiety in your life, making the forgiveness process easier, solving problems and increasing your self-acceptance? Meditation can be used to build your self-concept, strengthen your connection to your Inner Self and expand your self-aware-ness. You can even use meditation techniques to take a vivid and lively vaca-tion when you want, all right inside your mind.

Practicing meditation daily is a powerful tool that can be used to sharpen your other tools, and improve many aspects within your life. Unfortunately, some people have developed negative perceptions about meditation. With the New Age movement there have been a lot of harmful meditations that focus on spiritual beings other than God, like channeling through spirit guides and using a demonic chant for the mantra. These types of meditations that don't focus on God or the self can be unhealthy and dangerous. All the exercises contained in this chapter focus on the self. Meditations that focus on God can be considered a form of prayer and are described in the Prayer chapter.

The following items will help you sharpen your existing tools so they can be productively used in all your interactions. These items have been divided into two parts: The first part describes the actual mechanics of meditation – how to breathe, possession of the body and reaching a quiet state of mind. The second part describes some examples of different methods and styles of meditation and an explanation of their benefits.

The Mechanics of Meditation

Selecting the Time and Place

Try to find a convenient time to meditate on a regular basis. You will need a quiet, comfortable environment where you can concentrate. For many peo-ple the most convenient time is either early in the morning or late in the evening. Experiment with different times of day to find a time and place that works best for you. By meditating at a certain place and time on a regular basis, you will develop a natural rhythm that will promote deeper experiences.

Selecting the Length and Frequency

As you meditate, your ability to focus your mind and awareness will increase. If you are just beginning, it might make the process easier if you start with shorter sessions of around 10 minutes to 15 minutes. As you learn to gain control over your awareness, you can increase the length of your meditation period. Most people reach a quiet state of mind after about 20 minutes. Any time spent after that will deepen your experience. Don't try to force yourself for longer periods of time; more is not necessarily better. Simply trust your intuitive and instinctive ability when you naturally drift back into consciousness.

Breathing and Posture

It's important to be comfortable while meditating to prevent any unnecessary distractions that can be caused by aches or pains. If you're too comfortable or lying down, you run the risk of falling asleep. The best position is usually sitting in a chair or sitting on the floor in a lotus, half lotus or Indian-style position. Regardless of the position you choose, keep your back, neck and spinal column erect and straight. Relax your entire body, keeping it stable, still and comfortable. When you begin a meditation, focus on your breathing patterns. Take deep, slow breaths and hold them for a while before you slowly exhale. Some meditation styles focus solely on breathing, but most exercises allow you to breathe normally after the meditation has been started.

Concentration

Effective meditation requires discipline and the proper balance of awareness. It's necessary to create and maintain a state of awareness that is just right. If you become overly passive, it's possible to fall asleep. If you become overly intellectual, it will produce a thinking session. You will need to experiment through trial and error to achieve your own proper balance of awareness. When an interruption intrudes, like a past memory, a background noise or a random thought, simply let it go as quickly as it came. Gently guide your attention back to the subject of your focus. Don't allow these distractions any more awareness than possible. If a physical distraction like an itch arises, strengthen your disciplinary ability to ignore it and it will disappear. Equally apply the efforts of disciplinary focus to internal distractions (random thoughts and memories) and external distractions (itches and noises).

Different Meditative Methods and Styles

The following are examples of different meditative methods and styles. There are unlimited ways these examples can be converted or combined. Feel free to use or modify them any way that works best for you.

Physical Awareness Meditation

This exercise will help you become more relaxed and aware of your body. Begin by focusing awareness on each part of your body. Start with the top of your head and work your way down to your feet. Imagine your awareness in the form of an invisible source of energy. As this energy is effortlessly passed over different parts of your body, it helps you feel even the smallest sensations. Don't let the energy pass over any part of your body that isn't perfectly relaxed. Next, focus on the different groups of muscles. Allow yourself to become aware of every sensation you might be experiencing. Now focus your awareness on your skin. Notice any areas that are warmer, colder, softer or tighter. Don't try to change anything, just be aware. Now focus your awareness on your Inner Self. This center of your being is not part of your physical body, even though it resides at your body's special center. Just remain there noticing any sensations until you are ready to conclude the meditation.

Breathing Meditation

This exercise will help you feel better about yourself, promote more inner peace and promote a stronger state of self-acceptance. It's similar to the physical awareness meditation because it begins by focusing on your breathing patterns. Take deep breaths for a few minutes, and in your mind's eye imagine your physical self residing in a stream of very bright light. This light comes from God and is empowered with a specific form of energy. Depending on your own situation, this energy might bring *peace*, love, forgiveness or graces. (Pick one according to your needs.) As you breathe in this white light of *peace*, you can feel it enter your body. As you exhale, you release any negativity, tension, fear, anger or sadness you may be experiencing. Pretty soon your body begins to change color as you are completely cleansed by the bright light. Move your awareness of this process through every part of your body. After you are thoroughly cleansed, close the meditation.

Affirmation Meditation

This exercise can help improve your self-concept and self-acceptance. It works by focusing your attention on a group of words, sometimes referred to as a Mantra. Pick a Mantra with a personal meaning similar to an affirmation. Some examples might be I deserve to be loved, I love myself, God loves me, Blessed be God, I am safe. Next, silently voice these words along with your breathing pattern to find a rhythm that requires the least amount of effort. Allow these words to flow through your being. If your mind begins to wander, gently return your consciousness to the Mantra. After about 20 minutes close your meditation.

Self-Awareness Meditation

This exercise will help you uncover problems or situations in your life that need attention. Begin by focusing on your breathing as your mind and body relax for a few minutes. Then imagine your awareness in the form of a powerful detective. Be on the lookout for any clues. Carefully watch and examine any thoughts, feelings or perceptions that arise in your consciousness. Don't try to change or hide anything. Allow the detective to uncover any problems or distorted perceptions of reality that need attention. Allow the detective to ask questions. What might this mean? What would God want me to do here? Before you close your meditation, spend a few minutes picking out an assignment you can start in the next 24 hours that will help correct, fix or amend any problems you uncovered.

Spiritual Unity Meditation

This exercise will help you develop a stronger relationship with your Inner Self by viewing your true sense of self independent of your body, mind and actions. Begin by focusing your awareness on your Inner Self. Find the heart-like center where your spirit resides. Next, allow your awareness to enter your Inner Self and spend some time in that peaceful, loving and powerful part of your being. Then allow your Inner Self to float outside of your body. Imagine seeing your body in its meditative posture below. Study your body and realize that you have a body but you are more than that body. Study your thoughts. You have an intellect and mind, but you are more than what you think. Study your feelings and emotions. They are a part of you, but they do not govern you. Your truest sense of self is separate and independent from all these aspects, but at the same time it is connected. Now imagine your body getting up and going about its daily routine. Your Inner Self is still floating around outside of your body, studying its every move. Your Inner Self is evaluating the situation trying to identify ways your body, mind, emotions and spirit can coexist in more harmony. Maybe in an attempt to discover some areas in need of growth and change, your Inner Self will point out a situation where an angry emotion consumes your being. Maybe you watch as your body gets drunk in an attempt to control the mind, emotions and spirit. Allow your Inner Self to guide you anywhere it wants. Before you close your meditation identify some ways to create a more complete sense of harmony, unity and balance between the physical, mental, emotional and spiritual parts of your being.

Visualization Meditation

This exercise can be used to reduce anxiety, fear and stress, and strengthen your creative ability. There are many ways to use it, the simplest of which is to imagine a fixed image in your mind. It could be anything like a candle flame, a religious object, a flower or an entire meadow. By focusing your mind on this fixed object, you will strengthen your ability to control your thoughts. Many times your mind is accustomed to jumping from thought to thought. Focusing on a single object requires and builds discipline. If your awareness starts to drift away, gently bring it back to the fixed object. Another method is to imagine a peaceful setting when you need to relax. Simply take your own vacation in your awareness any time you need one. Imagine yourself floating off to the beaches, mountains, meadows or your favorite Bible scenes. Make sure you include all your senses in this journey. How does this experience smell, feel, look, sound, touch and taste? After taking a week-long trip in your mind – that only took 20 minutes – close the meditation and come back completely refreshed.

Forgiveness Meditation

This exercise will help promote self-forgiveness as well as the forgiveness of others. Begin by imagining yourself kneeling face-to-face before God. Use all your senses to make the situation real. What does everything look, smell, sound and feel like? Now in your awareness ask God for forgiveness for all your past mistakes. All you feel is His overflowing love and forgiveness. Now someone from your past who has hurt and violated you in some manner comes and kneels down beside you. They also ask for God's forgiveness and He grants it as well. God asks both of you to reconcile your differences, and to make amends and restitution to each other. So begin by studying the situation from the other person's point of view. You might need to vent some negative emotions first. God and the other person are there to listen, work through the pain and allow God's love and grace the opportunity to heal the situation.

Visions of Inspiration

I commune with my heart in the night; I meditate and search my spirit: I will meditate on all your work, and muse on your mighty deeds.
Psalm 77: 6, 12

I will meditate on your precepts, and fix my eyes on your ways. I will delight in your statutes; I will not forget your word. I revere your commandments, which I love, and I will meditate on your statutes.
Psalm 119: 15, 16, 48

Where there is charity and wisdom, there is neither fear nor ignorance. Where there is patience and humility, there is neither anger nor vexation. Where there is poverty and joy, there is neither greed nor avarice. Where there is peace and meditation, there is neither anxiety nor doubt.
St. Francis of Assisi

This art of resting the mind and the power of dismissing from it all care and worry is probably one of the secrets of energy in our great men.
Captain J. A. Hadfield

NEW COVENANT

TOOL 48

$\mathcal{T}$aking out an insurance policy on your car is not only a very wise thing to do, but is probably required by law where you live. For only a few dollars a day you can buy hundreds of thousands of dollars worth of coverage. When your car is insured, you can drive to your destination with confidence, knowing that if an accident happens, you are financially protected. Imagine what would happen if you didn't buy insurance and you were involved in an accident that was your fault. You would be financially responsible for both vehicles, ambulance charges, hospital bills, the anesthesiologist, x-rays, medical supplies, follow-up doctor bills, physical rehabilitation, permanent disability compensation, time lost from work and many other forms of compensation. Imagine what would happen if you were responsible for a multicar pileup where ten people went to the hospital.

Because insurance is so easy to afford and convenient to get, why would anyone drive through life uninsured? Do you and your relationship partner have insurance on your vehicles? Or are you willing to risk everything to save a few dollars?

The same insurance principle applies to our relationship with God as well. The insurance policy in this story represents the new covenant, the car that needs insurance represents our lives and the destination in life toward which we all are traveling is our afterlife existence. The new covenant is almost like an insurance policy issued by God. It's a contract we can enter into that insures our safe arrival at our afterlife destination. Without entering this contract, we are driving through life uninsured, risking everything. People buy insurance because it is easy to afford and will safely ensure their well-being. The new covenant, on the other hand, won't cost you a penny, is very simple to enter into and will insure your spiritual and afterlife well-being. If insurance policies weren't important and necessary, they probably wouldn't exist. If the new covenant were not important and necessary, God wouldn't have offered it to us. The question is, do you and your partner have insurance to cover your spiritual liability in the afterlife? If not, you might want to sign up on the deal God is currently offering before it's too late.

The new covenant is a Bible-based agreement we can enter into with God. Some people believe it is the only way to establish a genuine relationship with God. Others believe there are many roads in life that will all eventually lead to God. Unfortunately, the other roads in life don't come with a written guarantee from God. Just because you believe in God doesn't mean your afterlife existence is insured. You can also believe in the benefit of insurance, but until you pay the premium and bind the coverage in writing, you are driving around uninsured. Why take a chance on the other roads in life when the new covenant is written, guaranteed, simple, convenient, empowering and offers a lot of promises and benefits? Those benefits are outlined in the Bible as follows:

- ❖ Eternal life (John 3: 16);
- ❖ Abundant life (John 10: 10);
- ❖ Forgiveness of sins (Acts 2: 38);
- ❖ Gifts of wisdom (James 1: 5);
- ❖ To meet all our needs (Philippians 4: 19);
- ❖ To receive the gift of the Holy Spirit (Acts 2: 38);
- ❖ To become a child of God (John 1: 12).

To better understand how the new covenant works, you might find it helpful to look back through history to better understand God's relationship with His people. One of the first covenants God established was based on a set of laws known as the Torah, as described in the Old Testament in the chapters of Exodus, Leviticus, Numbers and Deuteronomy. In the first covenant God offers a blessing to all those who faithfully follow His laws. In Deuteronomy 28: 1-14, the promise reads: *"If you will only obey the Lord your God, by diligently observing all his commandments that I am commanding you today, the Lord your God will set you high above all the nations of the earth; all these blessings shall come upon you and overtake you, if you obey the Lord your God."* Then the promise continues with a list of available blessings. In Deuteronomy 28: 15-68, this covenant also comes with a list of curses for those who fail to follow God's laws: *"But if you will not obey the Lord your God by diligently observing all his commandments and decrees, which I am commanding you today, then all these curses shall come upon you and overtake you."* Then an extensive list of curses follows.

Now apparently the old covenant didn't work very well, because the people followed God's laws externally in their actions but failed to remain faithful internally in their hearts, thoughts and desires. God, being all-knowing, knew this would happen and set up the new covenant. In Jeremiah 31: 31-34, God talks about the coming of the new covenant: *"The days are surely coming, says the Lord, when I will make a new covenant with the house of Israel and the house of Judah. It will not be like the covenant that I made with their ancestors when I took them by the hand to bring them out of the land of Egypt – a covenant that they broke, though I was their husband, says the Lord. But this is the covenant that I will make with the house of Israel after those days, says the Lord: I will put my law within them, and I will write it on their hearts; and I will be their God, and they shall be my people. No longer shall they teach one another, or say to each other, "Know the Lord," for they shall all know me, from the least of them to the greatest, says the Lord; for I will forgive their iniquity, and remember their sin no more."*

God realized that it might be hard for His people to change their belief system from the old covenant to the new covenant. So He prepared them in advance by promising the coming of the Messiah, who was to present His people with the new covenant. The Messiah was predicted more than 300 times in the Old Testament and was promised by God to deliver His people from oppression by bringing them the new covenant. God provided proof of the identity of His chosen Messiah by using 60 major prophecies and 270 ramifications that were written in advance and to be fulfilled by God's chosen one.

Some of the prophecies that the Messiah would have to fulfill to prove His identity before He would deliver the New Covenant are:

In Genesis 9 and 10, all the nations of the world can be traced to the three sons of Noah – Shem, Jupheth and Ham. God eliminated two-thirds of all their descendants from which the Messiah would come by blessing the lineage of Shem. Then in the year 2000 BC, God called Abraham out of Ur of the Chaldees, and God stated in Genesis 12 and 17 that the Messiah will be one of Abraham's descendants. Abraham had two sons, Isaac and Ishmael, and half of Abraham's descendants were eliminated when God selected his second son, Isaac, in Genesis 22. Isaac had two sons, Jacob and Esau, and then God chose the line of Jacob in Genesis 28. Jacob had twelve sons, out of whom developed the twelve tribes of Israel, as per Genesis 35. God chose the tribe of Judah and eliminated eleven-twelfths of the Israelite tribes. Then from all the family lines in Judah's tribe, God chose the line of Jesse in Isaiah 11. Jesse had eight children and in Jeremiah 23: 5, God eliminated seven-eighths of Jesse's family line, where the Messiah will come from the house of David.

Then God eliminated all the cities of the world except Bethlehem as the birthplace for the Messiah in Micah 5: 2. Through a series of prophecies, God chose a time period in which the Messiah would enter the world in Malachi 3:1 and Haggai 2: 7-9, where the Messiah would come while the Temple of Jerusalem was still standing. (This Temple was destroyed in 70 AD and has not been rebuilt.)

God further defines the exact time in which the Messiah will enter the world in Isaiah 40: 3 and Malachi 3: 1, when there will be a forerunner who will precede him by announcing and declaring the Messiah's birth, as the voice in the wilderness, one preparing the way of the Lord.

In Isaiah 7: 14, God states how the Messiah will be born. In Zachariah 12 God set prophecies predicting the death of the Messiah. There are many other prophecies that define how the Messiah would be betrayed, how his own people would reject him and not believe in his miracles, how he would be called Emmanuel, and how his birthplace would suffer the Massacre of the Infants. These prophecies also state how the Messiah would deal kindly with the Gentiles and that many would believe in him, how he would speak in parables and heal many, how he would triumphantly enter the city of Jerusalem before his death and how his throne would be an Eternal Throne.

All these prophecies and many more were made by God and written through God's prophets, anywhere from four hundred years to thousands of years before they were all fulfilled by God's anointed Messiah, Jesus Christ. Jesus himself has also confirmed his identity, authority and partnership with God in presenting the new covenant. For it is written:

- ❖ If you knew me, you would know my Father also. (John 8: 19);
- ❖ Whoever sees me sees Him who sent me. (John 12: 45);
- ❖ Whoever hates me hates my Father also. (John 15: 23);
- ❖ All may honor the son just as they honor the Father. Anyone who does not honor the son does not honor the Father who sent him. (John 5: 23).

If you don't believe that Jesus Christ is God's chosen Messiah and new covenant, pray to God and ask Him to show you the truth. If anyone seeks after the truth with their whole being, body, mind and sprit, God will reveal Himself and the truth to that person. If you or your partner have not entered into the new covenant, you may be interested in the following items.

Entering Into the New Covenant

Faith and Confidence

Entering into the new covenant with God requires faith and confidence. Many people in life place their faith, confidence and search for meaning and purpose in various things like money, careers, reputation, other people, religious practices, laws, government and the self. But God calls everyone to develop their faith and confidence in Him above all. In Hebrews 11: 6 it states, *"Without faith it is impossible to please God."* Faith is more than a simple belief in something. Our faith needs to be real and built on every day. Belief in God and in God's son Jesus Christ is not enough, because in Hebrews 4: 2 it states, *"For indeed the good news came to us just as to them: but the message they heard did not benefit them, because they were not united by faith with those who listened."* When we combine what we believe with faith, our responses will become empowered by doing what God has asked of us, because in James 2: 17 it states, *"So faith by itself, if it has no works, is dead."* It's necessary to place faith and confidence in God the Father and in Jesus Christ, His son. In John 14: 6, Jesus states, *"I am the way, and the truth, and the life. No one comes to the Father except through me."*

Repentance

Entering into the new covenant requires repentance because man is sinful and that sin has separated us from God. In Romans 3: 23, it is written, *"Since all have sinned and fall short of the Glory of God,"* and in Ecclesiastes 7: 20, *"Surely there is no one on earth so righteous as to do good without ever sinning."* God created mankind in His image, with free will and freedom of choice. It is necessary to choose God first over our own self-willed or sinful ways. In Isaiah 59: 2, it states, *"Rather, your iniquities have been barriers between you and your God, and your sins have hidden his face from you so that he does not hear."* In Romans 6: 23 it states, *"For the wages of sin is death."* When we participate in behavior we know is wrong, we sin. When we fail to do what we know is right, we also sin. It's important to acknowledge the fact that sin has separated us from God. By acknowledging our sins and turning away from them, we can begin to grow toward God. In Acts 2: 38, it states, *"Repent, and be baptized every one of you in the name of Jesus Christ so that your sins may be forgiven; and you will receive the gift of the Holy Spirit."*

Receiving and Confession

Before you can enter into the new covenant, you will need to receive and confess Jesus Christ as your personal Lord and Savior. In Matthew 10: 32-33, Jesus states, *"Everyone therefore who acknowledges me before others, I also will acknowledge before my Father in heaven; but whoever denies me before others, I also will deny before my Father in heaven."* And in Romans 10: 9-10 it states, *"Because if you confess with your lips that Jesus is Lord and believe in your heart that God raised him from the dead, you will be saved. For one believes with the heart and so is justified, and one confesses with the mouth and so is saved."* It's necessary to invite Jesus into your life, to place your trust in Him and believe that He died for you and rose three days later in victory over death. Trusting Christ is more than mentally recognizing Him as your Lord and Savior by faith. In 1 John 5: 11-13, the testimony states, *"God gave us eternal life, and this life is in his Son. Whoever has the Son has life; whoever does not have the Son of God does not have life. I write these things to you who believe in the name of the Son of God, so that you may know that you have eternal life."*

Baptism

Before you can enter into the new covenant, you will need to be baptized. Being baptized is a visible God-chosen and God-commanded response to our faith. In the Greek language from which our New Testament was translated, the word baptize means "to dip, plunge, or immerse." The early churches baptized by immersion (see Acts 8: 35-39). Jesus was also immersed (see Matthew 3: 13-17). In Acts 22: 16, it is written *"And now why do you delay? Get up, be baptized, and have your sins washed away, calling His name."* In Matthew 28: 18-20, in Jesus' last words to his disciples He said, *"All authority in heaven and on earth has been given to me. Go therefore and make disciples of all nations, baptizing them in the name of the Father and of the Son and of the Holy Spirit, and teaching them to obey everything that I have commanded you. And remember, I am with you always, to the end of the age."* In John 3: 5, Jesus answered, *"Very truly, I tell you, no one can enter the Kingdom of God without being born of water and spirit."*

Service and Fellowship

Once you have been baptized and have accepted Jesus as your personal Lord and Savior, it is important to accept your responsibility for the task of helping others come to God. In Mark 16: 15, it states, *"Go into all the world and proclaim the good news to the whole creation."* In Romans 10: 14,15, it states, *"But how are they to call on one in whom they have not believed? And how are they to believe in one of whom they have never heard? And how are they to hear without someone to proclaim him? And how are they to proclaim him unless they are sent?"* As it is written, *"How beautiful are the feet of those who bring good news!"* It's helpful to study and meditate on the scriptures regularly. By reading the Bible daily, you will become more aware of what God wants to do for you and through you (see 2nd Timothy 2: 15). Make sure you talk frequently to God in prayer and share with Him your joys, sorrows, needs and all in your life (see Philippines 4: 6). Regular church attendance will also help you share in growth, worship, fellowship, counsel and teaching with others who have trusted the Lord Jesus Christ (see Hebrews 10: 25).

A PRAYER TO START

Lord Jesus Christ, I need you. I know I am a sinner. Thank you for dying on the cross for my sins. Forgive me and cleanse me. I am willing to open the door of my life and heart unto you to receive you as my personal Lord and Savior. Take control of my life and help me to be the kind of person you created and want me to be. Give me the courage and determination to get baptized immediately. Help me to seek after you through your teachings, with my whole life, being, body, spirit, heart, soul and mind forever always. Amen.

For any further information or questions,
please contact your local church.

Visions of Inspiration

I am the true vine, and my Father is the vinegrower. He removes every branch in me that bears no fruit. Every branch that bears fruit he prunes to make it bear more fruit. You have already been cleansed by the word that I have spoken to you. Abide in me as I abide in you. Just as the branch cannot bear fruit by itself unless it abides in the vine, neither can you unless you abide in me. I am the vine, you are the branches. Those who abide in me and I in them bear much fruit, because apart from me you can do nothing. Whoever does not abide in me is thrown away like a branch and withers; such branches are gathered, thrown into the fire, and burned. If you abide in me, and my words abide in you, ask for whatever you wish, and it will be done for you.

John 15: 1-7

PASSION

TOOL 49

*I*n most new cars a radio comes as standard equipment. Some radios only have AM stations, others have AM and FM and advanced models have AM/FM Cassette and CD capability. But just because your car is equipped with a stereo doesn't mean you will automatically appreciate its benefits. If you don't appreciate the equipment itself, you might have a hard time enjoying the music it can produce. If you don't know how to tune the radio and adjust all of its settings properly, it still might not be very enjoyable or pleasurable.

Everyone comes equipped with natural desires or drives, just like every car can come equipped with a radio. Your car's radio works just like your natural desires. The stereo equipment can produce music just like your natural drives can produce passion. People who invest time, energy and appreciation in their equipment usually produce more passionate music and listening experiences. Like music, passion can bring joy, pleasure and happiness if you respect it and use it in a proper manner. Passion can also produce problems and conflicts if you approach it with negative and unhealthy thoughts.

If you and your partner are interested in creating more passion, you may want to look at the following car radio examples to find out how:

❖ **Mechanical problems.** It's difficult to enjoy music on your car radio if you are having mechanical problems and are distracted while driving. If your car has a flat tire and the engine is overheating, all the songs on the radio would probably sound distracting and irritable. If your mind is consumed with negativity and frustration, it won't be possible to enjoy a really good song. The same is true in your relationships. If you and your partner are experiencing unmet emotional needs and resentment from the lack of forgiveness, you won't be able to enjoy the sweet sounds of that passionate music in your relationship.

❖ **Minor adjustments.** Some songs on the radio sound better with deeper bass settings and less treble. Other times the Dolby noise reduction or surround sound might help enhance your musical listening experiences. Making minor adjustments to the equalizer buttons on the stereo might make all the difference in the world. The same is true with the passion in your relationship. Maybe your partner would experience more passion if you were to make some minor adjustments to certain aspects of your life. Any time you help yourself or your partner become more attractive and desirable, you increase the amount of passion in the relationship.

- **Mental perceptions.** The difference between a good song and a bad song on the radio is the amount and type of your mental perceptions. If you can't find value and worth in country music, you might view it as unpleasant background noise; if you do find value and worth in country music, it's probably pleasant to your ears. The same is true with your partner. Passion is created by finding worth and value in your mate. If you can't think positive, loving and desirable thoughts about your partner, passion will turn to unpleasant background noise.

- **Internal desires.** If you sit around the office all day thinking about the sweet pleasure of music, once you get off work all the songs on the radio will sound great. That's because a strong desire to hear the radio will be programmed in your being by your mental activity. If you sit around the office all day wanting to hear songs on someone else's stereo equipment, you won't be able to enjoy music in your own car. The same is true in your relationships. Passion is created by feeding your internal desires with loving thoughts for another person. If you allow yourself to desire another person other than your committed partner, you produce lust. This unhealthy desire for a third person will deteriorate the passion in your own relationship.

- **Time together.** If you listened to the radio 24 hours a day, eventually nothing would sound good anymore. If you listened to your favorite song over and over again, you would get sick of that as well. The same is true of your relationship. If you and your partner are constantly smothering each other with too much time together, eventually you will get sick of each other and your passion will decrease. Passion is created by being away from your partner long enough to miss them and then coming back together again in a passionate sympathy of excitement.

Take a look at the amount of passion in your relationship. It's normal for some of the passionate feelings that you experience during the infatuation stage to develop into a more compassionate form of love for your partner. But passion or eros is still an important part of love. The lack of passion is usually a calling to think and act in a more loving way toward your partner. If you or your partner fail to enjoy the sweet rhythm of pleasurable music in your relationship, the following steps may help you get out to life's music festivals more often.

Steps to Restoring Passion in Your Relationship

Step 1: Maintain Your Relationship

The first step is constant relationship maintenance. It is difficult to maintain passion in any relationship when there is neglect in any of the following areas: unmet primary human needs, resentment from the lack of forgiveness, unresolved problems, lack of intimacy, poor communication or lust.

Step 2: List Your Attractive Qualities

The next step is for each partner to write a two-part list of attractive qualities. Begin the first part by describing all the qualities, attributes and characteristics you find attractive about your partner or other people. In the second part describe all the qualities, attributes and characteristics that are attractive about yourself. Include in both of these lists the physical, mental, emotional and spiritual aspects. When you finish, share and discuss these items with your partner. The purpose of this step is to develop a deeper understanding of what you and your partner find attractive.

Step 3: Become More Desirable

Becoming more desirable as a mutual event can be a fun way to create more passion in your relationship. Begin by creating another two-part list that suggests ways to become more attractive, sexy and desirable. Write the first list about yourself and the second about your partner. Try to make this a positive and productive event that brings out each other's attractiveness. Support all your suggestions with positive reasons and reassurances. Some examples might be: Agree to work out together on a regular basis. Agree to select items from each other's wardrobe to be donated to charity. Replace these items by shopping together and selecting items that bring out the best in each other. Consider anything else that can increase desirability, like hairstyles, self-esteem, cleanliness, attitude changes or role-playing.

Step 4: Change Your Perceptions

You can increase the passion in your relationship by evaluating, improving and maintaining healthy thoughts and perceptions about each other. In the beginning of a relationship when passion is strong, you usually hold positive mental perceptions about your partner. Usually when you first meet the person of your dreams, they can do no wrong. You worship the ground they walk on and think positive, loving and desirable thoughts about them all day. These thoughts create the passionate feelings you experience. Unfortunately, over time if you stop thinking the passionate thoughts, you will stop experiencing the passionate feelings. When you become consumed with negativity and focus on your partner's faults instead of their advantages, the passion fades away. Look at the following items to see if they can help you restore healthy thoughts and perceptions, which in turn will restore your passion for each other.

❖ Make a firm decision to never again criticize your partner in thought, word or action. See the Criticism chapter for more information.

❖ Build your passion by crediting positive situations to your partner. When you feel or experience a good situation in life, find a way to relate that to your partner. When you're feeling happy, successful, sexy, excited, playful or alive, simply give your partner the mental credit. For example, if you're at work feeling happy, tell yourself, "Wow, I feel great and I have (my partner) to thank."

❖ Make it a priority to regularly recognize your partner's efforts, ability, talents and accomplishments, and express your appreciation and respect every chance you get.

❖ Be specific and genuine with your verbal affirmations.

❖ Be sensitive to your partner's shortcomings and think of ways to help support them.

Step 5: Change Your External Behaviors

It's important that you don't spend too much time together, because passion is created by drawing close to your partner after being apart long enough to miss them. If you or your partner are always hanging around each other, the passion can decrease, just as it would if you listened to your favorite song over and over again. It might be beneficial to develop more friends, hobbies, interests and activities outside your relationship.

Another external method to increase passion is to change the ways you express your love and desire for each other. There are many ways you can express your internal desires: in words, physically by touching, externally with little things like notes, flowers or dating activities. Try a fun exercise by agreeing with your partner to use a different way of expressing your love for a certain period of time. Pick a method different from your normal expression patterns. If you're a verbal person, agree to show your love physically for a week. If you're a physical person, show your partner your love verbally or emotionally. At the end of the time period, share all the ways you recognized your partner's efforts.

Step 6: Do Past Healing Work

If you view your natural desires or sexuality in a negative or shameful manner, some past healing work will probably be necessary. Many times people from our past taught us that sexuality is dirty, bad, evil and sinful, in an attempt to keep us from discovering the unhealthy ways it can be used. God created our natural drives, bodies and sexuality and said, "It was all good." He only asks us to respect these gifts and use them in a respectful and healthy manner. If you don't like your sexuality, think it's dirty or shameful, or if you have experienced some form of sexual assault, incest or rape in the past, it's necessary to heal these negative past experiences before the gifts of passion can be fully appreciated. Trace any negative or unhealthy attitudes regarding your sexuality back in the past where they were learned. Then heal those issues by using the information listed in the Healing chapter.

Step 7: Practice This Passionate Fantasy Exercise

You can increase the amount of passion in your relationship by intentionally thinking sexy, romantic and passionate thoughts about your committed partner on a regular basis. Romantic books and movies are a good way to spark your imagination. Replace the fictional characters with your partner and create your own endings. When you experience sexual, romantic or passionate thoughts and feelings that don't involve your partner, stop yourself and include your partner in the mental scene.

After you have developed a healthy imagination, passion can be further increased by keeping a mutual fantasy journal. This journal works similar to the intimacy journal (see the Intimacy chapter for more information.), except the fantasy journal is a written story that describes you and your partner's wildest fantasies. Every day the story progresses as each partner adds their entries. Maybe your story starts out in a peaceful, secluded mountain setting or a tropical island setting. Include descriptive details about your passionate thoughts and expressions. Be sure to include all your senses. Vividly imagine and describe everything like sight, touch, feelings, smell, taste and sound. Living out your greatest fantasies together on paper will create more passionate music in real life. Allow your love, desire and passion for each other to grow as powerful as imagination itself.

Visions of Inspiration

Let love be genuine; hate what is evil, hold fast to what is good; love one another with mutual affection; outdo one another in showing honor.

Romans 12: 9-10

It is with our passions, as it is with fire and water, they are good servants but bad masters.

Sir Roger L'Estrange

On life's vast ocean diversely we sail, Reason the card, but passion is the gale.

Pope

PAST EXPERIENCES & TRANSFERENCE

TOOL 50

*I*magine driving a car with a crystal clear windshield. Then one day as you go traveling down the road, a rock suddenly flies up and puts a large crack in your line of vision. Would you take the time and effort to fix the damage, or would you just keep driving? Let's pretend you didn't have the resources or tools to fix the damage, so you kept driving. Then as you turn the next corner, another rock flies up and now there's another crack in your windshield. Didn't your view of the world just get a little more distorted?

Now imagine having driven the same car since childhood, and every time you suffered a negative or harmful past experience, your windshield developed another crack. How is all that damage going to affect your current view of the world? You can still see the road, but what happens when you become involved in a relationship and your partner is driving a car with a similar windshield? Do you think you could both look at the same road and see the same thing? Do you think you could maintain different views of the road and still maneuver your cars through the obstacle course of life without crashing into one another? If you became accustomed to the cracks in your own windshield, could your relationship partner – who is viewing the world through their own windshield – tell you any different?

The moral to this story is simple: Everyone views the world through their own windshield and everyone was born with a crystal clear view. When a negative experience happened in the past, a rock would chip the windshield. If we received the love and support we needed at the time, the chipped glass would be repaired and our natural view of the world would be restored. If we were hurt and never received the love and support we needed to heal that event, the chip in the glass would remain there distorting our perceptions and view of the road. This is called transference or projection because the hurt and pain from an unhealed event in the past would be transferred or projected onto people and situations in the present. These unhealed past experiences continue to distort our perceptions unless we do some glass repair work to heal the damage.

To understand how pain from the past is transferred to the present, let's look at the life of a girl who was emotionally abused by her alcoholic father. As you can imagine, her windshield got the gravel truck treatment. As an adult she will be conditioned to view the world through her distorted windshield. To her everything is fine and her childhood really wasn't that bad because, after all, she can still see the road. But her problems usually become apparent when she becomes involved in relationships.

Years later when this girl is dating there could be nine really nice guys who wanted to treat her like a princess and one jerk who wanted to abuse her. Unfortunately, she wouldn't be interested or attracted to nice guys and her first couple of boyfriends would probably exhibit the same abusive, alcoholic behavior her father did. To her this would be normal because that's how she was treated in the past and that's how she views the world. In time this girl would become tired of suffering in an abusive relationship and realize she doesn't deserve to be emotionally abused, criticized, beaten up or neglected. Slowly she would start loving that hurt part of herself that doesn't deserve to be abused and her windshield would get a little clearer. Eventually, when she embraced enough of the pain her father inflicted on her, she would say, "No way. I will never date another alcoholic again."

Her next relationship partner probably would not drink, but would probably be emotionally abusive, just like what she was accustomed to in the past. It's likely she would make a choice to suffer some more before she would begin to love that hurt part of herself. Once she repaired a little more of that glass by doing the necessary healing work, she would say, "No more emotionally abusive jerks."

Her next relationship partner would probably have a windshield similar to her own. But if her windshield were not crystal clear, she might overreact and imagine she was being abused, even though she wasn't. Once both people completed their healing work, they could drive through the relationship obstacle course of life without worrying about crashing because of transference issues.

Take a look at your current relationship problems, then look at your past relationship history. Are you still seeking the same partner? Which is more scary: to embrace the pain of your past, or to continue to allow it in the present? Unfortunately, no one escapes childhood without suffering pain, lessons and negative frightening experiences. The question is how much love and support did you receive when something negative happened? The only way to escape childhood with a clear windshield is if both your parents were around 100 percent of the time to make sure your feelings never got hurt. But even then your parents would need clear windshields themselves and enough of their own self-love to love you properly.

Fortunately, repairing your past is like repairing a broken bone. After it's healed, it grows back stronger than before. People who suffered a rough childhood and have successfully embraced their pain through healing work have the potential to be the strongest, most loving, caring and compassionate individuals on the face of this planet. That's because once you can embrace your own pain, you can successfully embrace the pain of others.

If you and your partner are sick of crashing into one another, the following steps will help you heal the negative past experiences that contribute to your present day transference issues.

Steps to Healing Transference Issues

Step 1: Overcome Avoidance Behaviors

The first step in the healing process is to overcome anything that keeps us from dealing with our negative past experiences. It's amazing how many forms of avoidance or denial we can create in an attempt to avoid dealing with unpleasant past memories, experiences and negative feelings. Addiction is one of the main methods we use, since all forms of addiction are mood-altering. We don't like how we feel or what our Inner Self is trying to say, so we attempt to make ourselves feel better through obsessive and compulsive behaviors.

There are numerous things to which we can become addicted in an attempt to distract ourselves from our problems. One of the simplest forms of avoidance is denial. These people might say, "I had a great childhood. Nothing bad has ever happened to me." But pleasure and pain go hand-in-hand. Everyone in life will experience pain. All children cry, and no one escapes childhood or life without their share of hurt, pain and trauma. A child can suffer just as much rejection from an alcoholic parent as they can from other kids on the playground at school. Both experiences have the same potential to distort the child's view of the world if they didn't receive the love and support they needed. So the question isn't, "How bad was your childhood?" but, "How loving, supportive, caring, sensitive, considerate and compassionate were your parents and role models?"

People who deny past issues are simply too scared to confront and deal with them in a healthy manner, or are so detached from their emotions and Inner Self that they can't feel anything. In either event, before anyone can fix their windshield, it will be necessary to get in touch with the Inner Self, and overcome addictions or forms of denial that keep them from acknowledging their negative past experiences.

Step 2: Connect the Past to the Present

Many times tracing your present situations of transference to their original source in the past is difficult, because when you experience conflict, you tend to view the situation through your own set of glasses and blame your partner. One way you can realize the damage in your own windshield is by looking for signs that you are overreacting in a negative manner.

For example, let's say that as a child you were abandoned by your parents. If these negative past experiences were never healed, they will be repressed behind the doors of your subconscious. Then every time your relationship partner is ten minutes late, you may be consumed by those same abandonment feelings you experienced in the past. When your partner is late, the door to your subconscious is opened and all the hurt from your past joins the present day hurt caused by your partner. After 15 minutes, when your hurt is overwhelming, you may find yourself saying, "How could my partner be so inconsiderate? What if they got in an accident? What if they never returned?" As soon as your partner walks through the door you blow up with 80 percent hurt from the past and 20 percent hurt from the present. The situation is very real to you, but your partner will accuse you of overreacting. After all, they were only 15 minutes late. So the next time you find yourself overreacting this way, trace your present day problems to their underlying source from your past.

It might also be helpful to keep a daily journal and record the times you experience overwhelming hurt feelings. Look for signs of overreaction and identify the underlying reasons behind your hurt feelings. Once you have identified how and why you were hurt, trace those feelings back to a similar situation in your past. Usually one event will lead you to another until you have uncovered the root causes or incidents. One of the fastest ways to trace your present transference issue to its root source in your past is to write your life story, or to make a list of the 100 worst events you ever suffered. Also try to keep an ongoing list of negative memories that keep recurring in your thoughts. If a negative past experience pops up in your memory for no apparent reason, it is likely your Inner Self asking you to remove it from your subconscious.

Sometimes the feeling of transference is different from other types of hurt or upset emotions. It might be beneficial to learn to identify that nasty transference monster as soon it shows up. Then stop yourself and take time to trace those feelings back to their source from your past.

Step 3: Heal Your Past

Once you have identified the source of your transference incidents, the next step is to heal situations where you have suffered negative past experience or a lack of love and support.

Once you have identified your issues, it's necessary to do some past healing work. To begin this process, go back in your memory and relive the negative experience or the experiences lacking love and support. It's necessary to feel, sense and vent all of your negative emotions. Make sure you work through your primary emotions of anger, fear, sadness, guilt, frustration, disappointment, concern and inadequacy. After you have felt, experienced and released those negative feelings, there will be room in your subconscious to replace them with positive emotions. Find a way to give yourself the love, support, caring, understanding, consideration, respect, patience, forgiveness, honesty, compassion, truth, gentleness, encouragement and acceptance you never received in the past.

Once you and your partner have identified the negative past experiences that are contributing to your relationship problems, make a commitment to each other to work together until every issue is healed. There are two different healing techniques that you can use and the instructions for both are listed in the Healing chapter. Even if the healing process takes you an hour a night for several months, you will both constantly and continually receive its benefits for the rest of your life. The more past healing work you do, the easier it will be to appreciate your past experiences and develop your ability to be stronger and more loving individuals.

Visions of Inspiration

The Lord passed before him, and proclaimed, "The Lord, the Lord, a God merciful and gracious, slow to anger, and abounding in steadfast love and faithfulness, keeping steadfast love for the thousandth generation, forgiving iniquity and transgression and sin, yet by no means clearing the guilty, but visiting the iniquity of the parents upon the children and the children's children, to the third and the fourth generation."

Exodus 34: 6-7

He called a child, whom he put among them, and said, "Truly I tell you, unless you change and become like children, you will never enter the kingdom of heaven."

Matthew 18:2-3

The repressed memory is like a noisy intruder being thrown out of the concert hall. You can throw him out, but he will bang on the door and continue to disturb the concert. The analyst opens the door and says, "If you promise to behave yourself, you can come back in."

Theodor Reik

PATIENCE

TOOL 51

*H*ave you ever watched an impatient driver at a stoplight? They take off at a high rate of speed only to have to stop again at the next intersection. They race their cars from one red light to another, almost like they think the light will turn green if they are the first one to get there. Have you ever driven your car in an impatient manner like this, speeding around and cutting people off only to end up at the same stoplight with everyone else? Have you ever been patient enough to time how fast your car is traveling so you hit all the green lights without having to stop? How much faster do you think an impatient driver arrives at their destination compared with a patient driver? Have you ever had to ride in a car with an impatient person? Did you enjoy the ride, or was it stressful and unpleasant?

Being impatient has its good points as well as its bad points. If you don't like yourself very much and don't enjoy living life, then being impatient is a great advantage, since it's just another distraction people use to avoid connecting with their true self. Many times the lack of patience is used to avoid personal growth, self-awareness and a connection with other people. But if you enjoy living life and being happy, then being impatient is a great disadvantage, since the lack of patience will only destroy your peace of mind, happiness and enjoyment of life. Haste makes waste, and the only way to conserve time is by thoughtful planning. Being impatient rarely conserves time and only makes people feel stressed. No one likes being around an impatient person because they project their frustration and anxiety on those around them.

Take a look at your driving habits. Do you race around, only to get frustrated at all the red lights life has to offer? Or do you enjoy the beautiful scenery while patiently hitting all the green lights? What about your relationship partner? If you or your partner could use more enjoyment, happiness and peace in your life, the following steps will help you obtain it by practicing more patience.

Steps to Practicing More Patience

Step 1: Identify the Lack of Patience

The first step is to identify the lack of patience in your life and the events where it most commonly occurs. It will be helpful to make a list of activities or situations in your life that promote your impatient attitude. Some possible items could be standing in line, traffic jams, children and their activities, coworkers, other people who appear slower, or activities where you are more efficient. By identifying these situations beforehand, you will be better prepared to change your future behaviors. Try to stop yourself as soon as you notice yourself growing impatient. The faster you are able to catch yourself, the easier it will be to modify your responses.

Step 2: Identify and Change your Perceptions

After you have noticed an uncomfortable lack of patience, the next step is to check your mental thoughts and perceptions. Many times you will find distorted thought processes or perceptions that contribute to your impatient attitude. Ten of the most common forms of distorted thinking are listed in the Perceptions chapter. It's helpful to identify distorted perceptions and replace them with healthy thoughts.

As an example of how distorted thoughts create an impatient attitude, let's pretend you're standing in line at a store. You may begin thinking to yourself things like: "This line is going to make me late and ruin my whole day (all or none thinking)," "What a bunch of incompetent people. Why can't they have their checks written before the clerk asks them for the dollar amount (name calling)?" "I probably won't have enough time to stop at the cleaners (predicting the future)," "It's all my partner's fault. Why didn't they stop in here last night (blaming)?" or "This shouldn't be happening to me. I'll never do this again. I must get out of here (authoritative)."

If you think and believe these distorted perceptions, you create your own impatient tendencies. By monitoring your thoughts and perceptions, making sure they accurately represent the truth, you will be better prepared to patiently enjoy life, even in the longest of lines. It might also be helpful to write a daily anxiety letter (see the Anxiety chapter for more information). Impatient feelings are closely related to feelings of anxiety. As you address any impatient situation in these letters, your ability to remain in emotional control will grow stronger.

Step 3: Change Your Focus

Next, it will be helpful to change the focus of your awareness. Many times impatient people become so consumed with the external focus on time, lines, people and being late they fail to notice how they are reacting internally. For example, if you are acting impatient while standing in line, your body is probably tense, breathing rate is shallow, you may be yelling at others and pacing back and forth, or you may be trying to distract yourself by tapping your foot on the floor or your keys on the counter. If that's the case, it will be helpful to change your focus from your external environment to your internal environment. Begin by relaxing your muscles, breathing deeply and trying to find pleasure in the little things that are all around you. Say a prayer or contemplate the amount of patience God holds for every one of us. Carry around your daily planner, books or laptop computer to convert downtime to productive time. Try working on your acting skills and pretend you have all the time and patience in the world. Try doing the opposite of what you are doing. If you're frowning, try smiling. If you're isolating yourself, try being friendly and talking to others around you. If you're yelling and acting frustrated, try speaking very softly and acting concerned.

Step 4: Do Healing Work

If your impatient tendencies persist after you have worked on the first three steps, it might be necessary to complete some healing work. No one was born impatient; it is either a learned response or a conditioned subconscious tendency. If your parents were impatient role models, you would probably grow up acting impatiently, just like them. If your role model's impatient behavior didn't hurt you, then your impatience is probably a learned behavior. New behaviors can be learned simply by acting differently over a period of time. If your parents treated you in a disrespectful, impatient manner, like acting rude or critical of your existence or not accepting you for who you are, or were overly demanding, or acted upset and hostile when you didn't perform to their expectations, or rushed around and stepped on your rights when you got in their way, you would probably feel worthless and disrespected. A child who grew up under these conditions would be deeply hurt by their parents' impatient behavior. Those negative past experiences could be repressed in that person's subconscious retention area, causing them to treat other people in the same hurtful, impatient way.

If this is the case, the best way to free yourself from the unhealthy past programming is to do some healing work. You can begin by writing down a large list of any unhealthy, violating and negative impatient behaviors you have suffered in the past from your parents or role models. If you know your parents acted in unhealthy ways but can't remember the specific incidents, it's possible to make a list of hypothetical situations and imagine how their hurtful behavior would affect a young child whose only desire was to be loved. Once you give yourself permission to blame the past, you can begin the process of reprogramming your subconscious tendencies by following the directions listed in the Healing chapter. Go back to all the situations in your past where you were treated in unhealthy, impatient manners. Experience again and vent the negative emotions, and replace them with the love, respect and support that you deserved but did not receive.

Visions of Inspiration

Knowing trees, I understand the meaning of patience. Knowing grass, I can appreciate persistence.

Hal Borland

For this reason, since the day we heard it, we have not ceased praying for you and asking that you may be filled with the knowledge of God's will in all spiritual wisdom and understanding, so that you may lead lives worthy of the Lord, fully pleasing to him, as you bear fruit in every good work and as you grow in the knowledge of God. May you be made strong with all the strength that comes from his glorious power, and may you be prepared to endure everything with patience, while joyfully giving thanks to the Father, who has enabled you to share in the inheritance of the saints in the light.

Colossians 1 :9-12

Patience serves as a protection against wrongs as clothes do against cold. For if you put on more clothes as the cold increases, it will have no power to hurt you. So in like manner you must grow in patience when you meet with great wrongs, and they will then be powerless to vex your mind.

Leonardo da Vinci

PERCEPTIONS

TOOL 52

*P*icture for a minute a highly advance prototype of a future car. This vehicle is different from any car ever built before because it doesn't have manual controls. There are no pedals to push, no levers to move and no buttons to turn. It doesn't even have a steering wheel. This prototype operates solely by the thoughts and perceptions of the driver. All you do is think a thought like "turn left," and the car automatically turns left. If you think thoughts like "go faster, turn up the radio and roll down the window," they all happen simultaneously.

Like other things in life, this highly advanced machine can be used in healthy or unhealthy ways depending on the driver's perception of the truth. For example, what do you think would happen if you were driving this futuristic car and you started thinking false thoughts about an imaginary object blocking the road? If your only option were to turn left into a ditch to avoid a collision, would the car automatically obey your mental orders? What would happen if you were driving at high speed over a bridge and you accidentally thought a "turn left" order? Would the car read your thoughts, turn left and send you tumbling into the river below?

The only way this car would be safe is if all your thoughts actually represented the truth. If you let your thoughts wander or started thinking false perceptions, you would probably experience a lot of accidents and auto body damage in life. The same situation applies to your life and relationships because your brain works just like that futuristic car. God created you with the same highly advanced automatic thought processing system. If you think distorted thoughts that don't accurately represent the truth, your brain will automatically produce the corresponding emotional and physical consequences. For example, if you are walking through a field thinking thoughts like, "I just know a big snake is going to jump out of the brush and bite me," you would probably find yourself checking behind every rock, listening for snake noises and looking for movement in the nearby bushes. You may even find yourself leaving the field in terror, all because your brain automatically produced the physical and emotional consequences of what you think.

If you think distorted thoughts that are not based on trust (like an imaginary snake), then you can expect a lot of negative reactions and physical damage running through the field. If you monitor your thoughts and perceptions to make sure they accurately represent the truth (like: I never saw a snake around here before, and I don't know if there are any.), then you will be better equipped to carry out your plans with a happy and peaceful mindset.

Another way to remember how this works is to use the A-B-C method. "A" is for action: You're waiting on someone who is late. "B" is for brain: You have the choice to give your brain two types of orders – one based on the truth, and the other based on false assumptions. "C" is for consequences: Your brain will automatically produce the appropriate consequences based on the orders and information it is given. For example, imagine you're waiting for someone who is late. If you think a truthful thought like, "I don't know why they're late, but I'll wait as long as I can and make good use of this time before I need to leave for my next appointment," then your brain will produce the appropriate consequences of peacefulness, relaxation and productivity. But if you give your brain a false and unrealistic perception of the truth like, "I know the other party has intentionally stood me up. If they really cared about me, they would be here early. They must be meeting people more important than me. I must not be very important at all." If you think these types of thoughts, your brain will produce the appropriate consequences of depression, hopelessness and anger. The types of messages you send to your brain will not change events outside of your control. The only difference is that distorted perceptions will leave you feeling unhappy, upset and hurt while realistic perceptions based on the truth will only leave you feeling that way only when it's unavoidable.

If you are experiencing negative emotions on a regular basis, it will be helpful to change your perceptions to more accurately represent the truth. Take a look at your own life and your relationship partner's life. How often do become upset with each other? How often do you experience anxiety, impatience, anger, fear, depression, jealousy, problems, conflicts and unmet expectations? Chances are that most of your problems and negative experiences can be greatly minimized simply by changing your perceptions so they accurately represent the truth. If you only try one exercise this book has to offer, put some effort into this one because you will notice incredible results almost immediately.

There are ten very common forms of distorted thinking patterns that most of us use every day. By using any of these regularly, we almost guarantee ourselves a dangerous ride in that highly advanced futuristic car. If you are tired of unnecessary accidents and emotional body damage in your life and relationships, learn to identify and avoid using these common forms of distorted thinking patterns. Then start seeking the truth because the truth will set you free. The following steps are designed to help you recognize and change unhealthy thinking patterns or perceptions in your life and relationships.

Steps to Preventing Unhealthy Forms of Distorted Perceptions and Thinking Patterns

Step 1: Monitor Your Thoughts and Perceptions

The first step is to monitor the thoughts that lead to your perceptions. We are all capable of thinking anything in unlimited amounts. Random thoughts alone don't influence our feelings and emotions; it's our belief in those thoughts that creates our perceptions. When our perceptions become distorted, we will experience unnecessary hurt, problems and difficulties in life. The best way to monitor your thoughts is to write them down when you're upset, unhappy, annoyed, hurt or feeling bad about yourself or others. It might be helpful to carry a small notepad where these thoughts can be recorded. Next, pay close attention to your emotions and the way you are feeling. When you feel upset or hurt, write down the thoughts that occurred before, during and after the situation. Once you are familiar with the basic principles of the exercise, it's possible to correct distorted thinking patterns in your mind without using the notepad. But because of the frequency of our thoughts and the stubbornness of preconditioned perceptions, this exercise will be more effective if you practice it in the written form until it's familiar.

Step 2: Identify Distorted Thinking Patterns

You can evaluate the accuracy of the thoughts you wrote down in Step 1 by checking them against this list of common distorted thinking patterns. These thinking patterns distort the truth in one form or another by focusing on the negative and not taking the entire situation into account. The ten most common forms of distorted thinking are:

A. **All-or-none thinking.** Viewing situations in black-and-white; known as dual-ity thinking. If one event falls short of your expectations, you view the whole situation in a negative manner or as a total failure. Everything is either all good or all bad, all right or all wrong.

B. **Perfectionism.** Picking a single negative event and dwelling on it exclu-sively. If the overall outcome of your goal is achieved, with the exception of one small mistake, you focus your attention on that insignificant part rather than on the successful whole.

C. **Predicting the future.** Predicting negative future events without proof, substantiation or facts to support your conclusion. For example, you might tell yourself, "Something bad is going to happen. I just know it," or "I know things will never work out."

D. **Blaming.** Perceiving problems in your life as another person's fault, and blaming other people for circumstances that are within your own control and responsibility. When this happens, you feel victimized and helpless because you have failed to acknowledge your own personal power and responsibility you need to resolve the situation.

E. **Failing to recognize the positive.** Denying, rejecting or discounting the positive events in your life. For example, you do a great job in another per-son's eyes but fail to acknowledge that fact yourself. You might tell your-self, "Anyone could have done that just as well, and probably better." These perceptions usually leave you feeling unrewarded and inadequate.

F. **Justification through feelings.** Perceiving or justifying events or situations in life through your own feelings and emotions. For example, you feel angry and therefore assume you have been treated in an unjust manner. You feel hopeless and therefore assume the situation is hopeless.

G. **Mind reading.** Assuming the thoughts and actions of others without first asking about their situations or intentions. If you assume another person was reacting negatively to your involvement or presence without any ver-bal or factual proof, you would be trying to read that person's mind. If your partner is late coming home and you automatically assume they are trying to avoid you or are having an affair, your thought may not accu-rately represent the truth.

H. **Martyrdom.** Automatically assuming personal responsibility for situations or events outside your control. For example, you assume you're being punished for a natural disaster or that you are a bad parent because your child got in a fight at school.

I. **Name calling.** Calling yourself or others names like "stupid" when a negative situation occurs. You might make mistakes and your actions in hindsight might be wrong, but you aren't stupid. Thinking that you are only leaves you feeling frustrated and hostile, or leaves you with low self-esteem and little hope for constructive improvement.

J. **Authoritativeness.** Using words like "should," "must," "always" and "never." Using these words generally sets you up for failure. These words focus your perceptions on an absolute reality which seldom is true. Using these words can lead to self-defeating thoughts and perceptions, and cause negative emotions for no apparent reason. For example, thoughts like, "I *should* have done better," may lead to guilt, "This *shouldn't* be happening," may leave you feeling frustrated, "I'm *always* falling behind," may leave you feeling depressed and, "That will *never* happen," may leave you feeling hopeless when it does.

It's important to recognize these ten forms of distorted thinking patterns in your everyday thoughts, perceptions, words and statements. If the thoughts you have recorded in your notebook coincide with one or more of these distorted patterns, it will be beneficial to replace that perception with one closer to the truth. If you and your partner are working on this exercise together, try to memorize the ten forms of distorted thinking and point out unhealthy statements during the natural course of your conversations. For example, if you're late coming home from work one day and your relationship partner says, "You're *always* late," you can point out the Authoritative perspective and say, "Yes, today I was late, but I'm not *always* late." This agreement may help make you and your partner more aware of unhealthy thinking patterns that cause unnecessary negative feelings in your relationship.

To check your ability to recognize distorted thinking, try to match the following statements with the ten examples of distorted thinking. The answers are located at the end of this chapter.

_____ It's your fault.
_____ I shouldn't be feeling this way.
_____ You're *never* on time.
_____ I just know I'm going to fail the test.
_____ These things are good and these things are bad.
_____ It's not good enough unless it's perfect.
_____ I can't find anything good about the situation.
_____ I know you're trying to avoid me.

_____ Look at the way that jerk is driving.
_____ It's my own fault that my husband beats me.

Step 3: Replace Distorted Thoughts and Perceptions

Once you have identified distorted perceptions (either by the notepad method, self-awareness or by having your partner point it out for you), you can replace those perceptions with ones that accurately represent the truth in a positive, realistic way. You can accomplish this by using the following methods:

❖ **Examine the facts.** Instead of assuming your thoughts and perceptions are true, try examining the actual evidence. The best way to test a negative theory is to confront your own fears, ask the proper questions and perform the necessary experiments to try to prove your assumptions.

❖ **Weigh the advantages.** You can consider the advantages and disadvantages of thinking in a distorted manner. For example, if you're in a traffic jam and late to an appointment, the disadvantages of thinking distorted thoughts are anxiety, stress and frustration; the advantages of replacing distorted thoughts are patience, acceptance and relaxation. Neither way of thinking will have an effect on the traffic jam – only on the way you feel.

❖ **Change your language.** Instead of thinking and speaking with authoritative words like "should," "never," "must" and "always," you can use statements like "I would prefer," "I would appreciate" and "Perhaps you might."

❖ **Practice self-compassion.** Instead of mentally beating yourself up in a harsh and critical manner, you can learn new ways to be more compassionate and understanding. See the chapters on Criticism, Compassion and Affirmations for more information. Another way to be more compassionate is to talk to yourself the same way you would to a close friend. For example, if you're going to take a test, some distorted perceptions and thoughts you have might be, "I'm going to fail," or "I'm not smart enough." But would you talk that way to your close friend?

❖ **Focus on problem solving.** Instead of being consumed with negative and distorted thoughts of guilt and blame, you can focus your attention, efforts and thoughts on solving existing problems. Find out what needs to be done and focus your time, energy and efforts on making it happen.

❖ **Think positively.** Instead of concentrating on plans that didn't work out, you can look at the advantages and gifts that are present in the learning experience. Instead of viewing situations as a total failure, you can evaluate them as a partial success and a valuable lesson.

* **Do past healing.** If you're having a hard time replacing recurring distorted thinking patterns with the truth, you might need to trace those thoughts back to their original repressed source in your past and do the necessary healing work before they will disappear from your life. For example, if you have unresolved issues about being abandoned as a child and are experiencing distorted thoughts every time your spouse is late coming home, you might need to trace those feelings and thoughts back in your past to when you were abandoned by your parents. Then work your way through the healing process so you can break the cycle of distorted abandonment perceptions. For more information see the Past Experience/Transference chapter.

* **Pray.** Turning to God in prayer is one of the most powerful ways of dealing with any situation life can throw your way. Ask God for assistance in providing the lessons necessary to clarify your stubborn distorted thinking patterns. Also try asking yourself the following questions: "What would God like for me to think regarding this situation?" "How would God perceive these events?" "What lesson can I learn from these situations if I view them in a positive, truthful way?"

Visions of Inspiration

No one after lighting a lamp puts it in a cellar, but on the lampstand so that those who enter may see the light. Your eye is the lamp of your body. If your eye is healthy, your whole body is full of light; but if it is not healthy, your body is full of darkness. Therefore consider whether the light in you is not darkness. If then your whole body is full of light, with no part of it in darkness, it will be as full of light as when a lamp gives you light with its rays.

Luke 11: 33-36

Finally, beloved, whatever is true, whatever is honorable, whatever is just, whatever is pure, whatever is pleasing, whatever is commendable, if there is any excellence and if there is anything worthy of praise, think about these things.

Phillipians 4: 8

Speak the truth by all means; be bold and fearless in your rebuke of error, and in your keener rebuke of wrongdoing; but be human, and loving, and gentle, and brotherly, the while.

W.N. Punshon

(Answers: D, F, J, C, A, B, E, G, I, H)

PERFECTIONISM

TOOL 53

$\mathcal{I}$magine what it would be like if God owned a new car dealership and He gave you a new vehicle off the showroom floor to use the rest of your life. God wanted you to take care of, fix and maintain the vehicle on a regular basis, as well as have fun, be happy and drive it around anywhere you wanted. In the beginning the car was in excellent condition, both internally and externally. But inevitably as cars are driven through life, they experience interior and exterior damage. The outside gets dirty, dented and maybe even rusted. Fast food winds up on the front seat, and eventually the interior upholstery starts to show signs of wear and tear. But that's okay – God knows how rough the road of life can be.

Now let's pretend your car experienced internal and external wear and tear. But instead of cleaning and maintaining the interior of your car, you simply tinted the windows so no one could see the mess inside. Then over time the interior got worse and worse. You justify the poor interior condition of the car by the immaculate condition of the exterior, and you make sure the outside of the car is spotless. It is always washed, waxed and perfectly polished. The very thought of the car's interior sends you for the wax and polish because the only way to distract yourself from the car's interior mess is to focus your attention on the car's external shine.

If you're wondering what wax and polish has to do with perfectionism, it's simple. Your car's interior represents your Inner Self. The trash, dirt and garbage inside your car represent negative self-concepts and unhealed childhood wounds. The exterior of the car represents your external environment. The obsessive and compulsive waxing, polishing and exterior maintenance represent the behavior of a perfectionist. Perfectionism is a calling to restore your car's internal condition by performing internal healing work.

Somewhere in every perfectionist's past, their self-worth and value got damaged. The perfectionist doesn't like how they feel on the inside, so they try to make themselves feel better through external accomplishments and rigid behaviors on the outside. Being a perfectionist is just like any other addiction, except that instead of trying to make themselves feel better with drugs and alcohol, they use wax and polish as a distraction. There is a huge difference between striving for excellence and being a perfectionist. Striving for excellence is maintaining an equal balance of maintenance between a car's interior and exterior conditions. Being a perfectionist is trying to cover up that hurt and damaged part of their interior through compulsive exterior activities. Striving for excellence is healthy because it is realistic and accepting when we fall short of our objectives. It is not driven, and allows for setbacks, mistakes and human error. A person who strives for excellence is able to make requests and knows their own internal value and worth regardless of their external environments.

Being a perfectionist is unhealthy because it sets up unrealistic expectations. It makes demands, gets very impatient, is self-condemning and doesn't allow for errors. If a perfectionist makes a mistake, there is no hope of self-worth. Even when projects are completed in a perfect manner, a perfectionist experiences very little self-worth because true self-worth comes from inside.

Living with a perfectionist as a relationship partner is extremely difficult because they usually impose the same strict standards on others as they impose on themselves. They criticize others' imperfections in the same ruthless way they criticize themselves. They also have a hard time accomplishing anything because it takes a lot of time to get things done perfectly. They might delay starting projects because the timing just doesn't seem to be "perfect." When they finally do manage to finish a project, they receive very little personal satisfaction because it never seems to turn out like they had hoped and planned. It just wasn't good enough, because somehow it could have been better.

On the road of life we will all experience internal and external damage. The question is, what are you going to do about it? Take a minute to look at your life. If you think it's perfect, you may be a perfectionist. If you're a perfectionist, some internal healing work will be beneficial to your car's condition. If your life is not perfect and you're aware of some internal damage, it will be beneficial to fix it immediately.

Steps to Overcoming Perfectionism

Step 1: List Items You Want Perfect

The first step is to identify any areas of your life where you want perfect results. Write down the situations where you try to achieve the ideal situation. What do you condemn yourself or others for when it's not done just right? What do you constantly blame yourself for? What aspects of your life do you find yourself unable to accept if they're less than perfect? What attributes do you find yourself constantly frustrated by or impatient with? Take a look at your work environment, test scores, parenting styles, correcting your children's behavior, searching for the perfect boyfriend or girlfriend, or winning a contest or any type of competition. Next, look at the order of your personal, household, or material possessions, your personal appearance, perfect hair and color coordination, pursuit of knowledge, education or degrees, sexual performance, unfinished projects, coming in second place, the bottom line, sales reports and your religious practices. Write down as many items as possible. If necessary, take several days to make the list and add new items as they arise.

Step 2: Modify Your Compulsive Behaviors

After you have identified them, the next step is to confront, correct and change your compulsive behaviors. There are many ways this can be accomplished. Take a look at the following suggestions and choose a method that will work best for your situation.

❖ **Reevaluate goals.** If you are a perfectionist, you may set unrealistic goals for yourself. You may strive to complete as many things as possible without any consideration for setbacks, mistakes, human factors, compromises, moderation, flexibility or balance. It will be helpful to redefine your goals based on what is really most important in your life. Instead of seeking self-approval through your overachiever or meticulous efforts, redefine your true purpose in life by focusing on what's really important. Why are you here on Earth? What would God want from you? What's most important for you to accomplish in a lifetime? Is it reorganizing canned goods in alphabetical order, or developing your ability to love as you make a difference in the lives of others? See the Direction/Potential and Goals chapters for more information on finding a greater purpose in life and a procedure for its accomplishment.

❖ **Reevaluate expectations.** Once you have some clearly defined goals that promote your ultimate purpose and direction in life, it's helpful to evaluate your expectations regarding their future outcomes. If you are a perfectionist, you may take on too many responsibilities and place extremely high expectations on the outcomes of your efforts. If so, it will be helpful to set an outcome rating for your goals. Begin by writing a description for each goal, and the outcome of the goal if you applied the minimum amount of effort and the maximum amount of effort. Then, establish your objectives to achieve a result that represents a balance between these two extremes. Make a list of instructions or substeps for your goals, instead of trying to accomplish everything at once. Rejoice and celebrate every substep that you have completed along the way. Allow yourself to feel good about the daily victories, as well as the final accomplishments.

❖ **Change unhealthy perceptions.** As a perfectionist, you may suffer from unhealthy and distorted forms of thinking. You might find yourself thinking things like, "If it's not done just this certain way, it's completely bad," "It's only good when it is done this way or my way," or "I'm either a bad mother or a good mother." When you use words like "must," "should" or "have to," you drive yourself in rigid ways. "I must do this because I feel obligated and driven," instead of, "I choose to do this because I am free and capable." If you find yourself thinking in this manner, you are participating in distorted perceptions. Distorted forms of thinking cause stress, anxiety and disappointment, and contribute to our perfectionist behaviors. See the Perceptions chapter to identify and correct unhealthy forms of thinking.

❖ **Practice self-acceptance and meditation.** It is important to schedule some quiet time alone every day for contemplation. Perfectionists usually use their external activities and accomplishments to avoid their internal feelings and their true self. When you spend quiet time alone, you can get in touch with your true feelings and begin to heal them. It is important to develop a positive sense of self through self-acceptance and self-concept, regardless or your external accomplishments. You are valuable, lovable and worthwhile. Simply start by acknowledging that. See the Self-Acceptance, Self-Concept and Meditation chapters for more information.

Step 3: Do Internal Healing

After you begin to change your external behaviors using the methods from Step 2, it will be helpful to heal the underlying internal conditions that you have been trying to avoid. Usually in every perfectionist's past, their sense of self-worth was damaged and usually becomes attached to their external accomplishments. This can happen in several ways:

Emotionally or physically neglected or abused children might blame themselves for the abuse they suffered. At an early age these children might believe that if they were valuable and lovable, they wouldn't have been treated in an unlovable manner. When they grow up, they might try to prove their self-worth and value through their perfect external accomplishments.

A perfectionist's self-worth could also be damaged by parents or role models who were overly strict, critical or demanding. Children who grew up under these conditions probably didn't hear very many positive words of reassurance and may have only received affection and approval when behavior was perfect. These children might grow up believing they are lovable only when they perform perfectly.

Parents might have used shaming techniques in an attempt to correct or control their children's behavior. If you have grown up under these conditions, you may have heard statements like: "Is this the best you can produce?" "Why can't you be more like your sister?" "What's wrong with you?" "You will never be good enough with that attitude!" or "Why can't you get good grades like the other children?" Other forms of shaming include name calling, silent treatment, looks of disappointment or disgust when your actions were judged and found wanting by another perfectionist. These children usually grow up lacking a healthy sense of self-worth for who they actually are. Adults who lack self-worth and value need some way to make themselves feel better, and a perfectionist tries to find it through their external accomplishments.

If you have suffered situations similar to these, it will be helpful to go back, search for and heal the past experience when your perfectionist tendencies were learned. Simply revisit the situation in your imagination, vent all the negative emotions and replace them with the love, support and encouragement you never received as a child. Once you have discovered the past events that injured your internal self-worth and value, follow the instructions in the Healing chapter.

Step 4: Make Daily Efforts

Overcoming perfectionist tendencies will require daily effort. It will be helpful to practice the compassion exercise or the self-awareness exercise every time you feel upset (see the Compassion and Self-Awareness chapters). Turning to God in prayer is also a powerful way to help yourself in all aspects of your life. Ask for patience when dealing with others, the wisdom that can be learned from mistakes, the power to accept your human limitation and the ability to accept yourself, regardless of your imperfections.

Visions of Inspiration

What we must decide is perhaps how we are valuable, rather than how valuable we are.

F. Scott Fitzgerald

I appeal to you therefore, brothers and sisters, by the mercies of God, to present your bodies as a living sacrifice, holy and acceptable to God, which is your spiritual worship. Do not be conformed to this world, but be transformed by the renewing of your minds, so that you may discern what is the will of God - what is good and acceptable and perfect.

Romans 12: 1-2

PERSONAL ABUSE

TOOL 54

*H*ave you ever walked up to your car after it's been parked in a trusted parking garage and noticed that someone has intentionally run their keys down the side? If someone vandalized your car by scratching the paint, what would you do? What would you think or feel? How would you deal with the hurt and pain?

If your car has been vandalized in the past, you may be faced with only three possible courses of action:

First, you can deal with your hurt and pain by violating another person's vehicle in the same way yours was violated. If you are an abusive person, you would take out your own keys and scratch the closest car in an attempt to make yourself feel better. Abusive people don't stop to think – they just act from a subconscious drive to hurt others in the same way they have been hurt.

Second, you can take the hurt and pain personally. If you are the type of person who allows yourself to be abused, after noticing the scratch on your car, you would make the damage worse by using your own keys. People who allow themselves to suffer abuse act from a subconscious drive that makes them believe they personally deserve to be abused.

Or third, you can take personal responsibility for the incident and forgive the accountable party. You can surrender the hurt and pain over to God in the forgiveness process and get your vehicle to the auto body shop for repairs.

Have you ever wondered why someone would vandalize your car in the first place? Do you find yourself wondering what makes one person abusive to others and another person abusive to themselves, when they were both born nonabusive, loving children? Unfortunately, both the abuser and the abused have learned their behaviors from the same sources in the past. These unhealthy tendencies usually start out in early childhood when parents, guardians or loved ones hurt us for some reason. If we didn't work through the forgiveness process or failed to receive the love and support we needed, these negative experiences were repressed in our subconscious. When an unhealed negative past experience is repressed in our subconscious, it has the power to affect our present behavior.

For example, if you take a young child and subject them to physical abuse long enough, eventually that child will believe they deserve to be abused. Their God-given natural programming will change through the painful experiences and negative thoughts they think about themselves. Once they have been conditioned to a life of abuse, as adults they usually seek abusive relationship partners because that's what feels comfortable and normal to them. Without healing work, abuse from these children's pasts has the power to change their subconscious programming and turn them into self-abusing martyrs. These people not only vandalize their own cars but continually put themselves in abusive situations.

In the same way, abusive people's subconscious programming has been distorted by their negative past experiences. If you take a young child and raise them in a physically abusive environment, they will believe that is how the world works. If the child's father has a bad day at work and deals with it by inflicting pain on his family, the child in turn will deal with their own pain the same way. Being smaller than the parents, the child will probably take the pain out on other family members or on the family dog. Children who have been abused will grow up hurting others the same way they themselves have been hurt. As adults these people usually seek relationship partners who enable their abusive tendencies.

Abuse from your past has the power to change your subconscious programming and turn you into an abusive person or a self-abusive person in the present. Abuse comes in many forms, including physical, sexual, mental, emotional and child abuse. Emotional abuse is just as destructive to the receiving party as physical abuse. It may not leave physical signs like broken bones, but it leaves emotional signs like broken spirits. All forms of abuse are equally destructive.

Try to identify any of the following forms of abuse in your present or past relationships so you can break the abuse cycle:

❖ **Mental and emotional abuse.** Do you or your partner withhold important information from the other or try to dominate or control the other in some way? Do you try to embarrass, humiliate, insult or ridicule each other? Does your partner say things like you're stupid, fat, lazy, good for nothing, worthless, ugly, crazy, not a good mother, or that you can't do anything right, that no one would ever want you or that you don't deserve anything? Do you say things to prove your partner's inadequacies? Does your partner make you feel worthless, not good enough or unlovable? Is there name calling, put-downs, negative criticisms or humiliation taking place in your relationship? Do you or your partner withhold the truth, distort the truth, tell lies or promise things to create false hopes? Do you or your partner attack one another for maintaining a different point of view or discount the seriousness of something that's important to each of you? Does your partner falsely accuse you of something they know isn't true or argue with you to prove their point of view, always trying to have the last word? Does your partner make you the brunt of their jokes, cutting in sensitive areas of your life and then trying to cover it up with humor? Does your partner order you around, threatening something that is important to you, or intentionally forget things as a form of manipulation? If so, it is considered emotional and mental abuse.

❖ **Physical abuse.** Do you or your partner hit, shove, slap, cut, choke, grab, kick, burn, throw things or spit on each other? Do you break furniture, destroy personal property like clothes, family pictures or possessions that are valuable to the other? Does your partner tamper with your car, causing it to break down? Does your partner hold you against your will, threaten you with a bat, hammer, frying pan, knife, gun or deadly weapon? Do you lock each other out of the house, or abandon or endanger one another? Is there any neglect of physical needs, like food, clothing, medical or dental care? What about negative behavior that prevents the other from fulfilling their primary human needs in a healthy way? Are there any forms of substance abuse, alcoholism, drug addiction or abuse of the elderly in your relationships?

❖ **Sexual abuse.** Do you or your partner force the other to have unwanted sex, or refuse to have sex as a form of punishment? Does your partner force you to have sex with other people, or force you to watch others having sex? Does your partner tell you about sexual relations with other people or brag about other love affairs? Do you or your partner falsely accuse one another of having affairs or criticize one another's sexual performance? Is there any type of behavior or attitude that relates pain and sex? Is there anything like incest or indecent exposure in or around your relationship?

❖ **Child abuse.** Children are defenseless victims when it comes to abuse. They can't defend or protect themselves and can't break the cycle of abuse. As adults it is up to us to offer our assistance. Here are some warning signals to look for:

- Unexplained bruises and burns that never seem to heal.
- Fractures or severe injuries to children under two years of age.
- A child who reacts by flinching or withdrawing in fear from the simplest of movements.
- Children who are afraid to go home or be with their parents.
- Considerably overweight, underweight, unclean or unsupervised children.
- Children who refrain from using the bathroom or complain of pain, swelling, itching or burning in their genital areas.
- Children who display strange, sophisticated or unusual sexual knowledge.
- Abnormal behaviors like self-harming actions, inappropriate emotional responses, rebelling against society or self-distracting habits.

Abuse in all of its forms is extremely painful, traumatic, crippling and damaging to all aspects of your life and relationships. Confronting personal abuse requires that you recognize it and do something about it. This will take courage, forgiveness and self-respect. God wants us to live a life free from abuse – from others and from ourselves. God will give you the strength, power and wisdom to overcome any obstacles that stand between you and a healthy relationship with yourself and His other beloved children. All you have to do is ask.

If you or your partner are expressing personal violations in your trusted relational parking garage, there are steps you can take to heal abuse. These steps are divided into two parts: the first set is for the abused and the second is for the abuser.

Healing Steps for Those Being Abused

Step 1: Recognize Abuse

The first step toward healing is to recognize abuse and the abusive situations that exist in your relationship. This is usually the hardest step because many people have slowly conditioned themselves to justify the abuse. We probably all have heard about the experiment to test how frogs grew accustomed to abuse. One frog was dropped in hot water and immediately jumped back out. It became uncomfortable too fast and immediately left the situation. A second frog was dropped in cold water where the heat was slowly increased. This frog stayed in the water, adjusting to the abuse until the water boiled.

Abuse is usually committed in private. Many times the victim begins to blame themselves for the perpetrator's behavior. Take the time to realistically evaluate your situation, life and relationships. Do you find yourself feeling worthless, inadequate or deserving of abuse? Do you find yourself constantly diminishing the seriousness of your situation? Do you recognize abuse in your current relationship and continue to put up with it, thinking that your love will conquer all? Do you fear the worst possible consequences if you were to do something to stop the abuse? Do you want to escape or run away? Do you find yourself wondering if you're crazy or if something is wrong with you? Do you notice a lack of self-confidence, self-esteem, spontaneity and enthusiasm in your life?

Step 2: Seek Confirmation

Once you have identified the issues, have accepted them and are willing to face them, the next step is to seek confirmation from a third party. Many times an outside source can view your situation more clearly than you can yourself. When you are deeply involved in a situation, your perception can become distorted. It is important to seek the assistance of a third party to verify and help you out of an abusive situation. Unfortunately, abused people might find themselves isolated because friends and family turn away in fear, rejection or disagreement. Friends and family may also have been forced away by the perpetrator in an attempt to gain further control of you through isolation. Try to confirm your beliefs regarding the abusive situation through friends, family, counselors, support groups, church, neighbors, crisis assistance centers, social services or battered women's alternatives. Reach out to others who can support and help you!

Step 3: Write a Letter of Facts and Feelings

It may be helpful to write a letter stating your facts and feelings regarding the abuse. Write this letter in private, in a safe and secure environment. Record in your letter all the situations, facts and circumstances regarding the abusive actions you have suffered. Search your past and document every situation of emotional, spiritual, mental and physical violation. For every situation write how you felt before, during and after the violation. Express all your negative feelings of fear, abandonment, guilt, anger and insecurity.

Step 4: Write a Letter of Self-Value

In addition, it will be empowering to write a letter confirming your own personal self-worth. Many times when people have been victims of an abusive relationship for an extended period of time, their self-worth and value are practically nonexistent. It's necessary to begin the process of rebuilding your self-concept and self-acceptance. See the Self-Concept and Self-Acceptance chapters for more information. It may also be helpful to write a personalized letter describing why you are no longer willing to tolerate the abuse. Explain how you don't deserve to be treated in violating ways and why you are no longer willing to participate in a destructive relationship. Begin by describing your own self-worth, value, integrity and love. Then list your rights, desires and expectations: you deserve to be loved; you deserve to be treated with respect at all times; you have the right to your own opinions and points of view; you have the right to live free of violence, threats, and fear; you don't deserve to be criticized, ridiculed, put down or devalued; and you deserve to be asked rather than ordered. Look at the items you wrote down in Step 3 and get in touch with your rights, desires, self-respect and value.

Step 5: Write a Letter of Proposed Changes

The next step is to write a letter specifically identifying the changes you want to happen in your relationship. Look at the items you listed in your letter from Step 3 and write down the ways you want to be treated. How would you like to see these situations stopped, change, improved on or worked out? What would you like to see different? Whose help will you need? How can counseling services, therapists, support groups, medical treatment, family crisis centers, shelters or substance abuse centers help you? Write down all your plans, ideas and proposals for correcting the abusive situation.

Step 6: Confront the Situation and the Abuser

After completing the five previous steps, you are ready to confront the situation and the person causing the abuse. It may be necessary to confront the individual with other people present. Gather all the people who are involved or affected in some way. If you are being physically abused and are afraid, you will need some support and assistance from others. Try asking the abusive person to see a counselor with you and the confrontation can take place in their office. If your partner is unwilling to do, this confront them in the safest environment possible. The purpose of your confrontation is to establish the facts regarding the seriousness of their behavior. Present your partner with your proposed changes and solutions to resolve the problems. You will need to firmly establish your unwillingness to suffer or participate in any further abuse. It might be helpful to have your letters from Steps 3, 4 and 5 available to assist in the confrontation process. If the abusive person is not willing to resolve the problems, correct and work on their issues, or seek professional help, your only alternative may be to temporarily or permanently remove yourself from the situation.

Step 7: Establish Healthy Boundaries

You will also need to establish healthy boundaries. If you have allowed yourself to be abused in the past, you probably lack healthy boundaries. It's necessary to describe what you will and will not tolerate in the future. You will need to decide what is healthy and unhealthy regarding your complete mental, physical, spiritual and emotional self. Set up some personal laws, just like society has laws. If the laws are broken, the consequences will need to be paid. Look at the items from your letter in Step 3 and create your own personal laws and boundaries. If these boundaries are crossed, you will need to take whatever action is necessary to protect yourself. See the Boundaries chapter for more information.

Unfortunately, you can't always change another person's destructive behavior. All you can do is set up and enforce healthy boundaries and remove yourself from unhealthy environments. Don't be afraid to take whatever action is necessary when it comes to removing yourself. If the abusive person truly cares about you, they will miss you and take steps to change. If they don't care, you don't deserve to be in that relationship anyway. It might be helpful to plan ahead in case you need to remove yourself from future situations. Consider keeping an emergency bag packed in case you need to leave in a hurry. Carry emergency money with you in case you need to remove yourself and get to a safe place. Carry phone numbers of friends and family so you will be prepared.

Step 8: Do Forgiveness and Healing Work

Next, it will be helpful to do some healing and forgiveness work as part of the recovery process. Usually people who allow themselves to be abused as adults have suffered an abusive childhood. If you want to restore your subconscious programming it may be necessary to go back in your past and heal situations where you were abused. The steps used in the healing process are the same for the abuser as they are for the abused, and are outlined in the following section. So to remove any self-abusing subconscious tendencies, proceed by working your way through "Step 2: Search Your Past," and "Step 3: Heal Your Past." You might also find it helpful to work through the forgiveness steps for every item listed in your letter from Step 3. See the Forgiveness chapter for more information.

Healing Steps for Those Who Cause Abuse

Step 1: Recognize the Abusive Behavior

The first step is to recognize your abusive behavior. It's very difficult for an abusive person to recognize their destructive behavior unless someone brings it to their attention. Abusive people usually react from a compulsive subconscious drive to hurt other people in the same way they themselves are hurting. Many times this is disguised with denial, blame toward the victim and projection. Try to look at your thoughts, actions and behaviors to see if they are violating another person mentally, physically, emotionally or spiritually. How would you react if the situation were reversed? If someone is accusing you of abuse, listen to them carefully. If you can't see the situation from their point of view, seek assistance from an outside third party, counselor or therapist.

Step 2: Search Your Past

Make a fearless and intense search of your past. People who abuse and people who allow themselves to be abused learned their destructive behavior from others who inflicted similar treatment on them. It's necessary to make a list of all the abuse you have suffered from others. It might be helpful to begin by writing the story of your life. Try to relate your current behaviors and attitudes to those from your childhood. Look at your family – is there anyone you want to leave out of the search? If so, it probably means that's where you need to be searching the most. Write down everything that didn't seem right. How were you hurt? Who wasn't there for you? Who made you feel powerless? How were you punished? How did your guardians deal with their anger? How were you treated? Ask God to help you remember and as you do, add those negative past experiences to the list.

Step 3: Heal Your Past

Next, you will need to heal the past experiences when you suffered abuse from others by following the directions in the Healing chapter. There are two techniques – a written letter exercise and an imagination technique. Use whichever technique works best for you, and keep working with every item on your list from Step 2 until you feel an internal sense of love and peace regarding each situation. When you can look back at a specific situation and feel love and compassion for both the victim and victimizer parts of yourself, you will know the situation has been healed. If you look back on it and feel some form of negativity, the situation will require some more work.

Step 4: Make Amends

The next step is to make a list of all the people you harmed in the past so you can make the necessary amends. Begin with your present relationships. How have you harmed your children, your spouse, family members, neighbors and coworkers? List all the ways you hurt, violated and abused them, then find a way to make amends and retribution for your actions. Try to offer your reconciliation in ways that are equivalent to the damage you caused. Sincere amends are a very important part of the healing process. Making amends will further your healing process in a way that almost transcends words. You will know its power when you look in the eyes of the person you have hurt and see your own pain and suffering. Be careful not to make any amends if doing so would cause additional harm as a result. See the Guilt chapter for more information.

Step 5: Make Daily Efforts

Overcoming the cycle of abuse will require daily effort and hard work. You will need to learn new ways to deal with your anger. See the Anger chapter for more information. Instead of surrendering yourself to powerful destructive forces, you will need to recognize them as they arise, and find a way to love and embrace that hurt, vulnerable and abused part of yourself. Practicing parental affirmations on a regular basis is also very effective. See the Affirmations chapter for more information. Outside support systems are very important to guide you and ensure your well-being. Seek assistance from professionals, friends, family, counselors, therapists, church organizations and medical providers as necessary. Pray to God for assistance, guidance and healing in every step of the way.

Visions of Inspiration

You shall not abuse any widow or orphan. If you do abuse them, when they cry out to me, I will surely heed their cry; my wrath will burn, and I will kill you with the sword, and your wives shall become widows and your children orphans.

Exodus 22: 22-24

On account of these the wrath of God is coming on those who are disobedient. These are the ways you also once followed, when you were living that life. But now you must get rid of all such things – anger, wrath, malice, slander, and abusive language from your mouth.

Colossians 3: 6-8

Whipping and abuse are like laudanum: You have to double the dose as the sensibilities decline.

Harriet Beecher Stowe

Those have most power to hurt us that we love.

Francis Beaumont

POWER

*W*ithout power our cars would be useless as a form of transportation. Our vehicles use power to move down the highway, and in the same way we use our personal power to fulfill our needs. Without personal power, we would be as helpless as a car without an engine. Just as car manufacturers design their products with an ample amount of horsepower, God designed each of us with an adequate amount of our own personal horsepower. When we experience a lack of horsepower in our lives and relationships, it usually means we're applying the power we already have in unhealthy and indirect methods.

When you are single and driving through life solo, you can take your car anywhere you want to go. If you want to go east, all you have to do is get on an eastbound road. The only thing you might worry about is not damaging your vehicle or another vehicle along the way. But once you marry or become involved in a relationship and start traveling in tandem with your partner's car, you may find yourself experiencing power struggles. If your partner wants to travel east and you want to travel west, what are you going to do? You could wrap a chain around the bumpers of both cars, and with your partner's car heading east and your car heading west, you could see who has the most horsepower. But don't you think this would cause damage to your relationship and burn out your car's transmission? Of course – not to mention the fact that no one would go anywhere, since everyone has an equal amount of personal power at their disposal.

God gave us our personal power as a great gift to make things happen in life. He wants us to use it to get where we want to go and to fulfill our needs, desires and wants. For all this He only makes one request of us: that we not use our personal power in a way that violates ourselves or others. This applies to solo drivers as well as those driving in tandem with their partners. Healthy use of our power promotes good in our lives and doesn't harm us or others. Unhealthy use of our power might seem to promote some types of good, but if it violates you or others in any way, it is negative and destructive. Let's look at three very common and unhealthy uses of personal power that can affect your relationship in a negative manner:

The first unhealthy use of power is the "Helpless Victim and Stranded Motorist." In this case your partner wants to go east and you want to go west, so you fake a helpless engine failure. You might say, "My car is broken down. Will you please tow me west to the repair shop?" This type of behavior is unhealthy because it uses, violates and takes advantage of your partner's car by putting extra stress on their drive train.

The second unhealthy use of power is the "Demanding Demolition Derby." Here, your partner wants to go east and you want to go west, so you threaten, coerce, manipulate or force your partner to change their mind. You say, "You go west because I said so! Going east is stupid, and only stupid people go east. You don't want to be stupid, do you? Besides if you don't go west, I will punish you by running my car into yours, causing damage to both vehicles." This is just as unhealthy as the first method because it also violates and abuses your partner's car.

The third unhealthy use of power is the "Self-Sacrificing, Enabling Tow Truck." This is when your partner wants to go east and you want to go west, so you misuse your personal power by sacrificing yourself over to your partner. You always hook up the tow truck and rush right in to tow your partner's car east. This can be a very loving act if you are not running your own car into the ground. Usually the self-sacrificing drivers deny their own wants and needs, hoping that their partner will return the favor someday. This behavior is clearly self-destructive because if your needs are not being met in your relationship, your partner will indirectly experience the repercussions later.

Take a look at the following list of power struggle characteristics to see if you or your partner are misusing your horsepower against one another:

❖ Making decisions for your partner or letting them make decisions for you.
❖ Trying to get even with each other.
❖ Stubbornly being set in your own ways.
❖ Needing to win and be right at all costs.
❖ Attempting to change each other instead of being willing to change yourself.
❖ Giving advice and not being able to accept it yourself.
❖ Not allowing your partner to solve their own problems.

- Failing to create win/win situations; putting your partner in a no-win situation.
- Using aggressive behavior like bullying, bribing, giving orders, demanding, threatening, anger tactics, holding grudges, abuses in all its forms.
- Having difficulty apologizing for your mistakes or admitting them.
- Having difficulty asking for support or reaching out to others.
- Giving one minute and taking it back in the next.
- Making promises and turning right around and breaking them.
- Any behavior that intimidates your partner, making one party superior and the other party inferior.
- Trying to defend any behaviors on this list to your partner.

Usually if you and your partner are experiencing any of these items, there is a good chance both of you are using one or all three unhealthy methods of struggling for power to get your needs met indirectly. If so, it will be very helpful for you and your partner to establish a balanced system of power. This system of give and take will be different for every relationship. When both parties feel respected, free and uncontrolled, you will have an easier time enjoying the tandem road trip throughout life. The following steps are designed to help you identify, confront and heal any power imbalances in your relationships.

Steps to Healing Power Imbalances

Step 1: Identify Past Problems

The first step is for both parties to make a separate list of items that describe areas of your relationship where you are experiencing power struggles. Try to pinpoint the exact items that are frequently disputed. You might be experiencing conflicts over issues like outside friendships, who makes the decisions, household chores, leisure activities or who speaks the last word. Write down as many items as possible. Address every issue where you feel controlled, demanded, expected, put down, punished, smothered, patronized, attacked, threatened, bullied or abused.

Step 2: Recognize the Damage

It's helpful to recognize the damage these power struggle issues cause to your relationship. For every item on your list from Step 1, make a written description that explains the damage, negative effects, loss of love and respect, and hurt feelings that these behaviors cause. For example, if you said in Step 1 that you feel controlled concerning your social activities and in the past you have experienced criticism, withdrawal and even threats, the damage these behaviors caused could be loss of respect, ruined evenings, resentment that lasted for days, anger or the loss of friendships. Look closely at every possible disadvantage concerning your power struggles and write them down on paper.

Step 3: Identify Unhealthy Roles

Next, it will be helpful to identify what types of unhealthy behavior roles are used in your power struggles. The three different roles are (a) the victim or helpless role, (b) the demanding or persecutor role, and (c) the enabled or rescuer role. You have probably experienced and participated in each of these behaviors at some point in your life. Try to identify which role you and your partner use most frequently by studying the following conversation:

Wife: "Why haven't you taken out the trash? It really smells bad." (B)
Husband: "I took it out yesterday. I'll do it again tomorrow." (C)
Wife: "Well, it needs to be taken out today." (B)
Husband: "Why don't you do it for a change?" (B)
Wife: "It's too hard and heavy. I can't get the lid off." (A)
Husband: "Well, I'm sorry. I wish I could help." (A)
Wife: "But if you don't do it today, it will smell up the house." (A)
Husband: "I don't want to, but I will anyway." (C)

Step 4: Heal the Past

Once you have identified your dominant role, the next step is to heal the past experiences where you learned these unhealthy behaviors. As children we all expressed our needs in a direct manner. For example, as infants we cried when we were hungry and as children we asked for ice cream directly before dinner. Unfortunately, no one could ever be there for us 100 percent of the time. We might have cried when we were scared and received a bottle or asked for ice cream and received a lecture. If you failed to have your needs met directly, it's possible you learned to get your needs met indirectly by using one of the three roles. Take a look at the following three examples that may explain how and why you have been conditioned with this type of behavior:

* **The Victim or Helpless Role.** All children by nature request their needs directly. If you didn't have your needs met, you might have begun to blame yourself and feel inadequate. A child might think to themselves, "If there wasn't something wrong with me, my parents would give me ice cream like the other kids." Or maybe as a child you were made to feel inadequate and were shamed for wanting ice cream when your parents said things like, "You don't need ice cream. You're too fat already." Or maybe as a child you learned that by playing helpless, you could quickly receive attention from others in the form of ice cream.

* **The Demanding or Persecutor Role.** If you requested your needs directly and didn't receive what you wanted, you may have learned to get it by throwing a fit. Some children learn at an early age to demand the attention they deserve and do what they think is necessary to achieve their desires, including violating others. This behavior could also have been learned from role modeling. Maybe a little boy witnessed his father getting what he wanted by bullying, threatening and physically overpowering others and learned to do the same.

* **The Enabled or Rescuer Role.** This type of unhealthy role can develop in children who requested their needs directly, but for some reason their parents were unable to fulfill them, perhaps due to physical disability, drug addiction, psychological or mental impairment, or dysfunctional problems. These children would eventually learn to repress their own needs for those of their parents. Maybe an older brother or sister from a single parent home felt responsible for a younger sibling's well-being. These children might learn to deny their own needs for those of another, always hoping someone would recognize their efforts and repay them. A child who was raised this way might find themselves giving, giving and giving until they were depleted, while justifying it with constant excuses.

After you have identified the unhealthy roles you are using in your relationship today, it's necessary to locate or re-create some childhood situations where you requested your needs in a direct and assertive manner and didn't receive them. As a child you were probably really hurt, confused and frustrated when your needs were not met. Instead of receiving the love and support you needed, you probably suffered with the pain and developed the unhealthy roles you're using today. The best way to reprogram those unhealthy subconscious tendencies is to make a list of your negative past experiences and heal them by following the directions in the Healing chapter. Go back in your childhood and comfort that hurt inner child part of yourself with lots of love and support.

Step 5: External Healing Techniques

The previous step will help heal any unhealthy subconscious tendencies programmed during childhood. But because old habits die hard, it might be necessary for you and your partner to work on these behaviors together. When you notice yourself acting in an unhealthy manner, stop, apologize, get in touch with your needs and wants, and express them directly. When you notice your partner acting in an unhealthy way, try to give them the support they never received in their past. For example:

❖ **If your partner is using the Victim or Helpless role:** Try to be empathetic with them. Acknowledge their needs, feelings and discomfort. Talk about how it's okay to feel any way they want. Reassure them of your care, respect and love. Try not to jump right in and solve their problems for them. Allow them the opportunity to deal with their own issues in a healthy way.

❖ **If your partner is using the Demanding or Persecutor role:** Try to set up boundaries, limits and structure in your arguments. It's necessary to confront unhealthy and hurtful behaviors. Let your partner know how their demanding actions make you feel. Try to get them to express their needs, vulnerability and fears directly.

❖ **If your partner is using the Enabled or Rescuer role:** Try to help them acknowledge and affirm their own needs. Create an atmosphere, system or environment that gives them permission to freely state their concerns and desires. Offer them the loving reassurances they may never have received as a child. Validate their requests and feelings in an atmosphere of unconditional love. Let them know you accept them just as they are.

Step 6: Make Daily Efforts

There are only three healthy alternatives for dealing with your needs:
- ❖ State them directly and reach out to others who can help you get relief. If your relationship partner is unable, try other sources.
- ❖ Fulfill your needs yourself.
- ❖ Accept the fact that you are unable to get your needs met at this time. Grieve the loss if necessary, and make alternative plans.

By accepting and acting on one of these three choices, you will avoid power struggles in your relationships. It might also be helpful to work with the exercises located in the Primary Human Needs, Behavior and Compromise chapters. Ask God for assistance, guidance, patience and understanding when expressing your own needs and dealing with those of your relationship partner.

Visions of Inspiration

The one who first states a case seems right, until the other comes and cross-examines. Casting the lot puts an end to disputes and decides between powerful contenders.

Proverbs 18:17-18

He did not care in which direction the car was traveling, so long as he remained in the driver's seat.

Lord Beaverbrook

Being powerful is like being a lady. If you have to tell people you are, you ain't.

Jesse Carr

PRAYER

TOOL 56

*I*magine for a minute that you're starting a new business. You're very talented and smart, but lack experience and the necessary financial backing for the venture. After serious consideration and many previous failed attempts, you decide to go into partnership with someone who can almost guarantee a successful enterprise. Your new partner has tremendous resources, abundant knowledge, excellent connections and a powerful ability for marketing. You feel honored to be considered a 50/50 partner. The only problem is you don't know your new partner very well and it will take some serious effort to establish a close working relationship.

Do you think a close working relationship is essential to the success of your new business? How important would it be for you and your partner to communicate on a regular basis? What would happen if you were going one direction and your partner was thinking the exact opposite? How many problems, conflicts and disasters do you think could be avoided if you and your partner knew exactly where the other stood on the issues?

Good communication is so important in the business world that we keep coming up with more efficient ways of keeping in touch with each other. We can exchange information verbally, in letters, over the telephone, by fax and e-mail and with voice mail, using cellular phones, pagers, the Internet and even satellite uplinks. Even though technology keeps advancing year after year, the fundamental principles behind the importance of good communication remain the same.

If you are wondering what all this has to do with prayer, it's simple. God is your senior business partner in life. When you and God go into business together, there isn't anything you can't handle. Besides, you're not going to be concerned with any other deal 100 years from now, except for your relationship with the Almighty Chief Executive Officer – God. The more you contribute to your 50/50 partnership with God, the more He will give back in return. The only way to maintain good communication with your 50/50 partner is through your direct satellite uplink system, known as prayer. In fact, God's technology far outperforms even the most advanced business communication system ever invented. There are no buttons to push or numbers to dial, and you don't even need to speak – all you need to do is acknowledge God in your mind and offer Him your full attention.

It is important to interact with God in the same way you talk to a close friend or any other business partner. Unfortunately, some people only turn to God in their times of need and don't bother to attend the regularly scheduled office meetings. People who pray to God without listening to His response can be compared to a business partner who calls on the phone but never lets you speak a word. Failing to pray on a regular basis is like making yourself available to God only at your convenience. If your partnership were 50/50, don't you think it would be important to return God's calls, whether you feel like it or not?

How would you define a close relationship with your partner? Would it be by sharing the good times, the bad times, your future plans, hopes and dreams, the current strategies and your everyday experiences? Or would you define a close relationship with your partner as turning to them only in an emergency? If you and your business partner had regularly planned office meetings, do you think your business would experience a lot fewer emergency crisis situations?

Maintaining a regular prayer life is extremely important to every single aspect of our lives and relationships. It's through our prayers and a close relationship with God that we enable ourselves to receive the gifts God generously bestows. Our prayers can bring guidance for the direction of our lives, strength to endure hardships, healing from our past experiences, forgiveness for ourselves and others and every other possible grace and gift imaginable. If your business is operating in the red, the following items will be of some assistance in developing and increasing your prayer life.

Receiving Guidance and Strength Through Prayer

Mental Preparation Before Prayer

Depending on the type and style of your prayer life, some mental preparation work might be beneficial. Using favorite mediation techniques before prayer can help create a sense of inner peace. Many times when we pray, our minds drift off to sleep or are distracted with the events of the day. Meditating before prayers can help us relax, get in touch with our Inner Self, release stressful events and help us focus all of our attention on God. If you find yourself distracted during prayer, try not to control distractions or feel guilty for having them; simply let them pass by as quickly as they entered. Help them along the way by returning attention to God's presence.

Physical Preparation Before Prayer

Depending on the type and style of your prayer life, the following items might be helpful:

❖ Find a quiet space in your environment to help create deeper, more meaningful prayer experiences.

❖ Set a specific time each day for your prayer life. In doing so, you are making yourself available to God on a regular basis instead of turning to Him at your convenience or when you want, need or feel like it.

❖ Designate a certain area of your home as a private sanctuary and decorate it to your taste with candles, religious articles, spiritual journal, prayer rugs, or kneeling pillows. This can make your praying experience more comfortable.

❖ Try to align your body posture with the way you are feeling and with what you are communicating. If you are feeling sad, use your entire being and body posture to express your sadness to God.

❖ You can keep a list of "things to do" in your prayer environment. It's not unusual for forgotten items to surface in our thoughts when we start to pray. Writing these items down will free up your concentration and allow you to focus your attention on God.

Contemplative Prayer

This is a process of praying for guidance, direction and answers to problems in your life, and listening closely to God's response. Contemplative prayer allows you to ask or meditate on certain questions in your prayer and wait for God's advice. It is usually prayed by making your free will and the desires of your heart open to what God has to say.

Begin by clearing your mind using a favorite meditation technique. After you have asked God your question or explained the difficult decision, focus your complete attention and being on His presence and quietly listen for His voice. During this process many voices will inevitably arise in your consciousness: things you forgot to do, things you wished didn't happen or things you could be doing better. Your purpose here among all these different voices is to recognize and distinguish God's voice from all the rest. God will speak to everyone differently. You will know His voice because it will somehow be different from all the other voices. The only true process of determining God's voice from the others is by trial and error. Once you think you have identified God's voice, remember the distinctive tone that was used and follow its advice. If the advice of the voice produces loving, positive and ethically sound results, the voice is probably God's. If the voice suggests any results that are harmful, violating or improper toward you or others, the voice can't be from God.

This process of contemplative prayer might take a lot of effort, patience and persistence, but regardless of your results, every attempt you make will strengthen your relationship with God.

Intercessory Prayer

This type of prayer is usually prayed out of love and concern for another person's well-being. Intercessory prayers are a very powerful way of helping others and yourself. Many times your own life is dramatically blessed and begins to change when you start praying for others. Intercessory prayers represent an unselfish act of putting the concerns, well-being and needs of others before your own. Keeping a prayer list is an easy way to remember all the people in need of your intercessory prayers.

Healing Prayers

These prayers can be prayed as a powerful method of healing negative past traumatic situations in life. They require the use of imagination techniques to envision a human representation of God in the past experience you wish to heal. God is the ultimate source of all healing and you can begin the healing process by asking Him for assistance.

In a state of prayer, go back in time to a negative experience from your past. Envision God in the form of a human being suffering the harmful situation right beside you. Work through and discuss your primary emotions of anger, frustration, sadness, disappointment, fear, concern, guilt and inadequacy with God. It's important to actually feel the emotions, not just logically think about them. Explain to God in detail every aspect of the events and how they apply to your primary emotions. After you have vented all your negative feelings, get in touch with your higher wants and needs. Explain to God what you wanted to happen that didn't. How can this past situation be beneficial in your life today? When you are finished sharing your concerns, God in His infinite wisdom will help you see the situation from the other person's point of view. Try to find a way in your imagination to love that hurt part of yourself.

Eventually God helps you find the higher road of forgiveness. Healing prayers will produce a deeper bond of understanding, love and compassion between you, those of your past, and your Heavenly Creator.

Everyday Prayers

The ways we can communicate with God are endless. We can start the day by embracing God with our morning prayers and conclude it with our evening prayers. We can recite formal prayers or pray using simple phrases. We can offer our sufferings to God in prayer or dedicate the work of our hands to Him in prayer. We can meditate on the scriptures or live our entire life as an ongoing prayer dedicated to God. A great way to pray is to talk to God as you would a close and dear friend. Talk about all the bad and good things that you are experiencing, events that make you happy and sad, your goals, dreams, or whatever is on your mind. You might even try talking to God out loud in private; it will add a new dimension to your conversations.

Written Prayers

You may have an easier time keeping your mind focused on God if you write in a special journal every day. Written prayers can be divided into several different parts:

❖ Praise: Where your daily praise is offered to God in a written form.
❖ Admission: Where you acknowledge and admit any shortcomings.
❖ Requests: Where you ask your petitions, needs and wants.
❖ Contemplation: Where you listen for God's guidance and write down His will for your life.
❖ Direction: Where you record your list of things to do for the day.
❖ Conclusion: Where your love for God is restated and reconfirmed.

Written prayers are a powerful way to bring God's healing guidance and strength into your daily life on a regular basis.

Inner Peace Prayer

When a negative or unwanted thought enters your mind, you can choose to either repress it in your subconscious, where it will become a hidden part of the way you view the world, or you can acknowledge its unwanted existence and surrender it over to God for his removal and replacement. The inner peace prayer works by asking God for His assistance in replacing an unwanted thought with a thought of His specific choosing. For example, if a thought of revenge enters your mind, stop yourself and acknowledge its unwanted presence. Then ask God to help you replace it with one of compassion and love toward that person. Pray with faith and trust God to take care of the situation.

Visions of Inspiration

So I say to you, Ask, and it will be given you; search, and you will find; knock, and the door will be opened for you. For everyone who asks receives, and everyone who searches finds, and for everyone who knocks, the door will be opened. Is there anyone among you who, if your child asks for a fish, will give a snake instead of a fish? Or if the child asks for an egg, will give a scorpion? If you then, who are evil, know how to give good gifts to your children, how much more will the heavenly Father give the Holy Spirit to those who ask him!

Luke 11: 9-13

Do not pray for easy lives. Pray to be stronger men. Do not pray for tasks equal to your powers. Pray for powers equal to your tasks. Then the doing of your work shall be no miracle, but you shall be the miracle.

Phillips Brooks

Pray then in this way: Our Father in heaven, hallowed be your name. Your kingdom come. Your will be done, on earth as it is in heaven. Give us this day our daily bread. And forgive us our debts, as we also have forgiven our debtors. And do not bring us to the time of trial, but rescue us from the evil one. For if you forgive others their trespasses, your heavenly Father will also forgive you; but if you do not forgive others, neither will your Father forgive your trespasses.

Matthew 6: 9-15

Pray as if everything depended upon God and work as if everything depended upon man.

Francis Cardinal Spellman

PRIMARY HUMAN NEEDS

TOOL 57

$\mathcal{D}$o you know what kind of oil is recommended for your car? There are many kinds – 10w40, 10w30, 15w50, 5w30, all with different API qualities – SH, SG/CC, CD, CE/SG. If you don't know which kind you need, that's okay. The point is that the vehicle you drive every day requires specific products, parts and fluids. Humans are similar to cars because all humans have the same set of primary human needs. Everyone's car requires oil, just as everyone in life requires emotional support. Different cars use different parts, just as different people require different forms of positive recognition from others. Understanding the needs of your car is relatively simple compared with understanding your own needs and those of your partner.

In life you can get a mechanic to service your car's needs, but who is going to recognize and fulfill your own individual and personal needs? It's nice to have a full-time mechanic to take care of your car, but unfortunately we are all responsible for our own individual and personal needs. Expecting your partner to automatically know your needs and instantly fulfill them is like expecting your car to perform its own maintenance procedures. Maybe someday automotive technology will be so advanced that your car will be able to drive itself to the local garage on autopilot, express its needs in a healthy manner, make decisions on your behalf, pay for the services and return to wherever it was last parked. Even if that were possible, you would still be responsible for fulfilling your own needs. Blaming your partner for your unfulfilled needs is like blaming your car for running out of gas. If you don't take responsibility for fulfilling your own needs, who will?

In the beginning stages of relationships, your partner may have automatically fulfilled all your needs. They might have acted perfectly, as they do and say all the right things. Usually everyone is on their best behavior during the infatuation stage. Your partner might have been extra attentive to keep other pursuers of the opposite sex from dating you. Maybe in the beginning stages of your relationship you didn't need to assume responsibility for fulfilling your own needs because your partner was so attentive. But eventually every couple passes through the infatuation stage as their relationship starts to grow and develop. As this happens, you will also need to grow and develop along with the relationship by assuming responsibility for your own needs.

If you fail to change the oil in your car, the engine will eventually blow up. When you neglect your own primary human needs, eventually the same things will happen. Unfulfilled needs is a major problem in most personal relationships. God gave each of us free will, and we are all responsible for our own lives and well-being. God wants everyone to live a life of contentment, peace and happiness. But that's not possible if we fail to assume responsibility for our own needs.

The following exercise will help you and your partner identify and fulfill your own needs in the future.

INSTRUCTIONS FOR PRIMARY HUMAN NEEDS EXERCISE

1) Look at the items listed in Column (A), and determine how these needs personally apply to your own life. Then look deep inside yourself to see if these needs are being fulfilled in a healthy and satisfactory manner, or if they are being repressed and neglected.

2) Next, in Column (B) through (E), rate on a scale of 1 to 10 (1 = unfulfilled and 10= very satisfied) how each need is being fulfilled in your life, and from which source. Rate columns (B) through (E) collectively so the total of all the columns will equal ten if the need is completely satisfied. If the need is only being partially satisfied, the total of column (F) might only be a 5. If any of these needs are being met in an excessive or unhealthy manner, place an asterisk in that column. For example: If your spouse is overly smothering, you might want to place an * in the "receiving affection" column.

3) After all the needs are rated and totaled, look inside yourself and search for the reasons that are preventing any low-scoring items from being fulfilled. Many times there are unspoken needs and expectations in relationships. Couples are afraid, or they don't feel worthy of being loved, or they don't want to inconvenience or burden another. These needs go unspoken

and when they aren't met, resentment and frustration builds. Other times people don't feel worthy, deserving or adequate in having needs or in making sure they are met. Yet other times these needs are denied or repressed because of fear of rejection or other past conditioning. Regardless of the reasons, it is important to find out why and record the information in Column G. Use additional paper if necessary.

4) After you have intensively searched and revealed the underlying reasons behind your unmet needs, make a commitment to start making changes. Write down all your proposed changes, ideas and plans in confronting these unmet needs, and in taking responsibility for their fulfillment in the future. Talk about ways to allow your partner more freedom on any items marked with an asterisk. Discuss your needs with your partner in an honest, flexible and compassionate manner. Make the necessary compromises and changes and record your proposed agreements in Column (H). Use additional paper if necessary and feel free to make enlarged photocopies of this form.

A	B	C	D	E	F	G	H
List of the primary human needs that are present in everyone.	Rate on a scale of 1 to 10 (1= unfulfilled and 10= very satisfied) how each need is currently being fulfilled in your life, and from which source. Place an * if need is excessively being fulfilled or being fulfilled in an unhealthy manner.					Describe all the reasons why these needs are not currently being met in your life. List any fears, insecurities or unspoken expectations that have been causing interference.	Make a specific list of proposed changes on how this need will be fulfilled in the future.
	Fulfilled by self	Fulfilled by partner	Fulfilled by others	Fulfilled by God	Total of columns B-E		
Physical Needs							
Satisfied hunger, medical care and shelter etc.							
Stability of environment							
Physical safety and security							
Responsible sexual contact							
Being held, touched, caressed							
Stimulation of physical senses like beauty and laughter							
Mental Needs							
Sense of excitement							
Mental stimulation							
Being challenged							
Peace of mind							
Experiences of pain							
Experiences of playfulness							
Experiences of pleasure							
Experiences of creativity							
Sense of security							
Sense of stability							

A	B	C	D	E	F	G	H
Emotional Needs							
Receiving encouragement							
Receiving praise							
Receiving affection							
Sense of feeling loved							
Sense of self-worth and value							
Receiving sense of worth and value from others							
Sense of spontaneity in life							
Affirmation of feelings from others							
Affirmation of needs from others							
Sense of understanding and being understood							
Sense of connection and unity with others							
Sense of independence from others							
Sense of being unique							
Social Needs							
Being regarded as special							
Time and friendships with others, outside of marriage or personal relationship							
Identification with significant other							
Receiving respect of others							

A	B	C	D	E	F	G	H
Social Needs (cont'd)							
Receiving recognition from others							
Receiving feedback and guidance from others							
Modeling and being a role model for others							
Sense of social predictability							
Sense of being accepted by others							
Sense of social limits							
Spiritual Needs							
Receiving forgiveness from others							
Receiving forgiveness from God							
Need to be connected with something greater than self							
Need to live up to one's ethics, values and morals							
Experiences of God and the gifts He bestows							
Giving and receiving mercy							
Need for sanctification							
Need for repentance							
Need for redemption							
Need for spiritual growth							

Visions of Inspiration

Understanding human needs is half the job of meeting them.

Adlai Stevenson

Necessity is the mother of invention.

Chinese Proverb

His divine power has given us everything needed for life and godliness, through the knowledge of him who called us by his own glory and goodness. Thus he has given us, through these things, his precious and very great promises, so that through them you may escape from the corruption that is in the world because of lust, and may become participants of the divine nature. For this very reason, you must make every effort to support your faith with goodness, and goodness with knowledge, and knowledge with self-control, and self-control with endurance, and endurance with godliness, and godliness with mutual affection, and mutual affection with love.

2 Peter 1: 3-7

No living being is held by anything so strongly as by its own needs. Whatever therefore appears a hindrance to these, be it brother, or father, or child, or mistress, or friend, is hated, abhorred, execrated.

Thomas W. Higginson

PROBLEMS & CONFLICTS

TOOL 58

*C*ars are a lot like relationships because all cars develop mechanical problems and all relationships develop personal problems. Cars are easier to deal with, though. When the transmission goes out, we simply call a tow truck and pay another person to make the repairs for us. But when the transmission goes out on your relationship, repairs can only be made by you. You can read this book, attend seminars or go to a relationship counselor for advice, but you are the only person who can make the necessary changes. There is a joke that makes this point: "How many relationship counselors does it take to change a lightbulb? One – but the lightbulb will need to change itself." Once you have accepted this fact, you can view the problems and conflicts you experience in life like a master mechanic.

Try to imagine what it would be like if you were the only car mechanic in the world. Everyone who owns a car will experience mechanical problems sooner or later, so it's safe to say your services would be in high demand. Because it's not possible for you to fix everyone's car at the same time, you decide to train one million new mechanics to keep up with the demand. In theory that sounds great, but how would you train so many people at once? Would you set up a school to teach each student individually? Or would you give the students old cars with mechanical problems to drive around, expecting each trainee mechanic to fix their own problems as they arose? That way, with the second option, if one of your students came up with a difficult problem, they could call for assistance, knowing you would point them in the right direction. Do you think your students would learn more in school, or would they learn more by getting their own hands dirty?

The best solution to any problem or conflict we face in life lies within the person experiencing the problem. The same is true with all relationship problems and conflicts. God is our Master Mechanic of love and we are His students. Instead of one million new apprentices to teach, God has the responsibility of teaching billions of us. Our mission is to develop our ability to love through personal growth, in an effort to be just like the Master Mechanic Himself. God could step in and fix all of our problems and conflicts for us, but He wants us to develop our own ability to love and personally grow through the natural course of the struggles that we experience every day.

The sole purpose of our problems and conflicts is to overcome them by being a better, stronger, wiser, more compassionate, more powerful, more understanding and more loving person. Without problems, we would have very little incentive to grow in the image and likeness of our Heavenly Father and Master Mechanic. Unfortunately, the problems and conflicts we experience in our lives and relationships are painful, and many times we try to avoid them at all costs. God designed them that way intentionally because if our problems didn't generate negative feelings, we probably wouldn't pay much attention to them. By meeting our problems and conflicts head-on with courage, we prevent them from growing bigger and also gain the gifts of personal growth. When we try to deny, avoid, repress or run away from our problems, they only grow worse, gain more power and eventually consume us.

Neglected and unspoken relationship problems won't go away or disappear. They only grow worse until the proper lessons are learned and the necessary changes are made. There is nothing to fear when facing problems and conflicts in life. God is right there with you, ready to point you in the right direction if you request. If you and your relationship partner are experiencing transmission problems, the following items will help you convert them into personal growth.

Problem and Conflict Resolution

Set Rules

Many times conflicts and arguments are unhealthy because they lack basic ground rules. Try setting up some boundaries and basic fair-fighting rules before discussing your next problem. Take a look at your past arguments and fighting history to figure out a list of unhealthy behaviors. Agree with your partner not to break any of these rules. Keep your rules available when an argument arises and update the list with new items when necessary.

Agree to One Subject at a Time

Many times during arguments and conflicts, different subjects arise. Try to stay focused on one subject at a time. When the first subject is resolved, move on to others if desired. Let your partner know what specific subject you would like to discuss before the discussion begins.

Define Your Intentions

When you are arguing, try to define your true intentions. Ask yourself and your partner the following questions: Are we trying to listen and support each other, or are we trying to win the battle at any cost? Are we trying to resolve the problem at hand, or are we blaming and accusing one another? Are we willing to compromise, or do we want to hurt each other to get our own way?

Dissipate Your Anger Prior to the Confrontation

Problems become very difficult to solve when anger or hostility is present. It's very helpful to vent your hurt, threatened or negative feelings to your partner before actually discussing the underlying problems or conflicts in your relationship. Many times in arguments there's not even a concrete problem to be solved, just hurt feelings that need to be expressed. But even if there is a concrete problem in need of change and compromise, it's helpful to release anger, resentment and hurt feelings first so both people can clearly see the issues. See the Anger chapter on releasing your hurt and threatened feelings.

Clarify Mutual Time Lines

When you experience a conflict with your partner, your mind has compiled information and facts that apparently conflict with the information and facts your partner's mind has produced. A small part of the dispute probably lies between the accuracy of the facts, assuming both people have good memories. A large part of the dispute is the length of time in which these facts have been collected. If your partner is compiling evidence against you based on your entire three-year relationship history and you are just using the facts and events since your last argument, it's safe to say there is going to be a difference of opinion. The length of time is irrelevant to your argument as long as both people are using the same measurements. Before your next argument heats up, determine the length of one another's time lines.

Pick the Right Times

Try to withhold your disagreement until both people are free of other activities. Fighting in the car or before a scheduled event is not conducive to solving problems.

Take Turns

The most important part of resolving conflicts and problems is listening to your partner. Make a commitment to take turns talking and listening without interruption. Let your partner start first, with one mutually agreed subject at a time. Make sure there is nothing left unspoken before the second person explains the situation from their point of view. Ask if there is anything else the other person would like to say because you are willing to hear it all. When you listen to others, they become willing to listen to you in return.

Keep it Positive

It is impossible to accomplish positive objectives through negative methods. No one feels good about themselves or their relationships when criticism, name calling, accusations or derogatory or demeaning remarks are made.

Make Win/Win Agreements

Usually when we resolve our problems and conflicts through manipulation and power plays, they can come back to haunt us later. Compromises where one person gets what they want this time and the other person has to wait until the next usually leaves the second person feeling used, cheated and unhappy. The best way to grow from problems and conflicts is to create win/win situations where both people get what they want by creating a greater reality in the relationship. Try to view situations in a united us/we perspective instead of a you/me alternative. See the Compromise chapter for more information.

Use Good Communication Skills

Try to explain how you are feeling by using "I" statements instead of "You" statements. For example, say, "I feel hurt when you show up a half hour late," instead of, "You are always late." The first statement will effectively communicate your feelings, while the second statement will put your partner in a defensive, argumentative position. Try to avoid statements like "you never," "you always," and "you should." Nothing escalates an unproductive argument like blaming, judging, condemning or trying to change another person. See the Communication chapter for more information.

Don't Repress

Conflicts and problems are best resolved when they are dealt with quickly as soon as they arise. When you wait, important facts and negative feelings can be repressed in your subconscious. If you are experiencing resentment from past problems and conflicts, please refer to the Healing and Forgiveness chapters for more information on resolving these issues permanently.

Schedule Mutual Growth Time in Your Relationship

It's helpful to agree on a mutual conflict discussion time in your relationship. Designate a period of time every day when you and your partner discuss problems together. Set a specific amount of time for the first person to listen while the other talks, and vice versa. Devise your own rules: maybe discuss one problem a night until it is settled, or maybe just listen and understand one another without finding any solutions.

Celebrate After Your Conflicts

Don't forget to celebrate your mutual victories. During an argument both people felt at odds with each other; through growth, patience, understanding and love the problems were mutually overcome. Take advantage of your closeness and celebrate your efforts after a mutual victory. Problems and conflicts are a valuable part of your mutual growth.

Work Through the Conflict Resolution Exercise

It can be helpful to fill out this conflict resolution form every time you or your family members experience an argument. Simply make some enlarged copies of this form and agree to fill it out when a conflict arises. (1) The first part describes the mutual problem and limits one subject at a time. (2) The second part involves the use of "I" statements and empathetic listening ability. (3) The third part involves creating a mutual compromise or win/win situation. (4) The fourth part recognizes responsibilities. (5) The fifth part moves you through the necessary apologies. (6) The sixth part expresses your higher wants and loving intentions. (7) The seventh part addresses any amends that will be necessary to restore the relationship back to its original condition. The next time an argument arises, have each involved person fill out their individual forms in an attempt to resolve the situation. Working through this written process together will solve most conflicts. But more important, it will help you understand the systematic order necessary to resolve future conflicts and problems in your relationships.

CONFLICT RESOLUTION EXERCISE

1. Description of mutual problem (one situation per page.)

| 2. How "I" feel statements, as you vent your negative emotions. | How the other person feels, use your empathetic listening skills. |

3. Compromises, win/win situations and future agreements.

| 4. The mistakes I made. | Mistakes of the other person. |

| 5. What I regret and apologized for. | What the other person apologized for. |

| 6. My higher wants and needs. | Other person's higher wants and needs. |

| 7. The form of amends or gifts of love I will make to myself. | My form of amends that I will make to the other person. |

Visions of Inspiration

A hasty quarrel kindles a fire, and a hasty dispute sheds blood. If you blow on a spark, it will glow; if you spit on it, it will be put out; yet both come out of your mouth.

Sirach 28: 11-12

Those conflicts and disputes among you, where do they come from? Do they not come from your cravings that are at war within you? You want something and do not have it; so you commit murder. And you covet something and cannot obtain it; so you engage in disputes and conflicts. You do not have, because you do not ask.

James 4: 1-2

A problem is something you have hopes of changing. Anything else is a fact of life.

C. R. Smith

RESENTMENT & REVENGE

TOOL 59

*H*as another driver ever pissed you off while you were driving and you couldn't do anything about it because of the circumstances? Imagine that you were driving to work one day and a coworker intentionally cut you off and endangered your life. Unfortunately, due to the circumstances you were unable to properly express your anger. Maybe at the time your boss was around, or maybe you just decided not to make a big deal of the situation. You're hoping the other person will apologize for their destructive behavior, but several weeks go by and they never do. Every time you think of this person you start to experience sick, hateful feelings because of what they did to you. If this situation has ever happened to you, you surely know what thoughts of resentment and revenge are like.

Resentment is unresolved anger turned outward, and revenge is unresolved anger outwardly acted upon. Resentment or revenge begin with another person's harmful actions that have hurt or threatened you somehow. If you fail to properly express your feelings at the time, they turn into anger. Once you are angry, you are faced with four choices:

- ❖ You can express yourself in a healthy way to the other person and your anger will turn into mutual understanding and personal growth.
- ❖ You can feed into your anger with positive loving thoughts and energy and turn your anger into forgiveness and understanding.
- ❖ You can do nothing, and your anger will be repressed into your subconscious, only to return later in the form of fear or transference.
- ❖ You can feed into your anger with negative thoughts and energy and your anger will turn into resentment or revenge.

Resentment is an internal anger that is backed by a lot of negative, hateful and destructive thoughts. When we attempt to get even by hurting the person who has hurt us, our anger turns into revenge. Resentment only hurts the person who holds the grudge by prolonging their suffering and robbing them of their happiness. Unfortunately, many people in life seem to think that revenge will make everything better. But it won't – revenge only makes things worse. After we try to get even, our anger is still unresolved, and we get the added bonus of guilt and the possibility of being further attacked by the other person in a continuous cycle of counter-revenge. Resentment and revenge are destructive to our lives and relationships. When we feed into anything with negative thoughts and emotions, we will reap the negative repercussions and consequences.

God asks that we leave judgment and vengeance to Him alone. He also says He will deal with us in the same way we deal with other people. If you are experiencing anger, resentment or revengeful feelings, it is best to feed into them with positive thoughts and energy. It takes the same amount of effort and it will promote your own personal peace and happiness.

The following steps will help you convert your resentful or revengeful thoughts into personal empowerment and well-being.

Steps to Converting Resentful or Revengeful Experiences

Step 1: Describe the Original Incident

The first step is to completely describe the original incident in writing. Write a letter that explains every detail regarding the people, places, events, behaviors and actions of the situation where your resentful or revengeful attitude was first developed. It's important to record only the facts you personally know to be true. Many times actual events are distorted and exaggerated if they are fed with negative energy and dwelled upon day after day.

Step 2: Vent Your Anger

Try to vent your anger by writing the meanest, cruelest "monster" letter possible. Usually after describing the events in Step 1, your angry emotions are ready to flow. Begin by writing a letter (one that should never be sent) to the person who hurt you. Tell them what you think of them and describe what type of person you perceive them to be. Feel free to use any applicable or appropriate language. Tell them how they hurt you. Tell them everything they deserve to hear. Keep writing until you don't have anything left to say.

Step 3: Recognize Your Personal Damage

It's necessary to recognize the amount of personal damage you are causing yourself over this incident. You may find it helpful to answer the following questions in written form to bring about a deeper understanding of this damage:

- How long have you experienced your angry, negative, hurtful and revengeful feelings?
- Do you think the person who has hurt you knows how much pain you are still feeling?
- How much of your time and life have these feelings consumed? Describe the daily suffering you continue to experience.
- If you act out in a revengeful way, what will be gained?
- If you get even and take revenge, what difference is there between you and the person described in the "monster" letter from Step 2?
- Do you want to remain consumed by your hurt and angry past, or do you want to free yourself from these self-imposed feelings through forgiveness?

Step 4: Forgive

After completing the first three steps, you are ready to work on forgiveness. It is very important to forgive all experiences where you have suffered harm in the past. If you don't forgive harmful past experiences, they will continue to haunt you and affect your well-being until they're resolved. Follow the instructions in the Forgiveness chapter and feed into your past experience with loving thoughts and energy.

Step 5: Make Daily Efforts

Avoiding resentment and revengeful feelings in the future will require daily efforts. It's helpful to work on your ability to express anger in a healthy manner. Anger is a valuable gift that lets us know when there is a hurt or threat present in our relationships. If we acknowledge our anger immediately and express ourselves in a healthy way, our everyday negative experiences might never develop into resentment or revengeful tendencies. If you continue to feel negative emotions regarding the situation you described in Step 1, try writing a healing letter by following the directions listed in the Healing chapter. Your relationship with God has a lot to do with your willingness to forgive. If you don't believe in God or fail to maintain a relationship with Him, you have very few reasons to work your way through the forgiving process. God is always there to help you in your relationships, especially when it comes to your own personal growth, healing and forgiveness.

Visions of Inspiration

It is folly to punish your neighbor by fire when you live next door.
Publilius Syrus

You shall not hate in your heart anyone of your kin; you shall reprove your neighbor, or you will incur guilt yourself. You shall not take vengeance or bear a grudge against any of your people, but you shall love your neighbor as yourself: I am the Lord.
Leviticus 19: 17-18

In taking revenge, a man is but even with his enemy; but in passing it over, he is superior.
Francis Bacon

Beloved, never avenge yourselves, but leave room for the wrath of God; for it is written, "Vengeance is mine, I will repay, says the Lord." No, "if your enemies are hungry, feed them; if they are thirsty, give them something to drink; for by doing this you will heap burning coals on their heads." Do not be overcome by evil, but overcome evil with good.
Romans 12: 19-21

RESPECT

TOOL 60

*I*magine trying to drive your car across a busy lane of traffic. It's rush hour and no one is letting you through. As you start to pull out, a large dump truck almost runs you down. The driver honks their horn in anger as they pass, creating a large cloud of dust. The next car that refuses to let you in is an expensive luxury automobile whose driver pretends not to notice you as they drive by with their nose in the air. The next car is a junker, the interior is trashed and the exterior is full of dents and damage. They obviously don't care about their own car, and as they pass, they give you the bird. The next car is a clean four-door sedan. It's a smaller economy car and the driver slows down and signals for you to merge into traffic.

Out of these four vehicles who has your respect? The dump truck is probably the most powerful, but doesn't their disrespectful actions cause you to disrespect them in return? The luxury automobile is probably the most prestigious, but doesn't their lack of respect toward anything other than themselves cause you to disrespect them as well? The junker is probably the most disrespectful and it's clear by the condition of their car that they don't respect anything. The only respectful car of the four is the clean economy sedan. They are respectful because they first acted in a respectful manner toward you.

The moral to this story is that if you want to be respected on the road of life, you need to respect yourself and other people first. If you don't respect yourself, other people won't respect you in return.

Lack of respect is a big problem in relationships. Do you think the big dump truck would have a very good relationship with the luxury sedan? How about the luxury sedan and the junker? Do you think the economy car could make friends with anyone? True respect is a good indication that everything in your relationship is functioning beautifully. Many times the lack of respect between partners is an early warning sign of future problems. Genuine respect requires you to uphold your own self-respect, maintain respectful mental thoughts and perceptions toward your partner and communicate that condition through your words, actions and behaviors.

Take a look at your life and relationships. Are you driving around in the dump truck, the luxury sedan, the junker or the economy car? Does your relationship partner regularly fail to let you merge in front of them? Could the lack of respect in your relationship be stemming from individual issues, negative thoughts and beliefs about each other, or lack of self-respect? Could the lack of respect be an early warning sign of future problems, unresolved resentments, control issues, power struggles and the lack of growth in your relationship?

If you or your partner find yourself traveling in the dump truck, luxury sedan or junker, the following steps will help increase the amount of respect in your relationship.

Steps to Increasing Relationship Respect

Step 1: List Disrespected Items

Start by listing things that you disrespect in your partner. Look at every aspect of their lives and write down as many items as possible. List any negative habits, addictions, compulsive behaviors, interactions with others, careless intentions, destructive behaviors or anything else about your partner you consider disrespectful. What don't you approve of? What do you feel is wrong, unhealthy or negative? If you're working with your partner, you might want to make sure both of your lists contain an equal number of items. This might help prevent the person with the longest list from feeling attacked. If you feel disrespected by your partner, figure out the exact issue and offer it to them as a potential candidate for their list.

Step 2: Confront and Resolve Each Issue

Next, it will be helpful to work your way through each issue that was listed in Step 1. You will need to make a decision concerning these items, and there are many possibilities from which to choose. Some possible situations might include working on changing these issues together, practicing forgiveness and making compromises, removing yourself from the situation and finding a more compassionate and positive way to view your partner's issues, or practicing acceptance by separating your partner's identity from their behaviors.

Some possible examples of disrespected items and their potential outcomes might be:

Being inconsiderate of others – Your partner might not be aware of their inconsiderate actions and may be willing to work with you to change and grow.

Smoking – Your partner might not be willing to quit, but maybe a compromise can be reached where they won't smoke in your presence. Or maybe you will need to accept the smoking issue by viewing your partner's true sense of self separate from the activities they choose to participate in.

Physical abuse – If your partner is unwilling to seek professional help, your only alternative would be to remove yourself from this situation.

Being rude to your friends – Maybe after discussing this issue, you realize your partner likes all of your friends and has not meant to intentionally act rudely toward them. An appropriate action on your part might be forgiveness.

Work together with your partner and come up with a plan for action, method of change or form of acceptance for every issue on both lists. Many times when you begin to respect others, you gain their respect in return.

Step 3: Heal the Past

To increase respect, you might find it helpful to heal negative past experiences where you were disrespected. Many times people who were disrespected by their parents grow up treating others in the same disrespectful manner. It's evident in today's society that some parents treat their children as objects to be owned and controlled. Maybe your parents told you what to do, how to do it and when to do it, without any consideration for your sense of self, your rights or your feelings. If you were treated disrespectfully by your parents, it will be helpful to go back, experience the feelings, and vent the negative emotions and replace them with the love, support and respect you never received. If you fail to love and embrace that disrespected, hurt part of yourself, it will continue to affect your subconscious programming and prevent you from treating others respectfully. Follow the instructions in the Healing chapter and go back, treating your child-self with the respect you deserved.

Step 4: Maintain Respectful Perceptions

The next step in the process is to monitor the mental attitudes and thoughts you have toward others. If you think disrespectful thoughts in your mind, you will produce disrespectful results in your reality. A good example of this would be to look at your feelings toward people in general. Are most people inherently good or bad? If you believe people are inherently good, you probably uphold a general respect for strangers unless they prove themselves unrespectable. If you believe people are inherently bad, you probably disrespect strangers until they prove themselves otherwise. In the same way, if you want to be more respectful in your relationships, it's necessary to eliminate disrespectful preconceived mental perceptions.

You can do this by monitoring your thoughts and attitudes toward other people for one hour each day. Make a commitment to carefully watch your thoughts for any forms of negativity during a specific time of day. You can move the allotted time around in your schedule so you can identify any areas of disrespectful outlooks. For example, you might find your thoughts more disrespectful during rush-hour traffic or in dealing with children than on a first date or in church. If you catch yourself participating in a thought or belief that is disrespectful, destructive, judgmental or negative, stop yourself and change it by focusing only on what you know to be true or on the positive aspects concerning the situation. Ask yourself what you would want others to perceive if the roles were reversed. The more you practice this monitoring exercise, the easier it will be to maintain respectful perceptions toward others, and your partner.

Step 5: Maintain Respectful Actions

You can also practice monitoring and correcting your words, behaviors and actions. Once you have an internal sense of respect for others in your thoughts and perceptions, it's rewarding to show it externally in your words and deeds. Try complimenting everyone you meet. Try treating children as though they are miniature adults. Often we feel comfortable telling a child what to do, but we would not consider ordering our friends around the same way. Take an hour each day to treat other people in your life the same way you want to be treated. The more respect you give others, the more respect you will receive in return.

Visions of Inspiration

You shall not make wrongful use of the name of the Lord your God, for the Lord will not acquit anyone who misuses his name.

Exodus 20: 7

Let love be genuine; hate what is evil, hold fast to what is good; love one another with mutual affection; outdo one another in showing honor. Do not lag in zeal, be ardent in spirit, serve the Lord. Rejoice in hope, be patient in suffering, persevere in prayer. Contribute to the needs of the saints; extend hospitality to strangers. Bless those who persecute you; bless and do not curse them. Rejoice with those who rejoice, weep with those who weep. Live in harmony with one another; do not be haughty, but associate with the lowly; do not claim to be wiser than you are. Do not repay anyone evil for evil, but take thought for what is noble in the sight of all. If it is possible, so far as it depends on you, live peaceably with all.

Romans 12: 9-18

When people do not respect us we are sharply offended; yet deep down in his heart no man much respects himself.

Mark Twain

If you want to be respected by others the great thing is to respect yourself. Only by that, only by self-respect will you compel others to respect you.

Fyodor Dostoevsky

SELF-ACCEPTANCE

TOOL 61

*H*ave you ever driven a truck that had two gas tanks but only one fuel gauge? Usually one tank holds the main fuel supply and the other stores the reserve supply. The vehicle has only one fuel gauge because it reads the level in the tank currently being used. The manufacturer designed the vehicle with two tanks to keep the driver from running out of fuel on the roadways of life. If your vehicle has ever run out of gas, you probably know just how worthless it becomes as a form of transportation.

What does this have to do with self-acceptance? It's simple. The world's most valuable energy source is not gas – it's LOVE. You could own all the gas in the world and still be the most miserable, empty and internally anguished person on the planet. Everyone needs love, just as vehicles need fuel. Without love you feel empty, valueless and useless, just like your truck would feel running on fumes. The truck's manufacturer created one fuel gauge and two fuel tanks just as your Manufacturer created you with one source of emotions and two love tanks. Your first love tank is the love you give yourself, otherwise known as self-acceptance. Your second love tank, the reserve tank, is the love you receive from others. Your vehicle comes with only one fuel gauge because you have only one source of emotions.

When one of our tanks is drained faster than the other, the fuel gauge will automatically sense a shortage and report the information through our feelings. This system works great, except that sometimes it's hard to determine which tank is empty when we are experiencing a lack of love in our lives. Many times in relationships we expect our partners to make us feel loved and to fill both of our tanks. Unfortunately, that is impossible, since no one can fill up our self-acceptance tank except us. Many times our partners provide us with enough love to fill up the reserve tank, but if our self-acceptance tank is empty, the gauge will sense a shortage and we may feel that our partner's love isn't good enough.

If you know that your partner loves you and are still experiencing a fuel shortage, it probably stems from a low self-acceptance tank. If you find yourself constantly looking for the perfect partner who makes you feel loved, you may want to check your self-acceptance tank. If you are unable to love yourself, you probably cannot find very much value and worth in your own life. If you are unable to recognize value and worth in your own life, why do you think you will be able to recognize value and worth in other people's lives? If you can't recognize and promote the value and worth in others, why would others want to be associated with you?

Basically the love of self and the love of others go hand-in-hand. The more value you can recognize in your own vehicle (self-love), the more potential you have to recognize value in other people's vehicles (love of others). Look at your own life and relationships. Do you feel like the richest person in the world when it comes to love? Are your love tanks full of the world's most valuable energy source, or are you feeling valueless, useless and empty most of the time? What about your relationship partner – is there a lack of balance in their tanks?

Healthy self-acceptance is being able to embrace, accept and value everything that makes us who we are. This involves embracing our hurt, unwanted and disadvantaged parts as well. We all have hurt, unwanted and disadvantaged parts we don't like very much. Self-acceptance is finding and using the positive sides of these unwanted parts and learning to value them more than the pain and inconvenience of their negative sides. Healthy self-acceptance promotes our own self-worth and value without causing harm to others. Unhealthy self-acceptance is a lot like narcissism, where we try to cover up and deny those hurt, disadvantaged parts of ourselves in an attempt to become something we aren't. Narcissism promotes the self at the expense of others and it doesn't promote the good of all.

The only way to get more love into your life and relationships is to love yourself first. The only way to love yourself is to humbly embrace your own pain and disadvantages because they are a part of who you are. If you or your partner could use some more love, the following exercise will help in its production.

INSTRUCTIONS FOR THE
SELF-ACCEPTANCE EXERCISE

1) The purpose of this exercise is to evaluate and increase your ability for self-love. To begin, study the list of internal aspects of love in column (1) and think about how you give yourself each of those qualities.

2) Next, take a look at the questions that are asked in columns (2) through (5). After you have asked yourself the questions, fill in a different word from the internal aspect list (column 1) into each of these questions. Then write down two different responses by answering the question. If it is applicable, try to find a different answer for each of the questions. There can be up to 88 different aspects of yourself if all the questions have been answered differently. Many times some of these questions will take a lot of deep thought and contemplation to answer. Some people only learn to love parts of themselves through negative experiences and losses. For example, you might not value and respect your ability to breathe easily until you have experienced asthma. Other times people will learn self-love through role modeling and be very strong in some areas of their lives, but weaker in other parts. Take your time in searching for these answers. If necessary, meditate on one set of questions until you come up with a comfortable answer.

3) After all the questions have been carefully answered, the next step is self-evaluation. Begin your self-evaluation by studying all the answers least loved about yourself. Then, if applicable, make a choice between the following two courses of action, and write down your discussion in column 6.

Making the changes. If there are aspects in yourself you don't like, you may want to take the necessary actions to change them. Try to determine if there are several answers that point to one specific area of your life that needs change. Then ask yourself what can you do to improve, change or correct those situations. By starting small and setting goals, you can slowly change anything you believe is possible.

Appreciating the gifts. If there are aspects in your life that are not changeable, it's important to find the advantages and gifts they add to your life. There are positive and negative qualities to every situation. By accepting and focusing on the positive, you will have an easier time releasing the negative. Write down the gifts that are present for every item listed in the least column that you choose not to change. By practicing affirmations, converting self-criticism and working on your self-concept, you will have an easier time recognizing and appreciating these gifts.

4) The next step is to find a way to further increase and appreciate all the good aspects that are already a part of yourself. Take a look at the items listed in the (most) columns. Then ask yourself how you can further increase and enhance these positive qualities in your life. How can you use these gifts to promote your own personal peace, happiness, well-being and success? How can you use these items to increase the amount of love you give and receive from others? Try to focus and think about them every day in an effort to increase your capacity for self-acceptance. Use additional paper if necessary and feel free to make enlarged photocopies of this form.

Column 1	Column 2	Column 3	Column 4	Column 5	Column 6
Study the different aspects of internal love within yourself and your life. Answer each question in columns 2-5 by filling in a different word from this internal aspects list.	What are your abilities that you (fill in word) the most and the least?	What types of mental thoughts do you (fill in word) the most and the least?	What types of emotional responses or feelings do you (fill in word) the most and the least?	What physical attributes about yourself do you (fill in word) the most and the least?	Evaluate every item in the *least* columns. Are these items changeable? If not, find and write down the gifts that are available in them. If they are changeable, write down the necessary plans, steps and goals to take action.
Internal Aspects of Love	**Most-Least**	**Most-Least**	**Most-Least**	**Most-Least**	**Appreciating Gifts and Making Changes**
Accept					
Acknowledge					
Admire					
Appreciate					
Approve of					
Encourage					
Respect					
Support					
Trust					
Understand					
Validate					

Visions of Inspiration

If I speak in the tongues of mortals and of angels, but do not have love, I am a noisy gong or a clanging cymbal. And if I have prophetic powers, and understand all mysteries and all knowledge, and if I have all faith, so as to remove mountains, but do not have love, I am nothing. If I give away all my possessions, and if I hand over my body so that I may boast, but do not have love, I gain nothing. Love is patient; love is kind; love is not envious or boastful or arrogant or rude. It does not insist on its own way; it is not irritable or resentful; it does not rejoice in wrongdoing, but rejoices in the truth. It bears all things, believes all things, hopes all thing, endures all things.

1 Corinthians 13: 1-7

To love oneself is the beginning of a life-long romance.

Oscar Wilde

SELF-AWARENESS

TOOL 62

*T*he warning lights and gauges on a vehicle's dashboard help inform the driver of the car's mechanical condition. If your car is overheating or running low on oil, the warning lights bring it to your attention so you can make the necessary corrections. These valuable gauges were installed by the car's manufacturer to help protect the vehicle from damage and protect the driver from experiencing dangerous situations. The signals and indications that the gauges reflect are neither positive nor negative; they only represent the car's internal condition.

The gauges and warning lights on your car's dashboard are similar to your eight primary emotions. God installed the eight primary emotions of anger/frustration, sadness/disappointment, fear/concerns and guilt/inadequacy in our dashboards because He doesn't want to see us overheat or run out of fuel on the highway of life. The signals these emotions reflect are neither positive nor negative; they only reflect your internal condition. Unfortunately, many people view the feelings generated by these primary emotions as negative. They've convinced themselves that negative emotions are harmful and should be avoided at all costs. Unfortunately, if you avoid your negative emotions, it can be just as dangerous as ignoring your car's temperature gauge when it indicates an overheated engine.

Let's say the needle is well into the red and smoke is trailing from behind your car. Would you stop the car and save the engine? Or would you perceive the temperature gauge's information in a negative way, as something to be avoided at all costs? Would you try to ignore the information by driving faster and playing with the air-conditioner? It happens every day as millions of people attempt to avoid their negative emotions through addictions, distractions and denial. Denial will resolve your car's mechanical problems just as fast as breaking out the lightbulb behind your warning light. When you ignore the underlying issues behind your negative emotions, they don't go away; they only grow more powerful with a consuming amount of force. The only way to free yourself from negative emotions is to determine their underlying source and deal with those issues.

Practicing good self-awareness requires a balance between spending too much time evaluating your emotions and avoiding your emotions altogether. People who spend too much time staring at the dashboard while driving are likely to cause an accident because they aren't paying proper attention to the road. Good self-awareness includes a constant acknowledgment of both your positive and negative emotions.

The following exercise will help you practice good self-awareness when you don't like what your gauges and warning lights are indicating. You can practice it when you're feeling hurt, annoyed, numb, upset, uncomfortable or negative. By using it regularly, you will find it easier to process and convert your negative emotions into positive emotions.

The Self-Diagnostic Exercise

Step 1: Do a Self-Diagnostic Check

First, it's necessary to commit yourself to working through the self-diagnostic check when you're feeling upset, unhappy, uncomfortable or negative. Stop what you're doing and force yourself to experience all eight primary emotions. You need only look deep inside yourself and find that angry, scared, sad or guilty part of yourself. If you can't find one of these emotions, try to create it. For example, let's say you're having a bad day and you don't know why. If you want to feel better, take a minute to get in touch with that angry and frustrated part of your being. Something is causing your bad day, so figure out what it is and give yourself permission to be angry and frustrated. Next, work your way through your fears/concerns, sadness/disappointment and guilt/inadequacy in the same way. It's necessary to actually feel your emotions. This exercise won't work if you just logically think about them. You can work through the eight primary emotions in any order, or in this order:

Anger/Frustration	Fear/Concerns
Sadness/Disappointment	Guilt/Inadequacy

Step 2: Dig Deeper

If you were almost involved in an accident on your way to work, your Inner Self would probably generate all eight primary emotions. If you don't acknowledge your anger, fears, sadness and guilt, these emotions may get trapped inside you and cause you to have a bad day. Usually the emotion you deny and refuse to express is the one that keeps you from getting back to the positive. For example, if you are in denial about your fears (the "I'm not afraid of anything mentality"), it's possible to be trapped in the sadness or anger stages.

If you're having trouble experiencing any of the primary emotions, it's necessary to dig deeper. Ask yourself the following questions to help draw out any repressed or denied emotions:

- Anger - What has happened that hurt or threatened your well-being?
- Sadness - What did you want to happen that didn't?
- Fear - What's the worst thing that could have happened?
- Guilt - What could you apologize for?
- Frustration - Does it seems like this is always happening?
- Disappointment - What would you have liked to happen?
- Concern - How have others been affected?
- Inadequacy - What could you have done differently?

Step 3: Evaluate

The next step is to evaluate the information you collected from your eight primary emotions. It's necessary to determine what those gauges and warning lights are actually trying to tell you before you can return to the positive emotions. By looking deep inside yourself and experiencing these feelings, you are getting in touch with your Inner Self. If you are well-connected to your spiritual source and have developed a trust in your intuitive ability, you probably already know what to do regarding the evaluation of your primary emotions. If you are unsure what to do, ask yourself what you could do to resolve the situation. How can you help yourself and others? What would God want you to do in this situation? Does your view of the situation represent the full truth, or are you assuming critical parts?

Many times it's necessary to talk to the person who lies at the root of your evaluation. These signals may be calling to make amends, take some action, or practice patience, forgiveness or assertiveness. Other times distorted perceptions of the truth will cause negative warning signals for no reason. If so, seek the truth and it will be automatically resolved. See the Perceptions chapter for more information. If you can't figure out what your internal indicators are trying to tell you, the chapters shown in parenthesis might be helpful:

❖ (Anger)-Frustration. Stems from being hurt or threatened.
❖ (Depression)- Sadness. Stems from the necessity to grieve a loss or to rise above it by focusing on the positive. It is also a calling to get in touch with your higher wants and needs.
❖ (Fear)-Concern. Stems from a proposed danger or threat, serves as a warning signal or a call for courage.
❖ (Guilt)-Inadequacy. Stems from actions that have hurt another or yourself, a call for amends and growth.

Step 4: Take Action

Once you figure out the underlying problems, it's necessary to follow through with a course of action to resolve the situation. For example, if the warning light indicates your car is too hot, the necessary evaluation would be to check the radiator. If the fluid is low, the necessary action would be to add coolant. If your internal warning light indicates anger, the necessary evaluation would be to figure out how and why you have been hurt and threatened, and express yourself in a healthy manner. By doing so, you will be quickly working through the negative so that you can return to the positive. After you know what actions are necessary, do what it takes to see them through.

Step 5: Acknowledge Your Gifts

After you complete the necessary actions, the next step is to acknowledge the gifts and rewards you are entitled to for completing the self-diagnostic exercise. When you successfully work through a negative emotion its positive counterpart is there waiting for you. Take a minute to look inside yourself, get in touch with the positive emotions and allow yourself to experience them. The gift and rewards that you are entitled to are:

Primary Emotions	Gift Received
Anger	Fulfillment
Sadness	Happiness
Fear	Confidence
Guilt	Freedom
Frustration	Satisfaction
Disappointment	Gratitude
Concern	Purposefulness
Inadequacy	Growth

Visions of Inspiration

Search me, O God, and know my heart; test me and know my thoughts.
See if there is any wicked way in me, and lead me in the way everlasting.

Psalm 139: 23-24

Your vision will become clear only when you can look into your own heart.
Who looks outside, dreams; who looks inside, awakes.

Carl Jung

Intellect is to emotion as our clothes are to our bodies; we could not very
well have civilized life without clothes, but we would be in a poor way if we
had only clothes without bodies.

Alfred Whitehead

SELF-CONCEPT

TOOL 63

*I*f you were the owner of a show car, how would you set up and display your priceless, valuable vehicle? Would you stand in front of your car and talk about it in a negative manner? Would you cut it down with criticism? Or would you work on improving the car's negative aspects, tying them with the positive qualities into one great package? Would you feel the need to hide your car behind material possessions to feel good about the display? How would you want your best friend or relationship partner to display their own car? How sad would it be to see a beautiful show car displayed in a disrespectful condition?

If life were a car show, then you would be the car on display. Your self-concept (sometimes referred to as self-esteem) would be the way you display yourself to the world. Just like the car, people who place a low self-worth and value on themselves will not do very well in the car shows or relationships of life. A negative self-concept will affect your feelings, behaviors and attitudes toward everything you do and say. A positive self-concept will promote your success, and a negative self-concept will bring about many painful lessons.

Usually at car shows there are many different types of vehicles – everything from cars to trucks – and they all have their advantages and disadvantages. If you have a really nice sports car to display, would you compare parts of your vehicle to another person's display? Would you look at your street tires and compare them to someone else's truck tires? The fastest way to destroy your self-concept is to compare parts of yourself to other people. There will always be someone who has it better, who is prettier, smarter or more talented than you are. But those are just parts that make up other people and they don't have any effect on your personal display and package.

God is the Master Car Show Creator. He doesn't make junk or mistakes; He only produces top-of-the-line, award-winning vehicles. All you have to do is put all your parts together into one loving package. A healthy self-concept is seeing yourself as God sees you. A healthy self-concept is based on the eternal and spiritual part of your being known as your Inner Self. It includes your true character, your integrity, your ability to be loving, your genuine intentions, your creativity and your spirituality. People with a positive self-concept are secure, confident, open to learning from others, appreciative of their individuality and accepting of other people's differences. An unhealthy self-concept is based on a false sense of self or ego. That is the logical part of your being that wants to be something you're not. The false self is something other people want you to be or what you want other people to think you are.

People with an unhealthy self-concept try to act superior to others because they feel insecure and needy. They frequently experience feelings of depression and hopelessness and try to maintain thoughts and feelings of overinflated righteousness. People who try to be something they aren't are fake and simply haven't discovered the true beauty that comes from putting all their parts together into a loving display. Some people make the mistake of basing their ego on outside sources. When we establish our identity and base our self-worth on relationships, the next promotion, careers or clothes, it might make us temporarily feel good, but eventually it leads to disappointments, insecurities and emptiness.

If your identity is based on your career, you aren't being true to your Inner Self. This ego-based identity will be damaged if you get fired. With a career-based identity you will think of yourself as worthless when something negative happens at the office. Unfortunately, people with a misplaced identity are not able to function freely. Their actions become limited by fear, insecurity and worry about losing who they think they are if they were to lose their job title. A person whose identity is based on their true sense of self can function as a valuable person regardless of their employment and economic conditions. The same destructive situation applies when you base your self-concept on any other type of outside source. If your identity and self-worth are based on owning a boat or on your husband, what will happen when the boat is not in use or your marriage experiences problems?

Once you have made a decision not to base your identity on external sources, your only option is to base it on internal sources. That isn't always easy and, like participating in car shows, it requires hard work. Many times there are parts of you and your car that you don't like very much. If your show car needs new paint, you can either love it and accept it as is, or you can do something about it. The same is true in your own life: You can either do something about the thing you don't like about yourself by making changes, or you can overcompensate in other areas of your life by promoting your positive qualities. It is even possible to learn to accept and love what you don't like.

If you find yourself not participating in the grand car show prize, you might find it helpful to work through the following steps to improve your self-concept.

Steps to Improving Your Self-Concept

Step 1: Make a Self-Identity List

Begin the process by making a list of everything that you base your self-identity on. Ask yourself the following questions to determine any ego-based external items. Try searching for as many different answers as possible, like your relationships, career, material possessions, assets, children or finances.

❖ What in your life do you need to be complete (Fill in)?
❖ If I only had more (Fill in), I would be satisfied.
❖ I can't live without my (Fill in).
❖ I am dependent on my (Fill in). Without it I would be hopeless.
❖ I am popular and others like me because of my (Fill in).

Step 2: Make a List of Consequences

If you have identified any external items that your self-worth, identity and value are based on, the next step is to write a couple of paragraphs that describe your feelings regarding the loss of that item. Because everything in life is constantly changing and nothing lasts forever, try to imagine the loss of each of these items on your list. Begin by writing a description of the imaginary events that could produce such a loss. Next, describe your feelings during and after this hypothetical situation. How will you survive? How will you react? What consequences will your self-concept and life suffer because of these ego-based outside sources? List all the ways your actions and feelings could be considered harmful to yourself and others. Write a separate description for every external item you discovered on your self-identity list from Step 1.

Step 3: Make a List of Internal Changes

Now write a couple of paragraphs regarding your internal value and worth after the loss. Describe how this imaginary loss would change who you are inside. How and why would it affect your value, worth, friendliness, intelligence or integrity? Would it have an effect on your ability to love, care, share, encourage, trust or respect others or yourself? List all the benefits that could be achieved by detaching your self-value and worth from any ego-based external item and basing them on your true self.

Step 4: Make a List of Self-Dislikes

The next step is to make a list of everything you don't like about yourself. List as many undesirable items about yourself as possible. These can include:

❖ Physical attributes like body parts, clothes and hair style.
❖ Mental attributes like intelligence and education.
❖ Environmental aspect like friends, popularity, family background and social prestige.
❖ Life events like work, play, rest, goals, relationships, plans and past history.

Step 5: Evaluate the Situation

Now you're ready to evaluate your list of dislikes. Look at the following four choices and choose a course of action that best fits your specific situation.

Choice A. Do nothing at all and continue to dislike these parts of yourself. You can try to ignore or repress these negative aspects of yourself, but it will only draw more negative attention to those parts of your life. Another option would be to feed into these aspects with more negative thoughts and energy, but this will only make matters worse.

Choice B. Do something about it. Commit yourself to making the necessary changes regarding what it is you don't like. This might include hard work, dedication and setting goals. It might also be necessary to seek help and assistance from others. Many times reaching out to other people is beneficial because everyone in life has to deal with their own self-concept and negative issues. You can find a lot of comfort and acceptance in sharing your concerns, desires and goals with others who have gone through similar experiences. See the Goals chapter for step-by-step instructions for accomplishing what it is you would like to change.

Choice C. Compensate for any aspects of yourself that you feel are negative by improving other areas of your life. Accept your disadvantages and make up for them by focusing on and strengthening your other talents and advantages. Get in touch with your talents, gifts and abilities and start using them for the greater service of yourself, others and God.

Choice D. Accept and learn to love any parts of yourselves you can't change. Begin by acknowledging the positive advantages that exist in every situation on your list of dislikes. If you study the opposite extremes, you can find their advantages. Keep your attention focused on the gifts. Have faith that God has great plans and purposes for these special attributes. Try to release negative thoughts about your uniqueness over to God. The Transformation and Transcendence chapter will help you rise above and find the positive aspects that exist in everything.

Step 6: Convert Negative Thoughts

It will be helpful to convert your negative self-criticism and to practice affirmations on a regular basis. Self-doubt and negative thoughts are very destructive to anyone's self-concept. By converting your self-criticism into its positive intentions, you will feel a lot better about every aspect of your life and being. Please refer to the chapters on Criticism and Affirmations for more information.

Step 7: Learn Self-Love and Acceptance

Self-love is the fundamental principle behind a positive self-concept. It's important to understand, accept and forgive yourself regardless of the circumstances. It's important to love and respect yourself the same way you would love and respect your closest friends and family members. It's also important to trust, listen and be patient with yourself. Please refer to the Self-Acceptance and Self-Awareness chapters for more information. Make plans to correct issues that might be preventing a positive self-concept.

Step 8: Do Past Healing Work

Nothing eats away a positive self-concept like unhealed past experiences. As children we receive a lot of verbal, non-verbal, subtle, direct and indirect messages about how we are viewed by others. If you received more positive messages, you probably grew up with a positive self-concept. If you received more negative messages, chances are you developed a negative self-concept. If you have been hurt by a negative past experience without receiving the love and support you needed from your parents, that experience has the power to distort your God-given natural programming and self-concept. If you can remember any negative situations from your past, it's very beneficial to go back and heal them. All you need to do is vent the negative emotions and give yourself the love and respect you deserved but didn't receive. See the Healing chapter for more information.

Step 9: Interact Socially and Help Others

The fastest way to recognize your own self-worth is through social interaction and helping others. This includes developing more friendships, seeking role models, joining support groups and other social activities. Anything that will establish feelings of common connection will be helpful. It's important to participate in events that you like and surround yourself with things that make you feel good about yourself. When you give to others, your own problems seem to disappear. By reaching out to others in need, you gain compassion and friendships, and your sense of uselessness quickly disappears. See the Loneliness/Isolation chapter for ways to develop additional friendships.

Visions of Inspiration

The Lord created human beings out of earth, and makes them return to it again. He gave them a fixed number of days, but granted them authority over everything on the earth. He endowed them with strength like his own, and made them in his own image.

Sirach 17: 1-3

For by the grace given to me I say to everyone among you not to think of yourself more highly than you ought to think, but to think with sober judgment, each according to the measure of faith that God has assigned.

Romans 12: 3

Believe in yourself! Have faith in your abilities! Without a humble but reasonable confidence in your own powers you cannot be successful or happy... Formulate and stamp indelibly on your mind a mental picture of yourself as succeeding. Hold this picture tenaciously. Never permit it to fade. Your mind will seek to develop the picture... Do not build up obstacles in your imagination... Do not be awestruck by other people and try to copy them. Nobody can be you as efficiently as YOU can. Remind yourself that God is with you and nothing can defeat him.

Norman Vincent Peale

She lacks confidence, she craves admiration insatiably. She lives on the reflections of herself in the eyes of others. She does not dare to be herself.

Anais Nin

SEX

TOOL 64

*H*ave you ever seen the bumper sticker that reads, "Sex, Drugs and Rock & Roll?" Isn't the order of those words backwards? Shouldn't they be, "Rock & Roll, Drugs and Sex?" Don't we usually turn on some music (rock & roll), have a glass of wine (drugs), and then the sex comes later?

Our bodies work internally this way as well. Rock and roll music represents the passionate messages we send our brains. The drugs represent the chemicals our brain releases that create our passionate and sensual feelings. But sex – sex can represent a beautiful act of love that transcends words, or it can cause a lot of damage and destruction to our relationships. Let's look at how this "Rock & Roll, Drugs and Sex" analogy may apply to a newly developed relationship, and then look at how it applies to an existing long-term relationship.

Usually after a couple goes on a few dates and gets to know each other, they find themselves on someone's couch. The kissing, touching and excitement of the new attraction sends certain messages to our minds (the rock and roll music). Once these messages are created, our brains automatically release the proper chemicals (the drugs) to prepare us for the upcoming situation. These brain chemicals are as powerful as any manmade drug. They are capable of overriding our logical reasoning and injecting an intoxicating amount of passion into our system. These chemicals don't care if our relationship is mentally, emotionally and spiritually mature enough to handle the responsibilities of sex. Once they are injected into our system, they will override our logical reasoning and send us into a passionate heat. If the couch scene turns into a bedroom scene, we might tell ourselves the next day, "It just happened."

To see how manipulative those brain chemicals can be, consider a "one-night stand." When your brain becomes intoxicated with thoughts of passion, it's easy to be overwhelmed by the heat of the moment. The next morning, after your brain chemistry has returned to normal, the usual response is shame, disrespect and regret. If you've ever experienced a one-night stand, you probably realize it's not a practical way to develop a healthy, fulfilling, lasting, respectable or loving relationship. In fact, a one-night stand would probably cause the same shame, disrespect and regret as if you had intentionally taken an illegal drug and lost control of your body.

There is little difference between putting yourself in situations that release natural brain drugs or taking manmade drugs if the end result is negative and destructive to your relationships. If your relationship is not developed enough to handle the responsibilities of sex, it's important to protect yourself from situations that can trigger the intoxicating brain chemicals of passion. That's because those brain chemicals have the power to override your logical reasoning and manipulate your body into doing almost anything.

The same brain chemistry analogy applies to established relationships as well. Let's look at a couple that's been married for 15 years and that are experiencing a lack of sexual passion in their relationship. Since the music we send to our brains releases the drugs that create the passionate feelings, couples having a hard time keeping the passion alive in their relationship may have a problem selecting the proper type of music. If we send songs of inadequacy like the "I can't perform well enough" or songs of resentment like the "I will never forgive you" acid rock concert, our brains will not release the proper chemicals to allow us to experience the passionate desires. If that's the case, it may be necessary to identify any past problems like anger, resentment, fear, shame, guilt, inadequacy, rape or incest that prevent you from listening to romantic, passionate music. Once you have identified these issues, go back into your past and heal those negative experiences using the techniques listed in the Healing chapter. Then the Passion chapter may help you increase and focus your desire, just like turning up the volume on the stereo.

Sex can be a very beautiful and powerful experience that strengthens the bonds of your relationship, or sex can cause a lot of problems and destruction in every aspect of your life. Everyone is responsible for their own actions and the corresponding consequences because we all have full control of our brain chemistry through the thoughts we think. God gave us the beautiful gift of sex and He asks us to honor it and use it respectfully for our greater good. If you and your partner have a newly established relationship or a long-standing marriage, the following exercise may help minimize the destruction sex can cause by clarifying any misunderstood sexual expectations.

INSTRUCTIONS

1) Look at the following list of sexual expectations. Study each issue to see how it affects your life, beliefs and relationships. Take the necessary time to deeply contemplate each issue.

2) Mark your answers in the corresponding boxes. There are two columns: one for partner (A) and one for partner (B). Feel free to photocopy and use separate forms if necessary. Answers are Agree, Disagree, Not Applicable and Problem Area. Use the additional space at the end of this chapter to rewrite any expectations or to create your own.

3) Once both you and your partner complete the exercise, it's important to come to some form of mutual understanding and agreement concerning any conflicting issues. Talk about any concerns. If you can't discuss sexual issues, it's probably not a good idea to be having sex. Listen empathetically to your partner and understand why they feel the way they do. Establish some form of mutual respect and values for your future well-being.

4) If you can't agree on important issues, it may be necessary to take some appropriate actions. This can include gathering more information, working on things together, seeking professional counseling or protecting yourself when necessary. For example, if you don't expect to die from AIDS, and a potential partner is unwilling to take a test, you might want to gather more information to determine how you can become infected. Or you might want to set some boundaries that will protect you from those types of risks. If you use sex as a way to deepen intimacy and your partner doesn't, you can always work on some additional intimacy exercises together. Once you know where you both stand on your expectations, you can make the necessary compromises to ensure your physical, mental, emotional and spiritual well-being.

SEXUAL EXPECTATION EXERCISE

	Partner A	Partner B
Agree		
Disagree		
N/A		
Problem		

Expectations About Monogamy

Do you expect your partner to be sexually monogamous? If so, how is your monogamous agreement defined? Is it clearly written, spoken only, or just assumed to be understood? Is it limited to sexual contact or does it include kissing and touching other men and women? If you have a monogamous agreement, how will you know if your partner violates that promise? If your partner wants out of the commitment, will they inform you beforehand or will they just act on their brain chemistry, hoping you find out later?

	Partner A	Partner B
Agree		
Disagree		
N/A		
Problem		

Expectations About Procreation

Do you respect the natural law of procreation? According to nature, the major function and design of sexual intercourse is to produce offspring. Nature has a powerful way of getting women pregnant every day, regardless of birth-control attempts. Are you and your partner prepared to bring a child into the world? What will you do if you or your partner is already pregnant? If your relationship can't handle the responsibility of procreation, can it handle the responsibility of sexual intercourse?

	Partner A	Partner B
Agree		
Disagree		
N/A		
Problem		

Expectations About AIDS

Do you expect to contract AIDS and die? Do you have AIDS right now? Does your partner? There is a specific blood test for AIDS. Just because the doctor draws blood and performs blood tests doesn't mean you have been tested for AIDS. The only way to be sure is to make an appointment for both of you to be specifically tested for AIDS. Should you engage in oral or genital contact, protected or not, if you are unsure? If you are not responsible enough to get a test, are you responsible enough to be having sexual relations?

	Partner A	Partner B
Agree		
Disagree		
N/A		
Problem		

Expectations About Commitment

Does sexual intercourse represent a form of nonspoken commitment? Should this intimate and vulnerable connection be shared by people who aren't committed to each other? If you are committed, how serious are your intentions? Are you committed until someone better comes along? Are you only committed until problems and conflicts arise or until you grow tired of each other, or are you committed for a lifetime? Should you be having sex with someone who is not committed to you?

	Partner A	Partner B
Agree		
Disagree		
N/A		
Problem		

Expectations About Birth Control

Do you expect your partner to be responsible for birth control? Do you speak about it? Does he provide it or does she? Which form do you prefer? Is it reliable and safe? What are your chances if it is properly used compared with not properly used? Are you comfortable with your partner's confidence regarding its proper use?

	Partner A	Partner B
Agree		
Disagree		
N/A		
Problem		

Expectations About Intimacy

Do you expect sex to take the place of genuine intimacy in your relationship? Many times sex generates powerful but temporary feelings of closeness. Do you expect it to take the place of real relationship work? Real intimacy starts by knowing your Inner Self and is created by sharing that true part or yourself with another. Do you use sex to make up with your partner after a fight instead of dealing with the real issues? Do you use sex as a shortcut to intimacy and feelings of closeness? Do you want to experience more closeness and intimacy in your relationship? How can you create this without using sex? How can you convert your sexual drive and energy into other forms of true intimacy?

	Partner A	Partner B
Agree		
Disagree		
N/A		
Problem		

Expectations About Respect

Do you participate in sex to gain respect or approval from your partner? Do you expect them to call the next day? Do you find yourself unable to say no when pressured? Do you need to prove yourself to others? Do you find yourself watching how your partner treats you the next day? Respect starts internally – if you don't respect yourself, no one else will either. When you respect yourself, you are better prepared to respect your own body sexually and that of your sexual partner. Do you think people who engage in one-night stands truly respect themselves?

	Partner A	Partner B
Agree		
Disagree		
N/A		
Problem		

Expectations About Safety

Do you want to feel safe before, during and after your sexual experience? Some people wait until the situation appears safe before they expose a vulnerable part of themselves. Other people expose an emotionally vulnerable part of themselves first and then want to feel reassured and safe later. Which do you and your partner represent? How can you help your partner feel safe before, during and after your sexual experience? Do your environmental conditions promote privacy, adequate time and security? Do your physical conditions promote relaxation, cleanliness and pleasurable enjoyment? Do your emotional conditions promote disrespect, criticism, rejection, disappointment or negative judgments?

	Partner A	Partner B
Agree		
Disagree		
N/A		
Problem		

Expectations About Performance

Do you expect to perform well and achieve climax for both yourself and your partner? Women generally need about 20 minutes of stimulation to reach orgasm; men generally need about three minutes of stimulation to reach orgasm. Men prefer to reach orgasm once they have been sexually stimulated; women don't always have to reach orgasm to enjoy a sexual experience. Depending on where they are in their sexual cycle, women may reach orgasm more easily at one time than at another; other times it might not be possible for women to reach a full orgasm at all. If you are male, do you wait for your female partner to experience her orgasm first?

Expectations About Touch

	Partner A	Partner B
Agree		
Disagree		
N/A		
Problem		

Do you expect your committed sexual partner to fulfill your primary human need for nonsexual touch? Eighty percent of a woman's need for physical touch is nonsexual. Are your needs for physical contact being fulfilled? How much time is spent holding hands, sitting close and touching each other in nonsexual ways? If your sexual partner is unwilling to fulfill your needs, who else can you turn to?

Expectations About Communication

	Partner A	Partner B
Agree		
Disagree		
N/A		
Problem		

Do you expect your sexual partner to openly express their needs, concerns, fears and vulnerabilities? Should you be having sex if you can't talk about these beforehand? Can you express yourself in a nonthreatening, and nonjudgmental way? Can your partner do the same? What do you and your partner need to talk about? What have you been holding back? Do you think it would be helpful to keep a sexual journal, where each person can make entries once a day? Would you like to discuss some specific subjects, express your wildest fantasies or address sensitive issues? If so, some topics to start the journal with might be what your greatest sexual fears are, what your parents' views on sex were, what you need from your partner sexually , what your greatest turn-ons are and how you could make your sex life better.

Expectations About Variety

	Partner A	Partner B
Agree		
Disagree		
N/A		
Problem		

Do you expect variety and excitement in your sexual activities? Are you bored by the same old mechanical procedures that lack creativity? How can different environments, procedures, methods of touch, positions, times, places and roles enhance your sex life?

	Partner A	Partner B
Agree		
Disagree		
N/A		
Problem		

Expectations About Power

What do you expect to give and receive when it comes to sex? Do you secretly give yourself to another hoping to receive special treatment, power or material positions? Do you withhold sex as a form of punishment? Do you reward your partner with sex for certain types of behaviors? Do you feel your partner uses sex as a form of manipulation? Many times there are a lot of hidden agendas behind our reasons for having sex. It is important to directly ask for what you want. Using sex as a weapon or tool can have serious repercussions and cause resentment in your relationship.

	Partner A	Partner B
Agree		
Disagree		
N/A		
Problem		

Expectations About Love

Do you expect sex to take the place of genuine love in your relationship? Do you expect to be loved by your partner before you will engage in sex? Do you need to love someone before you feel comfortable having sex with them? Do you and your partner respect, support, accept, encourage, comfort and care for each other outside of your sexual interactions? Do you want sex because it's a powerful way to feel loved? Or do you want to feel loved before you have sex? How can you increase and develop your ability to love without sex? What makes your partner feel loved? What does your partner do that makes you feel loved?

	Partner A	Partner B
Agree		
Disagree		
N/A		
Problem		

Expectations About Marriage

Do you think premarital sex is wrong? Should sex be confined to a seriously committed relationship? If both people were seriously committed to their relationship, should there be engagement or marriage plans? Do you hope your current sexual relationship will lead to marriage? Does your partner?

Expectations About Past Experiences

	Partner A	Partner B
Agree		
Disagree		
N/A		
Problem		

Do you expect your partner to free themselves from negative past experiences and emotional baggage that are causing problems in your sexual relations? Are you ashamed of your sexuality, desires, body or needs? What were your parents' attitudes or views toward masturbation, oral sex, premarital sex, adultery and pornography? Have you or your parents ever experienced incest, rape or other forms of sexual abuse? What are some of your adolescent sexually related experiences when you felt ashamed? Consider whether you have ever experienced any of the following shameful experiences that could be affecting your subconscious views on sex: getting an erection in public, playing doctor as a child, being teased for wearing a bra or for getting your first period, or getting caught and feeling ashamed for masturbating. Were you sexually shamed as a child? Were you taught that sex was dirty, bad or naughty? If so, please see the Healing chapter.

Expectations About Your First Experience

	Partner A	Partner B
Agree		
Disagree		
N/A		
Problem		

Are you expecting to have a good experience the first time you have sex? Many young adults would not choose the same first partner if they could do it over. Many times the first experience is awkward, messy, disappointing and unsafe due to lack of emotional maturity, planning and birth control. Some common reasons why young adults engage in sex when there not ready include being unable to say no when pressured; being curious about sex; wanting to see what it's like; trying to prove maturity, manhood or social prestige; being afraid of losing their boyfriend or girlfriend; feeling a sense of obligation or peer pressure; and experiencing a loss of control due to drugs and alcohol. Do you think any of these reasons justify rushing into a sexual relationship? If you are considering having sex for the first time, what are your reasons?

Expectations About Self-Worth

	Partner A	Partner B
Agree		
Disagree		
N/A		
Problem		

Do you expect to feel good about yourself after you experience sex with a new partner? Do you expect your partner to feel good about their own self-worth? When you become vulnerable to another person in an underdeveloped relationship, it's possible to experience feelings of emptiness, regret, being used or being disrespected, especially if the relationship quickly falls apart. By taking the time and effort to first establish a solid foundation of mutual respect, understanding, trust, friendship, intimacy and commitment, you will have a better chance in your relationship handling the vulnerable feelings and responsibility that accompany sex. It's easier to feel good about yourself when you haven't sacrificed a sacred part of your being to another person based solely on lustful desires. Have you damaged your own self-worth with frequent sex partners? Do you respect other people who frequently change sex partners? How can you rebuild a damaged self-concept?

	Partner A	Partner B
Agree		
Disagree		
N/A		
Problem		

Expectations About Social Life

Do you expect to maintain a healthy social life outside of your sexual relationship? Should your partner? Many times the powerful force of sex bonds people in a consuming and possessive way. Couples might want to be together all the time. Sex usually brings out insecurities, vulnerabilities, jealousies and fears. Are you trying to control your partner's social interactions? Are outside interests a threat to your relationship? Are you sacrificing friends, family and other social interests because of the powerful effects of sex? How can you deal with your primary human needs, insecurities and fears in a healthy manner?

	Partner A	Partner B
Agree		
Disagree		
N/A		
Problem		

Expectations About God's Law

Do you expect to not get hurt and avoid the natural consequences of premarital sex? God calls premarital sex fornication and says it causes a lot of damage and destruction to our lives and relationships. God doesn't want anything negative to happen to His children, so He set up some protective laws to ensure our safety. God designed sex to bond two people together. Do you think God wants you bonded to the wrong person? If your boyfriend or girlfriend slowly turned into an abusive person, do you think God would want you emotionally tied to that relationship? Sex also puts blinders on people. Do you think God wants you to marry the wrong person, just because the power of sex distorted your better judgment? Sex was designed to create new life. Do you think God wants you to bring new life into this world under conditions that would be destructive to the child's upbringing?

	Partner A	Partner B
Agree		
Disagree		
N/A		
Problem		

Expectations About Purpose

Do you expect your partner to hold the same views about sex as you? What are your own beliefs regarding the purpose of sex? What are your partner's? Is it to be used solely for personal pleasure? Or is it a profoundly deep gift from God that transcends words? Should it be respected, honored, used wisely and at the same time deeply valued and enjoyed? Is it the greatest gift one person can give another? Is it more than physical? Does it connect a part of your Inner Self and soul to your partner? What does sex represent and stand for in your life and in your partner's life?

Visions of Inspiration

You mustn't force sex to do the work of love or love to do the work of sex.
Mary McCarthy

The body is meant not for fornication but for the Lord, and the Lord for the body. And God raised the Lord and will also raise us by his power. Do you not know that your bodies are members of Christ? Should I therefore take the members of Christ and make them members of a prostitute? Never! Do you not know that whoever is united to a prostitute becomes one body with her? For it is said, " The two shall be one flesh." But anyone united to the Lord becomes one spirit with him. Shun fornication! Every sin that a person commits is outside the body; but the fornicator sins against the body itself. Or do you not know that your body is a temple of the Holy Spirit within you, which you have from God, and that you are not your own? For you were bought with a price; therefore glorify God in your body.
1 Corinthians 6: 13.5-20

SHAME

TOOL 65

*B*y taking care of a new car, you preserve its attractiveness and value. If you bought a new car and someone spray-painted it with graffiti, the car would lose value, wouldn't it? If you wanted to restore the value of a car vandalized this way, you would need to use a paint remover to carefully clean off the unwanted paint. Our lives are the same way. God created each of us with unlimited attractiveness and value. We all have the potential to vandalize other people's vehicles with spray paint and other people are capable of harming our valuable shine. Our cars can't remove unwanted graffiti by themselves. But God, being the Master Car Builder and Creator, has designed us with our own graffiti removal system. When something like graffiti covers up your natural shine, your body produces a natural paint remover called shame. This powerful system is designed to clean away unwanted graffiti so your life will shine again. Unfortunately, God didn't make this feature fully automatic. To neutralize the paint remover, we have to love and embrace that hurt part of ourselves. If we don't embrace the hurt and pain, the acid-like paint remover will continue to burn through the graffiti right into the original paint job.

Take a look at the shine on your personal vehicle. Can you see your smiling reflection in it from a block away? Or has that acid-like burning shame destroyed your vehicle's finish? If your vehicle's finish needs some restoration work, you may be interested in understanding how graffiti gets on your being in the first place.

As children we are all born with a powerful sense of internal value that radiates in the form of a natural shine. But for a number of reasons some of us learn to devalue ourselves. Usually the shame of our parents, families or role models gets spray painted all over us. Some parents even use shame as a form of control over their children. Maybe as a child we repeatedly asked for something we wanted, like ice cream. Instead of responding properly, a parent may have devalued us with shame-based spray paint by saying something like, "You're too fat already. You don't need any more ice cream." Pretty soon we won't ask for ice cream because that corrosive-like paint remover has already cleaned away the graffiti and continues to burn a hole into our valuable shine. Unfortunately, these children don't know how to love and embrace that hurt part of themselves and many grow up with a shame-based personality.

Family secrets can also cause graffiti-like destruction. Maybe your mother said things like, "Don't tell your father. Keep this a secret or he will get mad." This graffiti type of self-devaluation would say to the child: You are not completely accepted and loved by your father because of the secret you are keeping from him. This child may believe that if the father knew the secret, he would remove his love and get very angry. By being involved and withholding the secret, the child would be living in a self-devaluing way in the father's eyes.

Other times we might compare our family's or parents' behaviors with those of others. Maybe your family appeared severely dysfunctional or abnormal compared with other people's families. If so, you may have experienced shameful feelings for being associated with the family system.

Money can also cause self-devaluation. Maybe your parents were conservative or stingy with their spending habits and never bought you anything. This might have caused feelings of worthlessness.

Addictions have a lot to do with shame because they are the only thing powerful enough to cover up and hide those almost unbearable burning feelings. In fact, the number one underlying cause of substance abuse is shame. People don't like how they're feeling, so they turn to their addictions to feel better. Eventually their problems grow worse and they become even more ashamed because the addiction is slowly consuming whatever is left of their lives.

Unfortunately, self-devaluing or shameful beliefs can be developed from almost anything. Anytime something negative happens and covers up your natural shine, you can expect shameful spray paint on your vehicle.

Take a look at the automobile in your family's driveway. Does your car shine? How about your relationship partner's? What about your parents' vehicles? If you are experiencing self-devaluating shameful feelings, the following steps may help you trace, confront and heal the situations in your past when self-defeating beliefs and attitudes were learned.

Steps to Healing Shame

Step 1: Identify How You Hide Shame From Yourself

Try to identify anything you're using in your life to block out the painful feelings of hopelessness, inadequacy, uselessness, helplessness or worthlessness. These shameful feelings are extremely painful and almost unbearable, and you might turn to addictions or something else to alleviate the pain. It's necessary to confront and modify any behavior that keeps you from recognizing or dealing with your shameful feelings. See the Addictions and Substance Abuse chapters if necessary.

Step 2: Identify How You Hide Shame From Others

It's also helpful to identify ways you hide your shameful feelings from other people. That corrosive-like shameful substance is so painful you may find yourself doing anything to keep other people from knowing your true feelings. You may avoid intimacy in your relationships. Or you may criticize and blame other people in an attempt to divert attention from yourself. You may even try unrealistic ways of being perfect, thinking that if you're perfect, you can overpower the hurt and disown that part of your past. Other times you may try to fight to the bitter end to be right because you think that when you're wrong you lose, and when you lose it proves your worthlessness. Discover and confront the ways you're trying to hide your shameful feelings from other people in your life and relationships.

Step 3: Express Your Feelings

Once you have acknowledged the ways you hide your shame from yourself and others, you can begin to heal. Expressing your true feelings is a powerful and important step in this process because once these feelings are verbalized, you can begin to heal them. If they aren't verbalized and brought out into the open, they can't be healed. A good example of this is biodegradable trash. When your graffiti-based trash and shameful feelings are brought out into the open, they begin to decompose naturally. When you try to hide and repress these feelings, like trash in a plastic bag, it will grow slimy, rancid and stinky. If you poke a hole in this bag, what you smell is shame. Talking to a trusted friend in a safe environment or seeking out and joining a support group can be a very healing process.

Step 4: List Behaviors Causing Shame

The next step is to make a list of everything you are ashamed about. Include all types of behaviors that you view negatively – anything you naturally wanted to participate in but couldn't because you were expected by other people to behave differently. List all the natural parts of your personality, emotions and drives that you feel are unlovable. They could be almost anything you or other people don't approve of, like your sexuality, talents, ability, happiness, anger, sadness, playfulness, relaxation, appearance, ability and mistakes. List every part of your physical, mental, emotional and spiritual being that you are ashamed of, have disowned, can't stand or consider worthless, useless and inadequate.

Step 5: Evaluate Your List of Behaviors

After you have complied the list of inappropriate behaviors and disowned attributes, you can then evaluate these items. Begin by dividing the list into two separate columns (A and B). Separate all the items on your list that are intentionally harmful to yourself and others and put them in the (A) list. Put all the items that are not harmful to yourself or others on the (B) list. Items on the (A) list that are harmful and in your immediate control can be healed by making the necessary amends. To do so, please refer to the information in the Guilt chapter. The items on the (B) list can be healed by following the procedures in the next step.

Step 6: Heal Past Experiences

To heal any negative feelings or perceptions regarding the items on your (B) list, it's necessary to trace the negative beliefs of shame back to when they were learned. Somewhere in your past you taught yourself or you were given these unhealthy messages by your role models, parents or guardians. God created every aspect of your being and considers it all good. God asks you to use His creation, including every aspect on the (B) list, in a responsible manner. When you do, there is nothing to be ashamed of. Because you were not born with shameful feelings and God didn't create you as a shameful being, it's necessary to find the source of your shameful conditioning so you can heal it. Many times this search will lead you back to your childhood, when your parents passed along to you these shameful feelings in their words and actions. Pinpoint these events in your past and begin the healing process by working through one of the procedures located in the Healing chapter.

Step 7: Practice Self-Love and Acceptance

The next step is to reclaim, accept and love any part of yourself that was lost or disowned. You can begin by focusing your thoughts on the positive aspects of these items and changing your perceptions to match. The Self-Acceptance chapter has a powerful exercise and additional information that will help promote your self-love.

Step 8: Make Daily Efforts

The final step is to convert shameful feelings into the truth. This process works when you confront a shameful feeling immediately when it arises and ask yourself the following question: "How can I uncover this situation and convert it into the truth?"

For example, imagine you're in a business meeting and someone accuses you of doing something wrong. If shameful feelings arise in you, quickly ask yourself the question and respond with the truth. You might answer this person by saying, "Your question is a legitimate concern," "I may have made a mistake," or "Let's look at the situation closely." After acknowledging the truth openly, your shameful feeling will quickly disappear. Or imagine you're participating in a new activity for the first time, such as golf. If someone walked up to you on the golf course and questioned your ability, you might experience feelings of shame if you don't know what you are doing. You can either feed into the shame, or you can ask yourself the question to seek the truth. A truthful response might be, "You're right. I haven't tried this before," or "Can you help me?" Almost instantly the shame of being inadequate turns into a request for help.

If you continue to seek the truth when a shameful feeling arises, you will release and neutralize that natural solvent before it has a chance to burn its way into your shiny, valuable vehicle.

Visions of Inspiration

Nothing is covered up that will not be uncovered, and nothing secret that will not become known. Therefore whatever you have said in the dark will be heard in the light, and what you have whispered behind closed doors will be proclaimed from the housetops.

Luke 12: 2-3

We have renounced the shameful things that one hides; we refuse to practice cunning or to falsify God's word; but by the open statement of the truth we commend ourselves to the conscience of everyone in the sight of God.

2 Corinthians 4: 2

Do not make yourself low; people will tread on your head.

Yiddish proverb

For everything created by God is good, and nothing is to be rejected, provided it is received with thanksgiving; for it is sanctified by God's word and by prayer.

1 Timothy 4: 4

And, above all things, never think that you're not good enough yourself. A man should never think that. My belief is that in life people will take you very much at your own reckoning.

Anthony Trollope

STRESS

*S*tress is like putting your car in neutral and stepping on the gas, forcing the engine to run faster and faster. When you step on the gas pedal, it opens the fuel injection system and forces gas into the engine. The more fuel you give the engine, the more horsepower it will produce. If your car has to work extra hard, like when driving up a steep hill, it needs and consumes more gas. If your car is parked and you give it gas, the engine produces an overabundance of power. If you race an unloaded engine for very long past the red line, it will shake itself apart and blow up.

Stress works the same way in the human body. The car's engine in the scenario above represents your body. The chemicals your brain releases work just like the gas, and your thoughts and perceptions control the gas pedal. For example, pretend you're sitting at the office one day completely relaxed, just like a parked car. Then something happens that forces you to quickly adapt or adjust to a particular event, such as your boss threatening you with important deadlines. Next, your thoughts push down on the gas pedal in your head, and your brain releases the proper amount of chemical gas. This causes your body to work like the engine and prepare itself to handle the upcoming workload. If you sit around overestimating, worrying and placing great amounts of negativity on situations outside of your control, your brain will produce a lot of gas, which in turn will fire up your body. If it's not possible to use all the energy your body is producing, you will experience stress, just like an unloaded engine that's being pushed past the red line. The more negativity and worry you place on situations outside your control, the more gas and stress you place on your engine. If situations outside of your control were viewed as a calling for personal growth and opportunities to trust in God, you would use less gas and save your vehicle from unnecessary wear and tear.

The ideal condition when driving is to give your car the right amount of gas to match the workload of the engine. The ideal human condition is to use just the right kind of thoughts and perceptions needed to accomplish your agenda. Some situations in life require a full throttle, like if you were about to be eaten by a wild animal. In this emergency situation your fear would engage the chemical gas in your brain. Adrenaline would be released into your bloodstream, which would immediately prepare your body for action. Your heart rate, temperature, respiration and blood pressure would rise, and nonessential functions like digestion and reproduction would shut down to conserve energy. Your body would almost instantly be prepared to fight off the wild animal.

God gave everyone a high-performance engine for just such an occasion, but unfortunately very few situations require such a response. Many times when you are feeling stressed, you are doing nothing more than sitting around at the office thinking the stock market is going to eat your lunch like a wild animal. The chemicals in your brain, though, can't tell the difference between a life-or-death situation and an exaggerated situation outside your control. So be very careful with the thoughts and perceptions you have because excessive amounts of stress can cause severe damage to your health, life and relationships.

If you're experiencing headaches, sleeping disorders, insomnia, depression, anxiety, high blood pressure, irritability, a weak immune system or fatigue, you may be running your engine too hard for no reason. If you're experiencing ulcers, colitis, asthma, high blood pressure, eczema or heart problems, your engine might be close to the red line. A heart attack is a good indication that your engine just threw a rod. The only way to change the amount of stress you might be experiencing is by changing your thoughts, perceptions and attitudes that operate the chemical gas pedal in your brain.

If your engine is shaking itself apart, the following items may help you reduce the amount of stress in your life.

STRESS REDUCTION TECHNIQUES

- ❖ Set realistic goals and try to not overextend yourself.
- ❖ Manage your time using weekly and monthly agendas, which will allow flexibility in your schedule.
- ❖ Don't take everything personally.
- ❖ Don't blame anyone or anything. When you do, you surrender your personal power to them.

- ❖ Practice laughing regularly. It releases brain chemicals that counteract those of stress.
- ❖ Take time out of the day to discover and enjoy the simple joys and pleasures of life.
- ❖ Change your behavior to act assertively. Being aggressive or passive increases stressful problems.
- ❖ Allow yourself longer travel time when commuting.
- ❖ Surrender difficult situations in life that are outside your range of influence or control over to God.
- ❖ Try to create win/win situations and compromises in all your interactions. Anything else may produce conflicts, resentment and stress.
- ❖ Focus your attention on the positive aspects present in every situation of life.
- ❖ Motivate other people using positive intentions. Negativity and fear usually backfire and cause more stress.
- ❖ Take responsibility for your stress. Act appropriately in every situation; don't overreact or react recklessly.
- ❖ Don't attempt to control others. The only true control you have is over yourself – especially the unhealthy thoughts and perceptions that lead to stress.
- ❖ Practice relaxation, deep breathing and mediation techniques regularly.
- ❖ Take breaks when you're feeling tired, worn down or stressed.
- ❖ Take shorter but more frequent vacations.
- ❖ Schedule time daily for personal reflection, planning, journal writing and prayer.
- ❖ Maintain your physical health. A good exercise program and sound diet are essential.
- ❖ Get plenty of rest. It will help your body restore its balance.
- ❖ Manage your anger in a healthy way and practice forgiveness daily.
- ❖ Avoid rigid and controlling thinking patterns.
- ❖ Monitor your thinking patterns for distorted perceptions of the truth. They cause unnecessary emotional turmoil.
- ❖ Develop a healthy, positive, optimistic attitude and outlook in every aspect of your life.
- ❖ Be patient and understanding when dealing with others and yourself.
- ❖ Realize that stress is not worth dying for. Learn to control your stress instead of allowing stress to control you.

Visions of Inspiration

My brothers and sisters, whenever you face trials of any kind, consider it nothing but joy, because you know that the testing of your faith produces endurance; and let endurance have its full effect, so that you may be mature and complete, lacking in nothing.

James 1: 2-4

Irritations influence your mind and your mind influences your muscles. All the irritations of daily life subject your mind and nerves and then your muscles, to repeated tension. You can work out most of this tension with your exercise program, but if you are smart, you will try to avoid most of the tension to begin with.

Dr. Leon Root

SUBSTANCE ABUSE

TOOL 67

The Addiction chapter compared a car that leaked fuel with a person with an addiction problem. By ignoring the fuel leak, the car would require more and more gas to keep running, and the only way to keep the car running is to feed it more and more fuel. Unfortunately, the more gas you give the car, the greater the fuel leak becomes. This never-ending cycle only increases unless the underlying mechanical problems are fixed.

The addiction cycle works the same way. When we turn to mood-altering substances in an attempt to make ourselves feel better, our problems and negative emotions don't go away, they will only increase unless the underlying problems are resolved. If we compare an addiction to filling the gas tank twice a day to keep the car running, substance abuse is filling the car with jet fuel ten times a day. The risk of fire from leaking fuel is also ten times greater. When a car catches fire, most people are lucky to escape with their lives because jet fuel is highly flammable and extremely dangerous.

If you or someone you love is addicted to drugs or alcohol, your relationship will need outside assistance to recover. In addition, you may be interested in the following steps, which have been divided into two parts: The first part describes help for those who are involved in a relationship with someone who abuses drugs or alcohol; the second part describes help for those who are suffering from an addiction.

Part I: Helping Yourself and Others Who Are Addicted

If you are involved in a relationship with someone who abuses drugs or alcohol, you probably experience a lot of pain, grief and suffering along with your partner. Unfortunately it is impossible to change another person's unhealthy and destructive behaviors, although there are several things you can do to help your partner and yourself.

Step 1: Educate Yourself

Seek wisdom, knowledge and understanding regarding your partner's addiction. The better informed and better educated you are, the easier it will be to help you and your partner. There are many sources of information, including books, tapes, seminars, help hot lines and public libraries.

Step 2: Work on Forgiveness

Through their addiction your partner has probably caused a lot of problems and damage to your life, family and relationship. It's important for your own well-being to forgive them. It will be helpful to make a list of the ways they have hurt you and work through the steps listed in the Forgiveness chapter.

Step 3: Help the Addict See the Damage

An important step is to help your partner realize the damage they are causing themselves and others. Tell them how much you love them, but at the same time let them know how much pain and suffering they are causing. Try to express your message in ways that will motivate them to change their own behavior. Many times the addict was hurt by someone in their past in the same painful way they are now hurting others. As a form of self-protection, your partner may have learned to detach from that wounded part of themselves. Usually these people don't know how to recognize or embrace their own pain and they will have a hard time compassionately acknowledging the same pain in another. Try to create different ways to show your partner the pain and damage they are causing.

Step 4: Change Your Love

It may be necessary to change the way you express your love. It would be helpful if you could find that hurt, damaged part that remains in your partner and love it unconditionally, and to show that hurt little boy or girl inside of your partner just how valuable, lovable and special they are. But unfortunately that hurt, damaged part inside your partner would rather make itself feel better through the addiction. If you are unable to help your partner love themselves in this way, other forms of love might also be effective, such as tough love. Tough love doesn't rescue your partner from the problems they created themselves. Tough love helps you teach your partner to take responsibility for themselves and their actions. Tough love will let your partner spend the night in jail to sober up. Tough love tells your partner you are willing to see them stay in jail until they are ready to make the changes necessary to save their life. In a serious addiction, it's usually necessary for people to crash and hit rock bottom before they understand and are willing to make changes. Tough love says you will let that happen and still be there when your partner is willing to deal with the real issues.

Practicing detached love will help you separate your partner's actions from that hurt and damaged little boy or girl who resides within. With detached love it's possible to love your partner's true self, while at the same time disapprove of their destructive behavior.

Step 5: Help Your Partner Deal With Their Issues

It's necessary for an addict to deal with their problems, past issues and pain directly, instead of indirectly through their addiction. You can't force someone to deal with their problems, negative emotions or childhood issues, but you can offer your assistance. Try to work with your partner in any way possible. Anything that you can do to help them confront, embrace, accept, love and heal that hurt, damaged part of themselves will be beneficial. Try setting aside some healing time every night. Practice written or visualization techniques together. Show them how powerful and beneficial the exercise can be. Anything you can do to help repair or restore your partner's relationship with their parents and family will be helpful. Try helping their self-concept by giving them positive affirmations.

Step 6: Join a Support Group

For your own benefit, it will be helpful to join a support group to help you deal with your own issues as well as your partner's. Al-Anon groups are composed of people who love and care deeply about their substance-abusing partners. There is great comfort in expressing your pain and suffering with those who know exactly what you are experiencing. They will be able to help you. The corporate headquarters for Al-Anon and others support groups has been included in case you need additional assistance, support or resources. For information regarding the nearest chapter or meetings times and locations, check your local telephone book, churches, synagogues or newspapers.

Al-Anon Family Group Headquarters Inc.
1600 Corporate Landing Pkwy.
Virginia Beach, Va. 23454-5617
Main phone – (757) 563-1600
Meeting Information – (available Monday - Friday, 8:00 a.m. to 6:00 p.m. ET):
(800) 344-2666 (USA)
(800) 443-4525 (Canada)
Public Outreach – (For a free introductory packet of literature):
(800) 356-9996 (USA)
(800) 714-7498 (Canada)

Al-Anon Family Groups (Canada)
National Public Information
P.O. Box 6433, Station "J"
Ottawa, Ontario, Canada K2A3Y6
(613) 722-1830
(800) 443-4525

Adult Children of Alcoholics
P.O. Box 3216
Torrance, CA 90510
(310) 534-1815

Part II: Overcoming Substance Abuse

If you are addicted to alcohol or drugs, it's necessary to get help. These types of addictions are almost impossible to overcome on your own.

The recovery process starts by acknowledging and confessing the problem. Next comes a period of medically supervised detoxification in a hospital or treatment center, where the toxic addicting chemicals are allowed to leave your body and withdrawal symptoms are treated. This stage is followed by a period of rehabilitation, where you learn new skills to deal with your pain, problems, past issues, negative emotions and feelings. In this stage you work on restructuring your life to be free of unhealthy addictions. Individual psychotherapy and family or group counseling are also helpful in this process. The final stage is constant maintenance and work on living a life that is free of a future addiction cycle.

The 12-step program pioneered by Alcoholics Anonymous is the largest recovery program used today and is based on the healing power of God. The 12 Steps of Alcoholics Anonymous are:

1. We admitted we were powerless over alcohol – that our lives had become unmanageable.
2. We came to believe that a power greater than ourselves could restore us to sanity.
3. We made a decision to turn our will and our lives over to the care of God as we understood Him.
4. We made a searching and fearless moral inventory of ourselves.
5. We admitted to God, to ourselves and to another human being the exact nature of our wrongs.
6. We were entirely ready to have God remove all these defects of character.
7. We humbly asked Him to remove our shortcomings.
8. We made a list of all persons we had harmed, and became willing to make amends to them all.
9. We made direct amends to such people whenever possible, except when to do so would injure them or others.
10. We continued to take personal inventory and when we were wrong promptly admitted it.
11. We sought through prayer and meditation to improve our conscious contact with God as we understood Him, praying only for knowledge of His will for us and the power to carry that out.
12. Having had a spiritual awakening as the result of these steps, we tried to carry this message to alcoholics, and to practice these principles in all our affairs.

This twelve-step program has become the basis of our modern recovery movement. The steps have been used to deal with addictions ranging from sex addiction and overeating, to compulsive shopping, drugs and cocaine addiction. The corporate headquarters for A.A. and other substance abuse groups have been included here if you want additional assistance, support or resources. For information regarding the nearest chapter or meeting times and locations, check your local telephone book, churches, synagogues or newspapers.

Alcoholics Anonymous
Grand Central Station
P.O. Box 459
New York, NY 10163
(212) 870-3400

The Institute for Christian Living
12 Steps for Christian Living
P.O. Box 47482
Plymouth, Minn. 55447
(612) 593-1791

Cocaine Anonymous
World Service Office Inc.
P.O. Box 2000
Los Angeles, Calif. 90049-8000
(800) 347-8998 (24-hour referral line)
(310) 559-5833 (business office)

Moderation Management
Help for Problem Drinkers
P.O. Box 6005
Ann Arbor, Mich. 48106
(313) 677-6007
http://comnet.org./mm/

Narcotics Anonymous
World Service Office
19737 Nordhoff Place
Chatsworth, Calif. 91311
(818) 773-9999

Rational Recovery Systems
P.O. Box 800
Lotus, Calif. 95651-0080
(916) 621-4374 or (916) 621-2667

Overcomers Outreach (Christians)
520 North Brookhurst #121
Anaheim, Calif. 92801
(800) 310-3001

Men for Sobriety/Women for Sobriety
P.O. Box 618
Quakertown, Pa. 18951
(215) 536-8026

The names, addresses and telephone numbers of the organizations and support groups listed in this chapter have been reprinted with permission. Said permission does not imply these organizations have reviewed or approved the contents of this entire publication, or that they necessarily agree with the views expressed herein.

Visions of Inspiration

Wine drunk at the proper time and in moderation is rejoicing of heart and gladness of soul. Wine drunk to excess leads to bitterness of spirit, to quarrels and stumbling. Drunkenness increases the anger of a fool to his own hurt, reducing his strength and adding wounds.

Sirach 31: 28-30

The irony is that as the user gets sicker, he is less able to see it. The magic of the powder is that every noseful tells you that you don't really have a problem.

Dr. Joseph Purseh

TRANSFORMATION & TRANSCENDENCE

TOOL 68

*H*ow many times have you seen an automobile crash on television, in the newspaper or in real life? How many times have you been involved in, caused or nearly avoided a car wreck? How many times has your car been dented, scratched or damaged on the road of life? Unfortunately, auto body damage happens every day. When it affects you, what do you do about it? Some people accept the loss, make the necessary repairs and end up with a brand new car. Others make the damage worse and drive around in a wrecked car.

If your car's fender acquires a dent, a good auto body mechanic will use the necessary tools and repair the damage. When the road of life leads you into an unexpected wreck, a good relationship mechanic will repair the damage using the proper tools. In the auto body repair business there are two main tools for fixing dents: The first is a dent puller, used to change the form or appearance of a dent. The second is an auto body filler called bondo used to raise the dent to a new level. When life gives you a dent, it's going to be painful and unpleasant. You'll feel crushed, damaged and broken like a fender on your car when it meets someone else's bumper. You can either accept the loss and fix the damage using your tools, or you can make the damage worse and drive around in a wrecked car, bitter and angry.

The first tool – the dent puller – works for cars the same way transformation works for your life. The dent puller will reshape the damaged area of a car the same way transformation will help you change or reshape your perceptions of your damage. Once you can view the dent differently, you can get out the bondo and rise above the damaged area to a new level. The auto body filler will raise a dent to a new level, just like transcendence will help you rise above destructive situations. By using these powerful tools, you will be better equipped to deal with life's dents, losses, deaths, crises, disasters and traumas.

Both practices – transformation (changing your perceptions) and transcendence (rising above a situation) – are forms of personal and spiritual growth. The more you use and practice them to fix everyday dents, the better prepared you will be to deal with a major collision when one comes your way.

Transformation

You can transform a negative situation by making the necessary changes. Sometimes this includes physical changes like minimizing losses or mental changes like viewing the situation differently. Because this is not easy, it may be helpful to work through this process in a written form. Begin from a relaxed, meditative state of mind and ask God for assistance in your current struggles. Ask Him to show you the positive advantages and opportunities for growth regarding your situation.

Next, write down all the potential opportunities for growth with which you have been presented. What new skills have you learned in dealing with this situation? What personal skills, advantages or opportunities do you anticipate learning or growing from in the future? How has this experience helped you be a more loving, compassionate and understanding person? How will you relate to other people who have suffered a similar experience? How has this experience brought you closer to God, neighbors, friends or family members? How has this experience helped you value and appreciate the sacredness of life, instead of taking it for granted?

How has this situation helped other people in the world? For example, a hurricane or earthquake has the power to bond together an entire community. What about the opportunities to create a new life after a major loss? Try looking at your life and the world from a bigger picture. How do you think God views the situation? What changes would God like to see in your life, family, community and world?

If God is Love and He calls us all to be more loving, how can this situation help you increase your ability to be a more loving person? If you were to be more loving to yourself, others and God, how would it help your current situation? Try to find the greater meaning that lies in the painful situation you are experiencing.

How can you view the situation in a positive way? There are always positive and negative ways of viewing everything. Some people and cultures joyfully celebrate the death of a loved one as a passing from this world to the next. Other people allow it to destroy their lives because they refuse to view the situation in any way other than destructive, terrible and unpleasant.

Try making a list of positive and negative aspects regarding your situation. Write down all the advantages and disadvantages you can think of. When you have finished, take all the disadvantages and reword them into opportunities. For example, a disadvantage might be the loss of a good friend; the opposite or reverse side of that might be the opportunity to develop a closer friendship with another.

After you have converted the negative aspects and ways of viewing the situation into their positive counterparts, you can write down the ways you can begin to take action. Write down the ways you can improve the situation. How can you minimize your loss? What can you salvage from the experience? How can you convert the situation into a gain? If you have made a mistake, how can it be viewed as a learning experience and a lesson of what not to do in the future? Look deep inside yourself and get in touch with your true needs. Discover your need to be loved and to love others, and find a way to fulfill these needs through this experience.

Take your time working your way through the transformation process. Deeply contemplate each of these questions and find the answers that lie deep in your Inner Self. God will be there to help you; remember to trust Him every step of the way.

Transcendence

You can transcend your negative experiences by rising above them or by detaching yourself from their negative effects. Transcending the dents life throws your way will be difficult, and it's helpful to work your way through this process in written form. Begin from a relaxed, meditative state of mind and ask God for assistance in dealing with your current struggles. Ask Him for help in evaluating your life and rising above the negative situations.

We are all spiritual beings living in a physical world. If we live a life totally consumed by the physical and neglect the spiritual, we can expect additional pain and suffering. To transcend the situation, you will find it helpful to create a balance between the spiritual and the physical perspectives. So begin by writing down all your physical concerns regarding the loss or traumatic experience you are going through. Ask yourself what exactly are the material, financial, tangible or external aspects, consequences or concerns regarding the situation? Then make a list of all your spiritual concerns regarding the situation. What exactly are the emotional, loving and internal aspects, consequences or concerns regarding the recent dent life has thrown your way? After you have finished both lists, look at them to make sure they both have an equal number of items. If they don't, try to reverse the meanings of the items on the larger list by looking at the opposite extreme in an attempt to balance the other side.

For example, if you are experiencing a physical problem like cancer, it's possible to transcend, rise above or even overcome the situation from a spiritual realm. Instead of focusing your attention on your body and medical treatments, try to balance and improve your situation from a spiritual nature. Maybe you can develop a closer relationship with God. Have more appreciation for life. Secure your afterlife existence. Free yourself from the consumption of business, traffic and the daily grind.

If you are experiencing a problem related to financial issues in your relationship or marriage and have been trying without any success to overcome them solely from a spiritual perspective like prayer, it's possible to transcend the situation by focusing more attention on your physical actions and the financial solutions. By creating a balance between the physical and the spiritual, you will have an easier time rising above the dent.

It will also be helpful to transcend any situation life throws your way by comparing it to an eternal perspective. Because we are eternal spiritual beings living in a physical world, it's possible to become so consumed by the here and now that we fail to realize the greater good it may have on our eternal existence. We are only on this earth for a very short time. To get a better idea of your eternal existence in comparison to life on earth, look at the following timeline, where every half-inch represents 1,000 years of human existence. The earliest known record of human beings can be traced back to around 5000 BC, and a line approximately 3-1/2 inches long would take us to around 2000 AD.

				BC	AC		
5000	4000	3000	2000	1000	0	1000	2000
•	•	•	•	•	•	•	•

Now take a look at the length of time you, your friends and family are here on earth. If a half-inch represents 1000 years, how big a dot would you need to represent your earthly existence? Now imagine this timeline increasing off the page of this book and becoming twice as long. What is the spiritual and eternal part of your being going to be doing around 9000 AD? Now imagine the timeline stretching across the room, down the hall and half way around the world. After all that time has passed, your eternal existence will have just begun. As another example to demonstrate how brief our time on earth is in relation to our afterlife existence, imagine the tallest mountain in the world and every 100 years a raven flies by and brushes away a few stones with the tip of its wing. After the entire mountain has eroded, your eternal spiritual existence will have just begun.

By viewing your hardship from an eternal perspective, you will be better prepared to transcend the hurt, pain and damage. If you are more concerned about your physical situation, you can view things from an eternal perspective. If you are more concerned about your spiritual situation, you can view the world and all that resides in it as a great gift from God for all of life to enjoy, utilize and improve.

Another way to achieve transcendence is to realize the amount of harm you are causing yourself by dwelling on something outside your control. Begin by writing down all the emotional, physical, mental and spiritual damage you are suffering because of your inability to detach yourself from the situation. How is this situation affecting your attitude, happiness, livelihood, stress, peace of mind, contentment and your life? What could you gain by turning control of this situation over to God? How can you detach from it and let it go? When you dwell on the past or the future, you aren't truly living in the present. Where have the majority of your concerns, thoughts and worries been spent concerning this situation? Are you living in the present or suffering in the past and future?

After you have made the necessary evaluations, you can make your own personal affirmation statement. Write down the new ways in which you want to view this situation. When you start thinking or feeling in a way that runs contrary to the statement, simply take the time to read and reflect on the positive reassurances that you have created to transform and transcend this aspect of your life.

Try to surrender the situation over to God. Trust Him with your life and well-being. Make yourself available to His insight and surrender the direction of your life to His will. Walk in faith, knowing God will never let you down if you seek Him with all your heart. You may feel let down if your heart is consumed by your own self-willed ways, but not if you entrust God with your heart and walk in faith. Follow His lead and surrender your life to Him in a trusting way.

Visions of Inspiration

Very truly, I tell you, you will weep and mourn, but the world will rejoice; you will have pain, but your pain will turn into joy. When a woman is in labor, she has pain, because her hour has come. But when her child is born, she no longer remembers the anguish because of the joy of having brought a human being into the world. So you have pain now; but I will see you again, and your hearts will rejoice, and no one will take your joy from you. On that day you will ask nothing of me. Very truly, I tell you, if you ask anything of the Father in my name, he will give it to you. Until now you have not asked for anything in my name. Ask and you will receive, so that your joy may be complete.

John 16: 20-24

Do not love the world or the things in the world. The love of the Father is not in those who love the world: for all that is in the world – the desire of the flesh, the desire of the eyes, the pride in riches - comes not from the Father but from the world. And the world and its desire are passing away, but those who do the will of God live forever.

1 John 2: 15-17

Emotion is the chief source of all becoming conscious. There can be no transforming of darkness into light and of apathy into movement without emotion.

Carl Jung

Even a thought, even a possibility, can shatter us and transform us.

Friedrich Nietzsche

TRAUMATIC EXPERIENCES

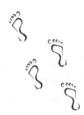

TOOL 69

I magine driving fast down one of life's unpredictable roads. Suddenly another car pulls in front of yours. You can't stop and you don't want to hit them head on, so you try to maneuver your car around them. There are only seconds in which to react, and before you know it, your car skids into the oncoming lane of traffic and rolls several times before hitting a large truck that rips off the front half of your vehicle. Your car's engine is lying in a near-by field on fire. If you're lucky, you will be lying on the pavement alive.

That's what it's like to experience a crisis, disaster or trauma, except it's much worse if there is loss of life involved. Life is full of these experiences. They can happen naturally in tornadoes, floods, earthquakes and disease, or they can be manmade such as accidents, bombings, wars or crimes.

Traumatic encounters can be the greatest and most beautiful situations in life, or they can be the worst and most destructive situations you will ever encounter. The sole factor determining how these experiences will affect your life is God. Some people embrace their hurt and surrender what is left of their life over to God and recover many times stronger than they were before. Other people start to hate life, curse God and themselves, and never recover. With every crisis, disaster or trauma life sends your way, God is right there with you! Every destructive experience you will ever encounter carries with it the seeds for growth and a new life. God will not allow negative experiences to happen in your life that don't carry with them an opportunity for your spiritual and personal growth.

When we are in the middle of a crisis, disaster or trauma, the pain can be unbearable. No one believes they can survive such an unfair, cursed, unjust, wretched experience. But when we experience one of these situations and things seem to be at their worst, remember they are actually at their best because it's when we lose everything that we have nowhere else to turn but to God. Life is not worth living without God. Many times when things are going well, we forget about God. It is in our deepest hurts, pains and miseries that we embrace God. By surrendering our life to God, we gain life to the fullest.

If you have suffered a crisis, disaster or trauma, don't bother asking God to make your life the way it was, because you probably would not have suffered this experience in the first place if that's what God wanted in your life. Don't ask God for special power beyond human capacity to fix your life, because God has already given you all the power you need. Don't ask God for miracles either; humbly ask God for the courage to embrace your pain. Ask God for the power to appreciate your new life and the strength to work your way through the grieving process. Ask God for the wisdom to understand His will for your life and the grace to unconditionally live it out. It's important to realize that you can't change or control the events of your past; you can only control your present. You have control over your perceptions, your relationship with God and your ability to work through the grieving process, all of which will help your emotional and psychological recovery.

There is a story about a man who suffered his share of tragedy here on earth. When he got to Heaven and looked back on his life, he compared it to two sets of footprints walking across a sandy beach. One set of footprints was God's and the other set was his own. During the times of his life when everything was going well, he noticed two sets of footprints in the sand. But when life was tough and the man experienced his share of crisis, disasters and traumas, he noticed only one set of footprints in the sand. The man was upset and asked God, "What's the deal? Why did you abandon me in my greatest times of need? I felt so alone – why did you leave me to walk through my greatest struggles and traumatic experiences all by myself?" God replied, "In your hardest trials and most traumatic experiences you only saw one set of footprints in the sand because during these times I was carrying you in my arms."

The following items will help you during the times when God is carrying you so once you're a little farther down the beach you can look back and again see two sets of footprints. But don't worry if you look down right now and only see one set of footprints – you're already in God's hands.

Recovering From Crises, Disasters and Traumas

The grieving, healing and growing process will be different for everyone because each loss is experienced in its own unique way. Regardless of the type of loss you or someone you are helping is experiencing, it's important to remember that you are still in control of your own thoughts, attitudes, actions and existence. Regardless of how hopeless or terrible the situation may seem, you ultimately have control over the way it is perceived in your mind. You will be required to make a decision regarding how you will let these events affect the rest of your life. The following items will assist you in grieving the losses, working your way through the healing and forgiveness process, and ultimately growing from the experience.

Mourning the Loss

It's important to mourn your loss. Many cultures set a predetermined number of days to be used entirely for this purpose. Allowing yourself the time and freedom to cry, vent your frustrations, scream or simply nurture yourself in a healthy manner will be helpful in the beginning stages of your loss. At first you might experience shock and disbelief. The sooner you are able to accept the actual reality of the situation, the sooner you can begin your grieving process. See the Grieving/Loss chapter for more information on this process.

Facing, accepting and expressing your emotions, regardless of how painful they may seem, is one of the most powerful ways of healing. Denying, repressing or failing to express your emotions is one of the most psychologically destructive things you can do. These negative emotions can be verbally expressed to others who are willing to listen, to God, who is always there for us, or by writing them out. The Death chapter contains a written healing procedure that might be very helpful for your situation.

Seeking Assistance From Others

It's almost impossible to work through your crisis, disaster or trauma alone. Although you might feel very alone, you are not. There are always resources, assistance programs, support groups and friends willing to help. You only need to ask the right people and you will receive the help you seek.

Check the Yellow Pages under Crisis Intervention, Hospitals, Counselors, Charities, Social Service Organizations, Human Service Organizations, Churches, Shelters, Support Groups, Community Services, Youth Organizations, Hot Lines, Help Lines, Blind Services and Disabled Assistance.

Minimizing the Losses

There are many ways to increase the losses you have just suffered, just like there are many ways to minimize your losses. Many times it's possible to get into a victim mentality and view the situation as hopeless when it isn't. It's very helpful to minimize your loss any way possible. Something can always be spared, fixed, improved, salvaged, assisted or comforted. Look at all aspects of physical, mental, emotional and spiritual loss to see how you can improve on it. At the very least, you can help others, which will eventually help you. It's important to start doing something positive or productive as soon as possible.

Working on Forgiveness

Forgiving is a necessity when you suffer a traumatic experience. It's important to forgive others, yourself, God and any other events or circumstances that were involved. It won't be possible to heal and grow from your traumatic experiences unless you can first create genuine forgiveness in your heart. Give yourself permission to blame. Then make a list of who is responsible and why. Next, get in touch with your resentment and work your way through the writing forgiveness process. See the Forgiveness chapter for more information.

Creating New Plans, Hopes and Dreams

Crises, disasters and traumas can be major turning points in your life. From this point forward the future is yours to create. It's helpful to take some time for deep contemplation and prayer to establish some new directions and potentials for your life. In the past you have invested a lot of time, love, energy and your very life into the people, places and things that are now considered lost. If you could go back and change the amount of your investment, would you give more or less? Would you lavish the loss with twice as much time, energy and love, or do you wish you had spread your time, energy and love more evenly among other sources? Regardless of your answer, nothing is stopping you from reinvesting your time, energy and love today in any way you desire. Take time to contemplate and create some new plans, hopes and dreams for your future investments.

Setting Goals

Many times traumatic experiences bring with them much sadness. It's very helpful to get in touch with these sad feelings and discover their underlying causes. Feed into your emotions and find out what you wanted to happen that didn't. Find out what you truly want and need right now. Once you discover what you want to make yourself feel better, you can set some goals and start working toward those items. The sooner you start setting plans to rebuild and recreate your future, the better you will feel. See the Goals chapter for step-by-step instructions once the desires of your heart are known.

Changing Your Perceptions

An important part of any healing process is understanding the lessons that were involved and finding the good in the situation. You will know that your healing process is complete when you can look back at the past and feel a source of peace, realizing and appreciating the meanings and purposes that were involved in your experience. The information listed in the Transformation/Transcendence chapter will help you find a positive way to view your experiences and grow from their invaluable lessons.

God is an important part of this process. Turning to God in Prayer is a powerful way to receive answers, assistance and awareness during life's struggles. Trust God with the new direction your life is heading, place your faith in Him and follow His lead. Ask God to change the desires of your heart so they line up with His will for your life. Ultimately that will be in your best interest.

Visions of Inspiration

Out of my distress I called on the Lord; the Lord answered me and set me in a broad place. With the Lord on my side I do not fear. What can mortals do to me?

Psalm 118: 5-6

We know that all things work together for good for those who love God, who are called according to his purpose.

Romans 8: 28

Let us be patient! These severe afflictions Not from the ground arise, But oftentimes celestial benedictions Assume this dark disguise.

Henry Longfellow

TRUST

*P*retend for a minute that you're about to buy a new car and your decision will be based solely on reliability. You experienced a lot of mechanical problems in the past and want a quality vehicle that will last a long time. After visiting several dealerships, you are unsure which car to choose because all the four-door sedans look the same, drive the same and are priced the same. How will you make a decision?

Do you realize that trust will be your determining factor? If you buy a car based on information listed in a consumer report, you will be trusting the information from that source. If you buy a car because the salesman swears his product is the most reliable, you will be placing your trust in his words. If your choice is based on a manufacturer's name, you are trusting their advertisements or trusting the company based on the past performance of its products. If your choice is based on your intuition, you are trusting your Inner Self.

Usually our trust is based on the source or combination of sources we feel best represent our perception of the truth. When we place our trust in the truth, we know what to expect and what not to expect. When we place our trust in something other than the truth, we usually get hurt. The problem lies in determining which truth to base our trust on. The car salesman might really believe his product is the most reliable and that he is speaking the truth. The writers of the consumer reports probably feel the same about their information. The person buying the car will have their own perception of the truth and that's what they will place their trust in.

It is also possible to base our trust on some form of commitment we believe to be true. The car salesman may make a verbal commitment when they speak of the vehicle's reliability. The manufacturer might offer a written warranty on the vehicle as their commitment to correct future problems. Trust is an essential element in all aspects of our lives and relationships, and all trust in life is based on a commitment or truth. Without trust it wouldn't be possible to maintain a healthy or lasting relationship with anyone. Who is going to buy a car from an untrustworthy source? Who is going to take a car on a road trip when they can't trust it to not break down?

The same thing also applies to your partner. Who is going to marry someone if they can't trust them to be faithful? If you can't trust your partner in small matters, how can you trust them in larger ones? The ability to trust your partner is one of the basic foundations that support your relationship. Broken trust or betrayal can cause severe damage in the form of anger, resentment and loss of love and respect for your partner. The inability to trust your partner on small issues will eventually eat away at your ability to connect with them on sensitive, vulnerable and important issues. Ultimately the lack of trust will destroy your relationship.

Knowing how important trust is, let's look at how trust can be broken, and then restored. We know trust is based on our own perceptions of the truth or a commitment. When our trust is broken, there's a misunderstanding between people on what both believe to be true or agreed on. For example, if we placed our trust in one of those four-door sedans by making the purchase and then later found we owned the most unreliable vehicle ever built, we would probably experience a lot of hurt feelings of betrayal because the truth on which we placed our trust has just proved itself differently.

Now who's to blame when this happens? Usually we just automatically blame the car salesman instead of taking responsibility for our own perceptions. The car salesman could have intentionally misrepresented the product or he might have honestly believed every word he spoke and just lacked knowledge. Or it might not be the other person's fault at all. We might have made our own assumptions by interpreting the salesman's words in a way we wanted to hear. He might have implied one intention and we heard and understood it differently. It's even possible for truth to change. The most reliable car of the '80s can't compare to cars of the '90s. The number of ways we can experience a breakdown in trust or betrayal is unlimited. Blaming other people usually only results in arguments.

If you had bought the unreliable four-door sedan would you go back and argue with the salesman? Would you try to get out of your commitment on a signed contract? Would you remain resentful and hate your new car? Or would you simply change your perceptions to those that more accurately represent the truth? If you choose to change your perceptions, it will be necessary to do some forgiveness work. That's because as soon as you acknowledge that you own an unreliable car, you'll need to forgive the salesman who misrepresented the product, or you'll need to forgive yourself for making the purchase. Either way, the only way to repair a broken trust is by forgiving the other person and aligning your perceptions with those that more accurately represent the truth.

If you have experienced a broken trust in your personal relationship, it will be necessary to work your way through the same process. For example, if you and your relationship partner have a spoken commitment that includes sexual monogamy and you find out your partner has been involved in an affair, your trust will be broken. You will probably feel betrayed, even if your partner claims it's over and says they're sorry. If you're interested in rebuilding your trust and saving your relationship, you will need to work through the following process.

First, it will be helpful to vent your negative emotions of anger and hurt. Next, it's necessary to abandon your old perceptions of the truth for something that better represents your current reality. The truth of the past might have been, "Your relationship partner loves you, would never do anything to hurt you and is not interested in other people." The current truth might be, "Your marriage has required a lot of work for many years and your partner has turned to other sources for the fulfillment of their needs." Once you have accepted the form of truth that best represents the current reality, it will be necessary to forgive your partner for hurting you. After the forgiveness work, it's possible to establish a new form of commitment that you and your partner can trust.

Steps to Rebuilding Trust

Step 1: Vent Negative Emotions

The first step in this process is to vent your negative emotions. Usually when you are confronted with betrayal or a broken trust, a lot of negative emotions arise. It's important to acknowledge and vent those emotions as soon as possible. You might experience anger, rage, frustration, depression, sadness, shame, guilt, vengefulness, confusion, disappointment, disgust, hopelessness, abandonment, rejection or emptiness. It will be helpful to write these negative feelings in a letter you never intend to send. Start by describing the events that led up to the betrayed trust. Explain how and why you believed the things you believed, how you found out about the betrayal or broken trust, along with every emotion that was involved. Look deep inside yourself and get all the negativity out in your letter.

Step 2: Confront the Truth

The next step is to search out and confront the truth. Many times after experiencing betrayal, you may find yourself holding onto perceptions that are different from reality. After you openly acknowledge the truth, it's important to discover the reasons why you perceived the situation differently. Have you been pursuing the truth all along, or has the betrayer intentionally been deceiving you? Have you been slowly deceiving yourself? Many times we deceive ourselves by creating a number of defense mechanisms that keep us from the truth. When we fear the truth and attempt to avoid or distort our perceptions of it, we usually end up hurting ourselves and others in the process. It's important to confront and change anything in your life that keeps you from acknowledging the truth to prevent a similar situation in the future. Use the steps in the Fear chapter to transform any fear that keeps you from acknowledging the full and complete truth.

Step 3: Forgive

The next step is to forgive the person who betrayed your trust. Forgiveness is an important part of life, especially in rebuilding trust. Many times we speak some forgiveness words, but fail to forgive the other person from our heart. The lack of forgiveness only hurts the person who continues to hold on to those negative, resentful, injured feelings. True forgiveness means that the relationship has been restored to its original condition. See the Forgiveness chapter for more information. Forgive your partner in writing and restore their rightful place in your heart.

Step 4: Heal the Past

The next step is to heal similar situations you have experienced in the past. We have all experienced some types of broken trust or betrayal in the past. Children who have been abused, mistreated, exploited or frequently lied to usually grow up with a limited ability to trust others. Maybe an old boyfriend or girlfriend has cheated on you in the past and this experience limits your ability to trust your current partner. An alcoholic parent might have made promises when sober and broken them when intoxicated. A sexual violator may have left you with the inability to trust men. You might even frequently find yourself looking for proof of untrustworthiness when no evidence exists. Children whose trust was betrayed will grow up learning it's not safe to trust anyone. All these incidents from the past will have a powerful effect on a person's ability to trust in the present. These painful experiences will continue to affect a person's subconscious programming the rest of their lives unless the issues are confronted, embraced and healed. Try to find as many broken trust issues as you can from your past. Write them down and work through them using one of the healing processes described in the Healing chapter.

Step 5: Establish a New Agreement

After you have completed some past healing work, you will have an easier time establishing a new agreement on which to base your future trust. Try to make a written agreement concerning what will and will not happen in the future. Sit down with your partner and establish a new form of agreement that addresses every little detail and technicality. Once you have a new agreement, you can begin the process of slowly reinvesting your trust in that person and situation.

Step 6: Develop Your Own Inner Trust

The next step is to develop the ability to trust yourself. If you can't trust yourself, it's almost impossible to trust another person. Internal trust is a firm belief in your own abilities. This includes the ability to protect yourself by setting the necessary boundaries, the ability to act in a reliable and responsible manner and the ability to make decisions based on everyone's best interests. When you trust in yourself and your own abilities, you develop an internal sense of faith and security. Through this process you can realize that no matter what commitments a partner breaks in the future, you will survive because you believe in your own internal strength to overcome the situation regardless of what happens. People with internal trust know they have the power to find forgiveness, make the necessary changes and, if necessary, remove themselves from the situation.

Setting healthy boundaries is an important part of your internal trust process. For example, if your relationship partner has an affair, a healthy boundary might be to leave them if it ever happened again. See the Boundary chapter for more information. You might not want to leave them, but if that boundary is crossed, you are prepared to act on your decision. Once you establish your boundaries and clearly communicate them to your partner, you will need to trust yourself enough to follow through with what is necessary. When you trust yourself to judge, accept and act on your own ability, you no longer have a reason to worry about or mistrust your partner. If they break their promise again, you will deal with it at that time. There's no need to dwell on it until the evidence presents itself. If you have questions, ask your partner in a healthy, direct and honest approach. Just be willing to accept the truth and act on it as necessary.

Step 7: Trust in God

The final step is to develop trust in God. Without a belief in a higher power of protection, safety and justice, the world would probably be viewed as a very unsafe place. Some things will happen to all of us that will test and increase our ability to be loving, forgiving and trusting. But God will not allow anything to happen to us that we cannot handle. God loves all of us and carefully watches out for everyone's best interests. We might not always understand His plans, but given time, everything works out for the best for those who love Him. God will provide the necessary lessons, strength, grace and assistance for you to work through anything. Ask God to help you develop your ability to internally trust yourself, externally trust other people in your life, and above all trust in His protection, intervention and guidance through life's natural processes.

Visions of Inspiration

You may be deceived if you trust too much, but you will live in torment if you do not trust enough.

Frank Crane

Blessed are those who trust in the Lord, whose trust is the Lord. They shall be like a tree planted by water, sending out its roots by the stream. It shall not fear when heat comes, and its leaves shall stay green; in the year of drought it is not anxious, and it does not cease to bear fruit.

Jeremiah 17: 7-8

The chief lesson I have learned in a long life is that the only way to make a man trustworthy is to trust him; and the surest way to make him untrustworthy is to distrust him and show your distrust.

Henry L. Stimson

TRUTH & HONOR

TOOL 71

*H*ave you ever driven your car down a steep mountain road? Usually the turns are very sharp as the road winds its way throughout the rugged terrain. The only way to safely navigate your vehicle down the mountain is to maintain a clear perception of reality. If your view of reality is distorted, you could envision the road continuing in a straight line when it actually veers to the left. Since the direction of your vehicle is determined by your perceptions of the road, what do you think would happen if your mind thought the road was straight when it actually cut to the left? Would you drive your car right off the side of the mountain?

The clearer your view of the road, the better equipped you are to deal with it safely and efficiently. If your relationship partner were trying to safely navigate your car down the mountain road, would you take out a can of spray paint and fog up their driving glasses? Do you think your partner could drive more safely with an accurate perception of reality, or with a distorted, spray-painted perception of reality?

What does this have to do with truth? The mountain road represents our ever-changing and unpredictable path through life. We all drive our own cars and the clearer our view and perception of reality, the better able we will be to keep our vehicle on the road. Being in a relationship with another person is just like traveling in the same vehicle with that person. When we lie to ourselves, we spray paint our own glasses. When we lie, withhold the truth or act dishonestly, we are blasting spray paint on another driver's glasses. Any time you distort the truth, you are distorting another driver's view of reality.

Which is more scary: Riding shotgun down the mountain in your relationship partner's car knowing you have intentionally distorted their perceptions of reality with spray paint? Or being honest, vulnerable and respectful enough to trust your partner to navigate the vehicle safely? Isn't your partner in control of the vehicle in both cases? Isn't the only difference between your two choices a destructive distortion? Living a life of honesty, integrity and honor is a lot safer for everyone involved, not to mention easier. Lying wastes a lot more time, effort and energy than telling the truth. When you lie, it becomes necessary to monitor a mental list of past lies so you don't get caught. It also becomes necessary to create new lies to conceal the old ones. Eventually this vicious cycle will damage the trust on which the relationship is built. Sooner or later you will get caught, or continue to drive blindly down the road of life in a never-ending cycle of danger. Telling the truth is free and healthy; distorting the truth wastes a lot of energy and produces a lot more pain.

Who do you want in your car riding shotgun: a fearful partner with a large can of spray paint? Or someone who respects, honors and trusts your ability to properly navigate the vehicle?

Maintaining Honesty and Honor in Your Everyday Interactions

Telling the Truth

There are two ways to lie to another person: The first is to make statements that are false. The second is to make statements that are true, but intentionally leave out important facts or details. Both ways are equally destructive, dishonest and deceptive. Many times we leave out important facts and details to be sensitive to another person's feelings. Parents often tell little white lies to their children in an attempt to protect them. Unfortunately, they only deprive the child of honest role models and distort important lessons behind what they are trying to hide. Distorting another person's perceptions of the truth limits their own personal growth and fogs up their glasses.

There are some situations in life where it may be in another person's best interests to withhold the truth. If you are confronted with such an experience, you may want to make sure your decision to withhold the truth is not based on a self-serving reason like the desire to be respected, liked or accepted, or on an attempt to fulfill your own needs, like the desire for power, control, financial gain or self-protection. Any decision you make to withhold the truth should be based solely on the needs of the other person in compliance with genuine and unconditional love, and then only after you have considered the person's ability to use the truth for their own personal growth. Any other time you are distorting another driver's perception of the road.

Treating Everyone With the Same Set of Standards

You can establish your own personal integrity by treating everyone with the same set of principles and standards. When you play favorites, gossip about others behind their back, tell white lies or share privileged information, you destroy the trust in your relationships. For example, picture yourself at work when a friend comes to you and criticizes a supervisor in a way that neither of you would do directly. If your friendship came to an end in the future, what do you think that person would do behind your back? Would this person assume you are criticizing them in the same way because you participated in the conversation regarding the supervisor? It's easy to see how malicious or deceptive actions destroy personal trust and integrity. What would happen if you treated everyone with the same set of principles and standards, regardless if your supervisor were present or not? What would happen if you agreed with some of your friend's concerns and suggested a meeting with your supervisor to discuss the company's problems? Actions such as that might not be very popular with others at first, but eventually those who maintain an honorable reputation become a trustworthy source for us all.

Keeping Your Promises

Keeping commitments, promises and obligations is an important part of building and maintaining personal honor. When you fail to do so, others lose trust and respect for you. For example, picture yourself at work again and a friend approaches you with confidential information that doesn't concern you. They say, "I really shouldn't tell you this, but since we're friends I will anyway." On the surface this conversation might appear to be building trust in your relationship, but in reality that trust is coming at the expense of another person. Your friend is betraying another person's trust in an attempt to promote your friendship. Do you consider this act honorable? Are you willing to trust them with your own confidential information? Are people who act this way considered honorable and honest? Any time you make a commitment or promise to another person, they place their trust in you. To maintain an honorable reputation, don't do anything that would jeopardize or break that trust. Be very careful when making a commitment, promise or obligation to another person. Make sure you study all the consequences beforehand. When something comes up, try not to make excuses. Ask the other person to release you from your commitment. This is the only honorable way to handle the situation.

Clarifying Mutual Expectations

Nothing undermines trust faster than misunderstood expectations. We usually base trust in others on whether they have fulfilled their responsibilities and commitments. If both people have differing expectations about those responsibilities and commitments, there is the potential for a broken trust in the future. It's important to establish a clear understanding right up front about who's responsible for what. Clarifying expectations many times requires courage and additional effort, but during the course of your relationship both people will benefit.

Visions of Inspiration

You shall not bear false witness against your neighbor.

Exodus 20: 16

You shall not spread a false report. You shall not join hands with the wicked to act as a malicious witness. You shall not follow a majority in wrongdoing; when you bear witness in a lawsuit, you shall not side with the majority so as to pervert justice; nor shall you be partial to the poor in a lawsuit.

Exodus 23: 1-3

Whoever is faithful in a very little is faithful also in much; and whoever is dishonest in a very little is dishonest also in much. If then you have not been faithful with the dishonest wealth, who will entrust to you the true riches? And if you have not been faithful with what belongs to another, who will give you what is your own?

Luke 16: 10-12

God offers to every mind its choice between truth and repose. Take which you please – you can never have both.

Emerson

And you will know the truth, and the truth will make you free.

John 8: 32

UNWANTED PREG-
NANCY & ABORTION

*I*magine you are driving down the highway when suddenly the brakes on your car fail. As you fly around the next curve in the road, a small child runs out in front of your vehicle. Panic stricken and terrified, you realize there are only two possible choices you can make, and unfortunately, both will end up in some type of loss. The question is, what type of loss are you willing to deal with for the rest of your life?

The first choice is to crank the steering wheel as hard as you can to avoid hitting the child. This decision will instantly change the course of your life as it sends your car off the road and down a hill. This choice will save the child's life, but you will experience physical losses in terms of wear and tear on your vehicle and financial losses in terms of your livelihood, career and medical expenses. The second choice is to keep your car on the road and run down the child. This choice produces less material loss, but you will need to deal with the emotional and spiritual consequences. There are no easy answers in this situation, and both decisions will have a serious effect on everyone who is involved in your life. Both choices appear to be legal: After all, you didn't intentionally put the child in the road and it's not really your fault the brakes on your car failed.

If you have had an abortion in the past for whatever reason, you need to heal the emotional and spiritual damage to prevent it from affecting the rest of your life. Many times the emotion and spiritual damage is denied, repressed and justified by focusing on the physical disadvantages that have been avoided. An abortion experience, like any other negative past experience, can be repressed in your subconscious if it's not properly grieved and healed. If you don't believe there are any consequences to losing a child, ask someone who has lost a child to miscarriage, still birth or sudden infant death syndrome – each of which was no fault of their own. If you are still denying the destructive emotional and spiritual consequences of abortion, you may be using one of the following defense mechanisms:

❖ **Rationalization.** Are you trying to deny emotional and spiritual damage by finding logical excuses or reasons to justify your actions? Do you say things to yourself like, "It wouldn't be fair to bring a baby into this world because I'm not ready to be pregnant, or be a mother or surrogate mother."

❖ **Repression.** Are you trying to repress emotional and spiritual damage by pushing down negative feelings or blocking them out when they arise? Do you find yourself saying things to yourself like, "I'm okay with my abortion. I can handle it. It doesn't bother me anymore." With constant mental persistence some women can repress these feelings for many years until they come back in the form of post-abortion syndrome.

❖ **Compensation.** Are you trying to make up for emotional and spiritual damage by doing good things like having an atonement baby soon after the abortion, or becoming deeply involved with charitable work or by being a "supermom"?

❖ **Distortion.** Are you trying to avoid emotional and spiritual damage by distorting your perceptions of the truth? Sometimes you might try to make yourself feel better by professing the exact opposite of what you know to be true. Instead of looking at the hurt and pain deep inside, you might deal with it by becoming extremely active in a pro-choice movement.

If you had an abortion in the past, take a minute and look deep inside yourself to notice what you are feeling. Are you angry, offended, upset, defensive or experiencing any negative feelings? If you are, some healing work will be necessary. These words are not creating your negative feelings; it is the repressed hurt and pain from your past abortion experience these words are stirring inside of you. If you are experiencing negative feelings, it's God's way of talking to you through your Inner Self, calling you to embrace your hurt and pain.

A past abortion can be a beautiful growth experience if you acknowledge, embrace and work through it. By doing so, you will become a deeper, stronger, more loving and connected individual in all your relationships with children, men, yourself, your parents and – most importantly – God. If you don't embrace the emotional and spiritual repercussions of an abortion, the pain and hurt will remain trapped in your Inner Self. It will affect (if it hasn't already destroyed) your relationship with the natural father. If you are hiding it from anyone in your present relationships, it is already having a negative effect on that person as well. There's probably a part of you that wouldn't feel lovable if that person knew, or you wouldn't be hiding it. If you can't love that hurt part of yourself, why would you believe anyone else could? If you can't fully love yourself, how can you expect another person to fully love you?

What about your relationship with God? If God is your Heavenly Spiritual Father and you are His beloved child, then whose child was standing in the road? How does that affect your relationship with God? The only way to justify it spiritually is to distort your relationship with God, which in time will affect every other aspect of your life.

Abortion is extremely destructive because it will affect a woman the same as war will affect a soldier. You can try to logically justify both acts of intentionally taking another being's life, but the emotional and spiritual damage can't be avoided. Both the acts of war and the abortion will generate huge amounts of anger, fear, guilt, grief and hopelessness. You may have experienced anger from being pressured into the decision, fear from what your parents would think, abandonment from the lack of support from others and guilt from your subconscious mothering instincts and religious beliefs. If these negative emotions are not dealt with properly, both the soldier and the would-be-mother will hurt for a short period of time before the negative feelings are repressed into their subconscious.

If that's not bad enough, both the soldier and the would-be-mother will also experience severe losses: the actual loss of a human life, the loss of your ability to trust, the loss of respect for life, the loss of self-worth and peace of mind, the loss of your relationship and perceptions of God, and the loss of approval and support from others, not to mention the loss of your parents' potential grandchild, and your future son or daughter. If all these losses are not properly grieved, the pain and sorrow will be repressed into the soldier's or would-be-mother's subconscious.

In war there is no time to do emotional healing work and all this negativity becomes repressed, only to come back at a later time in the form of transference. When the soldier returns home, they might be able to keep the negativity repressed by using defense mechanisms and logical justifications. But in a few years it will keep building until it explodes in the form of post-traumatic stress disorder. Would-be-mothers can also keep all that negativity repressed for five to seven years until it builds and explodes in what is known as post-abortion syndrome.

If you have experienced the pain of a past abortion, take a look at the following symptoms and characteristics of post-abortion syndrome and see if some healing work would be beneficial to your life and relationships:

❖ Guilt from violating the subconscious drives of your Inner Self.
❖ Anxiety from worrying about children, or avoiding anything to do with children.
❖ Depression from your everyday tasks in life.
❖ Dreams of nursing, of being pregnant, or of lost or dismembered children.
❖ Mood swings or sudden and uncontrollable crying episodes.
❖ Low self-esteem or feeling deficient or inadequate as a woman.
❖ Sexual disturbances, like the inability to experience orgasm or compulsive fears about another pregnancy.
❖ Anniversary syndrome, with terrible feelings around the date due or abortion date.
❖ Flashbacks and recurring memories of the events, smells and sounds.
❖ Having an atonement baby, or obsessively becoming pregnant again.
❖ Punishing yourself by deliberately harming yourself mentally, physically or emotionally.
❖ Degrading yourself by engaging in promiscuous actions or abusive relationships.

If you can relate to one or more of these post-abortion syndrome symptoms, the following steps will help you through the healing process.

Steps to Healing After an Abortion

Step 1: Write a Letter of Events and Feelings

First, it will be helpful to write a letter that describes all of the facts and your feelings surrounding your abortion. The purpose of this letter is to bring up all the forgotten or repressed events and emotions from your memory. Begin writing this letter in three parts: before, during and after.

In the 'before' letter describe in detail the quality of your relationship with the natural father of the child. What you were feeling when you first realized you were pregnant? How did your family and friends react? What internal messages did your Inner Self try to convey? Describe all your past circumstances, like income, job, school, medical insurance, physical health and living arrangements. How did you feel about the physical changes in your body? Who influenced your decision? What messages did friends, family and society directly and indirectly send you? The purpose of these letters is to get everything out in the open, so write as much as possible.

In the 'during' letter describe what you were feeling and how were you treated by the medical staff. Did you receive the support you needed? Describe what the procedure physically felt like, smelled like and sounded like? What did you feel like after the procedure?

In the 'after' letter describe your feelings toward the people who influenced or encouraged you to have the abortion. What was the relationship with the natural father like several weeks later? Describe all the losses you suffered by the experience. How did you feel about the loss of your security, trust, innocence, hope and dreams? Take your time writing these letters and add any additional thoughts that might surface later on. Make sure to include all the events, feelings, reasons, actions, emotions, fears, anger and resentment that you experienced.

Step 2: Do Healing and Forgiveness Work

The next step is to do some healing and forgiveness work. Take a look at your letter from Step 1 and list everything that needs to be healed. Who are the people who hurt you, who failed to support you or who forced your decision? Once you have identified those items and people, follow one of the procedures listed in the Healing chapter. Work to create a loving way to view the situation.

It will also be helpful to forgive yourself for any actions you regret or mistakes you made. Follow the instructions in the Forgiveness chapter to create a loving way to come to peace with the past.

Step 3: Write a Letter to Your Child

The next step is write a letter to your child. But before you can express your deepest emotions, it will be helpful to do some imagination techniques first. Imagine for a minute that God gave your aborted child a soul (or Inner Self) upon their conception. Now imagine your child hanging out with God up in heaven. Picture what they look like and give your child a name to establish their individual identity. After you have established an emotional connection to this little person, start your letter by addressing it to your child. Ask this little boy or girl for your forgiveness. Tell them about the world they never had a chance to experience. Explain to them all the circumstances and conditions that existed during that time in your life. Let them know how you felt once you realized they were growing inside of you. Let your child know if they are missed. Share with them in the body of your letter how you feel about everything that has happened. Express some of your dreams to them. Tell them what is going on in your life today. End your letter by acknowledging their happiness in the kingdom of God. Let them know how much you are looking forward to reuniting with them someday. Close your letter with a heartfelt goodbye for now.

Step 4: Write an Imaginary Response Letter From Your Child and God

The next step is to write an imaginary response letter in reply to the letter you wrote in Step 3. This is a pretend letter you write that states everything you would like to hear from your child and God. Start this letter out by addressing it to yourself. Envision your child being held in God's arms. Realize that because your child is in God's presence, they can only radiate God's unconditional love, compassion and forgiveness. Next, have your child reconfirm that forgiveness and express their happiness and joy, telling you a little bit about their new home in God's kingdom. Build the body of the letter with anything you wish to hear from your child or from God Himself. Conclude the letter with God's blessings and reconfirming statements of His unconditional love, compassion and forgiveness. Close with some special words from your child.

Step 5: Come to Acceptance and Conclusion

The final step is to create a memorial for your child. The purpose of the memorial is to honor, respect, reconcile and commemorate the little person whom you loved and lost. This can be done by writing a poem, painting a picture, buying and giving toys to children, erecting a cross in the mountains, sealing and burying your healing letters, planting a tree or dedicating a special place in your heart. Choose anything that seems appropriate at the time.

Visions of Inspiration

For it was you who formed my inward parts; you knit me together in my mother's womb. I praise you, for I am fearfully and wonderfully made. Your eyes beheld my unformed substance. In your book were written all the days that were formed for me, when none of them as yet existed.

Psalms 139: 13-14.5, 16

Before I formed you in the womb I knew you, and before you were born I consecrated you.

Jeremiah 1: 5-5.5

But Jesus, aware of their inner thoughts, took a little child and put it by his side, and said to them, "Whoever welcomes this child in my name welcomes me, and whoever welcomes me welcomes the one who sent me."

Luke 9: 47-48.5

Author Biography

A financial crisis inspired *The Relationship Toolbox.*

An unstoppable force led Robert Abel to a spiritual mountain retreat after he experienced a commodities future and options loss in 1994. Called during the retreat to write "the most valuable lessons in life you don't learn in school," Abel returned with an overwhelming peace and an inner motivation that inspired him to write twelve hours a day for more than three years. Recognizing that the deepest issues in life surface in an intimate connection between two people, Abel developed these lessons into relationship tools.

Abel is director of Relationship Rebuilders, a marriage and family psychotherapy counseling practice in Colorado. He works with couples and families helping them heal the emotional wounds of the past and incorporate spirituality into their lives. A member of the American Psychological Association with extensive studies in psychology and sociology, one of Abel's highest goals is to dramatically reduce the current divorce rate by encouraging couples to develop the tools to rebuild, maintain and strengthen their relationships.

A former real estate developer and mortgage banker who has been self-employed since age 18, Abel is a native of Denver, Colorado. To relax, he takes his boat out on the calm Colorado waters where he enjoys water skiing.

A portion of the proceeds from *The Relationship Toolbox* benefits St. Malo Retreat Center near Estes Park, Colorado, where Abel made his spiritual retreat that inspired *The Relationship Toolbox.*

Making a Difference

I hope the procedures, information and exercises in this book have made a positive and beneficial difference in your life and relationships. If so, I would like to personally invite you to join our ministry by sharing this information with your friends. If you would rather keep your own personal copy, you can order books through the mail for your friends. They make great gifts, and for only two dollar more we will gift wrap a copy and enclose a personalized note of your design. If you would like to distribute several copies of this book to people in a support group or other work-related situation, consider joining our distributor program. This allows you to acquire copies of the book on consignment or at wholesale cost. Please use the following forms to place an order or to send a written inquiry. Thank you, and may God bless all of your endeavors.

Standard Order Form

Please send me _____ copy (copies) of
The Relationship Tool Box.

Price $18.95 per copy.
Please add $3.00 shipping for the first book,
and $1.50 for each additional copy.

_____
NAME (PLEASE PRINT)

_____
SHIPPING ADDRESS

_____
CITY / STATE / ZIP

_____
ATTENTION

Return this order form and payment to:
Relationship Rebuilders LLC.
P.O. Box 27422
Lakewood, Colorado 80227

Gift-Wrapped Order Form

Please send one gift wrapped copy of
The Relationship ToolBox
to my friend at the following address:
(Price $18.95 plus $5.00 for shipping, handling,
and the gift-wrap service.)

TO:

_____

YOUR FRIEND'S NAME (PLEASE PRINT)

_____

YOUR FRIEND'S SHIPPING ADDRESS

_____

YOUR FRIEND'S CITY/STATE/ZIP CODE

FROM:

_____

YOUR NAME, OR LEAVE BLANK IF ANONYMOUS

_____

YOUR ADDRESS

_____

YOUR CITY/STATE/ZIP CODE

You may enclose a brief note that will be included with the book. Please use only one form per order. If you would like to send several friends a gift, feel free to photocopy this form as necessary.

Return this order form with the payment to:
Relationship Rebuilders LLC.
P.O. Box 27422
Lakewood, Colorado 80227